Ed. David Choquet

1000
game heroes

TASCHEN

KÖLN LONDON MADRID NEW YORK PARIS TOKYO

Contents

Fearless Heroes
014

Fighting Heroes
052

Funny Heroes

088

Heroes of the Future 156

Kings of Action
230

Legends
of Video Games
298

Licensed Heroes
380

Magical Heroes
430

Sexy Heroes
504

Strange Heroes
542

«David Choquet»

1000 Game Heroes

Throughout history, humanity has elected heroes. From the demi-gods of mythology to the giants of cinema, they have attained the status of legends. Not least among them are the real-life heroes of war, politics or sport. Another breed of heroes was created by cartoon strips. And since the late 70s, a further category has emerged. These new-comers, born of the new technologies, have not merely come to rival the heroes of the past; they have elbowed their way to the front.

These new heroes can rightly claim to be closer to their admirers, for their fame hangs on a playful but intimate relationship with fans who, for hours, days, and even weeks at a time, assume their roles and destinies. The universe that they share is one of pixels and polygons: video-games.

Only an elite found anything to admire in the rudimentary graphics and simple concepts of the earliest games. Indeed, in those days gamers seemed pretty eccentric. Today, video-games are superb microcosms, complex and rich in detail, and gamers of all ages take intense pleasure in immersing themselves in these cornucopian virtual worlds. The computer or television screen, no longer a barrier to the imagination, has become a window onto new continents; virtual continents, in which everyone can live out their dreams. And like all coherent worlds, those of the video-game have their own landmarks and models: their heroes. Every one of them, large or small, human or animal, good or evil, peaceful or bellicose, reflects some facet of human dreams and aspirations. And so they, too, have attained to legendary status.

John Lennon once reflected that the Beatles were as popular as Christ. Given their increasing renown, you can bet that Mario, Lara Croft, Pac-Man and the others will soon be as celebrated as the Beatles. These and many other figures from digital culture foregather here. Charming, violent, sexy or mechanical, newcomers or imports from other fields, the majority of the icons of video-gaming are for the first time brought together in this volume.

Another breed of heroes deserves a mention here. Less famous they may be, but to them the virtual characters owe their very existence. They are, of course, the game creators and developers. Let us salute their extraordinary talents, offering special thanks to those who share their vision and passion in these pages. Nor should we forget those who, over the years, have made it possible to enter the gates of dream in the comfort of one's own home: the manufacturers of the Nintendo, Sony, Sega and Microsoft consoles, and the engineers who bestowed such immense technical resources on computerised gaming. Above all, we should not forget the builders of 3D graphics cards, such as Nvidia; they have endlessly expanded the visual possibilities of a device not originally designed for entertainment: the computer.

Tout au long de son histoire, l'être humain s'est choisi des héros. Des demi-dieux issus des différentes mythologies aux géants du cinéma, en passant par les surhommes nés sous les crayons des dessinateurs de bandes dessinées, sans oublier ceux qui se sont distingués par leurs hauts faits dans la vie réelle – qu'ils soient guerriers, politiciens ou même sportifs –, maints se sont hissés au rang de légendes. Depuis la fin des années 70, ces héros voient d'étranges trublions rejoindre leurs rangs. Ces nouveaux venus, nés des nouvelles technologies, non contents de s'installer aux côtés des « vieux » héros dans leur Panthéon, méritent la jalousie de leurs aînés.

Ces nouveaux héros peuvent se targuer d'être plus proches de leurs admirateurs que bon nombre de leur aînés : la source de leur célébrité est une relation intime et ludique entre eux et leurs adorateurs, ces derniers ayant pris en main pendant des heures, des jours voire des mois ou des années, le destin de ces héros. L'univers qu'ils partagent, fait de pixels ou de polygones, est celui du jeu vidéo.

Si les premiers jeux aux graphismes simplistes et aux concepts limités ne trouvaient qu'une élite d'admirateurs, souvent montrés du doigt, ceux d'aujourd'hui sont devenus des mondes superbes, riches et complexes, dans lesquels un nombre sans cesse grandissant de joueurs, du plus jeune au plus âgé, plongent avec délectation. L'écran d'un moniteur d'ordinateur ou de télévision, qui était autrefois une barrière peu engageante, est devenu une fenêtre ouverte sur de nouveaux continents, certes virtuels, mais dans lesquels chacun peut désormais vivre ses rêves comme il l'entend. Et comme tout univers cohérent, celui des jeux vidéo possède des repères et des modèles : ses héros. Qu'ils soient grands ou petits, humains ou animaux, bons ou méchants, pacifiques ou combatifs, ils reflètent tous une ou plusieurs facettes des rêves et aspirations de chacun, aussi était-il évident qu'ils entreraient à leur tour dans la légende.

John Lennon a un jour déclaré que les Beatles étaient aussi célèbres que le Christ. Vu leur célébrité grandissante, gageons que les Mario, Lara Croft ou autres Pac-Man seront à leur tour aussi célèbres que les Beatles dans les années à venir. Ces figures de la culture digitale et bien d'autres encore se sont donné rendez-vous ici. Qu'ils soient mignons, violents, sexy ou mécaniques, nouveaux venus ou transfuges des autres univers héroïques, la majorité des icônes du jeu vidéo sont pour la première fois rassemblés dans cet ouvrage.

Il convient également de mentionner d'autres héros du jeu vidéo, moins célèbres, mais sans qui ces personnages virtuels n'existeraient pas : leurs créateurs, bien évidemment. Saluons-les tous pour leur incroyable talent, et plus particulièrement ceux qui ont accepté de partager leur vision du jeu vidéo – et leur passion – tout au long de ces pages. N'oublions pas non plus ceux qui ont permis depuis des années d'ouvrir les portes des univers virtuels dans les foyers, constructeurs de consoles Nintendo, Sony, Sega et Microsoft ou ingénieurs ayant rendu le jeu sur ordinateur capable d'atteindre des sommets de puissance, notamment les constructeurs de cartes 3D, tel Nvidia, qui ont repoussé les limites des possibilités visuelles sur ces machines, dont la vocation était bien éloignée du divertissement à l'origine.

Solange es Menschen gibt, haben sie sich Helden gesucht. Angefangen bei den Halbgöttern aus der Mythologie über die Giganten aus der Feder von Comic-Zeichnern bis hin zu den Leinwandgrößen und – nicht zu vergessen – zu all jenen, die sich durch ihre Großtaten im wirklichen Leben einen Namen als Krieger, Politiker oder Sportler gemacht haben: So mancher von ihnen ist zur Legende geworden. Seit Ende der 70er Jahre haben sich merkwürdige Gestalten zu ihnen gesellt, die die Heldenruhe massiv stören. Diese Neuzugänge in der Ruhmeshalle sind aus den neuen Technologien hervorgegangen und geben sich nicht damit zufrieden, sich neben den alten Helden einzureihen. Und ganz zu Recht werden sie von den Alten beneidet.

Die neue Heldengeneration kann von sich behaupten, ihren Fans näher zu sein, als viele der alten Helden es waren. Ihre Berühmtheit resultiert aus einem intensiven und spielerischen Miteinander. Schließlich wird den Bewunderern das Schicksal ihrer Helden über Stunden, Tage, ja sogar Monate oder Jahre anvertraut. Die aus Pixeln und Polygonen geschaffene Welt, die sie miteinander teilen, ist die Welt des Videospiels.

Die ersten Spiele hatten grafisch und konzeptionell kaum etwas zu bieten und fanden deshalb nur einige wenige Anhänger, auf die häufig noch mit dem Finger gezeigt wurde. Inzwischen jedoch warten die Spiele mit fantastischen und komplexen Welten auf, in die eine stetig wachsende Zahl von Spielern jeglicher Altersklasse genussvoll abtaucht. Der Bildschirm eines Computers oder Fernsehers, der früher noch eine Barriere darstellte, ist das Fenster zu neuen, wenngleich virtuellen Kontinenten geworden, in denen jeder seine Träume nach Lust und Laune ausleben kann. Und wie jedes Universum hat auch die Welt der Videospiele ihre ganz eigenen Vorbilder, ihre ganz eigenen Helden eben. Ob groß oder klein, menschlich oder tierisch, gut oder böse, friedliebend oder kämpferisch: Sie alle spiegeln die Träume und Sehnsüchte jedes Einzelnen in Facetten wider. Und so ist es nur allzu verständlich, dass sie zur Legende werden.

John Lennon hat einmal gesagt, die Beatles wären inzwischen populärer als Jesus. Was die Popularität der virtuellen Helden angeht, so werden Mario, Lara Croft, Pac-Man und wie sie alle heißen bald mindestens so populär sein wie die Beatles. Diese und viele andere digitale Kultfiguren geben sich hier ein Stelldichein. Ganz gleich, ob sie lieb und nett oder gewalttätig, sexy oder mechanisch sind, ob sie neu entwickelt oder aus anderen heroischen Welten übernommen wurden: Die meisten Ikonen des Videospiels sind zum allerersten Mal in einem Buch versammelt.

Eine Erwähnung haben auch jene Helden des Videospiels verdient, die zwar nicht so berühmt sind, ohne die es die virtuellen Charaktere aber nicht gäbe: Gemeint sind die Entwickler. Hut ab vor ihrem überwältigenden Talent und Hut ab insbesondere vor jenen, die uns in diesem Buch an ihren Visionen und an ihrer Begeisterung teilhaben lassen. Nicht zu vergessen all jene, die den Spielern überhaupt erst den Zugang zu den virtuellen Welten ermöglichen: Konsolenhersteller wie Nintendo, Sony, Sega und Microsoft oder Ingenieure, die dafür gesorgt haben, dass die Spiele auf den Computern zur Höchstform auflaufen – allen voran die Hersteller von 3-D-Karten, wie Nvidia. Sie haben die visuellen Möglichkeiten der Rechner, die anfangs weit davon entfernt waren, zum Unterhaltungsmedium zu taugen, ins Unermessliche gesteigert.

NAME
FRÉDÉRICK RAYNAL

BORN
1969

HOME TOWN
LYON, FRANCE

OCCUPATION
CREATIVE DIRECTOR

WORK
TOY COMMANDER (1999) NO CLICHÉ / SEGA
TWINSEN'S ODYSSEY (1997) ADELINE SOFTWARE
TWINSEN'S ADVENTURE (1995) ADELINE SOFTWARE
ALONE IN THE DARK (1992) INFOGRAMES

«Fearless Heroes»
Frédérick Raynal

The Birth of Alone in the Dark

The story of Alone in the Dark begins in 1991. I was fascinated by real-time 3D, which had finally become viable thanks to the 'demon' new 33mhz PCs, and had set about developing a tool for modelling and animating articulated objects in 3 dimensions. I was particularly attracted by certain techniques then unavailable in real time: 'skinning', which builds a convincing object from several components rather than a composite of ill-coordinated parts, and time interpolation, which adjusts animation quality to the power of the computer. Though I had never seen a professional modeller, I managed to construct a tool whose commercial equivalent appeared only many years later. The tool made it possible to animate monsters and characters with unprecedented 3D rendering. Technical as all this sounds, it was precisely the constraints of this technology that gave me an idea - an idea that transformed what might have been a simple 3D game into a new category of entertainment.

Horror films were one of my great passions at the time, so I wanted the basic horror scenario to underpin the game: a man is willingly or unwillingly plunged into a terrifyingly hostile environment and tries to escape with his life. Sadly, the computers of the time lacked the power to simultaneously display several complex animated characters (150 polygons with no texture and 15 articulations per character!) and realistic real-time 3D environments. The total number of polygons available for display (around 1,000 per image at 60 images per second) ruled out a reproduction of characters and environment sufficiently realistic to create the "haunted house" atmosphere of horror films. To bypass this problem, I decided that the entire polygon-power of the computer would be devoted to displaying the heroes and monsters in 3D. For the background, then, there was only one solution: bitmapping to represent the backgrounds (the environment). But these needed to be perspectival if they were to match the 3D actors. So a second tool came into being: a background modeller. I was then able to use it to map the house in 3D wireframe. All of the forms of the furniture and walls were drawn in white lines on a black background, forming a tangle of cubes and other hollow parallelograms. Then I could use the mouse to move through the line-laden spaces of the house and choose locations for the 170 fixed cameras that would film the scenes of the game. Once the position of each "camera" was established, the tool would generate an image composed of geometrical wireframe shapes in perspective, which the graphic designers could clothe and colour in, thus transforming it into a setting through which the game's characters could move. A synthetic image rendering programme would have been perfect to create the 3D background, but at the time such applications were the merest pipe dream.

When, for the first time, I saw a character moving through these early backgrounds, it was a revelation. I had wanted to draw on horror films for the scenario and combat-scenes with monsters (my main technological challenge was real-time 3D animation) and there I was, looking at shots that might have been filmed with cameras. The cinematic aspect of this form of visual rendering was obvious. At this point, everything became clear: the sinister atmosphere would also derive from the way in which things were filmed. Alone in the Dark was born.

All the same, I had to bear in mind that this was a game not a film. The ergonomics of character-movement and object-manipulation had to reach the same standard. The positioning of the cameras then answered two different imperatives, that of creating or disturbing an environment aesthetic, as circumstances demanded, and that of maximum coverage of the game-area to assist the gamer's orientation. The criterion for real-time camera selection - virtual direction - was to avoid reverse shots whenever possible by filming the hero's movements as much as possible from behind. Abrupt changes of viewpoint would disorientate the gamer.

In addition to all this technology, which was the most remarkable aspect of Alone in the Dark, I put everything into the gameplay and ergonomics I then considered obligatory for a game. At that particular point in the history of videogames, technical innovations were an important factor. But the goal of the game, borrowed as it was from horror movies, remained, in my eyes, essential: battling to survive in a situation of pure terror.

La naissance d'Alone in the Dark

L'histoire de ce jeu a commencé en 1991. Passionné par la 3D temps réel, devenue enfin exploitable grâce à la puissance « démoniaque » des PC à 33mhz de l'époque, j'ai entrepris la réalisation d'un outil capable de modéliser et d'animer des objets articulés en trois dimensions. Quelques techniques, inexistantes en temps réel à l'époque, m'attiraient particulièrement : les peaux continues (skinning) qui permettent d'avoir un objet composé de plusieurs sous-parties bien jointes entre elles plutôt qu'un assemblage d'objets mal imbriqués et l'interpolation dans le temps qui adapte la qualité des animations en fonction de la puissance de calcul de l'ordinateur. Alors que je n'avais jamais vu de modeleur professionnel, j'ai construit un outil qui ne trouva d'équivalent dans le commerce que bien des années plus tard. Grâce à cet outil, il devenait facile d'animer monstres et personnages avec un rendu 3D jamais atteint. Tout ceci est bien technique me direz-vous, mais c'est pourtant grâce aux contraintes de cette technologie que j'ai eu l'idée qui transforma ce qui aurait pu être un simple jeu en 3D en une nouvelle catégorie de divertissement.

Les films d'horreur étaient une de mes grandes passions à cette époque ; il fallait que ce jeu soit basé sur le même moule que beaucoup d'entre eux : un homme pénètre de gré ou de force dans un milieu hostile et effrayant et son seul objectif est de s'en sortir vivant. Malheureusement, les faibles capacités de traitement des ordinateurs à ce moment-là n'autorisaient pas l'affichage simultané de plusieurs personnages animés complexes (150 polygones sans texture et 15 articulations par personnage !) et de décors réalistes en 3D temps réel. Le nombre total de polygones affichables (environ 1000 par image à 60 images par seconde) ne permettait pas de reproduire l'ensemble avec le réalisme nécessaire à l'ambiance d'une maison hantée façon films d'épouvante. C'est pour palier à cet inconvénient que j'ai décidé que toute la puissance polygonale de l'ordinateur devait être réservée à l'affichage du héros et des monstres en 3D. Il ne restait alors qu'une solution pour les décors : des images dessinées en « bitmap » pour représenter efficacement les fonds d'écran qui constitueraient les lieux d'évolution, mais ceux-ci devaient être en perspective pour coller à la 3D des acteurs. C'est alors que naquit un deuxième outil, le modeleur de décors. Grâce à lui, les plans de la maison furent saisis en 3D fil de fer. Toutes les formes du mobilier et des murs étaient dessinées avec des lignes blanches sur un fond noir formant un enchevêtrement de cubes et autres parallélogrammes creux. Il suffisait alors de se déplacer à la souris dans ces espaces pleins de traits qui représentaient la maison afin de choisir les emplacements des 170 caméras fixes qui filmaient les scènes du jeu. Une fois la position de chaque caméra établie, l'outil générait une image composée de formes géométriques filaires en perspective que les graphistes pouvaient alors « colorier » et habiller pour la transformer en une scène du jeu dans laquelle les personnages évoluaient. Un programme de rendu d'images de synthèse aurait parfaitement fait l'affaire pour fabriquer les décors en 3D, mais à cette époque, ce type d'applications nous était totalement inaccessible. Lorsque pour la première fois, j'ai vu un personnage évoluer dans les premiers décors, ce fut la révélation. Je voulais m'inspirer des films d'horreur pour la construction scénaristique et pour les scènes de combats contre les monstres (mon vrai défi technologique était l'animation 3D temps réel) et je me retrouvais avec des prises de vue comme filmées par des caméras. L'aspect cinéma de ce rendu visuel était évident. Tout devenait alors clair et limpide, l'ambiance angoissante allait aussi provenir de la manière de filmer. Alone in the Dark était né.

Cependant, il ne fallait pas oublier que c'était un jeu, pas un film. L'ergonomie des déplacements et de la manipulation des objets devait atteindre le même niveau que le reste. Le positionnement des caméras était un savant mélange de prises de vues destinées à offrir une mise en scène esthétique ou inquiétante selon les cas, mais aussi une recherche de couverture maximale de la surface de jeu afin que le joueur ne se perde pas. La sélection en temps réel des caméras, sorte de réalisateur virtuel, essayait d'éviter au maximum les champs contre champ en filmant les déplacements du héros le plus possible de dos. Ceci dans le but de ne pas perturber le joueur avec les inversions violentes de direction.

Voilà, en plus de toute cette technologie qui a été l'aspect le plus remarquable de ce jeu, j'ai mis dans le gameplay et l'ergonomie, tout ce que je considérais comme obligatoire à l'époque pour un jeu. A ce moment-là de l'histoire des jeux vidéo, les innovations technologiques étaient un facteur important. Mais pour moi, un des points essentiels restera le but du jeu emprunté aux films d'horreur : surmonter une situation terrifiante et survivre à tout prix.

Die Entstehung von Alone in the Dark

Die Geschichte dieses Spiels begann im Jahre 1991. Begeistert von den 3-D-Spielen in Echtzeit, die dank der „dämonischen" Leistung der damaligen 33-MHz-Computer endlich Verbreitung fanden, begann ich ein Werkzeug zu entwickeln, das in der Lage war, bewegliche Objekte in 3-D zu modellieren und ihnen Leben einzuhauchen. Einige bis dato in Echtzeit noch nicht vorhandene Techniken faszinierten mich besonders: das Skinning, mit dem statt einer Montage von in sich schlecht verschachtelten Objekten ein aus mehreren, gut zusammenpassenden Einzelteilen zusammengefügtes Objekt erzielt werden kann, sowie die Interpolierung in der Zeit, die die Qualität der Animationen an die Leistung des Rechners anpasste. Obwohl ich noch nie mit professionellen Modellisten zu tun hatte, ist es mir gelungen, ein Werkzeug zu konstruieren, das im Handel erst Jahre später seinesgleichen fand und mit dem Monster und Figuren in einer bisher noch nie erreichten 3-D-Wiedergabequalität animiert werden konnten. Das ist sehr technisch, werden Sie sagen, aber eben diese bisher ungelösten technischen Probleme brachten mich auf die Idee, nicht ein simples 3-D-Spiel, sondern eine neue Kategorie der Unterhaltung zu kreieren.

Eine meiner großen Leidenschaften damals waren Horrorfilme. Deshalb sollte das Spiel ihrem Prinzip angepasst werden: Ein Mann dringt in ein feindliches und schreckliches Milieu ein. Sein einziges Ziel ist es, wieder lebend aus der Sache rauszukommen. Leider ließen die schwachen Computerleistungen von damals nicht mehrere komplex animierte Figuren (150 texturlose Polygone und 15 Bewegungen pro Figur!) und realistische 3-D-Bilder in Echtzeit zu. Die Gesamtzahl sichtbarer Polygone (ungefähr 1000 pro Bild bei 60 Bildern pro Sekunde) vermochte es noch nicht, das vollständige Bild mit dem für die Atmosphäre eines Spukhauses erforderlichen Realismus im Stile von Horrorfilmen wiederzugeben. Deshalb entschloss ich mich, die gesamte polygonale Leistung des Rechners auf die Sichtbarmachung des Helden und der Monster in 3-D zu konzentrieren. So blieb nur eine Lösung für das Dekor: gezeichnete „Bitmap"-Bilder, um den jeweiligen Hintergrund, der den Ort des Geschehens darstellt, so wirkungsvoll wie möglich, aber auch perspektivisch darzustellen, damit er im Einklang mit den 3-D-Szenen der Akteure steht. Auf diese Weise entstand ein zweites Werkzeug, der Dekormodellierer. Der Aufriss des Hauses konnte mit Hilfe eines 3-D-Rasters erfasst werden. Sämtliche Umrisse des Mobiliars sowie der Wände wurden als weiße Linien auf schwarzem Hintergrund gezeichnet und bildeten eine Verflechtung von Würfeln und anderen hohlen Parallelogrammen. Jetzt musste nur noch die Maus in diesen von Linien durchzogenen Bereichen, die das Haus darstellten, hin- und herbewegt werden, um die Stellungen der 170 unbeweglichen Kameras auszuwählen, die die Spielszenen filmen sollten. Sobald jede Kamera platziert sein würde, ließe sich mit dem Werkzeug ein netzartiges, aus geometrischen Formen zusammengefügtes, perspektivisches Bild erzeugen, das die Grafiker dann „ausmalen" und füllen könnten, um es in eine Szene des Spiels einzubringen, in der sich die Figuren bewegen würden. Zwar wäre ein Programm zur Wiedergabe synthetisierter Bilder ausreichend gewesen, um den umgebenden Rahmen dreidimensional darzustellen, doch diese Anwendungen waren uns noch nicht uneingeschränkt zugänglich. Als ich das erste Mal die Bewegung einer Figur vor diesem Hintergrund sah, war es eine Offenbarung. Das Ergebnis war umso erstaunlicher, als ich mich für das Szenario und die Kampfszenen mit den Monstern von Horrorfilmen hatte inspirieren lassen (meine wahre technologische Herausforderung war die 3-D-Animation in Echtzeit), jedoch vor Aufnahmen stand, die von Kameras gefilmt worden zu sein schienen. Der kinematografische Aspekt dieser visuellen Wiedergabe war offensichtlich. Alles wurde klar und einleuchtend, die angsterfüllte Atmosphäre ergab sich nicht zuletzt aus der Art zu filmen. Alone in the Dark war geboren.

Bei alldem durfte nicht vergessen werden, dass es hier um ein Spiel und nicht um einen Film ging. Die Ergonomie der Bewegungen und die Handhabung der Objekte musste mit der übrigen Spielintention in Einklang stehen. Die Kameraeinstellungen mussten geschickt arrangiert werden, um von Fall zu Fall entweder das Ästhetische oder das Bedrohliche der Szenen in den Vordergrund zu stellen, die aber vor allem einer ausgeklügelten Gestaltung der Spieloberfläche bedurften, um dem Spieler die Orientierung zu ermöglichen. Die Wahl der Kameras in Echtzeit, eine Art virtuelle Regie, sollte häufige Schuss-Gegenschuss-Situationen weitestgehend vermeiden helfen und den Helden möglichst oft in Rückenperspektive zeigen, um die Konzentration der Spieler nicht durch abrupte Richtungswechsel zu beeinträchtigen.

Diese Technologie war der wohl bemerkenswerteste Aspekt dieses Spieles. Aber ich bedachte auch das Gameplay und die Ergonomie mit all jenen Faktoren, die ich damals für ein Spiel als notwendig erachtete. Zu diesem Zeitpunkt in der Geschichte des Videospiels waren die technologischen Neuerungen ein wichtiger Faktor. Aber für mich war nach wie vor auch der spielerische Aspekt relevant. Meine Devise habe ich den Horrorfilmen entlehnt: Rette sich, wer kann, um jeden Preis lebend aus einer Grauen erregenden Situation.

NAME
AGARTHA

PLATFORM
DREAMCAST

RELEASE
TO BE RELEASED

EDITOR
NEVER RELEASED

DEVELOPER
NO CLICHE

COPYRIGHTS
© NO CLICHE/SEGA

FACT
97 MILLION DOLLARS: TOTAL VALUE
OF USA SALES OF DREAMCAST IN THE
FIRST TWENTY-FOUR HOURS OF SALES.

Agartha

The creation of Frédérick Raynal, considered by many the father of the survival/horror actioner genre since his *Alone in the Dark*, *Agartha* was an ambitious project, a spell-binding scenario whose realisation seemed full of promise. In 1929, in a remote village of Romania, our hero, Kirk, discovers a dimensional rift between Earth and Agartha, a world dominated by evil. Kirk must choose whether to help its monstrous hordes invade his own planet, or, on the contrary, attempt to seal the portal forever.
Sega was to publish the game, but suspended its contract. Raynal meanwhile claimed that there had been excessive censorship. *Agartha* was finally abandoned in 2001. Frédérick Raynal said at the time: "Our concept and starting point was precisely to go beyond the politically correct and completely immerse the gamer in a disquieting and sinister universe" (Source: Interview, GameKult.com).
« »

Créé par Frédérick Raynal, considéré par beaucoup comme le père du genre survival/horror (jeu d'action-aventure horrifique) avec le premier *Alone In the Dark*, *Agartha* était un projet ambitieux, au scénario envoûtant et à la réalisation prometteuse. En 1929, au cœur d'un village perdu de Roumanie, Kirk, le héros de cette aventure, se trouve face à une déchirure dimensionnelle entre la Terre et Agartha, un monde dominé par les forces du mal. Kirk aura le choix entre aider les hordes monstrueuses à envahir la Terre ou, au contraire, tenter de sceller définitivement le portail entre les dimensions.
Suite à une cessation de contrat avec Sega (qui devait éditer le jeu), mais aussi, d'après Frédérick Raynal lui-même, une trop grande censure, *Agartha* fut abandonné définitivement en 2001. Frédérick Raynal déclarait d'ailleurs : « Notre concept et notre idée de départ était justement d'outrepasser les limites du politiquement correct pour immerger totalement le joueur dans un univers sombre et inquiétant. » (source : interview sur GameKult.com).
« »

Aus der Feder von Frédérick Raynal, der für viele als der Vater des Survival-Horrors gilt (grauenerregende Adventure-Action-Spiele) und bekannt ist für seinen ersten Titel *Alone in the Dark*, stammt *Agartha*, ein ehrgeiziges Projekt mit einem aufwändigen Szenario und einer vielversprechenden Inszenierung: 1929, mitten in einem Dorf in den Weiten Rumäniens, steht Kirk, der Held des Abenteuers, plötzlich vor einem Riss zwischen der Erde und Agartha, einer von den Kräften des Bösen beherrschten Welt. Kirk hat die Wahl, den monströsen Horden dabei zu helfen, die Erde zu überfallen, oder andernfalls für immer und ewig das Tor zwischen den Dimensionen zu schließen.
Nachdem Sega sich von ihrer Tochterfirma No Cliché getrennt hatte (ursprünglich Herausgeber des Spiels), aber auch, so Frédérick Raynal, wegen einer allzu einschneidenden Zensur, landete *Agartha* im Jahre 2001 endgültig in der Schublade. Frédérick Raynal erklärte dazu: „Unser ursprüngliches Konzept und unsere Ausgangsidee bestanden eben darin, die Grenzen der Political Correctness zu überschreiten, um den Spieler in ein finsteres und schauderhaftes Universum eintauchen zu lassen." (Quelle: Interview unter http://www.gamekult.com)

NAME: ALONE IN THE DARK:
THE NEW NIGHTMARE

PLATFORM: PC-DREAMCAST
PLAYSTATION-PLAYSTATION 2

RELEASE: 2001

EDITOR: INFOGRAMES ENTERTAINMENT

DEVELOPER: DARKWORKS

COPYRIGHTS: © DARKWORKS/INFOGRAMES

FACT: 517,078: THE NUMBER OF COPIES OF ONIMUSHA:
WARLORDS SOLD IN JAPAN WITHIN THREE DAYS
OF ITS RELEASE (25–28 JANUARY 2001).

Alone in the Dark

Frederick Johnson has commissioned Charles Fiske to investigate the mysterious Shadow Island. When Fiske disappears, Johnson calls in Fiske's best friend, the famous detective of the paranormal, Edward Carnby, to continue the investigation. Alice Cédrac, a specialist in of dead languages, is recruited to help him. As their seaplane approaches Shadow Island, they encounter a strange force field and have to bail out. Thus separated, they explore Shadow Island. And in the island's shadows lurk a myriad of dangers: terrifying ghosts, the living-dead, unspeakable monsters and other threats to their lives and sanity. The awful truth is revealed: the owners of the island, the Mortons, have opened a portal onto a shadow world, and Carnby and Cédrac - if they can - must seal it forever by ancestral rites.

« »

Charles Fiske, le meilleur ami d'Edward Carnby, célèbre détective de l'étrange, a disparu lors de l'enquête qu'il menait sur la mystérieuse Shadow Island pour le compte de Frederick Johnson. Ce dernier demande à Carnby de poursuivre l'enquête et lui adjoint Alice Cédrac, spécialiste des langues disparues. En approchant de Shadow Island, l'hydravion qui transportait les deux protagonistes est attaqué par une force étrange, obligeant Carnby et Cédrac à sauter en parachute sur l'île où ils atterrissent séparés. Ils vont chacun devoir explorer Shadow Island de son côté, affrontant seul les mille dangers tapis dans l'ombre : fantômes effrayants, morts-vivants épouvantables, monstres innommables et autres périls qui menaceront aussi bien leur vie que leur équilibre mental. Ils découvriront que les propriétaires de Shadow Island, les Morton, ont ouvert un portail vers un monde de ténèbres que Carnby et Cédrac devront sceller à jamais grâce à des rituels ancestraux.

« »

Charles Fiske, der beste Freund des berühmten Detektivs Edward Carnby, ist verschwunden, während er auf der geheimnisvollen Insel Shadow Island für Frederick Johnson Ermittlungen durchführte. Letzterer bittet nun Carnby, die Untersuchungen fortzusetzen, und stellt ihm Aline Cedrac, eine Expertin für ausgestorbene Sprachen, zur Seite. Beim Anflug auf Shadow Island wird ihr Wasserflugzeug von einer geheimnisvollen Macht angegriffen, so dass die beiden mit dem Fallschirm abspringen müssen und getrennt auf der Insel landen. Jeder für sich muss nun Shadow Island erkunden und den Gefahren trotzen, die hinter jedem Schatten lauern: Unheimliche Gespenster, grässliche Untote, unzählige Monster und andere Gefahren bedrohen nicht nur beider Leben, sondern setzen auch ihrer Psyche gehörig zu. Carnby und Cedrac finden heraus, dass die Eigentümer der Insel, die Mortons, ein Tor zu einer Welt der Finsternis geöffnet haben, das es für immer zu schließen gilt, und zwar mit Hilfe von althergebrachten Ritualen.

NAME
BLOOD OMEN 2
PLATFORM
PC - PLAYSTATION 2 - HBOH
RELEASE
2002
EDITOR
EIDOS INTERACTIVE
DEVELOPER
CRYSTAL DYNAMICS
COPYRIGHTS
© CRYSTAL DYNAMICS/
EIDOS INTERACTIVE

Blood Omen

Four centuries have gone by since the reign of Kain the Vampire plunged the world into chaos. Sacrificing himself, Kain restored world peace and attained redemption, thereafter ruling over his vampire armies in the world of Nosgoth, remote from all contact with the living. But the Sarafan humans, a mysterious leader at their head, invade Nosgoth, decimate Kain's lieutenants, steal his accursed sword, Soul Reaver, and thrust him into a fathomless void. After two centuries in Limbo, Kain is resuscitated by another vampire survivor, Umah. But Kain has lost his memory and powers, and during his long exile, the Sarafans have taken firm control of Nosgoth, imposing a tyrannical regime. Kain is set on vengeance, but must first recover his powers and rally the surviving vampires to his cause.

« »

Quatre siècles ont passé depuis que Kain le Vampire, après avoir régné sur le monde en le plongeant dans le chaos, s'est sacrifié pour faire revenir la paix sur la terre pour sa rédemption. Depuis, Kain s'est résigné à ne plus s'immiscer dans le monde des vivants et dirige le monde des Nosgoth et ses armées de vampires. Menés par un mystérieux leader, les humains Sarafan envahissent Nosgoth, déciment les servi-teurs de Kain, lui volent son épée maudite, la Soul Reaver et le précipitent dans un gouffre sans fond. Après deux siècles d'errance dans le Néant, Kain est ressuscité par un autre vampire rescapé, Umah, mais se retrouve amnésique et privé de ses pouvoirs. Durant son long exil, les Sarafan ont pris possession de Nosgoth, et règnent en tyrans. Bien décidé à se venger, Kain devra trouver un moyen de recouvrer ses pouvoirs et rallier à sa cause les rares vampires qui ont survécu au massacre.

« »

Vier Jahrhunderte sind nunmehr verflossen, seit sich Kain, der Vampir, aufopferungsvoll zurückzog: So schenkte er der Welt, über die er bis dahin geherrscht hatte und die er für seine Pläne dem Chaos preisgegeben hatte, den erlösenden Frieden. Seitdem meidet er die Welt der Lebenden und herrscht mit seinen Vampir-Armeen über Nosgoth. Angeführt von einem geheimnisvollen Lord dringen die Sarafanen in Nosgoth ein, töten Kains Diener, rauben sein verwunschenes Schwert, das legendäre Soul Reaver, und stürzen ihn eine Klippe hinunter. Nach einer zwei Jahrhunderte währenden Irrfahrt im Jenseits wird Kain von einem entlaufenen Vampir namens Umah wieder zum Leben erweckt, büßt dabei jedoch sein Gedächtnis und seine Kräfte ein. Während seines langen Exils haben die Sarafanen weite Teil von Nosgoth unterjocht. Kain, wild entschlossen, sich zu rächen, muss ein Mittel finden, um seine Kräfte wiederzuerlangen, und die wenigen Vampire, die das Massaker überlebt haben, auf seine Seite ziehen.

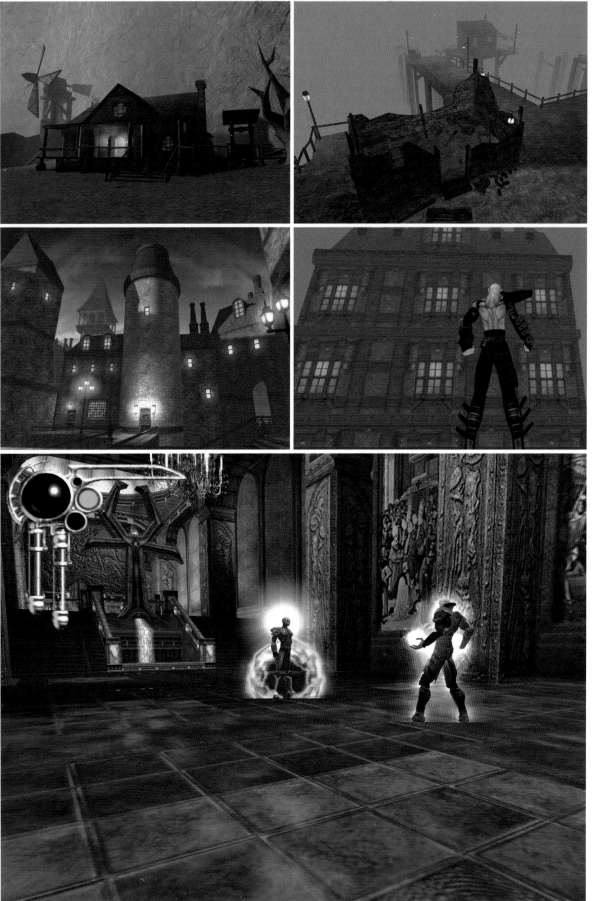

NAME CASTLEVANIA CHRONICLES
PLATFORM PLAYSTATION
RELEASE 2002
EDITOR KONAMI
DEVELOPER KONAMI
COPYRIGHTS © KONAMI
FACT 450 MILLION: THE NUMBER OF GAME BOY/ GAME BOY COLOR GAMES SOLD BETWEEN THE APPEARANCE OF THE CONSOLE AND MID-2001.

Castlevania

Simon Belmont comes of a long line of vampire-, sorcerer- and demon-hunters. Now he takes on Dracula and his henchman in the heart of Dracula's own castle, just as his ancestors before him have done. Simon also hopes to break the spell by which the vampire resuscitates every 100 years. His predecessors, Sonia, Trever and Christopher have each in their turn defeated Dracula, armed, like Simon with the Belmont "family" weapon, a fearsome magic whip that can throw fire or cast supernatural energy projectiles. Simon's hunt through the fortress leads him to other magical arms and artefacts: an enormous axe made of jet, spring-heeled boots, and a strange razor-sharp boomerang, which he can throw into the hordes of living dead, werewolves and other infernal monsters unleashed on him by Dracula.
« »

Descendant d'une longue lignée de chasseurs de vampires, sorciers et démons, Simon Belmont affronte le comte Dracula et ses sbires au cœur même du château du mort-vivant, comme le firent ses ancêtres. Simon espère également briser la malédiction qui permet au vampire de ressusciter tous les 100 ans. Chaque fois, ses prédécesseurs Sonia, Trevor et Christopher ont su vaincre Dracula, armés comme lui de l'arme de prédilection de la famille Belmont, un redoutable fouet pouvant détenir des pouvoirs magiques comme l'embrasement ou l'envoi de missiles d'énergie surnaturelle. Sa quête dans les profondeurs de la forteresse du comte lui permettra également de récupérer d'autres armes et artefacts magiques, comme une énorme hache de jet, des bottes lui permettant de sauter à des hauteurs phénoménales, ou encore un étrange boomerang tranchant comme un rasoir qu'il pourra lancer contre les hordes de morts-vivants, loups-garous, gargouilles et autres créatures infernales aux ordres de Dracula.
« »

Simon Belmont, dessen Familie seit vielen Generationen Vampire, Zauberer und Dämonen jagt, stellt sich Graf Dracula und seinen Häschern auf dem Schloss der Untoten, wie es schon seine Vorfahren getan haben. Auch er hofft den Fluch zu brechen, der den Vampir alle hundert Jahre zu neuem Leben erweckt. Seine Vorgänger Sonia, Trevor und Christopher haben es jedes Mal geschafft, Dracula zu bezwingen, und zwar mit Hilfe der Lieblingswaffe der Familie Belmont, einer gar fürchterlichen Peitsche, die mit magischen Kräften ausgestattet ist und unter anderem Raketen abschießen kann. In den Tiefen des Schlosses von Graf Dracula stößt Simon auf weitere Waffen und magische Hilfsmittel wie eine gewaltige Wurfaxt, Stiefel, mit denen er riesige Höhen überwinden kann, oder auch einen rasiermesserscharfen Bumerang, den er den von Dracula befehligten Horden von Untoten, Werwölfen und anderen höllischen Kreaturen entgegenschleudern kann.

NAME
HOUSE OF THE DEAD 3

PLATFORM
DREAMCAST - ARCADE

RELEASE
2002

EDITOR
SEGA

DEVELOPER
SEGA

COPYRIGHTS
© SEGA

FACT
HANG ON: FIRST YU SUZUKI ARCADE
GAME FOR SEGA.

House of the Dead

The living-dead and a myriad of other demonic creatures have awoken and invaded the earth, feeding off the flesh of the living. These hordes of vampires, werewolves and other gargoyles are, naturally enough, spreading panic. Only the AMS agents, with their long experience of supernatural forces, have the courage to take on and take out the shadowy beings who have summoned these terrifying minions. Top dogs at AMS are the mysterious Harry Harris, an impassive marksman with integral shades, and the charming Amy Crystal, who despite her tender years, has squelched innumerable magic creatures. The *House of the Dead* games are famous arcade and console shooters; they leave the gamer no respite; aim well and shoot fast, or the zombies will soon be sinking their teeth into you!

« »

Les morts et maintes créatures démoniaques se sont réveillés et envahissent le monde, se nourrissant de la chair des vivants. Ces hordes de zombies, de gargouilles et autres créatures surnaturelles sèment la panique, et seuls les agents de l'AMS, rompus aux combats contre ces forces surnaturelles, ont le courage de les affronter et de défaire les êtres ténébreux qui ont invoqué ces terrifiantes armées et leurs lieutenants. Au premier rang de ces agents, on retrouve le mystérieux Harry Harris, redoutable tireur inexpressif qui ne quitte jamais ses lunettes noires, et la charmante Amy Crystal qui, malgré son jeune âge, a en maintes occasions affronté et vaincu d'innombrables créatures maléfiques. Célèbres jeux de tir en salle d'arcade et sur consoles de salon, les *House of The Dead* ne laissent aucun répit au joueur qui doit viser vite et juste, au risque de voir les innocents atrocement dévorés par les zombies... ou de se faire lui-même croquer par les monstres.

« »

Die Toten und etliche andere Dämonen sind wieder erwacht und überfallen die Erde. Sie ernähren sich vom Fleisch der Lebenden. Diese Horden von Zombies, gurgelnden Monstern und anderen übernatürlichen Kreaturen verbreiten Panik, und lediglich die im Kampf gegen diese mystischen Kräfte erprobten Agenten der AMS haben den Mut, ihnen zu trotzen und die finstern Wesen, die ihre grauenhaften Armeen und ihre Commander herbeigerufen haben, zu vernichten. Zu den besten Agenten gehören der mysteriöse Harry Harris, ein gefährlicher Schütze mit ausdrucksloser Mine, der sich nie von seiner schwarzen Sonnenbrille trennt, und die charmante Amy Crystal, die trotz ihres jugendlichen Alters zahllosen Unheil bringenden Kreaturen die Stirn geboten und sie in die Knie gezwungen hat.
House of the Dead, dieses beliebte Ballerspiel für Spielhallen und die Heimkonsole, zieht den Spieler in eine atemberaubende Atmosphäre. Dabei muss er Schnelligkeit und Treffsicherheit unter Beweis stellen, sonst werden Unschuldige von den Zombies grausam verschlungen ... oder er selbst wird von Monstern gefressen.

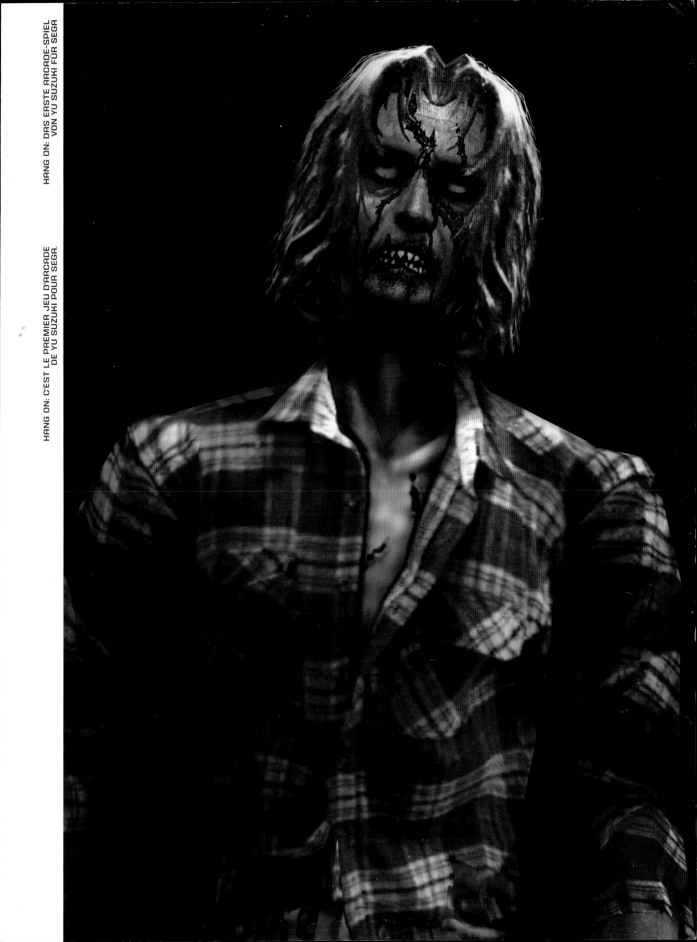

NAME
SHADOWMAN 2

PLATFORM
PLAYSTATION 2

RELEASE
2001

EDITOR
ACCLAIM ENTERTAINMENT

DEVELOPER
ACCLAIM ENTERTAINMENT

COPYRIGHTS
© ACCLAIM ENTERTAINMENT

FACT
400: THE NUMBER OF DIFFERENT
MOVEMENTS AVAILABLE FOR WRESTLERS IN
THE GAME WWF ATTITUDE ON NINTENDO 64.

Shadowman

Michael LeRoi is a NYPD officer. His partner hands him a mysterious book of ancient magic before being brutally offed by a terrifying demon in search of the volume. Some years later, the magic of the book invades LeRoi as he approaches New Orleans. He becomes Shadow Man, a supernatural voodoo-inspired creature whose mission is to protect Earth against infernal forces. And Shadow Man faces a new danger: Asmodeus has returned to earth after two thousand years of exile to unite the fanatical hordes led by Papa Morte, the Grigori. The world is threatened with voodoo apocalypse. Shadow Man must do battle in the worlds of the living and the dead, moving from one to another to vanquish the fanatics and demons who serve Papa Morte and Asmodeus.

« »

Avant d'être sauvagement assassiné par un effrayant démon, le partenaire de Michael LeRoi, policier de New York, lui confie le mystérieux livre de magie ancienne que convoite la créature. Quelques années plus tard, la magie du livre envahit LeRoi alors qu'il approche de la Nouvelle-Orléans, le transformant en créature surnaturelle animée par la magie vaudou, le Shadow Man. Investi d'une mission de protection de la Terre contre les forces infernales, Shadow Man doit aujourd'hui affronter un nouveau péril : Asmodeus, un être maléfique, revient sur terre après deux millénaires de bannissement, rassemblant des hordes de fanatiques menés par le sorcier Papa Morte, les Grigori, et s'apprêtant à plonger la planète dans un cauchemar vaudou apocalyptique. Pour vaincre les Grigori, Shadow Man devra se battre aussi bien dans le monde des vivants que dans celui des morts, passant d'un univers à l'autre afin de terrasser les fanatiques et les démons au service de Papa Morte et d'Asmodeus.

« »

Unmittelbar bevor der New Yorker Polizist und Partner von Michael LeRoi auf abscheuliche Weise von einem Dämon ermordet wird, vertraut er Michael LeRoi noch das alte Zauberbuch an, auf das es der Dämon abgesehen hatte. Einige Jahre später, als Mike sich auf dem Weg nach New Orleans befindet, greift der Zauber des Buches auf LeRoi über und verwandelt ihn in eine übernatürliche, vom Voodoo-Zauber getragene Kreatur, den Shadow Man. Mit der Mission beauftragt, die Erde gegen die dämonischen Kräfte zu verteidigen, muss Shadow Man einer neuen Gefahr trotzen: Asmodeus, der Höllenfürst, will auch seiner zwei Jahrtausende währenden Verbannung wieder auf die Erde zurückkehren. Dazu heuert er die vom Zauberer Papa Morte befehligten Horden von Fanatikern an, die Grigori, die sich anschicken, den Planeten in einen apokalyptischen Voodoo-Albtraum zu stürzen. Um die Grigori zu besiegen, wird Shadow Man ständig zwischen der Welt der Lebenden und der Toten pendeln müssen, um die im Dienste von Papa Morte und Asmodeus stehenden Fanatiker und Dämonen zu überwältigen.

400: SO VIELE VERSCHIEDENE BEWEGUNGEN
KÖNNEN DIE CATCHER IN WWF ATTITUDE
AUF NINTENDO 64 AUSFÜHREN.

400: C'EST LE NOMBRE DE MOUVEMENTS
DIFFÉRENTS POUR L'ENSEMBLE DES CATCHEURS
DU JEU WWF ATTITUDE SUR NINTENDO 64

NAME
SILENT HILL 2

PLATFORM
PLAYSTATION 2
XBOX

RELEASE
2001

EDITOR
KONAMI

DEVELOPER
KONAMI

COPYRIGHTS
© KONAMI

FACT
26: THE NUMBER OF MONTHS SPENT
ON DEVELOPING BIOHAZARD, RENAMED
RESIDENT EVIL FOR THE USA AND EUROPE.

Silent Hill

The happy, normal life of James Sutherland takes a tragic turn when his beloved wife, Mary, dies of a grave illness. Three years later, James receives a letter from his dead wife, telling him to meet her in the little abandoned town of Silent Hill. There follows a voyage into the heart of darkness; the little town is submerged in mist and haunted by vile creatures and disturbed individuals, like Eddie, a psychopathic young fatty. James is constantly on the point of going mad himself. Why has his wife returned from the dead? What superior power has drawn her to this accursed spot? The truth is buried at the heart of Silent Hill, and defended by hideous monsters. Silent Hill has an atmosphere worthy of the finest horror films; the scenario of this gut-wrenching game tests the gamer's nerve to its limits.

« »

La vie heureuse et ordinaire de James Sutherland bascule en ce jour tragique où son épouse adorée, Mary, décède d'une grave maladie. Trois ans plus tard, James reçoit une lettre de sa défunte épouse, lui donnant rendez-vous dans la petite ville perdue de Silent Hill. S'ensuivra un périple au cœur de l'horreur dans une ville perdue, noyée dans le brouillard et hantée par des créatures innommables, de troubles individus, tel Eddie, le jeune garçon obèse psychopathe. James risquera à tout moment de basculer dans la folie : pourquoi son épouse est-elle revenue de l'au-delà ? Quelle puissance supérieure l'a attirée dans ce lieu maudit ? La vérité est tapie au cœur de la ville de Silent Hill, baignée dans une sombre atmosphère digne des plus angoissants films d'horreur. Un jeu qui prend au tripes, un scénario qui entraîne le joueur à la limite du malaise, des monstres effroyables à combattre : tel est l'univers de la ville de Silent Hill.

« »

Das zufriedene und recht normale Leben von James Sutherland bekommt einen gehörigen Knacks an dem Tag, als seine geliebte Frau an einer schweren Krankheit stirbt. Drei Jahre später erhält der Witwer einen mysteriösen Brief von seiner verstorbenen Frau, in dem sie ihn um ein Treffen in dem verschlafenen Ferienressort Silent Hill bittet. Nun beginnt eine Horrorreise in einer ausgestorbenen, im Nebel versunkenen Stadt mit wild gewordenen Zombies und einzelnen Störern - mit dem kleinen, dicken Eddi zum Beispiel, der ein Psychopath ist. James droht jeden Moment wahnsinnig zu werden. Warum ist seine Frau aus dem Jenseits zurückgekehrt? Welche höhere Macht hat sie an diesen Ort des Grauens befohlen? Die Wahrheit verbirgt sich in dem Städtchen Silent Hill, wo eine so düstere Atmosphäre wie in den schlimmsten Horrorfilmen herrscht. Ein Spiel, das an die Nieren geht, mit einem Szenario, das einen an den Rand des Wahnsinns treibt, mit schaurigen Monstern, gegen die man ankämpfen muss: Das erwartet den Spieler in Silent Hill.

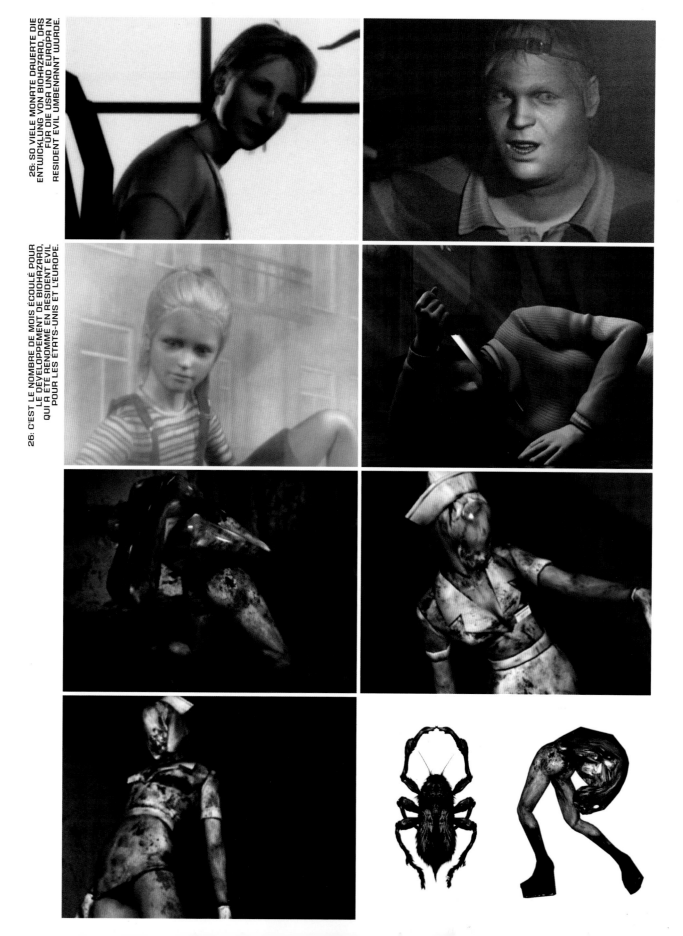

26: SO VIELE MONATE DAUERTE DIE ENTWICKLUNG VON BIOHAZARD, DAS FÜR DIE USA UND EUROPA IN RESIDENT EVIL UMBENANNT WURDE.

26: C'EST LE NOMBRE DE MOIS ÉCOULÉ POUR LE DÉVELOPPEMENT DE BIOHAZARD, QUI A ÉTÉ RENOMMÉ EN RESIDENT EVIL POUR LES ÉTATS-UNIS ET L'EUROPE.

NAME
SOUL REAVER 2
PLATFORM
PLAYSTATION 2 · PC
RELEASE
2001
EDITOR
EIDOS INTERACTIVE
DEVELOPER
CRYSTAL DYNAMICS
COPYRIGHTS
© CRYSTAL DYNAMICS/
EIDOS INTERACTIVE

Soul Reaver

Betrayed by his master Kain, Lord of the Kingdom of Nosgoth, for acquiring powers exceeding his own, Raziel is condemned; he will be immersed in the Lake of Lost Souls, fatal to the vampire kind. Miraculously escaping this fate, Raziel swears vengeance on his former master. But Kain's powers have grown, while Raziel's have been eroded by the fatal waters; his face perpetually masked by a ragged cloth, Raziel must regain his strength by fighting a myriad of creatures and absorbing their damned souls. Over the course of his adventure, Raziel discovers time portals and can seek through different epochs of Nosgoth an era when Kain had not yet put on his recently-acquired invincibility. But Raziel's quest gradually takes on a completely different dimension... Ultimately, the very existence of Nosgoth lies in his hands.

« »

Trahi par son maître Kain, seigneur du royaume de Nosgoth, parce qu'il avait acquis un pouvoir supérieur au sien, Raziel est condamné à être exécuté et plongé dans l'eau du lac des âmes perdues, fatale à son espèce. Echappant par miracle à son destin fatal, Raziel jure de se venger de son ancien maître. Mais, alors que le pouvoir de ce dernier s'est affirmé, celui de Raziel, suite aux dommages causés par les eaux, s'est amoindri. Le vampire au visage éternellement masqué par une étoffe usée devra retrouver sa puissance en combattant maintes créatures et en absorbant leur âme damnée. Au cours de son aventure, Raziel découvrira des portails temporels qui lui permettront de voyager dans différentes époques de Nosgoth et peut-être de trouver Kain dans le passé, avant qu'il ne devienne invincible... Mais la quête de Raziel prendra petit à petit une toute autre dimension, et de ses actes dépendra l'existence même du royaume de Nosgoth.

« »

Raziel, der von seinem Gebieter Kain, dem Herrscher über die Welt von Nosgoth, verraten wurde, weil er als sein Statthalter inzwischen mächtiger geworden war als dieser, wird mit zerfetzten Flügeln in den See der Toten geworfen. Für einen seines Schlags ist das tödlich. Doch wie durch ein Wunder entgeht Raziel seinem verhängnisvollen Schicksal und schwört dem einstigen Gebieter ewige Rache. Während Kain seine Macht vorerst erneut festigen konnte, hat Raziel im Wasser an Macht eingebüßt. Um seine alten Fähigkeiten wiederzuerlangen, muss der Vampir, der sein Gesicht stets hinter einem alten Stofffetzen verbirgt, gegen eine Vielzahl von Kreaturen kämpfen und sich ihre verdammten Seelen einverleiben. Im Laufe der Zeit stößt Raziel auf Zeittore, durch die er in verschiedene Epochen von Nosgoth reisen kann. Und vielleicht trifft er in der Vergangenheit auf Kain, bevor dieser unbesiegbar wird... Nach und nach nimmt die Suche nach Kain ungeahnte Dimensionen an, und von Raziels Vorgehen hängt bald sogar die Existenz von Nosgoth ab.

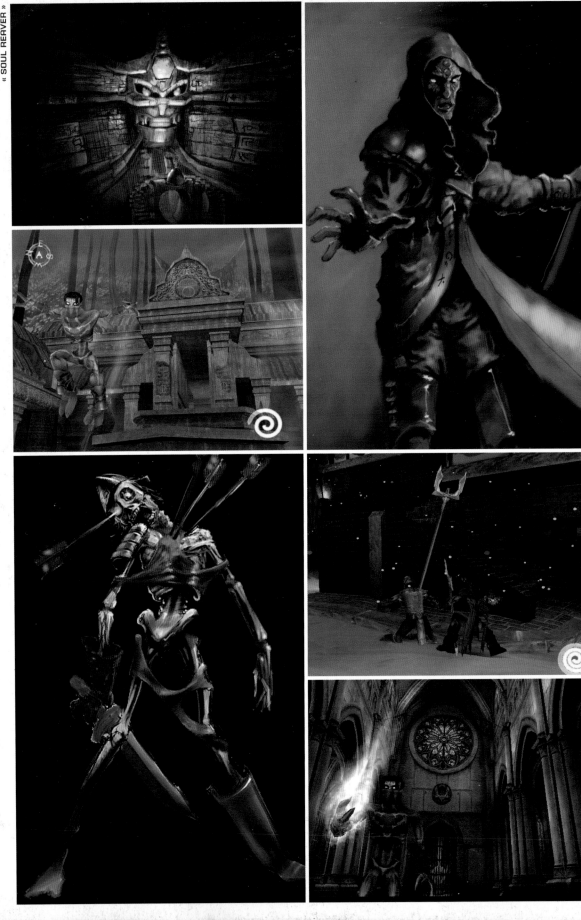

«Fighting Heroes»

Combat games are not simply safety-valves for testosterone-release. The combatants may spend their time unleashing avalanches of blows on their adversaries 'human' or virtual, but the games themselves are almost invariably based on Asian martial-art traditions. Sagas such as Sega's Virtua Fighter, Tecmo's Dead or Alive and Namco's Tekken combine spectacle and realism in a homage to existing martial arts.

They may be less eye-catching than games in which the protagonists are endowed with magical arms or supernatural powers, but these 'traditional' duels are no less dazzling for the fact that the blows and holds are taken from reality. Indeed, they go beyond combat to become veritable ballets; the choreography of expert combat is impressive, and to see two masters of virtual martial arts face off is a very striking spectacle.

Combat games don't just base themselves on martial-art techniques, they also tend to incorporate the values of those arts. The fighters in these virtual tournaments have a moral grounding and their reasons for entering the fray are not reducible to the quest for adrenaline: self-perfection, constraints of honour, clan tradition and other such motivations are always to the fore. Some games place these values at the heart of their narrative; in Bushido Blade, for instance, the quest cannot be completed unless the gamer competes honourably and respects his adversaries.

Expertise in martial arts, virtual or real, cannot be acquired overnight. The gamer learns through combat which tactics and combinations are effective and must, with every new duel, assess his adversary and adjust his style accordingly. Thus every gaming novice can, by persevering, expect to become a virtual master.

« »

Loin de n'être que de simples défouloirs dans lesquels les joueurs ne font qu'asséner des avalanches de coups à leurs adversaires (entièrement virtuels ou dirigés par d'autres joueurs), les jeux de combat, dans leur grande majorité, s'inspirent des traditions martiales asiatiques. Les sagas Virtua Fighter de Sega, Dead or Alive de Tecmo ou Tekken de Namco allient le spectaculaire au réaliste, s'appuyant sur des arts martiaux existants.

S'ils sont moins pyrotechniques que les combats d'autres jeux où les protagonistes se défient à coup de pouvoirs surnaturels ou d'armes magiques, les duels « traditionnels » sont tout aussi éblouissants avec des frappes et des prises calquées sur la réalité. Plus que de simples combats, ces affrontements sont aussi de véritables ballets : les chorégraphies de combat sont impressionnantes et voir des maîtres en arts martiaux virtuels mesurer leurs arts respectifs est un spectacle souvent étourdissant.

Les jeux de combats ne se contentent évidemment pas de s'inspirer des techniques martiales, mais intègrent également leurs valeurs. Les combattants de ces tournois virtuels ont un sens moral et des raisons de s'affronter qui vont au-delà de la simple envie de se battre : accomplissement de soi, dette d'honneur, tradition de clan et autres motivations du même ordre sont toujours au rendez-vous. Certains jeux ont même mis ces valeurs au cœur de leur principe, comme Bushido Blade, où le joueur ne peut achever sa quête que s'il a combattu dans l'honneur, en respectant ses adversaires.

La maîtrise de ces arts martiaux virtuels ne s'acquiert pas en un instant, tout comme dans la réalité. Le joueur apprend au fil des combats les tactiques et enchaînements efficaces et doit à chaque duel jauger son adversaire et agir en conséquent. Aussi tout joueur novice peut-il espérer devenir maître des arts martiaux de son ou ses jeux, par persévérance et ouverture d'esprit.

Kampfspiele sind in den allermeisten Fällen von den asiatischen Kampfkünsten inspiriert und weit davon entfernt, der Kategorie simpler Spiele zum Abreagieren anzugehören, in denen die Spieler permanent Schläge austeilen (völlig virtuell oder von anderen Spielern gesteuert). Sagas wie Virtua Fighter von Sega, Dead or Alive von Tecmo oder Tekken von Namco verbinden Spektakuläres mit Realistischem.

Zwar sind die „traditionellen" Duelle weniger effektvoll angelegt als viele andere Spiele, in denen sich die Protagonisten mit übernatürlichen Kräften oder magischen Waffen messen, dennoch beeindrucken auch sie mit Schlägen oder Griffen, die der Realität abgeschaut sind. Sie präsentieren mehr als nur einfache Kämpfe, sie präsentieren regelrechte Ballettvorführungen. Die Kampf-Choreografien sind beeindruk-kend, und den virtuellen Meistern zuzuschauen, wie sie ihre virtuellen Kampfkünste im Duell zum Besten geben, ist meist ein überwälti-gendes Schauspiel.

Die Kampfspiele sind nicht bloß von den Kampftechniken inspiriert, sie integrieren auch die ihnen zugrunde liegenden Werte. Die Kämpfer vertreten meist moralische Prinzipien und ihre Motive für die Teilnahme an den Kämpfen liegen jenseits der simplen Kampfeslust: So suchen sie beispielsweise Selbstverwirklichung, wollen ihre verlorene Ehre wiederherstellen oder in den Traditionen ihres Clans leben. Diese oder ähnliche Motive wurden für einige Spiele zum Prinzip erhoben, so auch für Bushido Blade, wo der Spieler erst dann erfolgreich seine Mission erfüllt hat, wenn er ehrenvoll gekämpft und seinem Gegner den nötigen Respekt entgegengebracht hat.

Die sichere Beherrschung dieser virtuellen Kampfkünste erwirbt man, ganz so wie in der Realität, nicht im Handumdrehen. Der Spieler erlernt im Laufe der Kämpfe Taktiken und nützliche Kombinationen und muss bei jedem Kampf die Fähigkeiten seines Gegners einschätzen lernen und dementsprechend handeln. So darf jeder Anfänger hoffen, durch Ausdauer und Aufgeschlossenheit zum Meister der ver-schiedenen Kampfkünste aufzusteigen.

NAME
PLATFORM
RELEASE
EDITOR
DEVELOPER
COPYRIGHTS

Dead or Alive

The combatants of *Dead or Alive* are past-masters of their disciplines. They include Jann-Lee, Chinese adept of Jeet Kune Do, Bass, the American wrestler, Zack, the Thai Boxing master, and Hayate the Ninja, and the variety of their combat styles is matched only by their sleight of hand: devastating blows, fast and furious combinations of kicks and punches, immobilisation holds and counter-attacks follow so close on each other that the spectator is witness to a dazzlingly lethal choreography in which Queensberry rules definitely don't apply. The fighters find themselves duelling now in the heart of snow-bound forests, where tree-trunks serve to parry a blow, now on the summit of immense mountain-ranges where the least slip means death. There are no rules, and gallantry is not on the menu, since the men of *Dead and Alive* are regularly faced by charming young women whose beauty and bra-popping forms disguise mean combat skills.

« »

Les combattants de la trilogie *Dead or Alive* sont tous passés maîtres dans leurs arts martiaux respectifs. De Jann-Lee, Chinois adepte du Jeet Kune Do à Bass, le catcheur américain, en passant par Zack, maître du Thaï Boxing ou Hayate le Ninja, la variété de leurs façons de se battre n'a d'égale que leur rapidité : coups fulgurants, enchaînements furieux de coups de poings et de pied, prises d'immobilisation et contre-attaques se succèdent et offrent aux spectateurs un ballet sauvage éblouissant, une mortelle chorégraphie où tous les coups sont permis. Les affrontements entre ces guerriers peuvent aussi bien se dérouler au cœur d'une forêt enneigée où les troncs d'arbres permettent de bloquer un adversaire qu'au faîte de montagnes immenses où le moindre faux pas peut entraîner une chute vertigineuse. Aucune règle n'est à respecter, ni même la galanterie, les combattants de *Dead or Alive* se retrouvant régulièrement face à de charmantes jeunes femmes dont la beauté et les formes généreuses masquent des talents guerriers hors pair.

« »

Die Kämpfer der Trilogie *Dead or Alive* sind allesamt Meister in ihrer jeweiligen Kampfsportart. Angefangen vom chinesischen Streiter Jann-Lee, einem Anhänger von Jeet Kune Do, über Zack, den Thai-Boxing-Meister, bis zu Bass, dem amerikanischen Catcher, oder dem Ninja Hayate wird die Vielfalt der Kampfdisziplinen nur noch von der Reaktionsschnelligkeit übertroffen: Blitzschnelle und scharfe Schläge, eine Aufeinanderfolge von heftigen Faustschlägen und Fußtritten, Blockierungsgriffen und Gegenangriffen bieten den Zuschauern das bestechende Bild eines wilden Balletts, einer tödlichen Choreographie, in der alle Schläge erlaubt sind. Schauplatz dieser Gefechte können verschneite Wälder sein, in denen die Baumstämme einen Gegner in die Enge treiben, aber auch die Gipfel mächtiger Berge, wo ein falscher Schritt einen Schwindel erregenden Sturz zur Folge hat. Regeln sind dabei nicht einzuhalten, nicht einmal Rücksichtnahme oder Ritterlichkeit zählt, obwohl die Kämpfer von *Dead or Alive* ständig charmanten jungen Damen gegenüberstehen, deren Schönheit und deren üppige Formen mit meisterlichen Kampfkünsten einhergehen.

女優なんぞ許さん…

お前に奴は倒せん

偉くなったなハヤテよ

NAME

PLATFORM

RELEASE

EDITOR

DEVELOPER

COPYRIGHTS

FACT

Smash Brothers

The Nintendo heroes come in all shapes and sizes, but this party is no family love-fest: it's one massive all-against-all! Of course, they're all members of the same family, so killing is out, and the idea is to have a wild time without inflicting too many scrapes and bumps; the losers are chucked straight out of the astounding combat arenas as soon as they are KO'd. Pikachu, Mario, Yoshi, Donkey Kong, Link, Fox, Kirby and many others thus take part in duelling games, each with their own secret moves, and with the assistance of the various objects with which the terrain is littered. Pokeballs, laser swords, small bombs, massive packing-cases, anything goes in the effort to knock out your adversary or shove them out of the arena. Unlike most combat games, *Super Smash Brothers Melee* has a strong vein of humour and brings to life the dream of millions of gamers worldwide who have grown up with the Nintendo universe: to see their idols brought together in a single game.

« »

Venus de tous les horizons, des différents univers façonnés par Nintendo au fil des années, les héros de la compagnie se retrouvent non pas pour une fête entre amis… mais pour une grande bagarre généralisée ! Bien sûr, tous sont de la même famille, aussi n'est-il pas ici question de s'entre-tuer, mais de se défouler ensemble sans grand bobo, les vaincus étant éjectés des incroyables arènes de combat lorsqu'ils sont mis K.O. Pikachu, Mario, Yoshi, Donkey Kong, Link, Fox, Kirby et bien d'autres s'affrontent ainsi par jeu, armés de leurs bottes secrètes, mais aussi aidés par les nombreux objets disséminés sur le terrain. Petites bombes, pokeballs, épées laser, caisses massives : tous les coups sont permis pour sonner les adversaires, voire les pousser hors de l'arène. Loin de la grande majorité des jeux de combats, *Super Smash Brothers Melee* prend le parti de l'humour et concrétise le rêve de millions de joueurs qui ont grandi avec les mondes de Nintendo : voir leurs idoles rassemblées dans un seul et même jeu.

« »

Aus allen Himmelsrichtungen und aus den verschiedenen von Nintendo im Laufe der Jahre geschaffenen Welten kommen die Helden zusammen, aber nicht etwa zu einem Fest unter Freunden, sondern zu einer allgemeinen Prügel-Orgie! Weil alle der gleichen Familie angehören, geht es hier nicht um ein gegenseitiges Abschlachten, sondern einfach darum, sich ohne größeren Schaden gemeinsam auszutoben und abzureagieren und die Besiegten aus den Kampfarenen zu werfen. Pikatchu, Mario, Yoshi, Donkey Kong, Link, Fox, Kirby und andere treten, ausgestattet mit ihren Zauberstiefeln, in einzelnen Spielpartien gegeneinander an. Dabei bedienen sie sich zahlreicher auf dem Feld versteckter Gegenstände. Kleine Bomben, Pokeballs, Laserschwerte, massive Kisten: Alles ist erlaubt, um den Gegnern einen tüchtigen Schlag zu versetzen oder sie gar aus der Arena zu werfen. Völlig anders als die meisten Kampfspiele verschreibt sich *Super Smash Brothers Melee* dem Humor und setzt den Traum von Millionen Spielern in die Tat um, die mit der Welt von Nintendo aufgewachsen sind. Hier sehen sie ihre Idole in einem einzigen Spiel vereint.

NAME
PLATFORM
RELEASE
EDITOR
DEVELOPER
COPYRIGHTS

P – 66

Soul Calibur

Soul Edge, a demon-sword, offered its holder phenomenal power by bestowing the soul-strength of defeated adversaries. The sinister Cervantes possessed it but was worsted by the beautiful Sophitia, who smashed the accursed weapon. Don't crow too soon! From the fragments of Soul Edge a still more dreadful weapon may arise: Soul Calibur.

Many warriors have devoted their lives to discovering the Soul Edge fragments. Resolved to destroy its powers or bent on acquiring them, they find in their path other claimants to the arm, who attack without mercy. Of those, a mere handful can hope ultimately to lay hands on the demon-blade. They fought over Soul Edge. Now they are again pitted against each other. Cervantes, Astaroth, Hwang, Inferno, Ivy, Kilik, Lizardman, Maxi, Mitsurugi, Nightmare, Rock, Seung Mina, Siegfried, Sophitia, Taki, Voldo, Xianhua and Yoshimitsu are all contenders. But who will finally brandish Soul Calibur?

« »

Soul Edge, l'arme-démon, offrait à son détenteur un pouvoir phénoménal, le dotant de la force des âmes des adversaires vaincus. Le sombre Cervantes qui possédait l'épée autrefois fut vaincu par la belle Sophitia, et celle-ci brisa l'arme maudite. Mais des fragments de Soul Edge peut naître une arme encore plus redoutable : Soul Calibur.

De nombreux guerriers ont voué leur existence à la découverte des fragments de l'arme. Qu'ils se soient juré de détruire son effroyable puissance maléfique ou qu'ils la convoitent, leur quête les amènera chacun à affronter les autres prétendants, dans de formidables duels sans merci. Mais si les prétendants sont nombreux, seule une poignée de combattants peut espérer s'emparer de l'arme-démon. Ces quelques hommes et femmes se sont déjà affrontés pour Soul Edge, et vont de nouveau se mesurer : qui de Cervantes, Astaroth, Hwang, Inferno, Ivy, Kilik, Lizardman, Maxi, Mitsurugi, Nightmare, Rock, Seung Mina, Siegfried, Sophitia, Taki, Voldo, Xianghua ou Yoshimitsu prouvera qu'il est capable de brandir Soul Calibur ?

« »

Soul Edge, die Dämonen-Waffe, bot seinem Besitzer eine außergewöhnliche Macht, da sie ihm die Kraft der Seelen besiegter Gegner verlieh. Einst war sie im Besitz des finsteren Cervantes. Aber die schöne Sophitia besiegte ihn und zerstörte die fluchbeladene Waffe. Die Splitter von Soul Edge lassen sich jedoch in eine noch gefährlichere Waffe verwandeln: Soul Calibur.

Auf der Suche nach den verschollenen Teilen sind zahlreiche Krieger sogar bereit, ihr Leben zu opfern. Ganz gleich, ob sie sich schwören, diese entsetzliche und böse Macht zu zerstören oder ob sie sie begehren: Auf ihrer Suche werden die Krieger immer in fürchterliche, gnadenlose Duelle gegen die anderen Mitstreiter verwickelt. Die Zahl der Suchenden ist groß, aber nur ein paar Kämpfer können hoffen, der Dämonen-Waffe habhaft zu werden. Obwohl die wenigen Männer und Frauen bereits im Kampf um Soul Edge ihre Kraft unter Beweis gestellt haben, müssen sie sich erneut einer Prüfung unterziehen. Angetreten sind Cervantes, Astaroth, Hwang, Inferno, Ivy, Kilik, Lizardman, Maxi, Mitsurugi, Nightmare, Rock, Seung Mina, Siegfried, Sophitia, Taki, Voldo, Xianghua oder Yoshimitsu. Wer wird der legitime Besitzer des Schwertes Soul Calibur sein?

NAME
PLATFORM
RELEASE
EDITOR
DEVELOPER
COPYRIGHTS
FACT

Tekken

Whether it's the call of glory or the whopping prizes, the greatest martial artists have all foregathered for the greatest competition, the Iron Fist Tournament, also known as 'Tekken'. Each must fight eliminators for the right to take on the fearsome Heihachi Mishima. The redoubtable Mishima, who heads up a huge financial consortium, Mishima Zaibatsu, is the tournament-organiser. But all the candidates have ulterior motives, not all of them savoury. Yoshimitsu and his rival, Kunimitsu, the Ninjas, are attracted by the prize money. Marshall Law has come for the glory, like Paul Phoenix; Paul is shadowed by Kuma, who has sworn to kill him. Kazuya Mishima, Heihachi's son, is a karate champion who would love to supplant his father. Michelle Chang, American by birth, seeks revenge: Heihachi had her father assassinated. The Russian cyborg Jack aims to kill all the members of the Mishima family, as does the Irish woman Nina Williams; in Nina's footsteps comes her sister Anna, a bad case of sibling rivalry. To these must be added the mysterious King, his face concealed by a jaguar mask, the sumo warrior Ganryu, the karateka Lee Chaolan and the old master Wan Jinery. They're all here, folks, let combat begin!

« »

Attirés par la gloire ou par la confortable récompense qui gratifiera le vainqueur, les plus grands maîtres en arts martiaux du monde entier se retrouvent pour la plus grande des compétitions, le tournoi Iron Fist, aussi connu sous le nom de Tekken. Ces guerriers s'affronteront pour savoir lequel d'entre eux pourra se mesurer au grand Heihachi Mishima, redoutable guerrier, dirigeant du plus grand empire financier, le Mishima Zaibatsu et organisateur du tournoi ; mais tous ont également d'autres motivations, parfois obscures. Yoshimitsu et son rival, Kunimitsu, tous deux guerriers Ninja, sont attirés par la récompense. Marshall Law est venu pour la gloire, tout comme Paul Phoenix, ce dernier étant suivi par Kuma qui a juré de le tuer. Kazuya Mishima, fils de Heihachi et champion de karaté, veut faire mainmise sur l'organisation de son père. Michelle Chang, américaine d'origine, veut se venger d'Heihachi, qui fit assassiner son père. Le cyborg russe Jack a pour but de tuer les membres de la famille Mishima, comme l'Irlandaise Nina Williams, suivie par sa sœur Anna, désireuse de se mesurer à son aînée. Restent les mystérieux King au visage dissimulé sous un masque de jaguar, le sumo Ganryu, le karatéka Lee Chaolan et le vieux maître Wan Jinery. Les participants sont tous là, que le tournoi Iron Fist commence !

« »

Mit der Aussicht auf Ruhm oder eine ansehnliche Belohnung für den Sieger treffen sich die weltbesten Allroundkämpfer beim „King of the Iron Fist"-Turnier, das auch unter dem Namen Tekken bekannt ist. Sie wollen herausfinden, wer sich messen kann mit Altmeister Heihachi Mishima, einem Furcht erregenden Krieger, der das größte Finanzimperium leitet, oder mit Mishima Zaibatsu, dem Organisator des Turniers. Gleichzeitig haben die Kämpfer noch andere, zum Teile niedrige Beweggründe. Yoshimitsu und sein Kontrahent Kunimitsu, ihres Zeichens Ninja-Kämpfer, sind wegen der hohen Belohnung angetreten. Marshall Law ist auf Ruhm aus, ebenso Paul Phoenix. Letzterem ist Kuma auf den Fersen, der geschworen hat, ihn zu töten. Kazuya Mishima, der Sohn von Heihachi und Karatemeister, will sich das Imperium seines Vaters einverleiben. Michelle Chang ist amerikanischer Abstammung und will sich an Heihachi rächen, weil der ihren Vater umgebracht hat. Der russische Cyborg Jack hat vor, alle Angehörigen von Mishima auszulöschen, dasselbe Ziel verfolgt auch die Irin Nina Williams. Deren Schwester Anna will sich unbedingt mit ihrer älteren Schwester messen. Nicht zu vergessen der geheimnisvolle King, der sein Gesicht hinter einer Jaguarmaske verbirgt, der Sumoringer Ganryu, die Karatekämpferin Lee Chaolan und Altmeister Wan Jinery. Alle Haudegen sind versammelt: Das Iron-Fist-Turnier kann beginnen.

NAME

PLATFORM

RELEASE

EDITOR

DEVELOPER

COPYRIGHTS

FACT

Virtua Fighter

The World Fighting Tournament is the world's most secretive martial arts competition; only the greatest dare compete for the title of ultimate fighter. Six mega-industries affiliated under the codename Judgement 6 have chosen the tournament to test their creation, Dural, half-man, half-machine, who has been programmed with fighting skills of unimaginable efficiency. If Dural wins the tournament, Judgement 6 will mass-produce cyborgs and use them to take over the world. The finest representatives of the different martial arts are here, all thirteen of them: the massive Jeffry Wild, the athletic Vanessa Lewis, Lei Fei the Shaolin monk, the agile Pai Chan, the wrestler Wolf Hawkfield, the devastating Akira Yuki, the graceful Aoi Umenokouji, the unpredictable Shun Di, the dazzling Sarah Bryant and her brother Jacky, the feline Lion Rafale, the sage Lau Chan, and Kage-Maru the Ninja. Which of them will win through to the final and take on Dural?
« »

Le World Fighting Tournament est le plus secret des tournois d'arts martiaux, où seuls les plus grands osent s'inscrire et briguer le titre de combattant ultime. Les six méga-industries regroupées sous le nom de code Judgment 6 ont choisi ce tournoi pour mettre à l'épreuve leur dernière création, Dural, mi-homme, mi-machine, doté de talents de guerrier inimaginables. Si Dural remporte le tournoi, Judgement 6 lancera la fabrication de cyborgs à grande échelle et se lancera à la conquête du monde. Qui des treize meilleurs guerriers des différents arts martiaux réussira à vaincre Dural, après avoir triomphé des autres participants ? Tous ont leur chance : le massif Jeffry McWild, l'athlétique Vanessa Lewis, Lei Fei le moine shaolin, l'agile Pai Chan, le catcheur Wolf Hawkfield, le fulgurant Akira Yuki, la gracieuse Aoi Umenokouji, l'imprévisible Shun Di, la fulgurante Sarah Bryant ou son frère Jacky, le félin Lion Rafale, le sage Lau Chan, et Kage-Maru le ninja.
« »

Das World Fighting Tournament gilt als das geheimste Turnier der Kampfkünste. Nur die Besten wagen eine Teilnahme, um den Titel des Ultimate Fighter zu erringen. Die sechs Megaindustrien, die unter dem Codenamen Judgment 6 zusammengeschlossen sind, haben sich für dieses Turnier entschieden, um ihre letzte Kreation zu testen. Dural, halb Mensch, halb Maschine, besitzt unvorstellbare kriegerische Talente. Sollte Dural das Turnier gewinnen, wird Judgment 6 mit der seriellen Produktion des Cyborgs beginnen, um die Welt zu erobern. Welchem der dreizehn besten Krieger der verschiedenen Kampfkünste wird es gelingen, die anderen Teilnehmer und schließlich Dural zu besiegen? Jeder bekommt eine Chance: der massige Jeffry McWild, die athletische Vanessa Lewis, der Shaolin-Mönch Lei Fei, der geschickte Pai Chan, der Catcher Wolf Hawkfield, der blitzschnelle Akira Yuki, die anmutige Aoi Umenokouji, der unberechenbare Shun Di, die schnellfüßige Sarah Bryant oder ihr Bruder Jacky, die Raubkatze Lion Rafale, der weise Lau Chan oder der Ninja Kage-Maru.

250: ANZAHL DER PERSONEN, DIE ÜBER EINEN ZEITRAUM VON DREI JAHREN AN DER ENTWICKLUNG VON SHENMUE MITGEWIRKT HABEN

250: C'EST LE NOMBRE DE PERSONNES QUI ONT PARTICIPE AU DEVELOPPEMENT DE SHENMUE PENDANT 3 ANS.

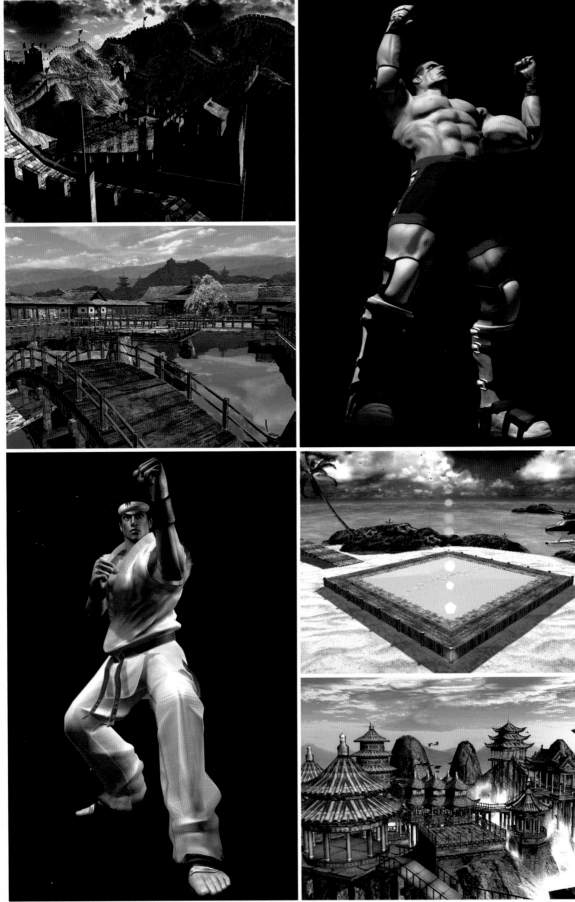

NAME
JASON RUBIN

BORN
1970

HOME TOWN
LOS ANGELES, USA

OCCUPATION
C.E.O.

WORK
JAK & DAXTER :: THE PRECURSOR
LEGACY (2001) NAUGHTY DOG
CRASH BANDICOOT 2 :: CORTEX
STRIKES BACK (1997) NAUGHTY DOG
CRASH BANDICOOT (1996) NAUGHTY DOG
WAY OF THE WARRIOR
(1994) NAUGHTY DOG
KEEN THE THIEF (1989) NAUGHTY DOG

«Funny Heroes»
Jason Rubin

Humour came honestly to Naughty Dog's early video games attempts: they were laughable. Our first published title, Ski Crazed, was notable for two reasons. First, it came very close, but didn't quite create the opposite of a siing experience. And second, it relished that fact, throwing about images of ski bunnies and cartoon studs in lieu of gameplay. In an era when gamers were on serious quests and defending the world from alien attack, Ski Crazed was stupid, and proud of it. If only our publisher at that time hadn't been.

We tried to leave humour behind with our third title, Keef the Thief, but it was not meant to be. Angered by the idea that we had been assigned a "professional" writer, we put sarcastic placeholder text in the Beta version and then sent it off to slaughter. Inspired by our insults, the hack wrote 1650 lines of what was very close to, but not quite, the opposite of humour, and our title was transformed over-night into a parody. Based on Keef's sales, the joke was on us.

Naughty Dog's first successful title was Way of the Warrior. Sure, we ripped off Boon and Tobias' Mortal Kombat, but we tried to make the characters and actions so over-the-top that the gore was more slapstick than visceral. We tried to imbue the game with our trademark Naughty Dog humour. But the United States House of Representatives didn't get the joke, and WOTW was mentioned as one of the top ten worst games for kids that year. For the first time in our careers we weren't smiling. Naughty Dog decided that every game we made from that point on would lift spirits, not lower them. Thus we began Crash Bandicoot.

I am convinced that Crash's success as a character is directly linked to his physical comedy, especially his facial expressions. Sure, the gameplay was good, but it was the humour, in my opinion, that sold the games. Mario never really had a personality. Sonic's persona, if you will call it that, is that he is fast. Crash began his first game by pulling his nose out of the sand, shaking off, turning around and giving you the most vacant stare seen in a video game to date; and then he braced himself for the tasks ahead. There it was. Crash isn't too bright, he isn't infallible, but he has a big heart. He's just like you and me. We love him. Crash was put through more gruesome deaths than the Way of the Warrior characters, but this time everyone laughed. Sony Computer Entertainment sold over 24 million copies of the four Naughty Dog developed Crash games, we were mentioned in Congress three games in a row as a family-friendly title, and most importantly, we made a lot of gamer's days brighter.

The PlayStation 2 opened new frontiers for us as developers so we took our latest characters, Jak and Daxter, in a different direction than Crash. Sure, there is physical absurdity in the game, but most of the comedy lies in Daxter's wit. It was a big risk, we were betting an entire product on our ability to write good gags. If Daxter bombed, so would the game. Daxter won "New Character of The Year" in the 2001 Developers Choice Awards. Apparently, we didn't get the gong.

As technology gives developers the ability to push limits and compete evenly with other entertainment medium, game players excuse less and the stakes get higher and higher. If we want to compete against motion pictures, television, and music then we must provide the same entertainment they do when they hit, and burn as badly as they do when they miss.

Five years ago bad jokes were part of the kitsch of gaming. These days, bad humour can kill a game. Being successful today making video games on the lighter side ain't no joke. But ask an aged comedian what's the secret to a long career, is and he can only provide you with the same advice I can: "You had better be funny."

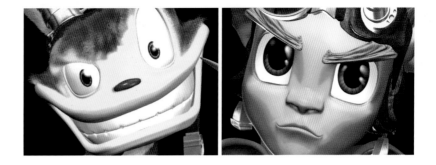

L'Humour s'imposa le plus naturellement du monde dans les premiers essais de jeux vidéo chez Naughty Dog. Notre premier titre à être publié, Ski Crazed, méritait l'attention pour deux raisons. Tout d'abord, le jeu était proche d'être l'opposé d'une simulation de ski, mais pas tout à fait. Ensuite, le jeu s'appuyait avec délectation sur des images de jolies bunnies en ski et des myriades de dessins plutôt que sur la jouabilité. A cette époque où les joueurs étaient lancés dans de sérieuses quêtes ou défendaient le mode d'une attaque extraterrestre, Ski Crazed était stupide et fier de l'être. Si seulement notre éditeur de l'époque ne l'avait pas été.

Nous avons essayé de laisser l'humour de côté pour notre troisième titre, Keef the thief, mais nous aurions dû éviter. Agacés par l'idée qu'on nous avait assigné un auteur « professionnel», nous avons mis dans la version Bêta des textes intermédiaires sarcastiques avant de les envoyer au massacre. Inspiré par nos insultes, l'écrivaillon écrit 1650 lignes de texte qui étaient assez proches, mais pas tout à fait, de ce qui était l'opposé de l'humour et le jeu fut transformé en une parodie. Les volumes de vente du jeu, par contre, furent une vraie blague.

Way of the Warrior fut le premier succès de Naughty Dog. Evidemment, nous nous sommes largement inspirés du Mortal Kombat de Boon et Tobias, mais nous avons essayé de faire en sorte que l'action et les personnages soient si réussis que le gore soit plus une farce qu'un écœurement. Nous voulions que le jeu soit imbibé de l'humour caractéristique de Naughty Dog. Mais la United House of Representatives ne comprit pas la blague, aussi le jeu fut-il mentionné parmi les dix pires jeux pour enfants de cette année. Pour la première fois de notre carrière, nous ne souriions pas. Naughty Dog décida alors qu'aucun de ses prochains jeux ne rabaisserait les esprits, mais au contraire les élèverait. C'est ainsi que nous commençâmes à travailler sur Crash Bandicoot.

Je suis convaincu que le succès de Crash en tant que personnage est directement lié à son aspect comique et principalement à ses mimiques. Bien sûr, la jouabilité était bonne, mais c'est à mon sens l'humour qui, avant tout, a fait vendre les jeux.

Mario n'a jamais vraiment eu de personnalité. Celle de Sonic, si tant soit qu'on puisse la définir ainsi, est sa rapidité. Dans son premier jeu, Crash apparaît en extirpant son nez du sable, se secoue, se retourne et vous jette le regard le plus inexpressif qu'on ait pu voir dans un jeu vidéo à ce jour... avant de se reprendre afin d'affronter les tâches qui l'attendent. Tout était dit : Crash n'est pas très brillant, n'est pas infaillible, mais a un grand cœur. Il est comme vous et moi. On l'adore.

Crash subissait des morts plus atroces que les personnages de Way of the Warrior, mais cette fois-ci, tout le monde en riait. Sony Computer Entertainment a vendu plus de 24 millions d'exemplaires des quatre jeux Crash développés par Naughty Dog ; nous fûmes mentionnés trois fois de suite par le Congrès pour des titres familiaux et plus important encore, nous avons rendu plus radieux les jours de nombreux joueurs.

La PlayStation 2 ouvrit de nouvelles frontières aux développeurs que nous sommes, aussi avons-nous emmenés nos derniers personnages en date, Jak et Daxter, dans une direction différente de celle de Crash. Bien sûr, il y a beaucoup d'absurdité physique dans le jeu, mais l'humour vient en grande partie de l'attitude de Daxter. Baser entièrement un produit sur notre capacité à écrire de bons gags était un gros risque. Si Daxter faisait un bide, le jeu en ferait autant. Daxter reçut la récompense du « Meilleur nouveau personnage de l'année » aux Developers Choice Awards 2001. Apparemment, nous n'avons pas raté le coche.

Aujourd'hui, la technologie permet aux développeurs de repousser les limites et même d'entrer en compétition avec d'autres types de loisirs, avec lesquels les joueurs sont plus exigeants. Si nous voulons rivaliser avec le cinéma, la télévision et la musique, nous devons être tout aussi divertissants que ces loisirs lorsqu'ils réussissent et nous brûler tout autant les ailes lorsque nous échouons.

Il y a cinq ans, les mauvaises blagues faisaient partie du folklore du jeu vidéo. Aujourd'hui, un mauvais humour peut tuer un jeu. Aujourd'hui, avoir du succès en faisait un jeu vidéo est loin d'être de la plaisanterie. Mais demandez à un vieux comédien le secret d'une longue carrière : il ne pourra que vous donner ce même conseil : « Tu as intérêt à être drôle ».

Die ersten Spiele, die Naughty Dog produzierte, waren – was den Humor betraf – wirklich lachhaft. Unser erster Titel Ski Crazed war aus zweierlei Gründen bemerkenswert. Erstens war die Simulation so schlecht, dass sie fast genau das Gegenteil von dem erzeugte, was das Erlebnis des Skifahrens ausmachte. Und zweitens schien dies auch noch gewollt zu sein, denn anstelle eines ordentlichen Gameplays wimmelte es von Skihäschen und Pistenhengsten. Zu einer Zeit, als Spieler knifflige Quests bewältigen mussten, um die Welt vor außerirdischen Angreifern zu schützen, war Ski Crazed einfach nur dumm und auch noch stolz darauf. So wie unser damaliger Produzent.

Bei unserem dritten Titel Keef the Thief versuchten wir den Humor außen vor zu lassen, aber es sollte einfach nicht sein. Wir waren verärgert darüber, dass man uns einen „Profi"-Schreiber zugewiesen hatte, und also packten wir einen sarkastischen Blindtext in die Beta-Version und stellten ihn damit an den Pranger. Unsere Beleidigungen schienen den Schreiberling so inspiriert zu haben, dass er in 1650 Zeilen etwas beschrieb, was so ziemlich das Gegenteil von Humor war und unseren Titel über Nacht zu einer Parodie machte. Was die Verkaufszahlen von Keef betraf, waren wir die Dummen.

Der erste erfolgreiche Titel von Naughty Dog war schließlich Way of the Warrior. Natürlich klauten wir ordentlich bei Mortal Kombat von Boon und Tobias, aber wir versuchten, die Charaktere und Missionen so überzogen darzustellen, dass das Blut eher was von Slapstick als von Eingeweide hatte. Wir wollten das Spiel mit dem speziellen Naughty-Dog-Humor tränken. Doch das amerikanische Repräsentantenhaus verstand keinen Spaß und so wurde War of the Warriors noch im selben Jahr auf den Index gesetzt. Zum ersten Mal in unserer Karriere als Entwickler verging uns das Lachen. Naughty Dog beschloss, dass fortan jedes von uns entwickelte Spiel die Menschen aufheitern und nicht deprimieren sollte. Und so nahmen wir Crash Bandicoot in Angriff.

Ich bin fest davon überzeugt, dass der Erfolg von Crash in unmittelbarem Zusammenhang mit seiner witzigen körperlichen Erscheinung steht, vor allem mit seiner Mimik. Sicher, das Gameplay war gut, aber meines Erachtens lag es an der Komik, dass dieses Spiel sich so gut verkaufte. Mario hatte eigentlich nie eine eigene Persönlichkeit. Sonics Eigenart, wenn man sie überhaupt als solche bezeichnen kann, besteht darin, dass er schnell ist. Der erste Auftritt von Crash begann damit, dass er den Kopf aus dem Sand zog, sich schüttelte, umdrehte und den Spieler mit einem derart leerem Blick anstarrte, wie er bis dato noch in keinem Videospiel zu sehen gewesen war. Dann rüstete er sich für die Aufgaben, die vor ihm lagen. Das wars. Crash ist nicht besonders intelligent, er ist auch nicht unfehlbar, aber er hat ein großes Herz. Er ist wie du und ich. Wir mögen ihn halt.

Crash starb mehr schreckliche Tode als die Charaktere aus Way of the Warrior, doch diesmal lachten alle. Sony Computer Entertainment verkaufte über 24 Millionen Kopien der vier Crash-Episoden von Naughty Dog. Der amerikanische Kongress stufte gleich drei unserer Spiele als familienfreundlich ein, und das Schönste war, dass wir viele Spieler damit aufheiterten.

Mit PlayStation 2 eröffnete sich uns Entwicklern eine ganz neue Welt. Und so gaben wir unseren neuesten Charakteren Jak und Daxter eine andere Richtung als Crash. Bestimmt gibt es auch alberne Sequenzen in dem Spiel, doch die Komik basiert größtenteils auf Daxters Schlagfertigkeit und Witz. Es war ziemlich riskant, wir verließen uns bei diesem Produkt ganz auf unsere Fähigkeit, gute Gags zu schreiben. Wäre Daxter bei den Spielern nicht ankommen, das ganze Spiel wäre ein Misserfolg geworden. Doch Daxter erhielt 2001 als „Neuer Charakter des Jahres" einen der begehrten Game Developers' Choice Awards. Offensichtlich waren wir doch nicht so schlecht.

Während die Technologie die Grenzen für Entwickler immer weiter ausdehnt und sie die Konkurrenz mit anderen Unterhaltungsmedien nicht mehr scheuen müssen, ist von den Spielern weniger Nachsicht zu erwarten; ihre Ansprüche werden immer höher. Wenn wir uns gegen das Kino, das Fernsehen und die Musik durchsetzen wollen, müssen wir dieselbe Unterhaltung bieten wie diese Medien, wenn sie einen Treffer landen, und ebenso bluten wie sie, wenn sie ihr Ziel verfehlen.

Vor fünf Jahren gehörten schlechte Witze zum Spielen dazu. Heutzutage kann schlechter Humor für ein Spiel tödlich sein. Unterhaltsame Videospiele zu produzieren und damit Erfolg zu haben ist keine Kleinigkeit. Fragen Sie doch mal einen alten Komiker nach dem Geheimnis seines Erfolgs. Er wird Ihnen denselben Rat geben wie ich: „Du solltest besser witzig sein."

NAME

JAK & DAXTER THE PRE...

PLATFORM

PLAYSTATION 2

RELEASE

EDITOR

SONY COMPUTER
ENTERTAINMENT OF AMERICA

DEVELOPER

NAUGHTY DOG

COPYRIGHTS

© 2001 SONY COMPUTER
ENTERTAINMENT INC.
© REJP/SCPRCSWU ALL
RIGHTS RESERVED. DEVELOPED
BY SONY COMPUTER

FACT

SIDO AND D.T-SHIRT. WHAT SAY...
COMPUTER ENTERTAINMENT AMERICA GAVE
ITS EMPLOYEES FOR PASSING THE 10 MILLION
SALES-BARRIER FOR CONSOLES.

Jak & Daxter

Jak and his friend Daxter are two young boys who have never left Sand Village, but they dream of great adventures. Awed by the strange buildings of the Precursors, a long-since-vanished race, and encouraged by the sayings of Samos the sage, the two buddies decide to explore the island in quest of new wonders. But they soon come face to face with an unknown army and have to hide in a dark cavern. The clumsy Daxter falls into a strange black swamp and is transmuted into a bizarre animal: half-rat, half-kangeroo. To save his friend and protect his village, Jak has to collect up the energy cells scattered across the place by the Precursors. The island is a triumph of animated graphics, full of astonishing creatures, weird traps, and bizarre machinery.
« »

Jak et son ami Daxter, jeunes garçons qui ne connaissent du monde que leur Village des Sables, rêvent de grandes aventures. Emerveillés par les étranges constructions des Précurseurs, race aujourd'hui disparue, et poussés par les élucubrations du vieux sage Samos, les deux compères décident d'explorer l'île à la recherche d'autres merveilles. Nos deux jeunes héros tombent nez à nez avec une armée inconnue et se cachent dans une sombre caverne. Sa maladresse fera choir Daxter dans une étrange mare noirâtre qui le transformera en étrange animal à mi-chemin du rongeur et du kangourou. Afin de sauver son ami et de protéger son village de l'armée qui les menace, Jak devra rassembler les cellules d'énergie disséminées par les Précurseurs sur toute l'île, véritable monde de dessin animé peuplé de créatures plus étonnantes les unes que les autres et truffé de pièges et de machines extraordinaires.
« »

Jak und sein Freund Daxter kennen außer ihrem Sanddorf nichts von der Welt und träumen deshalb von großen Abenteuern. Fasziniert von den seltsamen Bauten der Precursor, einer inzwischen untergegangenen Rasse, und angespornt durch die Hirngespinste des alten weisen Samos, beschließen die beiden Jungen, ihre Insel nach weiteren Wunderwerken zu durchforsten. Auf einmal sehen sich unsere jugendlichen Helden einer unbekannten Armee gegenüber und können sich gerade noch in eine dunkle Höhle retten. Ungeschickt wie er ist, fällt Daxter in einen merkwürdigen schwärzlichen Tümpel, wo er in einen haarigen Nager verwandelt wird. Um seinen Freund zu retten und sein Dorf vor der bedrohlichen Armee zu beschützen, muss Jak die Energiezellen finden, die die Precursor überall auf der Insel versteckt haben. Ein Spiel in bester Comic-Optik – mit einer Vielzahl von Figuren, eine erstaunlicher als die andere, und gespickt mit fiesen Fallen und spektakulären Maschinen.

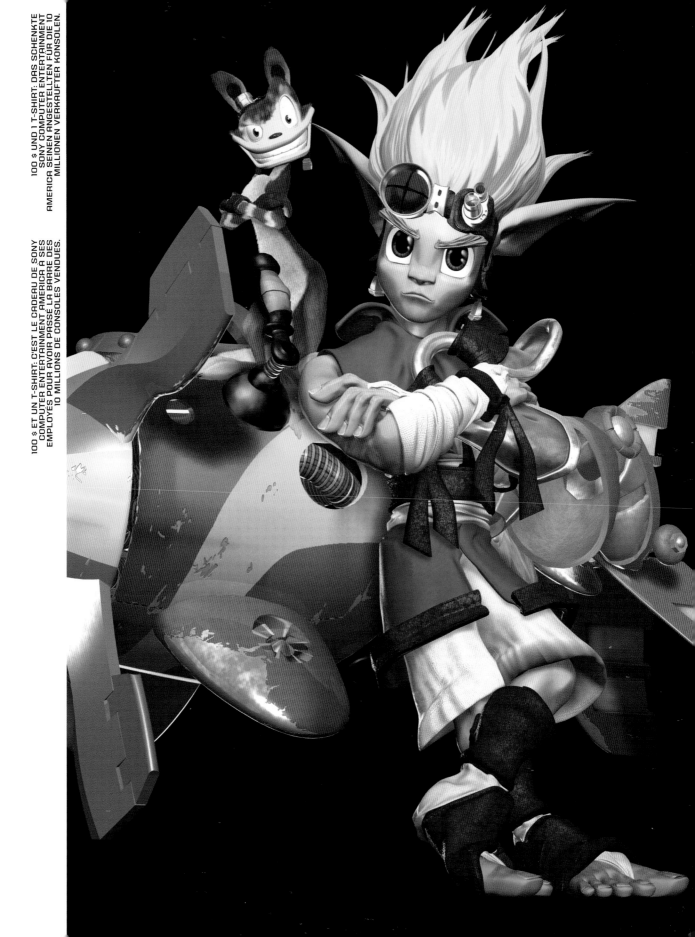

100 $ UND 1 T-SHIRT: DAS SCHENKTE
SONY COMPUTER ENTERTAINMENT
AMERICA SEINEN ANGESTELLTEN FÜR DIE 10
MILLIONEN VERKAUFTER KONSOLEN.

100 $ ET UN T-SHIRT: C'EST LE CADEAU DE SONY
COMPUTER ENTERTAINMENT AMERICA À SES
EMPLOYÉS POUR AVOIR PASSÉ LA BARRE DES
10 MILLIONS DE CONSOLES VENDUES.

NAME

PLATFORM

RELEASE

EDITOR

DEVELOPER

COPYRIGHTS

FACT

Banjo-Tooie

Our heroes, that charming bear, Banjo, and his confederate, Kazooie the bird, thought they had seen the last of the ugly witch Gruntilda. Burying her under a huge rock really should have done the trick. Wrong! Their enemy has escaped. She's on the warpath, and they're on her hitlist. She's just going about her usual business: sucking up the lives of the island's peace-loving folk to help her become beeyootiful! She has two accomplices, her sisters Mingella and Blobbelda - both of them, like her, pretty repellent - so this time the danger factor is multiplied by three. Just as well that Banjo and Kazooie have an ally, the astonishing Mumbo-Jumbo, a shaman with feathers on his scalp. His magic comes in awfully useful. And then there's Humba-Wumba, the witch; she has a soft spot for them, and she's no slouch at magic. If need be, she can turn Banjo and Kazooie into submarines, snowballs, or even washing-machines, just like that...
« »

Le sympathique ours Banjo et son compère, l'oiseau Kazooie, croyaient s'être définitivement débarrassés de la très laide sorcière Gruntilda après l'avoir enterrée sous un immense rocher. Mais leur ennemie s'est, on ne sait comment, sortie de ce piège et est aujourd'hui bien décidée à se venger du duo et à atteindre son objectif de toujours : aspirer la vie des paisibles habitants de l'île et utiliser cette énergie pour devenir belle. Pour ce faire, Gruntilda s'est alliée à ses deux sœurs Mingella et Blobbelda, dont l'apparence est également peu flatteuse. Trois fois plus de dangers attendent donc Banjo et Kazooie, qui seront heureusement aidés dans leur quête par l'étonnant Mumbo-Jumbo, le petit chaman au crâne emplumé, dont les talents magiques seront bien utiles. La gentille sorcière Humba Wumba sera aussi une alliée de choix, ses pouvoirs lui permettant, si besoin est, de transformer l'ours et l'oiseau en sous-marin, en boule de neige ou en machine à laver...
« »

Der sympathische Bär Banjo und seine gefiederte Freundin Kazooie glauben, die garstige Hexe Gruntilda nun ein für alle mal los zu sein, nachdem sie sie unter einem riesigen Felsblock begraben haben. Doch irgendwie konnte die hässliche Alte zu entkommen. Nun ist sie fest entschlossen, sich an den beiden zu rächen und ihr altes Ziel weiter zu verfolgen: die friedlichen Inselbewohner auszusaugen und mit deren Lebensenergie zu einer echten Schönheit zu mutieren. Zu diesem Zweck hat sich Gruntilda mit ihren ebenfalls nicht sehr ansehnlichen Schwestern Mingella und Blobbelda verbündet. Eine Menge Gefahren lauern also auf Banjo und Kazooie, doch zum Glück ist da der fabelhafte Mumbo-Jumbo: Der kleine Schamane mit dem Federschmuck auf dem Kopf hilft ihnen mit seinen magischen Kräften aus so mancher Notlage. Eine weitere Verbündete ist die freundliche Hexe Humba Wumba. Sie kann bei Bedarf dank ihrer Zauberkräfte den Bären und den Vogel in ein U-Boot, einen Schneeball oder eine Waschmaschine verwandeln.

1,4 MILLIONEN: REKORD AN INNERHALB VON EINER WOCHE VERKAUFTEN SPIELEN, DER VON POKEMON GOLD UND POKEMON SILVER IN DEN USA GEHALTEN WIRD. DEN VORHERIGEN VERKAUFSREKORD HIELT POKEMON GELB MIT 600.000 EXEMPLAREN.

1,4 MILLION: C'EST LE RECORD DE VENTES DE JEUX EN UNE SEMAINE DETENU PAR POKEMON GOLD ET POKEMON SILVER AUX ETATS-UNIS. LE PRECEDENT RECORD ETAIT DETENU PAR POKEMON JAUNE AVEC 600.000 EXEMPLAIRES VENDUS.

NAME CRAZY TAXI
PLATFORM DREAMCAST · PLAYSTATION 2 · GAMECUBE
RELEASE 2000
EDITOR SEGA
DEVELOPER HITMAKER
COPYRIGHTS © SEGA/AM3

Crazy Taxi

Someone gave them a licence?! Forget the Highway Code. Never mind other vehicles, passers-by, and suchlike obstacles, these drivers have just one thing in mind: to get their clients where they want to go ASAP. And their passengers actually like them to drive like lunatics; they delight in shunts; the more risks the driver takes, the better they tip. So the taxis defy one-way systems, cut in, and take off-road short-cuts, just to impress the client. Beware: if you run into the scenery or oncoming traffic and come off unscathed, the passengers complain. And if you frighten them too much or too little, they'll just bail out en route!

« »

Quel inconscient a bien pu valider les permis de conduire des conducteurs de *Crazy Taxi* ? Oublié, le code de la route ! Peu importent les autres véhicules, les passants, les trottoirs : ces fous du volant ne connaissent qu'une règle : emmener leurs clients à bon port le plus vite possible, sans se soucier de quoi que ce soit d'autre. Après tout, leurs passagers les encouragent à piloter sans contrainte, poussés par le temps mais aussi par le plaisir que leur procurent les cascades de leurs taxis. Plus le pilote prend de risques, plus ils sont heureux et ont la main lourde pour le pourboire. Aussi les taxis ne se gênent-ils aucunement pour rouler à contresens, couper à travers champs, effectuer des queues de poisson ou tout autre cascade périlleuse, afin d'impressionner les clients. Mais gare : si un choc avec un élément du décor ou un autre véhicule n'occasionne aucun dégât, les passagers se plaindront, seront moins enclins à payer voire même, s'ils craignent trop pour leur vie ou s'ennuient fermement, sauteront en marche !

« »

Welcher verantwortungslose Mensch hat den Fahrern in *Crazy Taxi* bloß den Führerschein ausgestellt? In diesem Spiel wird die Straßen-verkehrsordnung komplett außer Kraft gesetzt. Ohne sich um andere Fahrzeuge, um Passanten oder Bürgersteige zu scheren, haben die verrückten Taxifahrer nur eines im Sinn: ihre Fahrgäste so schnell wie möglich an das gewünschte Ziel zu bringen. Und ihre Passagiere ermuntern sie geradezu zum rücksichtslosen Fahren, denn die meisten haben es sehr eilig und finden zudem auch noch Spaß an den rasanten Fahrten. Je waghalsiger der Taxifahrer fährt, desto mehr freuen sie sich und lassen ihm ein ordentliches Trinkgeld zukommen. Und so fahren die Taxis ungeniert verkehrt in die Einbahnstraße, nehmen Abkürzungen querfeldein, schneiden andere Fahrzeuge oder verhalten sich sonst wie verkehrsgefährdend, nur um ihre Fahrgäste zu beeindrucken. Doch Vorsicht: Bei einem Zusammenstoß mit irgendwelchen Gegenständen am Wegesrand oder mit einem anderen Wagen gibt's Schelte von den Passagieren. Sie sind dann weniger spendabel mit dem Trinkgeld. Und wenn sie allzu sehr um ihr Leben fürchten oder sich während der Fahrt zu Tode langweilen, machen sie sich gar ohne zu bezahlen aus dem Staub.

NAME · FUR FIGHTERS: VIGGO'S REVENGE
PLATFORM · PLAYSTATION 2
RELEASE · 2001
EDITOR · ACCLAIM ENTERTAINMENT
DEVELOPER · BIZARRE CREATIONS
COPYRIGHTS · © ACCLAIM ENTERTAINMENT
FACT · 100: THE NUMBER OF OFFICIAL VEHICLES IN THE GAME 4X4 EVOLUTION; THEY COMPRISE EIGHT MAKES: CHEVROLET, FORD, DODGE, GMC, LEXUS, MITSUBISHI, NISSAN AND TOYOTA.

Fur Fighters

Having fought off the life-threatening attacks of General Viggo, the Fur Fighters have returned to a peaceful existence, putting aside their martial talents to bring up their children. They thought Viggo was dead: no, he returns to revenge himself in fearsome fashion. Not only does he kidnap the Fur Fighters' families, but he forces them to fight their parents after transforming them into soulless psychotic warriors. The six Fur Fighters have no choice; they must take up arms again if they are to defeat Viggo and save their nearest and dearest. Bungalow the Kangaroo (who can leap vast distances), Juliette the Cat (who can climb anything), Tweek the Dragon (who glides for miles on his little wings), Roofus the Dog (who can dig like an excavator), Rico the Penguin (no one swims faster) and Changa the contortionist panda all shoulder arms once again, and prove to Viggo that a few years' rest has done nothing to blunt their formidable martial talents.
« »

Après avoir affronté l'infâme général Viggo au péril de leur vie, les Fur Fighters sont revenus à une existence paisible, laissant leurs talents guerriers de côté pour voir grandir leurs enfants. Mais Viggo, que l'on croyait mort, revient se venger de la plus horrible façon : il kidnappe non seulement les familles des Fur Fighters, mais les oblige à se battre contre leurs parents après les avoir transformés en combattants psychotiques sans âme. Les six Fur Fighters n'ont d'autre choix que de ressortir les armes et d'affronter de nouveau Viggo afin de sauver leurs proches. Bungalow le kangourou (capable de sauter sur d'incroyables distances), Juliette la chatte (grimpeuse de talent), Tweek le dragon (doté de petites ailes, il peut planer sur de longues distances), Roofus le chien (peut creuser le sol à grande vitesse), Rico le pingouin (nageur d'élite) et Chang le panda contorsionniste reprennent du service et vont prouver à Viggo que leurs années de repos n'ont en rien émoussé leurs talents de guerriers.
« »

Nachdem sie dem abscheulichen General Viggo unter Einsatz ihres Lebens die Stirn geboten haben, kehren die Fur Fighters zu einem friedlichen Dasein zurück. Derweil sie ihre kämpferischen Talente ruhen lassen, widmen sie sich der Erziehung ihrer Kinder. Aber der tot geglaubte Viggo kehrt zurück, um sich fürchterlich zu rächen. Er entführt nicht nur die Familien der Fur Fighters, sondern verwandelt sie auch in seelenlose, geisteskranke Krieger, die unter seinem Einfluss die Hand gegen ihre Eltern erheben. Um ihre Angehörigen zu retten, haben die sechs Fur Fighters keine andere Wahl, als ihre Waffen wieder herauszuholen und erneut gegen Viggo in den Kampf zu ziehen. Bungalow, das Känguru (das Sprünge über riesige Entfernungen vollbringen kann), Juliette, die Katze (ein wahres Klettertalent), Tweek, der Drache (der mit seinen kleinen Flügeln weite Entfernungen zurücklegen kann), Roofus, der Hund (der blitzschnell Löcher buddelt), Rico, der Pinguin (ein Ass im Schwimmen), und Chang, der akrobatische Pandabär, nehmen wieder ihren Dienst auf und werden Viggo beweisen, dass die Jahre der Rast in keiner Weise ihre Talente als Krieger geschmälert haben.

100: C'EST LE NOMBRE DE VÉHICULES OFFICIELS IMPLANTÉS DANS LE JEU 4X4 EVOLUTION, QUI SONT RÉPARTIS SUR HUIT CONSTRUCTEURS : CHEVROLET, FORD, DODGE, GMC, LEXUS, MITSUBISHI, NISSAN ET TOYOTA.

100: ANZAHL DER OFFIZIELL VERWENDETEN AUTOS IM SPIEL 4 X 4 EVOLUTION, DIE SICH AUF ACHT HERSTELLER VERTEILEN: CHEVROLET, FORD, DODGE, GMC, LEXUS, MITSUBISHI, NISSAN UND TOYOTA.

NAME **HERDY GERDY**

PLATFORM **PLAYSTATION 2**

RELEASE **2002**

EDITOR **EIDOS INTERACTIVE**

DEVELOPER **CORE DESIGN**

COPYRIGHTS **© EIDOS INTERACTIVE/CORE DESIGN**

FACT **1.1 MILLION: THE NUMBER OF POLYGONS THAT PLAYSTATION 2 CAN GENERATE WHEN THE GAME IS RUNNING AT 60 FRAMES PER SECOND.**

Herdy Gerdy

Who is to be the next Guardian of the Acorn of Life? The Acorn has immense powers, and every five years, there's a competition on the magic island for the Guardianship. But, can you believe it? The Keeper of the Acorn has long since proven unworthy of his role. The wicked Sadorf has several times acquired the post by trickery. His neglect of the island is turning this haven of peace into a landscape of desolation. The hopes of the island's denizens rest with master-shepherd Gedryn, but Sadorf's black magic puts him to sleep shortly after the off. The islanders are down-hearted, but all is not lost. Gedryn's lore has passed to his crafty son Gerdy, who takes up the baton and prepares to match Sadorf and his henchman in the, ehem, terrifying ordeals of the competition!

« »

Tous les cinq ans, sur l'île magique, un tournoi est organisé pour savoir lequel des habitants de ce petit monde paisible méritera de devenir le gardien du Gland de vie, fruit magique au pouvoir incommensurable. Hélas, depuis longtemps déjà, le détenteur du Gland est loin de mériter son rôle : l'infâme Sadorf se l'est plusieurs fois accaparé par roublardise, et néglige l'île, transformant ce havre de paix en paysage de désolation. Les habitant de l'île se préparent donc pour le prochain tournoi, farouchement décidés à ravir le Gland à Sadorf. Tous les espoirs des êtres pacifiques de l'île se tournent vers le maître berger Gedryn, que Sadorf endort par magie noire peu avant le coup d'envoi. Le découragement gagne les habitants de l'île, mais tout n'est pas perdu : Gedryn a pu enseigner à son jeune et ingénieux fils, Gerdy, une bonne partie de ses talents, aussi l'enfant reprend-il le flambeau, et se prépare-t-il à se mesurer à Sadorf et ses sbires lors des nombreuses et périlleuses épreuves du tournoi !

« »

Alle fünf Jahre wird auf Bally Island ein Turnier ausgetragen, um unter den Bewohnern der friedlichen Zauberinsel den Hüter der heiligen Eichel zu ermitteln. Der jetzige Besitzer der Eichel, einer magischen Frucht mit unermesslichen Kräften, ist ihrer schon lange nicht mehr würdig. Bereits mehrmals konnte sich der gemeine Sadorf mit List und Tücke der Trophäe bemächtigen. Doch statt für Harmonie zu sorgen, lässt er die Insel verkommen und verwandelt den friedlichen Zufluchtsort in eine wüste Landschaft. Die Bewohner von Bally Island bereiten sich auf das kommende Turnier vor, wild entschlossen, dem Fiesling Sadorf die Eichel zu entreißen. Alle ihre Hoffnungen ruhen auf dem Meisterhirten Gedryn, den Sadorf jedoch kurz vor Turnierbeginn mittels schwarzer Magie in einen Tiefschlaf versetzt. Enttäuschung macht sich unter den Bewohnern breit, doch noch ist nicht alles verloren. Gedryn hatte zuvor seinen kleinen, gewitzten Sohn instruieren können. Und so setzt das findige Kind das Werk des Vaters fort und schickt sich an, gegen Sadorf und seine Häscher beim Turnier anzutreten, wo zahlreiche und gefährliche Wettkämpfe auf ihn warten.

1,1 MILLION: C'EST LE NOMBRE DE POLYGONES QUE LA PLAYSTATION 2 EST CAPABLE DE GÉRER LORSQUE LE JEU TOURNE À 60 IMAGES PAR SECONDE.

1,1 MILLIONEN: ANZAHL DER POLYGONE, DIE DIE PLAYSTATION 2 GENERIEREN KANN, WENN DAS SPIEL MIT 60 BILDERN PRO SEKUNDE ABLÄUFT

NAME
KIRBY 64

PLATFORM
NINTENDO 64

RELEASE
2000

EDITOR
NINTENDO

DEVELOPER
NINTENDO

COPYRIGHTS
© NINTENDO

FACT
51‰ PERCENTAGE INCREASE IN NINTENDO'S PROFIT ON 30 SEPTEMBER 2000 RELATIVE TO THE PREVIOUS YEAR, MEANING 235 MILLION DOLLARS - TO TURN MAINLY INTO POKEMONS!

Kirby

Among the many immortal video-game heroes from Nintendo, Kirby is certainly the most multifarious. By swallowing other objects or creatures, this protean sphere takes on their characteristics, and has, as such, presided over any number of platform games. But form is fate, and Kirby has also played the role of pin- or golf ball. However, most of his adventures take place in Dream Land, a magic universe light-years from earth. The daily fare of this pastel-coloured world is games, picnics and siestas, but from time to time, wicked creatures fetch up there, intent on stealing its legendary energy source, the Star Rod. And of course, Kirby is always there to thwart them with his courage, ingenuity, and amazing mimetic powers.

« »

Parmi les nombreux personnages Nintendo qui ont toujours su garder une place de choix dans le monde du jeu vidéo, Kirby est certaine-ment le plus polyvalent. Cette étrange petite boule rose, capable d'avaler n'importe quel objet ou créature et d'en acquérir ainsi les parti-cularités a en effet officié dans de nombreux jeux de plates-formes, mais a aussi, forme sphérique oblige, joué le rôle d'une bille de flipper ou d'une balle de golf. La plupart de ses aventures se déroulent dans le Dream Land, un univers magique se trouvant à des années-lumière de la terre. Le quotidien des habitants de ce monde aux couleurs pastel est fait de jeux, de pique-niques et de siestes, mais de temps en temps, de peu recommandables créatures, jalouses de la vie paisible des habitants du Dream Land, tentent de dérober leur source d'énergie, le légendaire Star Rod. Bien évidemment, Kirby sera toujours prêt à protéger son monde, grâce à son courage, son ingéniosité et, bien sûr, ses très utiles pouvoirs de mimétisme.

« »

Von den zahlreichen Nintendo-Spielfiguren, die sich einen Spitzenplatz in der Welt der Videospiele erobern konnten, ist Kirby sicherlich eine der vielseitigsten. Die kleine rosafarbene Kugel, die jeden Gegenstand und jede Kreatur aufsaugen kann und dadurch deren Eigentümlichkeiten annimmt, hat ihren Sieg nicht nur in zahlreichen 2-D-Spielen gefeiert, sondern auch die Rolle einer Flipperkugel oder eines Golfballs gespielt – die runde Form verpflichtet. Die meisten Abenteuer von Kirby spielen in Dream Land, einer magischen, ganz in Pastellfarben gehaltenen Welt, die Lichtjahre von der Erde entfernt ist. Der Tagesablauf ihrer Bewohner besteht aus Spielen, Picknicken und Siesta halten. Hin und wieder jedoch versuchen finstere Kreaturen, die den Bewohnern von Dream Land ihren Frieden missgönnen, sich ihrer Energiequelle, des legendären Star Rod (Sternenstab) zu bemächtigen. Aber natürlich ist der rosafarbene Knuddelheld allzeit bereit, seine Welt zu beschützen. Das verdankt er seinem Mut, seinem Erfindungsreichtum und nicht zuletzt seinen überaus nützlichen Fähigkeiten der Mimikry.

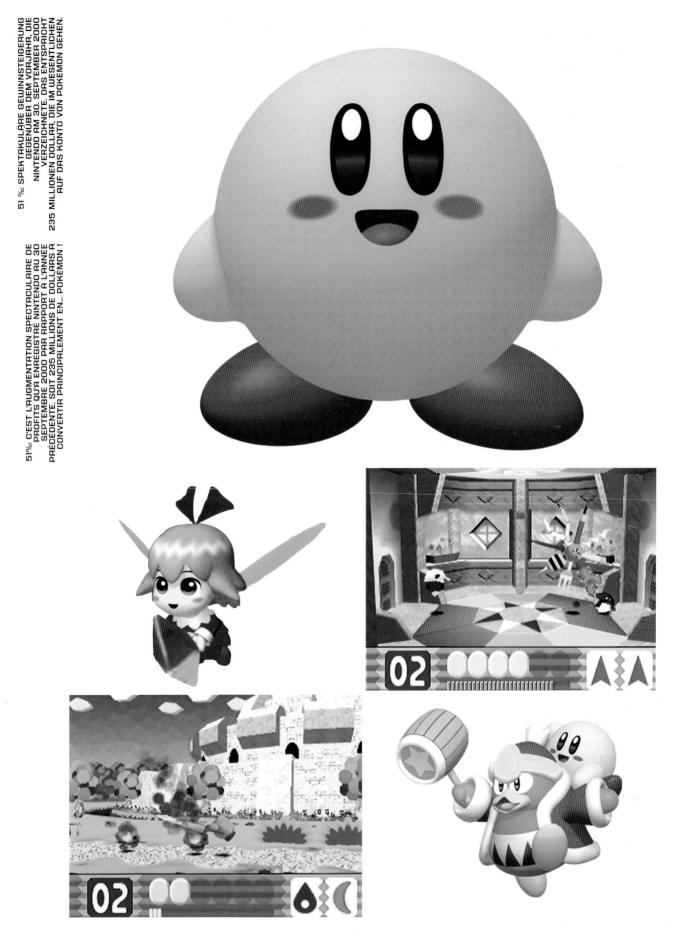

51 %: SPEKTAKULÄRE GEWINNSTEIGERUNG GEGENÜBER DEM VORJAHR, DIE NINTENDO AM 30. SEPTEMBER 2000 VERZEICHNETE. DAS ENTSPRICHT 235 MILLIONEN DOLLAR, DIE IM WESENTLICHEN AUF DAS KONTO VON POKÉMON GEHEN.

51%: C'EST L'AUGMENTATION SPECTACULAIRE DE PROFITS QU'A ENREGISTRÉ NINTENDO AU 30 SEPTEMBRE 2000 PAR RAPPORT À L'ANNÉE PRÉCÉDENTE. SOIT 235 MILLIONS DE DOLLARS À CONVERTIR PRINCIPALEMENT EN... POKÉMON !

NAME

PLATFORM

RELEASE

EDITOR

DEVELOPER

COPYRIGHTS

FACT

KLONOA 2 LUNATEA'S...

400,000: THE NUMBER OF SITES FOUND ON
(SUPER NINTENDO). SOLD IN JAPAN ON
THE DAY IT WAS PUT ON THE MARKET

Klonoa

What an enchanted planet is Lunatea! Its magic is protected by the four Bells of Harmony, each ensuring the stability of one of Lunatea's regions. But legend cites a Fifth Bell, which carries within it the power of Chaos. If this Bell fell into power-hungry hands, Lunatea's very existence would be threatened. Well, what do you know? All of a sudden the Fifth Bell does appear, and under its baleful influence, the peaceable inhabitants of Lunatea are starting to turn into ferocious monsters. Baguji the Wise, greatest of Lunatea's priest-guardians, sees his peers and powers ailing; he prays for the fulfilment of a prophecy concerning the advent of the Dream Traveller. For only the Dream Traveller, equipped with his amazing magic ring, can free Lunatea from the menace of the Fifth Bell. Yo! Klonoa, a young Lunatean with big flappy ears, is revealed as the Dream Traveller. He sets out to save Lunatea, assisted by his inseparable friends Lolo and Popka.

« »

Lunatea est un monde enchanté, dont la magie est protégée par les quatre Cloches d'Harmonie, chacune garantissant l'équilibre des quatre régions de Lunatea. Une légende mentionne cependant l'existence d'une cinquième Cloche qui porte en elle le terrible pouvoir du Chaos. Si cette cinquième Cloche tombait dans les griffes de mauvais individus avides de pouvoir, l'existence même de Lunatea serait en danger. Cette catastrophe se concrétise hélas : la cinquième Cloche apparaît on ne sait pourquoi, et sa sombre puissance commence à transformer les paisibles habitants de Lunatea en monstres agressifs. Baguji le sage, le plus grand des prêtres-gardiens de la planète, voit ses pairs tomber malades, et prie pour que s'accomplisse la prophétie annonçant la venue du Dream Traveler, un héros qui seul pourra libérer Lunatea de la menace de la cinquième Cloche grâce à un étonnant anneau magique. Klonoa, jeune autochtone aux grandes oreilles, s'avérera être le Dream Traveler et devra sauver Lunetea, aidé par ses deux inséparables amis Lolo et Popka.

« »

Lunatea ist ein Zauberland, eine schöne Welt voller Träume und Ruhe. Beschützt wird es von vier geheimnisvollen Glocken namens „Harmony Bells", den Frieden in die den vier Königreichen von Lunatea sichern. Es geht jedoch das Gerücht, dass noch eine fünfte Glocke existiert und diese die Macht hat, das Chaos zu entfesseln. Würde diese fünfte Glocke bösen und machtgierigen Individuen in die Hände fällen, dann wäre die Existenz von Lunatea bedroht. Die Katastrophe nimmt ihren Lauf, denn aus unerfindlichen Gründen taucht die fünfte Glocke auf und ihre dunkle Macht lässt die friedlichen Bewohner von Lunatea allmählich zu aggressiven Monster werden. Der uralte Weise Baguji muss als höchster Priester und Hüter von Lunatea mit ansehen, wie seine Gefährten nach und nach erkranken, und so betet er, die Prophezeiung möge sich erfüllen. Danach soll ein Dream Traveler, ein Traumreisender kommen, der mit Hilfe eines magischen Ringes Lunatea als Einziger vor der unheilvollen fünften Glocke bewahren kann. Dieser Traumreisende erscheint in Gestalt von Klonoa, einem katzenartigen Comicwesen mit sternförmigen riesigen Schlappohren, das nun mit Unterstützung seiner beiden unzertrennlichen Freunde Lolo und Popka das Traumland Lunatea retten soll.

400.000: ANZAHL DER VERKAUFTEN SUPER
FAMICOM (SUPER NINTENDO) IN JAPAN
AM TAG DER MARKTEINFÜHRUNG

400000: C'EST LE NOMBRE DE SUPER
FAMICOM (SUPER NINTENDO) VENDUES LE
PREMIER JOUR DE SA DISPONIBILITÉ AU JAPON.

NAME LUIGI'S MANSION

PLATFORM GAMECUBE

RELEASE 2001

EDITOR NINTENDO

DEVELOPER NINTENDO

COPYRIGHTS © NINTENDO

FACT 108,870: THE NUMBER OF COPIES OF MARIO TENNIS SOLD IN JAPAN AFTER TWO WEEKS ON THE MARKET.

Luigi's Mansion

Luigi is worried; his famous brother Mario has disappeared while plumbing a ruined manor. When Luigi goes to look for him, he runs into a ghost and is saved - at the last moment - by a strange little fellow, a loony scientist who specialises in hunting ectoplasm. Luigi thinks Mario has been kidnapped by ghosts. Determined to set him free, he returns to the spook-house with a ghostbuster's toolkit: a torch to blind phantoms, and a vacuum cleaner to suck 'em up with. Luigi has to be fast and cunning to flush out all the ectoplasm in the cupboards, vases, u-bends and other strange ghost-holes of the manor.

Nintendo's "Luigi's Mansion" was inspired by the *Ghostbuster* films. If you like your fun with a frisson, this is the game for you...

« »

Luigi a de quoi s'inquiéter : son célèbre frère Mario a disparu pendant qu'il travaillait dans un mystérieux manoir en ruines. Alors qu'il se rend sur place pour essayer de retrouver son frère, Luigi se retrouve nez à nez avec un fantôme et est sauvé in extremis par un drôle de petit bonhomme, un scientifique farfelu spécialiste de la chasse aux ectoplasmes. Persuadé que Mario a été kidnappé par les fantômes, et bien décidé à le libérer, Luigi retourne dans l'angoissante bâtisse, non sans s'être préalablement équipé de l'attirail du parfait chasseur d'ectoplasmes : une torche électrique pour aveugler les revenants et un puissant aspirateur pour les emprisonner. Luigi devra faire preuve d'ingéniosité et de rapidité pour débusquer les fantômes cachés dans les nombreux recoins de la maison tels placards, vases, siphons de douche et bien d'autres endroits encore. S'inspirant des célèbres films de la série *Ghostbusters*, Nintendo signe ici un jeu original qui s'adresse à tous les publics désirant s'amuser à se faire peur.

« »

Luigi hat allen Grund zur Sorge: Sein berühmter Bruder Mario ist verschwunden, während er sich in einem mysteriösen und völlig verfallenen Landsitz zu schaffen machte. Luigi, der loseilt, um seinen Bruder zu retten, steht plötzlich vor einem Gespenst. Ein kleines drolliges Männchen, ein verdrehter, auf die Verfolgung von Ektoplasmen spezialisierter Gelehrter, rettet ihm in letzter Minute das Leben. Überzeugt, dass Mario von den Gespenstern entführt wurde, und fest entschlossen, ihn zu befreien, kehrt Luigi in das Furcht erregende Gebäude zurück. Bewaffnet ist er mit einer Taschenlampe, um die Gespenster zu blenden, und einem starken Staubsauger, um sie zu fangen. Luigi muss Einfallsreichtum und Schnelligkeit unter Beweis stellen, um die in den zahlreichen Schlupfwinkeln des Hauses, in den Wandschränken, den Vasen, den Duschabläufen und anderen Ecken versteckten Gespenster aufzustöbern.

Inspiriert von den berühmten Filmen der *Ghostbuster*-Serie, signiert Nintendo hier ein originelles Spiel, das sich an ein Publikum mit Spaß am Nervenkitzel wendet.

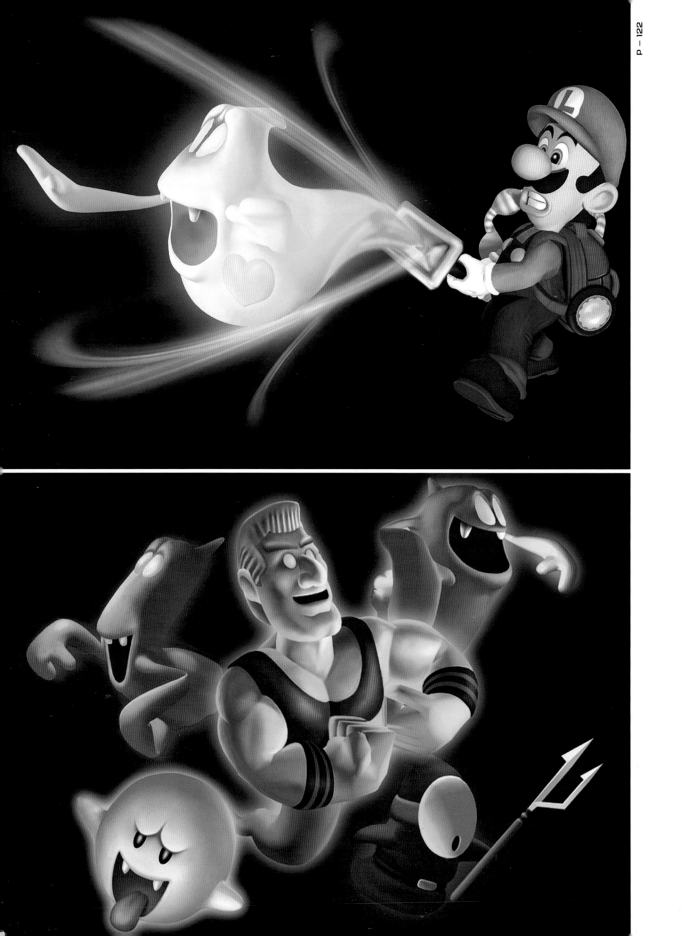

NAME ODDWORLD, MUNCH'S ODDYSEE

PLATFORM

RELEASE 2001

EDITOR MICROSOFT

DEVELOPER ODDWORLD INHABITANTS

COPYRIGHTS © ODDWORLD INHABITANTS/ MICROSOFT

Oddworld: Munch's Oddysee

For generations the puny Mudokons were enslaved by the Glukkons, vile capitalists without a moral sentiment between them. And the Glukkons didn't just exploit the Mudokons in their factories - they ate them too. A while ago, Abe, a Mukodon, liberated his own kind; most of them now live free lives, but many are still captives of the Glukkons and their enforcers, the Vykkers and Sligs. So Abe has become Glukkon Public Enemy Number One. And the Glukkons are not finished yet, not by a long chalk. To start with, they don't just oppress Mukodons... In the course of his mission, Abe also liberates Munch. Munch is the last of the Gabbits, and becomes Abe's right-hand man as he saves Mukodons and Fuzzles, little hairballs used by the Glukkons to polish their shoes and paint their faces. So Abe and Munch, with Glukkons, Scrabs, Paramites, Slogs and other local carnivores in hot pursuit, run the gauntlet of this droll, dingbat world.

« »

Pendant d'innombrables générations, les frêles Mudokons ont été les esclaves des horribles Glukkons, créatures immorales et capitalistes à l'extrême qui exploitaient les Mudokons dans leurs usines et les utilisaient également comme matière première pour leurs conserves de nourriture. Libérés par un des leurs, Abe, la plupart des Mudokons vivent enfin libres depuis peu, mais nombre d'entre eux sont encore prisonniers des griffes des Glukkons et de leurs sbires, les Vykkers et les Sligs. Abe, logiquement devenu Ennemi Public numéro Un, est loin d'en avoir terminé avec ses adversaires de toujours, d'autant que d'autres espèces sont elles aussi sous le joug des Glukkons. Au fil de sa quête, Abe libérera ainsi Munch, le dernier des Gabbits, qui l'épaulera dans sa quête et l'aidera à sauver Mudokons et Fuzzles, petites boules de poils, utilisés comme cirage à chaussures et produit cosmétique par les Glukkons. Pourchassés par les exploiteurs, mais aussi par les Scrabs, Paramites, Slogs et autres créatures sauvages et carnivores du coin, Abe et Munch vont affronter de multiples dangers dans un univers aussi drôle que décalé.

« »

Seit vielen Generationen werden die schwachen Mudokons von den bösen Glukkons als Sklaven gehalten. In ihren Fabriken beuten diese ruchlosen und geldgierigen Kreaturen die Mudokons aus und benutzen sie als Rohstoff für ihre Dosennahrung. Nach der Befreiung durch ihren Artgenossen Abe leben zwar die meisten Mudokons endlich in Freiheit, aber trotzdem befinden sich noch viele in der Gewalt der Glukkons und ihrer Schergen, den Vykkers und den Sligs. Abe, der logischerweise zum Staatsfeind Nummer eins avanciert ist, hat seinen alten Widersachern Rache geschworen, zumal auch andere Tierarten von den Glukkons unterjocht werden. Während seiner Mission befreit Abe den letzten Überlebenden der Gabbits, Munch. Dieser unterstützt ihn bei seinem Rachefeldzug und hilft ihm bei der Rettung der Mudokons und der Fussles, kleinen Wollknäueln, die von den Glukkons als Schuhcreme und Kosmetikartikel benutzt werden. Doch nicht nur die bösen Ausbeuter, auch Scrabs, Paramites, Slogs und andere wilde Kreaturen sind ihnen dabei dicht auf den Fersen, und so müssen die beiden Helden Abe und Munch in einer wahnwitzigen Welt vielen Gefahren trotzen.

ODDWORLD
Munch's
Oddysee

100%
UNNATURAL
ODDITIVES

REFRESHINGLY
TWISTED

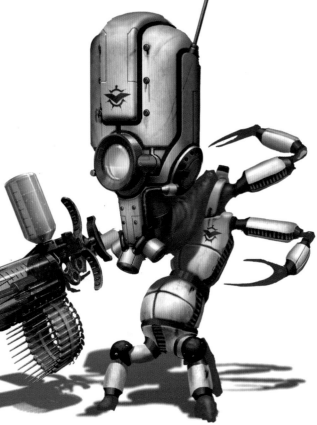

NAME
PLATFORM
RELEASE
EDITOR
DEVELOPER
COPYRIGHTS

FACT

PaRappa

PaRappa and his friends PJ Berri and Sunny are upstanding young rap-lovers living in peaceful smalltown America… or so it seems. But a strange plot is being hatched. PaRappa registers the ultimate truth: all he eats is noodles. Resolved to change his ways, he sets his heart on a hamburger. Nothing doing. No one in his home town eats anything but noodles - all other forms of food are mysteriously transformed! PaRappa launches an ultra-serious enquiry. Massive noodle-attack! What lies behind it? Can adversaries like Beard Burger Master, Chop Chop Master Onion, Guru the Ant, the teacher Moosesha (she should know better), and Colonel Noodle thwart the rapman? PaRappa can only progress by out-rapping them to the funkiest tunes. A wacky game with racy rhythms, singalong songs and vibrant visuals.

« »

PaRappa et ses amis PJ Berri et Sunny sont de braves jeunes amateurs de rap sans histoire habitant dans une petite ville paisible… du moins en apparence, car un étrange complot se fomente. PaRappa se rend en effet compte que toute la nourriture qu'il ingurgite se limite à un seul et unique aliment : la nouille. Bien décidé à changer de régime alimentaire, PaRappa décide de s'offrir un hamburger ; mais quelle n'est pas sa surprise lorsqu'il découvre que la ville entière ne mange que des nouilles ! Toute nourriture se transforme systématiquement en pâtes. PaRappa se lance alors dans une enquête humoristique, à la recherche de l'individu coupable de l'invasion de nouilles. Afin de progresser dans son enquête, PaRappa devra vaincre maints adversaires (Le Beard Burger Master, le Chop Chop Master Onion, Guru la fourmi, l'instructrice Moosesha, le Colonel Noodle) en rappant mieux qu'eux sur de nombreuses musiques frénétiques. Un jeu loufoque au rythme endiablé, servi par des chansons originales entraînantes et une réalisation graphique étonnante.

« »

Der Hund PaRappa und seine Freunde PJ Berri und Sunny Funny sind brave junge Rap-Freaks, die in einer kleinen friedlichen Stadt aufwachsen… zumindest scheint es so, bis sich ein eigenartiges Komplott zusammenbraut. Langsam wird PaRappa nämlich bewusst, dass er eigentlich nur noch ein einziges Nahrungsmittel in sich hineinstopft: Nudeln. Fest entschlossen, seinen Speiseplan etwas zu bereichern, beschließt PaRappa, sich einen Hamburger zu leisten. Aber wie groß ist sein Erstaunen, als er merkt, dass alle in der Stadt nur noch Nudeln essen! Sämtliche Nahrungsmittel verwandeln sich automatisch in Teigwaren. PaRappa nimmt es mit Humor und geht diesem Fall nach, er verfolgt die Spuren des für diese Nudelinvasion verantwortlichen Individuums. Um in seinen Ermittlungen voranzukommen, muss er so manchen Gegner besiegen (Beard Burger Master, Chop Chop Master Onion, Guru Ant, die Lehrmeisterin Musheisha, Colonel Noodle) und zu frenetischen Klängen rappend in den Schatten stellen. Ein verrücktes Spiel zu besessenen Rhythmen, mitreißenden Originaltiteln und einer coolen Grafik.

NAME
SAMBA DE AMIGO

PLATFORM
DREAMCAST

RELEASE
2000

EDITOR
SEGA

DEVELOPER
SONIC TEAM

COPYRIGHTS
© SONIC TEAM/SEGA

FACT
128 IS THE CAPACITY OF A DREAMCAST GD-ROM

Samba de Amigo

The Rio Carnival has a serious console-based rival: *Samba de Amigo*, a musical game dedicated to South American rhythms. Whipping up a sheer tornado of music, it invites the gamer to slip into the role of maraca-wielding dancer (the two electronic maracas, along with a sensor strip and foot mat, are part of the package). Dozens of famous pieces have been re-orchestrated in South-American-style for this game, so that the player can jig along in time to the rhythmic coloured circles shown on-screen. But even when *Samba de Amigo* is played simply on the D-pad: the visuals and the music are so compelling that the player can't help being caught up in the festive atmosphere of this virtual carnival, led by an MC called Amigo – an adorable monkey. It's even more fun with two players, whether they compete or team up; and various modes and levels of versatility are available. This is a highly original and very sensual game, which should attract all ages and all kinds of players, from the ultimate gamer to the newcomer.

« »

Le Carnaval de Rio a trouvé un sérieux challenger sur consoles. *Samba de Amigo* est un jeu musical dédié aux rythmes sud-américains ; il entraîne le joueur dans une tornade musicale endiablée et le met dans la peau d'un danseur armé de maracas électroniques (disponibles en tant qu'accessoires spécifiques, capteur et tapis inclus). Des dizaines de musiques célèbres, réorchestrées pour l'occasion à la sauce sud-américaine, sont au programme du jeu, qui amènent le joueur à reproduire des mouvements circulaires de maracas affichés à l'écran, en rythme, évidemment. Si *Samba de Amigo* n'est jouable qu'à la manette, la réalisation et la musique sont spécialement conçues pour plonger le joueur dans l'ambiance festive de ce carnaval virtuel orchestré par le sympathique singe Amigo. L'expérience est encore plus divertissante à deux, que ce soit en compétition ou en coopération voire dans un mode supposé définir le degré de complicité des participants. Un jeu original, physique, qui saura séduire tous les publics, petits et grands, joueurs invétérés ou occasionnels.

« »

Der Karneval in Rio hat auf den Spielkonsolen einen ernsthaften Herausforderer gefunden. *Samba de Amigo* ist ein Musikspiel, das den südamerikanischen Rhythmen gewidmet ist. Es entfacht einen leidenschaftlichen musikalischen Wirbelsturm und lässt den Spieler in die Rolle eines Tänzers mit zwei elektronischen Maracas-Rasseln (als Spezialzubehör, inklusive Sensorleiste und Matte) schlüpfen. Im Programm sind Dutzende berühmter Kompositionen, allesamt südamerikanisch aufbereitet, die den Spieler dazu bringen sollen, die Bewegungen der auf dem Bildschirm abgebildeten Kreise rhythmisch umzusetzen. Doch auch wenn *Samba de Amigo* nur mit dem DC Pad gespielt wird: Die Bildschirmgestaltung und die Musik sind wie geschaffen, um den Spieler hineinzuziehen in die festliche Stimmung dieses virtuellen Karnevals, durch den der sympathische Affe Amigo führt. Das Musikerleben ist zu zweit noch unterhaltsamer, egal ob man gegeneinander oder miteinander oder in einem der verschiedenen Modi spielt, bei denen der Schwierigkeitsgrad zuvor von den Teilnehmern festgesetzt wird. *Samba de Amigo* ist ein originelles und sinnliches Spiel, das ein breites Publikum begeistern wird: Alt und Jung ebenso wie Spielbesessene und Gelegenheitsspieler.

1,2 GIGA: SPEICHERKAPAZITÄT EINER
GD-ROM VON DREAMCAST.

1,2 GIGA: C'EST LA CAPACITÉ DE STOCKAGE
D'UN GD-ROM VON DREAMCAST.

NAME	SPACE CHANNEL 5
PLATFORM	DREAMCAST, PLAYSTATION 2
RELEASE	2000
EDITOR	SEGA
DEVELOPER	RM9
COPYRIGHTS	SEGA and UGA
FACT	5. THE NUMBER OF GAMES IN WHICH MICHAEL JACKSON APPEARS (MOONWALKER, SPACE CHANNEL 5, AND READY TO RUMBLE ROUND 2).

Space Channel 5

Shock horror! Vile extraterrestrials have invaded planet earth! And their evil goal is to enslave all humans and force them to partner them in the dance: dance, dance, dance to the point of exhaustion - and if attraction is mutual, it may not stop there... Must humanity forever jitterbug to alien rhythms? Is there no escape? Yes! Ulala, Space Channel 5's ace reporter, takes up the cause of humanity, and shows those pesky aliens that we can step it out without them! The *Space Channel 5* universe is a surprising but rather appealing mix: a futurist world of dazzling colours and wonderfully kitsch architecture, all set to the funkiest rhythms. The sublime Ulala soon sets fingers tapping with her peerless dancing. In short, a great eyeful and a great earful: enjoy!

« »

Ô malheur ! D'infâmes extraterrestres envahissent la terre ! Leur but : faire des humains leurs esclaves, et les obliger à danser avec eux jusqu'à épuisement, voire plus si affinités ! Les xénomorphes hypnotisent les humains en effectuant d'étranges danses fascinantes. L'humanité est-elle perdue, vouée à se mouvoir sur des rythmes extraterrestres jusqu'à la fin des temps ? Non, car Ulala, reporter pour Space Channel 5, est en première ligne de défense et va montrer aux extraterrestres qu'on n'a pas besoin d'eux pour danser ! L'univers *Space Channel 5* est un cocktail aussi surprenant qu'efficace : un monde futuriste aux couleurs chatoyantes, une architecture kitsch à souhait, le tout rythmé par de la musique funky endiablée. La sublime Ulala, danseuse émérite et au charme incontournable, fait bouger les consoles de jeu et leurs utilisateurs avec autant de grâce que d'humour. Bref, elle va vous en mettre plein les yeux et les oreilles, pour votre plus grand plaisir !

« »

O weh! Gar schändliche Außerirdische bedrohen die Erde. Ihr Ziel ist es, die Menschen zu versklaven und sie zu zwingen, bis zur Erschöpfung und sogar noch darüber hinaus mit ihnen zu tanzen. Die Fremden aus dem All hypnotisieren die Menschen, indem sie ihnen seltsame, aber faszinierende Tänze vorführen. Ist die Menschheit rettungslos verloren? Dazu verdammt, sich bis in alle Ewigkeit zu außerirdischen Rhythmen zu bewegen? Nein, denn Ulala, Reporterin für Space Channel 5, geht voll in die Offensive und wird den Außerirdischen zeigen, dass man zum Tanzen nicht auf sie angewiesen ist. Das Universum von *Space Channel 5* ist ein so beeindruckender wie wirkungsvoller Mix. Gezeigt wird eine futuristische Welt in schillernden Farben und ein denkbar kitschiges Design, das Ganze rhythmisch unterlegt von einer tollen funkigen Musik. Die reizende Ulala, eine begnadete Tänzerin mit unnachahmlichem Charme, animiert Spielkonsolen und Tänzer mit so viel Anmut wie Humor. Kurz und gut: Ein Augen- und Ohrenschmaus, der großes Vergnügen bereitet.

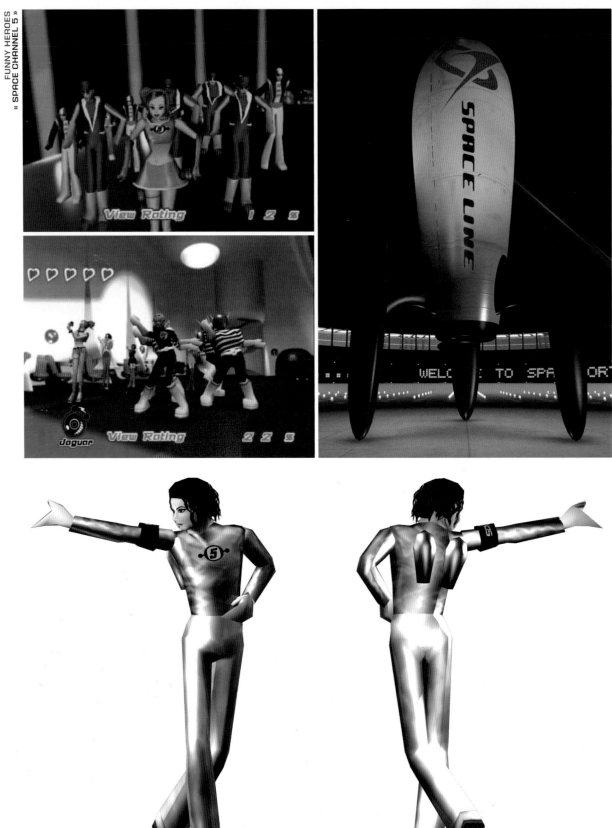

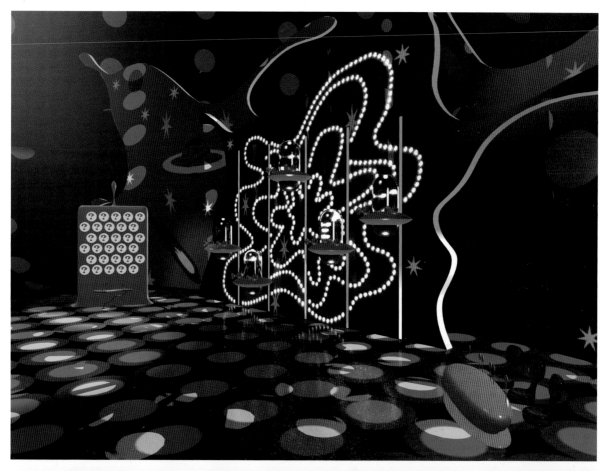

NAME SPYRO: SEASON OF ICE

PLATFORM GAME BOY ADVANCE

RELEASE 2001

EDITOR UNIVERSAL INTERACTIVE STUDIOS

DEVELOPER DIGITAL ECLIPSE

COPYRIGHTS "SPYRO: SEASON OF ICE", SPYRO THE DRAGON
AND RELATED CHARACTERS TM AND
© 2001 UNIVERSAL INTERACTIVE STUDIOS, INC.
ALL RIGHTS RESERVED

P – 140

Spyro

The dreadful Rhinos have not only captured the exquisite fairies of the Dragon kingdom, but shut them up in blue crystals and scattered them through the land. Now, the fairies' friends are just not the kind to take up arms, but, good-hearted as they are, they must do their best to free them. At their head is the violet dragon, Spyro. In point of fact, he's no fiercer than the others, but there are undoubtedly a few pluses to being a dragon; only Spyro can fly across the vast canyons that divide the different regions, and, if you are faced by a Rhino, breathing fire is a handy little skill.

Even with these talents, Spyro has never acquired quite the prestige of other great video-game figures like Crash Bandicoot, Mario or Sonic, but he still has a high place in the affections of many gamers old and young, who have had a lot of fun playing Spyro in quality platforms for PlayStation and Game Boy Advance.

« »

Les infâmes Rhinos ont capturé toutes les gentilles fées du royaume du Dragon puis les ont enfermées dans des cristaux bleus, disséminés de par le royaume. Et si tous les amis des fées, plus gentils les uns que les autres, ne sont pas du genre à prendre les armes, ils vont devoir les libérer. A leur tête, Spyro, un jeune dragon violet. Ce n'est pas qu'il soit plus belliqueux que les autres, mais être un dragon a des avantages dans de telles situations : lui seul sait voler et peut franchir les gouffres qui séparent les différentes régions, mais surtout, les flammes qu'il peut cracher s'avèrent ô combien utiles pour affronter les Rhinos.

S'il n'a encore jamais bénéficié du même prestige que d'autres grandes figures du jeu vidéo, comme Crash Bandicoot, Mario et autres Sonic, Spyro a su se faire une place dans la ludothèque de bien des joueurs, petits et grands, qui ont adoré l'incarner dans des jeux de plates-formes de qualité sur PlayStation et Game Boy Advance.

« »

Die frechen Rhinos haben alle guten Feen des Drachenreiches entführt, sie in blaue Eisblöcke eingesperrt und diese überall im Reich verstreut. Auch wenn es nicht ihre Art ist, gleich zu den Waffen zu greifen, so sind die Freunde der Feen doch fest entschlossen, sie zu befreien. Allen voran Spyro, ein junger lilafarbener Drache. Nicht, dass er kampfeslustiger wäre als die anderen, aber ein Drache ist in solchen Situationen einfach unschlagbar: Er allein kann fliegen und mühelos die Abgründe überwinden, die die verschiedenen Regionen voneinander trennen. Vor allem aber kann er Feuer spucken, und das ist äußerst nützlich, um den Rhinos zu trotzen.

Auch wenn Spyro nicht das gleiche Ansehen genießt wie die anderen großen Charaktere des Videospiels, Crash Bandicoot etwa, Mario und Sonic, hat er bei Jung und Alt einen festen Platz in der Videospiel-Sammlung, die ihm in anspruchsvollen Konsolenspielen auf PlayStation und Game Boy Advance ihr Herz geschenkt haben.

NAME

PLATFORM

RELEASE

EDITOR

DEVELOPER

COPYRIGHTS

FACT

Super Monkey Ball

Encased in transparent spheres, the monkeys in *Super Monkey Ball* are, well, obviously, having a ball; all kinds of fast and furious action is available when you roll up in a translucent superbowl. They sweep through wild switchbacks (where their ability to compensate for inertia in the bends is the key to victory), fly down gigantic bowling alleys, shoot across giant golf courses and enormous billiard tables - and the smile never leaves their faces. Intoxicated by speed, thrilled by harmless collisions and addicted to the chase, these monkeys have just two aims in life: having fun, and snatching up the tasty bananas scattered over the various monkey-ball courses.

« »

Ce n'est pas parce qu'ils sont enfermés dans des boules translucides qu'il faille s'apitoyer sur les singes de *Super Monkey Ball*. Bien au contraire, les petits animaux sont ravis de leur situation qui leur permet de s'amuser sur diverses épreuves frénétiques. Roulant à grande vitesse dans leurs boules sur des circuits délirants, où leur aptitude à compenser l'inertie dans les virages est leur principal atout les menant à la victoire, sur de gigantesques pistes de bowling où ils doivent viser les quilles, sur des terrains de golf géants ou de grandes tables de billard, les primates n'ont pas le temps de s'ennuyer, et ont un éternel sourire aux lèvres. Grisés par la vitesse, excités par les chocs sans danger et enivrés par le jeu, les singes n'ont que deux buts dans leur vie : s'amuser et, bien évidemment, attraper les savoureuses bananes éparpillées sur les différents terrains de jeu qui s'offrent à eux.

« »

Es besteht kein Grund, mit den in lichtdurchlässigen Kugeln eingesperrten Affen von *Super Monkey Ball* Mitleid zu haben. Ganz im Gegenteil, die Tierchen sind über ihre Lage begeistert, weil sie sich ausgelassen allein dem Spiel hingeben können. Ob sie nun in ihren Kugeln über Schwindel erregende Bahnen rasen und dabei siegesgewiss ihre Fähigkeit austesten, die Trägheit in den Kurven auszugleichen, ob sie gigantische Bowlingbahnen entlangrollen, um die Kegel zu treffen, oder ob sie auf riesigen Golfspielplätzen und übergroßen Billardtischen herumtollen: Zeit für Langeweile haben sie nicht, dafür aber stets ein fröhliches Gesicht. Ganz benommen von der rasanten Geschwindigkeit, aufgestachelt von den harmlosen Schocks und berauscht vom Spiel, haben die Affen nur zwei Ziele im Leben: Sie wollen sich amüsieren und, natürlich, die leckeren Bananen einsammeln, die überall auf den verschiedenen Spielfeldern verstreut sind.

1963: JAHR, IN DEM NINTENDO BESCHLOSS, SEINE PRODUKTION ZU ERWEITERN UND SPIELE ZU ENTWICKELN, NACHDEM SICH DIE FIRMA 71 JAHRE LANG AUF DIE HERSTELLUNG VON TRADITONELLEN KARTENSPIELEN KONZENTRIERT HATTE.

1963: C'EST L'ANNÉE OÙ NINTENDO A DÉCIDÉ D'ÉLARGIR SA PRODUCTION ET DE CRÉER DES JEUX APRÈS S'ÊTRE CONCENTRÉE SUR LA FABRICATION DE CARTES À JOUER TRADITIONNELLES PENDANT 71 ANS

NAME

PLATFORM

RELEASE

EDITOR

DEVELOPER

COPYRIGHTS

FACT

5 YEARS: THE TIME ELAPSED BETWEEN
THE LAUNCH OF SUPER MARIO BROS (1985)
AND THE FILM MARIO BROS (1990)

Twinsen

Twinsen, a young Quetch, won fame by saving his planet Twinsun from the tyrant FunFrock. Now he lives on the citadel island with his charming wife Zoé. But a new danger beckons: a powerful storm has injured DinoFly, Twinsun's lifelong friend. Determined to help him, Twinsen sets out to find the magus Kar'aaoc, the only man who can save DinoFly. His quest leads him to a terrible discovery. A danger threatens Twinsun: Dark Monk, the god of the Esmers, wants to destroy the planet and exploit its energy. To overcome him, Twinsen must take ship for the emerald moon; there the Dark Monk is fabricating gigantic jets, which will fire the moon directly into Twinsun's orbit. Humorous, thought-provoking, and action-packed, *Twinsen* also features endearing secondary characters and a delightful pastel environment: no wonder it's been such a hit.

« »

Après avoir déjà sauvé sa planète, Twinsun, des griffes du tyran FunFrock, Twinsen, jeune Quetch désormais célèbre, vit paisiblement sur l'île de la citadelle avec sa charmante épouse Zoé. Mais un nouveau danger approche : un puissant orage éclate et blesse le DinoFly, ami de toujours du jeune Quetch. Bien décidé à soigner son ami, Twinsen part à la recherche du mage Kar'aaoc, seul capable de soigner le DinoFly. Sa quête l'amènera à découvrir la terrible menace qui pèse sur sa planète : Dark Monk, le dieu des Esmers, veut détruire Twinsun et s'emparer de son énergie. Afin de vaincre ce nouvel adversaire, Twinsen devra s'embarquer vers la lune d'émeraude, sur laquelle l'infâme Dark Monk fabrique de gigantesques réacteurs qui lui permettront d'envoyer le satellite se fracasser sur Twinsun...
Humour, action et réflexion ont fait le succès des aventures de Twinsen, servies par des personnages attachants et une réalisation poétique aux teintes pastel.

« »

Endlich herrscht wieder Frieden auf dem Planeten Twinsun. Der inzwischen berühmt gewordene Twinsen, ein junger Quetch, der den Tyrannen FunFrock besiegt hat, lebt nun friedlich mit seiner charmanten Gattin Zoe auf der Zitadelleninsel. Doch es droht erneut Gefahr: Ein heftiges Unwetter bricht aus und verletzt den DinoFly, den treuen Begleiter des jungen Quetch. Fest entschlossen, seinen Freund zu heilen, macht sich Twinsen auf die Suche nach dem Wunderheiler Kar'aaoc, der als einziger den DinoFly retten kann. Auf seiner Suche entdeckt er jedoch die Katastrophe, die über dem Planeten schwebt: Dark Monk, der Gott der Esmerier, will Twinsun zerstören und sich seiner Energie bemächtigen. Um diesen neuen Gegner zu überwältigen, muss Twinsen zum Smaragd-Mond fliegen, auf dem der schändliche Dark Monk gigantische Reaktoren produzieren lässt, mit deren Hilfe er den Satelliten losschickt, um Twinsun zu zerstören...
Humor, Action und Reflexion begründen den Erfolg der Abenteuer von Twinsen, dem sympathische Figuren zur Seite stehen. Das pastellfarbene Design ist ansprechend und poetisch.

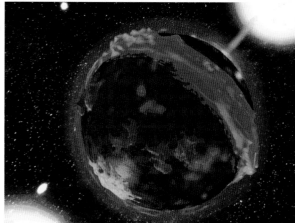

8 JAHRE: ZEITRAUM ZWISCHEN DEM ERSCHEI-
NEN DES SPIELS SUPER MARIO BROS (1985)
UND DEM FILM MARIO BROS (1993)

8 ANS: C'EST LE TEMPS QUI SÉPARE LA SORTIE
DE SUPER MARIO BROS (1985) ET CELLE
DU FILM MARIO BROS (1993)

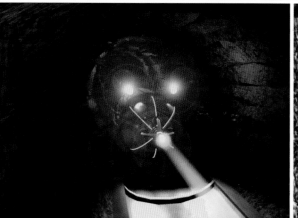

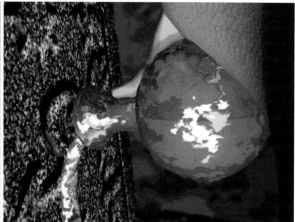

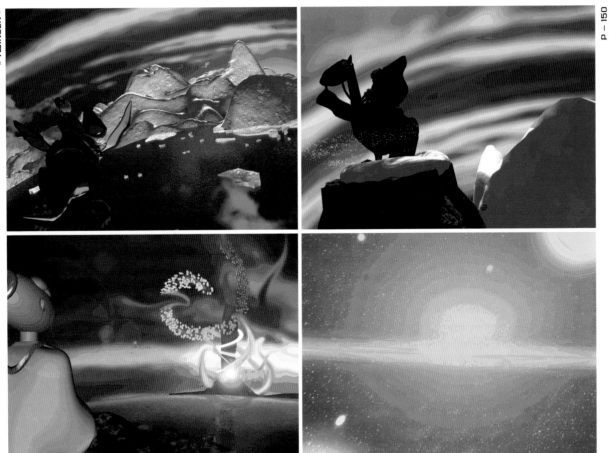

QUAND LES BLAFARDS SONT AU SOLEIL, ILS DEVIENNENT DE TOUTES LES COULEURS

KOUFLES

LE MOINE BLAFARD ET SON APÔTRE

LE BLAFARD

NAME
PLATFORM
RELEASE
EDITOR
DEVELOPER
COPYRIGHTS

Worms

So, how warlike is the average earthworm? Really? Beneath your feet, at this very instant, violent vermiform clan-conflicts rage, and redoubtable as the weaponry is, it does have a comic side... Alongside bazookas, machine guns, fragmentation grenades and other endearments, there are less conventional weapons: exploding flying-sheep, mad cows, holy grenades (shades of Monty P's *Holy Grail*), the worm-seeking pigeon, *Star Trek*-style teleporters and various ninja rope-tricks. All these feature in the worm-soldier's backpack. Thanks to this unlikely repertoire, worm-combats are as unpredictable as they are hilarious. Chain reactions - not easily foreseen - can undo your plans in a second: shells return to sender on adverse winds, grenades are awfully bouncy, and explosions can send worms into orbit...

« »

Qui aurait cru que les lombrics étaient des animaux aussi belliqueux ? Sous nos pieds se déroulent de violents conflits entre clans de vers de terre, et ceux-ci s'entre-tuent grâce à un arsenal redoutable... mais surtout farfelu. A côté des bazookas, mitraillettes et autres grenades à fragmentation, des armes peu conventionnelles sont aussi au rendez-vous : le mouton volant explosif, la vache folle, la sainte grenade (clin d'œil au film *Holy Grail* des Monty Python), le pigeon à tête chercheuse, les téléporteurs à la *Star Trek* et autres cordelettes de ninja sont aussi dans les besaces des lombrics. Grâce à cet incroyable inventaire, les combats entre vers sont toujours aussi surprenants que radicalement drôles. Les effets en cascade, difficiles à anticiper, peuvent souvent avoir un résultat inverse de ce qui était attendu : un obus qui retombe sur l'envoyeur à cause d'un vent contraire, des grenades qui rebondissent un peu où elles veulent ou des souffles d'explosion qui lancent des vers en orbite en sont quelques exemples amusants.

« »

Wer hätte gedacht, dass Regenwürmer so kampflustige Tiere sind? Unter unseren Füßen spielen sich brutale Auseinandersetzungen zwischen verschiedenen Regenwurm-Clans ab, die sich mit Hilfe eines furchtbaren, vor allem aber furchtbar komischen Waffenarsenals gegenseitig niedermetzeln. Neben Bazookas, Maschinenpistolen und Splittergranaten geben sich auch eher unkonventionelle Waffen ein Stelldichein: das fliegende Explosiv-Schaf, die verrückte Kuh, die heilige Granate (in Anlehnung an die Granaten der heiligen Hand in dem Monty-Python-Film *Die Ritter der Kokosnuss*), die Taube mit Zielsuchkopf, die Transmitter à la *Star Trek* und Ninja-Seile befinden sich im Besitz der Regenwürmer. Angesichts dieses unglaublichen Waffenbestandes nehmen die Kämpfe zwischen den Würmern immer einen ebenso überraschenden wie überaus witzigen Verlauf. Die Dominoeffekte, die schwer vorhersehbar sind, zeitigen oft ein Ergebnis, das keineswegs beabsichtigt war. Beispiele dafür sind Granaten, die durch Gegenwind zu dem zurückfliegen, der sie geworfen hat; Granaten, die einfach irgendwo abprallen; oder ein gewaltiger Explosionsdruck, der die Würmer ins All schleudert.

«Heroes of the Future»

Astonishing as it seems, although sci-fi video-games are common currency, very few are inspired by cyberpunk, the branch of sci-fi literature one might think closest to computerised entertainment. The commonest genre is the Space Opera, with its spaceships, giant combat-robots, laser weapons, monstrous aliens and distant universes. Is video-game afraid of its close relative, cyberpunk, and its recurrent themes of symbiosis between man and machine, all-powerful computer networks ruling over humanity and A.I endowed with consciousness?

Among the few games to celebrate its connection with cyberpunk is Dreamweb (Empire Interactive, 1994), a veritable pioneer in which the gamer must take on a sort of world Internet whose stability has been lost through human influence.

Also rooted in cyberpunk is Westwood Studio's Blade Runner (1997), which plunges the gamer into the dark universe of Ridley Scott's film - whose scenario was itself inspired by Philip K. Dick's novel, Do Androids Dream of Electric Sheep? This was one of the first great cyberpunk novels, and preceded the consecration of the genre in the work of authors such as William Gibson or Bruce Sterling.

We should finish by citing one of the most recent cyberpunk games, Ion Storm's exceptionally fine Deus Ex. Here is a world in which mega-corporations reign and humans can be cybernetically modified; in short, a game in the great tradition of the cyberpunk genre.

« »

Etonnamment, bien que les jeux vidéo de science-fiction soient légion, rares sont ceux inspirés du cyberpunk, branche de la littérature de S-F a priori la plus proche de l'informatique de loisirs. Le Space Opera et ses cortèges de vaisseaux spatiaux ou de robots de combat géants, d'armes laser, d'extraterrestres prodigieux et d'univers lointains, est en effet plus couramment employé. Le jeu vidéo aurait-il peur de son plus proche parent et de ses thèmes récurrents, tels la symbiose entre l'homme et la machine, les tout-puissants réseaux informatiques qui régissent l'humanité ou les intelligences artificielles conscientes ?

Parmi les rares jeux qui revendiquent leur appartenance au cyberpunk, citons Dreamweb (Empire Interactive, 1994), véritable précurseur où le joueur affronte l'équivalent d'un Internet mondial devenu instable suite à l'influence des forces et faiblesses d'être humains.

Tout aussi ancré dans le cyberpunk, Blade Runner de Westwood Studios (1997) plonge le joueur dans l'univers du film de Ridley Scott, lui-même tiré du roman de Philip K. Dick, Do Androids Dream of Electric Sheep?, qui pour beaucoup fut l'un des premiers grands romans cyberpunk, avant la consécration du genre amenée par des auteurs comme William Gibson ou Bruce Sterling.

Terminons avec l'un des plus récents jeux cyberpunk, l'exceptionnel Deus Ex de Ion Storm. Le joueur est dans ce jeu plongé dans un univers où les méga-corporations règnent, où les êtres humains peuvent être cybernétiquement modifiés bref, dans un monde cyberpunk dans la plus grande tradition du genre.

Obwohl die Zahl der Science-Fiction-Videospiele beträchtlich ist, gibt es erstaunlicherweise nur wenige, die sich vom Cyberpunk inspirieren lassen, einer der Unterhaltungsinformatik nahe stehenden Spielart der SF-Literatur. Viel häufiger nehmen sie sich die Space Opera mit ihren Raumschiffen oder riesigen Kampfrobotern, mit Laserwaffen, ungeheuren Aliens und weit entfernten Galaxien zum Vorbild. Fürchten Videospiele sich denn etwa vor ihren nächsten Verwandten und den ureigensten Sujets, als da wären die Symbiose zwischen Mensch und Maschine, die allmächtigen Datennetze, die die Menschheit beherrschen, oder die bewusst handelnden künstlichen Intelligenzen?

Von den wenigen Spielen, die sich ihrer Zugehörigkeit zum Cyberpunk nicht schämen, sei hier Dreamweb (Empire Interactive, 1994) genannt, ein echter Wegbereiter: Der Spieler sieht sich mit einer Art weltweitem Internet konfrontiert, das durch den Einfluss menschlicher Stärken und Schwächen instabil geworden ist.

Ebenso im Cyberpunk verwurzelt ist Blade Runner (Westwood Studios, 1997), das den Spieler in das Universum des Ridley-Scott-Films eintauchen lässt, gedreht nach dem Roman von Philip K. Dick. Diesen Buch Do Androids Dream of Electric Sheep?, war für viele einer der ersten großen Romane des Cyberpunk war, noch bevor Autoren wie William Gibson oder Bruce Sterling diesem Genre ihre Weihen verliehen.

Nicht zu vergessen das absolut spannende Deus Ex von Ion Storm: Es ist eines der neuesten Cyberpunk-Spiele. Der Spieler betritt hier eine Welt, die von Megakonzernen beherrscht wird und in der die Menschen cybertechnisch modifiziert werden können. Kurz: Er betritt eine Welt des Cyberpunks, die nach allen Regeln der Kunst entwickelt wurde.

NAME
DEUS EX

PLATFORM
PC - PLAYSTATION 2

RELEASE
2000

EDITOR
EIDOS INTERACTIVE

DEVELOPER
ION STORM AUSTIN

COPYRIGHTS
© EIDOS INTERACTIVE/ION STORM

FACT
10,000: THE NUMBER OF LINES OF DIALOGUE
THAT SHELDON PACOTTI WROTE FOR
THE GAME DEUS EX.

Deus Ex

In a none-too-distant future, in which nanotechnology is in everyday use, the global economy has hit rock-bottom. The majority live lives of wretched poverty, while an epidemic of new-species plague is sweeping the world. Dissident factions are fomenting terror in order to overthrow the established power; one such faction is the NSF, the biggest rebel group in the US. To bring order to this chaos, the UNO has created a unit of cybernetically modified elite soldiers, the UNATCO, whose mission is to eradicate the rebellion. UNATCO's new generation of nano-combatants are indistinguishable from ordinary mortals, and, for the moment, there are only two of them: Paul and JC Denton, two brothers who have been commissioned to take down the NSF rebellion. Over the course of the adventure, JC Denton's astonishing investigation, punctuated by gory fights, reveals the dark purposes of the UNATCO; it may even lead JC to defect to the rebels…
« »

Dans un futur proche, où la nanotechnologie est reine, l'économie mondiale est au plus bas. La majorité de la population vit dans la misère et souffre d'une épidémie de peste nouvelle génération qui s'étend sur l'ensemble de la planète. De plus, des factions terroristes sèment la terreur pour renverser les pouvoirs en place, comme la NSF, le plus grand regroupement rebelle des Etats-Unis. Afin de lutter contre ce chaos général, l'ONU a créé une unité de soldats d'élite cybernétiquement modifiés, l'UNATCO, dont la mission est d'éradiquer purement et simplement toute rébellion. Les nouveaux nano-combattants de l'UNATCO, dont les modifications cybernétiques sont invisibles à l'œil nu, ne sont pour l'instant qu'au nombre de deux : Paul et JC Denton, des frères qui ont pour directive principale de démanteler la NSF. Au cœur de l'aventure, JC Denton mènera une étonnante enquête, régulièrement ponctuée de combats d'une grande violence, qui l'amènera à découvrir les noirs desseins de l'UNATCO et peut-être à rejoindre la cause des rebelles…
« »

In der nahen Zukunft regiert die Nanotechnologie, während die Weltwirtschaft kurz vor dem Zusammenbruch steht. Der Großteil der Bevölkerung lebt im Elend und leidet unter einer Seuche, die sich über den gesamten Planeten ausbreitet. Hinzu kommt, dass terroristische Gruppen unaufhaltsam die Saat der Gewalt streuen, um an die Macht zu kommen, so zum Beispiel die NSF, der größte Zusammenschluss von Rebellen in den USA. Im Kampf gegen das allgemeine Chaos hat die UNO eine Elite-Einheit kybernetisch aufgerüsteter Soldaten zusammengestellt: die UNATCO, deren Mission darin besteht, jede Art von Rebellion ein für alle Mal niederzuschlagen. Die neue Generation der zur UNATCO zählenden Nano-Kämpfer, deren kybernetische Veränderungen auf den ersten Blick nicht zu erkennen sind, besteht im Augenblick nur aus den beiden Brüdern Paul und JC Denton, die die Weisung haben, die NSF zu zerstören. JC Denton macht bei seinem Einsatz erstaunliche Entdeckungen und wird dabei immer wieder in äußerst brutale Kampfhandlungen verwickelt. Dabei kommt er auch einer Verschwörung der UNATCO auf die Spur. Wird er jetzt ins Lager der Rebellen wechseln?

NAME
EMPIRE EARTH

PLATFORM
PC

RELEASE
2001

EDITOR
SIERRA ENTERTAINMENT

DEVELOPER
STAINLESS STEEL STUDIOS

COPYRIGHTS
© 2001 SIERRA ENTERTAINMENT, INC.
ALL RIGHTS RESERVED.

Empire Earth

War has punctuated the entire history of humanity. In every period, somewhere in the world, men have been at war over hunting grounds, wealth or political and religious issues. And this is still true today...

Mixing the ingredients of two legendary video-game sagas, *Civilization* and *Age of Empires*, *Empire Earth* allows you to play the eternal general. You guide the nation through wars distributed over nearly half a million years, from prehistory to the nano-age of the 22nd century. You must build villages and manage natural resources, construct buildings in which to drill your troops, and guide the developing nation. Now your staff-wielding soldiers give way to terrifying robots firing laser-salvoes. On sea and land and in the air, you must lead your troops to world-domination.

« »

Les guerres rythment l'histoire de l'humanité. A toute époque, il y a eu quelque part sur notre planète des hommes qui se battaient, pour un territoire de chasse, parce qu'ils convoitaient les richesses du voisin ou pour des raisons politiques et religieuses. Et cela n'est hélas certainement pas terminé...

Mêlant les ingrédients qui ont fait le succès de deux sagas légendaires du jeu vidéo, *Civilization* et *Age of Empires*, *Empire Earth* offre au joueur le rôle de l'éternel général des armées, lequel doit guider sa nation au fil de guerres s'étalant sur près d'un demi-million d'années, de la préhistoire au 22e siècle, le Nano-Age. Le joueur devra également bâtir des villages, gérer les ressources naturelles qui permettront de construire des bâtisses où entraîner ses troupes et guider sa nation dans l'évolution, permettant à de simples guerriers armés de bâtons de laisser progressivement la place à de terrifiants robots de combat tirant de redoutables salves laser. Sur terre, air et mer, le joueur devra mener ses troupes à la conquête de la planète.

« »

Die Menschheit wird in regelmäßigen Abständen von Kriegen heimgesucht. In jeder historischen Epoche hat es auf unserer guten alten Erde Menschen gegeben, die gegeneinander gekämpft haben, sei es um ein Jagdrevier, sei es aus Neid, weil der Nachbar größere Reichtümer besaß, oder aber aus politischen oder religiösen Gründen. Und das ist heute noch immer so...

Mit *Empire Earth*, einem Mix aus Zutaten, die den Erfolg der legendären Spiele-Klassiker *Civilization* und *Age of Empires* begründet haben, kann der Spieler in die Rolle des ewigen Generals schlüpfen und seine Armee in die vielen Kriege führen, die sich über einen Zeitraum von knapp einer halben Million Jahre erstrecken – von der Altsteinzeit bis ins 22. Jahrhundert, das Nano-Zeitalter. Außerdem hat der Spieler die Aufgabe, Städte zu errichten, die Ressourcen zu verwalten, die zum Bauen benötigt werden, seine Truppen auszubilden und die Entwicklung seines Volkes voranzutreiben. Dazu gehört auch, dass einfache, nur mit einem Stock bewaffnete Krieger nach und nach ersetzt werden durch Furcht erregende Kampfroboter, die mit Laser-Kanonen aufeinander losgehen. Zur Eroberung des Planeten muss der Spieler seine Truppen zu Land, zu Wasser und in der Luft kämpfen lassen.

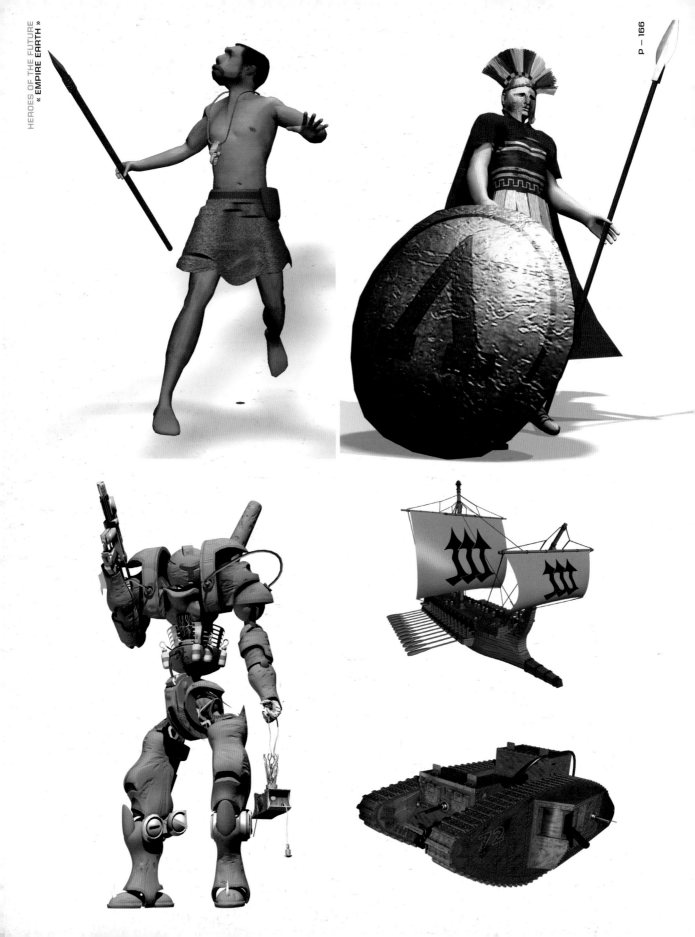

NAME
FINAL FANTASY X
PLATFORM
PLAYSTATION 2
RELEASE
2001
EDITOR
SONY COMPUTER ENTERTAINMENT
DEVELOPER
SQUARESOFT
COPYRIGHTS
© SQUARESOFT

Final Fantasy

In a high-tech future, everyone's favourite sport is Blitzball; Tidus is its greatest star, adored by young and old. During a match in Zanarkand, the city is attacked by a fearsome magic power, the Sin. Auron, a friend of Tidus' late father, saves him from a horrible death, but Tidus is swept up in a supernatural whirlwind created by the Sin, which propels him a thousand years into the future. In this future, the earth is held in an iron grip by the Sin, which ravages the cities and hunts down the few surviving humans, who have safeguarded only fragments of their former technological prowess. In their relentless battle against the Sin, the resistants have rediscovered magic, which forms part of the combat repertoire of strange warriors called Summoners. Determined to return to his own era, Tidus joins a little group of warriors bent on eliminating the Sin: the beautiful young Rikku, the athletic Wakka, the sorceress Lulu, the Summoner Yuna and her bodyguard Kihmari.

« »

Dans un futur hautement technologique, le loisir préféré de tous est le Blitzball, sport dont Tidus est la grande célébrité, adulé des petits et des plus grands. Alors qu'il joue un match dans la ville de Zanarkand, la cité est attaquée par une redoutable puissance magique, le Sin. Sauvé in extremis d'une mort horrible par Auron, ami de son défunt père, Tidus est projeté dans un siphon surnaturel créé par le Sin, qui le propulse à travers le temps, un millénaire plus tard. Dans cet avenir, le Sin domine la terre entière, ravageant les cités et pourchassant les rares humains survivants, qui n'ont sauvegardé que des fragments de leur ancienne glorieuse technologie. N'ayant cesse de combattre le Sin, les résistants ont redécouvert la magie, que d'étranges guerriers, les Invocateurs, utilisent dans leur combat quotidien. Porté par sa volonté de rentrer dans son ère, Tidus rejoint un groupuscule de guerriers farouchement décidés à éliminer le Sin : la belle et jeune Rikku, le sportif Wakka, la magicienne Lulu, l'Invocatrice Yuna et son garde du corps Kihmari.

« »

In einer technologisch sehr hoch entwickelten Zukunft heißt die von allen bevorzugte Freizeitbeschäftigung Blitzball. Tidus ist der große Star dieser Sportart und wird deshalb von Jung und Alt vergöttert. Während eines Matches in Zanarkand wird die Stadt von einem gefürchteten Ungeheuer, dem magischen Sin, angegriffen. Nachdem Tidus in letzter Minute durch Auron, einen Freund seines verstorbenen Vaters, vor einem schrecklichen Tod gerettet wird, schleudert ihn ein von Sin erzeugter übernatürlicher Sog durch die Zeit ins nächste Jahrtausend. Dort, in einer Welt namens Spira, verwüstet Sin als uneingeschränkter Herrscher die Städte und jagt die wenigen Überlebenden, von deren einst ruhmreicher Technologie nur Bruchstücke übrig geblieben sind. Die unermüdlich gegen Sin ankämpfenden Bewohner von Spira haben die Magie wiederentdeckt, die geheimnisvolle Krieger, die Summons, bei ihren täglichen Kämpfen einsetzen. Beseelt von dem Wunsch, wieder in seine Zeit zurückzukehren, schließt Tidus sich einer kleinen Gruppe von wild entschlossenen Kämpfern an, die das Ungeheuer Sin vernichten wollen, darunter die schöne, junge Rikku, der sportliche Wakka, die Zauberin Lulu, das Medium Yuna und ihr Leibwächter Kihmari.

NAME **GUNVALKYRIE**
PLATFORM XBOX
RELEASE 2001
EDITOR SEGA
DEVELOPER SMILEBIT
COPYRIGHTS © SMILEBIT/SEGA

FACT SPACE INVADERS, THE FIRST ARCADE PORTED TO THE HOME CONSOLE, ATARI 2600.

Gunvalkyrie

In a parallel universe, in a period like that of the earthly 19th century, a solitary scientist, Dr Hebble, has discovered an incredibly advanced technology. It is, however, founded on a new and unstable form of energy, and creates a terrible risk: if this energy fell into the wrong hands, the catastrophe might annihilate the universe. To protect his discoveries, Dr Hebble and the government have created the Gun Valkyrie organisation. When Dr Hebble disappears and hordes of nightmare creatures suddenly appear out of nowhere, Gun Valkyrie is summoned to retrieve the scientist and destroy the monsters. Thanks to their hyper-efficient arsenal and rocket-packs, the Gun Valkyrie units can save the cosmos - if, that is, the gamer at the controls is up to the task...

« »

Dans un univers parallèle, à une époque semblable à notre 19ᵉ siècle, un scientifique solitaire, le Dr Hebble, découvre une nouvelle technologie incroyablement avancée. Mais celle-ci, fondée sur une nouvelle forme d'énergie instable, risque à tout moment de créer une catastrophe risquant d'annihiler l'univers si elle tombait entre de mauvaises mains. Afin de protéger ses découvertes, le Dr Hebble et le gouvernement créent une unité spéciale, l'organisation Gun Valkyrie. Lorsque le Dr Hebble disparaît et que des hordes de créatures de cauchemar, venues d'on ne sait où, font leur apparition, la Gun Valkyrie est appelée pour retrouver le scientifique et détruire les monstres qui menacent l'équilibre de l'univers. Grâce à leur arsenal surpuissant et leur aptitude à se propulser dans les airs, les unités Gun Valkyrie sont l'unique chance de salut de l'humanité... du moins si le joueur qui prend les commandes est à la hauteur de la tâche qui lui incombe.

« »

In einer Parallelwelt, in einer Zeit, vergleichbar unserem 19. Jahrhundert, entdeckt ein einsiedlerischer Wissenschaftler namens Dr. Hebble eine neue, unglaublich hoch entwickelte Technologie. Diese basiert auf einer bisher unbekannten, instabilen Energieform, die, geriete sie in unbefugte Hände, jederzeit eine Katastrophe auslösen und das Universum vernichten könnte. Zusammen mit der Regierung gründet Dr. Hebble eine Spezialeinheit, die Organisation Gun Valkyrie, die den Auftrag hat, seine Erfindungen zu schützen. Als Dr. Hebble verschwindet und Horden von gruseligen Kreaturen auftauchen, deren Herkunft völlig ungeklärt ist, bekommt die Gun Valkyrie Order, den Wissenschaftler aufzuspüren und die Monster, die das Gleichgewicht der Welt bedrohen, zu vernichten. Durch ihr überdimensionales Waffenarsenal und ihre Fähigkeit, sich in der Luft fortzubewegen, sind nur die Kämpfer der Gun Valkyrie in der Lage, die Menschheit zu retten zumindest, wenn der Spieler, der die Hebel in die Hand nimmt, seiner Aufgabe gewachsen ist.

SPACE INVADERS: ERSTES ARCADE-SPIEL, DAS AUF EINE KONSOLE, DEN ATARI 2600, ÜBERTRAGEN WURDE.

SPACE INVADERS: C'EST LE PREMIER JEU D'ARCADE PORTÉ SUR UNE CONSOLE DE SALON, L'ATARI 2600.

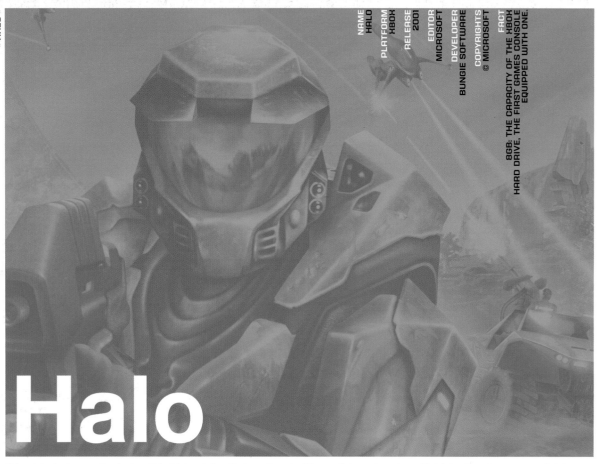

NAME HALO
PLATFORM XBOX
RELEASE 2001
EDITOR MICROSOFT
DEVELOPER BUNGIE SOFTWARE
COPYRIGHTS © MICROSOFT
FACT 8GB: THE CAPACITY OF THE XBOX HARD DRIVE, THE FIRST GAMES CONSOLE EQUIPPED WITH ONE.

Halo

A fearful mission awaits the handful of interstellar Marines disembarking on Halo, a gigantic artificial ring hanging in space. Halo's inner side is covered in plains, forests, and mountains, studded here and there with mysterious constructions. It is also swarming with extra-terrestrial creatures of a highly evolved kind, equipped with amazing aircraft, who laser-blast you on sight. Humanity, determined to acquire the funky technologies of Halo, has sent out its elite forces, the ultra highly trained Marines. Given extra-terrestrial hordes and a myriad dangers lurking on and beneath the surface, the Marine's blockbusting arsenal is just the thing. *Halo* is the first major title for the recent Microsoft console Xbox: it offers a complete sci-fi scenario, explosive action, and amazing visual spectacle.

« »

Une mission aussi périlleuse qu'extraordinaire attend la poignée de Marines intersidéraux s'apprêtant à débarquer sur l'étrange Halo, gigantesque anneau artificiel flottant dans l'espace, dont la face interne est recouverte de plaines, forêts et montagnes où l'on peut obser-ver, ci et là, de mystérieuses constructions. Mais surtout, Halo est peuplé d'innombrables créatures extraterrestres évoluées et violentes, défendant l'anneau, armées de fusils laser et de véhicules aériens étonnants. Bien décidés à acquérir par tous les moyens les prometteu-ses technologies avancées qu'offre le monde de Halo, les humains décident d'y envoyer leurs forces d'élite, des Marines surentraînés. Face aux hordes d'extraterrestres et aux mille dangers insoupçonnés qui les guettent à la surface et dans les entrailles de Halo, l'arsenal sur-puissant des Marines ne sera pas de trop...

A la fois jeu d'action explosif, récit de science-fiction à part entière et spectacle visuel incroyable, *Halo* est le premier grand titre de la récente console Xbox de Microsoft.

« »

Eine ebenso lebensgefährliche wie außergewöhnliche Mission erwartet eine Hand voll Marines, die zur Landung auf dem seltsamen Planeten Halo ansetzen: Der Halo ist ein gigantischer künstlicher Ring, der im All schwebt und Täler, Wälder und Berge beheimatet; hier und da sind auch ein paar mysteriöse Konstruktionen zu erkennen. Vor allem aber wird Halo von zahlreichen außerirdischen und gewalttätigen Kreaturen bevölkert, die den Ring mit Lasergewehren und Luftfahrzeugen verteidigen. Fest entschlossen, des vielversprechenden High-Tech-Systems mit allen Mitteln habhaft zu werden, beschließen die Menschen, ihre Elitetruppen, extrem durchtrainierte Marines, auf den Planeten zu entsenden. Angesichts der Horden von Außerirdischen und der tausendfachen Gefahren, die sie auf Halo und in seinem Inneren erwarten, dürfte wohl keiner der vielen Marines fehl am Platz sein...

Halo, der erste große Titel für die neue Xbox von Microsoft, ist ein nervenaufreibendes Action-Spiel und zugleich eine unglaublich gut konzipierte Science-Fiction-Erzählung. Dieses irre visuelle Spektakel sollte sich niemand entgehen lassen.

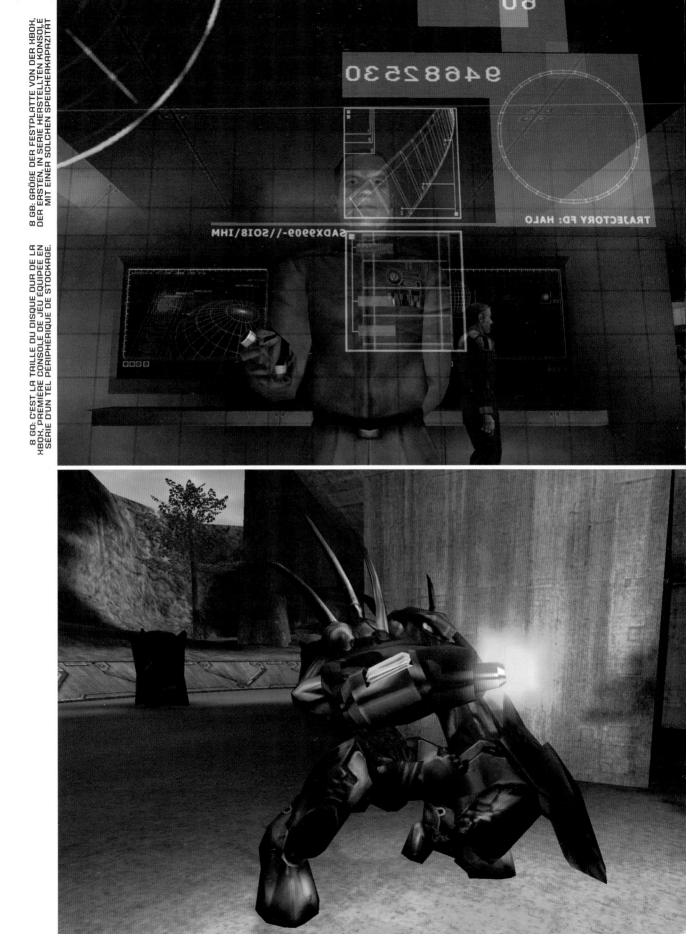

NAME
JET SET RADIO
JET SET RADIO FUTURE

PLATFORM
DREAMCAST - XBOX

RELEASE
2001

EDITOR
SEGA

DEVELOPER
SEGA

COPYRIGHTS
© SEGA

FACT
102: THE NUMBER OF GRAFFITI IT IS POSSIBLE
TO INSCRIBE IN THE GAME JET SET RADIO, NOT
COUNTING THE GAMER'S OWN INVENTIONS.

Jet Set Radio

In the Tokyo of 2024, roller-gang warfare is raging. But these are peaceful contests, fought with graffiti; each gang takes possession of a part of the town by making its mark there. The gangs are competing, but they have a common enemy, the Rokkaku Corporation, which wants to ban roller-skates from the city. So their spray-paint quests are subject to interference from the police under the orders of the Rok Corp. The CG gang must therefore protect its territory from the three rival gangs, the Immortals, the Posion Jam and the Noisetanks, while playing cat and mouse with the security police of the Rok, who are led by officer Hayashi, the right-hand man of the Corp's president, Gouji.

« »

À Tokyo, en 2024, la guerre des gangs en rollers fait rage. Mais ces affrontements sont pacifiques et se déroulent à coups de graffiti, chaque gang prenant possession d'un quartier de la ville en y apposant sa marque. S'ils sont antagonistes, les membres de ces gangs ont aussi un but commun : empêcher la Rokkaku Corporation de leur ôter leur liberté de s'éclater en rollers en ville. Aussi la course au Tag est-elle parasitée par les interventions des forces de police, sous les ordres de la Corpo. Ainsi, le Clan des GG, dirigé par le célèbre DJ K. et composé des acrobatiques Cron, Gum, Beat, Yyo, Roboy, Combo, Clutch, Jazz, Garam et Soda, doit non seulement protéger son territoire des deux équipes rivales, les Immortals, les Poison Jam et les Noisetanks, mais aussi jouer au chat et à la souris avec les forces policiè-res de la Rokkaku, que dirige l'officier Hayashi, bras droit de Gouji, président de la Corporation.

« »

Im Tokio des Jahres 2024 tobt der Bandenkrieg auf Rollerskates. Doch die gegenseitigen Angriffe sind friedlicher Natur und erfolgen aus-schließlich über Graffiti, wobei jede Gang sich eines Stadtviertels bemächtigt und dort ihre „Tags" hinterlässt. Obwohl sie Gegner sind, ver-folgen die Bandenmitglieder ein und dasselbe Ziel: Sie wollen verhindern, dass die Rokkaku Corporation ihnen verbietet, auf Rollerskates durch die Stadt zu brausen. Die „Tag"-Strecke wird im Auftrag der Corporation polizeilich überwacht. Der GG-Clan, mit dem bekannten DJ Professor K an der Spitze und den akrobatischen Skatern Corn, Gum, Beat, Yyo, Roboy, Clutch, Jazz, Garam und Soda, muss nicht nur sein Territorium gegen zwei gegnerische Teams – die Immortals und die Poison Jam und Noisetanks – verteidigen, sondern auch noch Katz und Maus mit den Polizeikräften von Rokkado spielen. Deren Chef ist Officer Hayashi, die rechte Hand von Gouji, dem Präsidenten der Corporation.

102: ANZAHL DER GRAFFITI, DIE MAN
IM SPIEL JET SET RADIO BEKOMMEN
KANN, AUSSCHLIEßLICH DERER, DIE MAN
SELBST KREIEREN KANN.

102: C'EST LE NOMBRE DE GRAFFITI QU'IL EST
POSSIBLE D'AVOIR DANS LE JEU JET SET RADIO,
SANS COMPTER TOUS CEUX QUE L'ON PEUT
CRÉER SOI-MÊME.

NAME
MECHWARRIOR 4
PLATFORM
PC
RELEASE
2001
EDITOR
MICROSOFT
DEVELOPER
FASA INTERACTIVE
COPYRIGHTS
© FASA INTERACTIVE/
MICROSOFT
FACT
40%: THE PERCENTAGE OF PC OWNERS
WHO USE THEIR COMPUTER EXCLUSIVELY
FOR VIDEO-GAMING.

Mechwarrior

We have entered the Third Millennium. The universe is in thrall to warrior clans, who duke it out for clan honour and planetary conquest in their Mechs: monstrous biped robots, heavily armed, very fast and highly manoeuvrable. Steel giants, capable of launching waves of missile strikes or laser-slicing through enemy armour, they are, nevertheless, just machines. The true combatants are their pilots, the Mech-Warriors, intrepid fighters pushing the machinery to its limits in search of the ultimate blow.

Licensed from FASA's *BattleTech* boardgames, *MechWarrior* has been considerably modified for video-gaming, with combat sims placing the gamer in the cockpit of the robots, and wargames in which whole battalions of Mechs form up under your command.

« »

Le troisième millénaire. L'univers est déchiré par des guerres entre clans de guerriers, les MechWarriors, qui s'affrontent sans répit pour la conquête de planètes, mais aussi pour l'honneur. Leurs véhicules de combat, les Mechs, sont de monstrueux robots bipèdes surarmés, rapides et très manœuvrables. Mais ces géants d'acier, capables de noyer l'ennemi sous des nuées de missiles ou de le couper en deux d'un simple tir de rayon laser surpuissant, ne sont que des machines : les véritables guerriers sont leurs pilotes, les MechWarriors, témé-raires combattants capables de pousser leurs machines au-delà de leurs limites dans l'espoir d'asséner le coup fatal à l'adversaire. Tiré de la licence des jeux de plateau BattleTech de la société FASA, l'univers des MechWarriors a bénéficié de maintes adaptations en jeu vidéo, principalement avec des simulateurs de combat plaçant le joueur dans le cockpit des robots guerriers et des wargames où l'utilisateur dirige des bataillons entiers de Mechs.

« »

Wir schreiben das 3. Jahrtausend. Das Universum ist zerrissen durch die Kriege zwischen kriegerischen Clans, den MechWarriors, die unaufhörlich um die Herrschaft über fremde Planeten, aber auch um die Ehre willen kämpfen. Als Kampfmaschinen benutzen sie die Mechs, riesige Kolosse in der Gestalt von Robotern, die bis an die Zähne bewaffnet, sehr schnell und überaus wendig sind. Doch diese Stahlkolosse, die den Gegner im Raketenhagel untergehen lassen oder ihn mit einem einzigen übermächtigen Laserstrahl in zwei Hälften teilen, sind nichts weiter als Maschinen. Die wahren Helden sind ihre Kommandanten, die MechWarriors, tollkühne Krieger, die ihren Kampfmaschinen das Äußerste abfordern, in der Hoffnung, dem gegnerischen Mech den Todesstoß zu versetzen.

Entwickelt von den Schöpfern des *BattleTech*-Universums der Spielefirma FASA, hat *MechWarrior* 4 erheblich von seinen Vorgängerversionen profitiert, vor allem bei den Gefechtssimulationen, wenn der Spieler im Cockpit eines Mechs sitzt, oder bei den Kriegsspielen, wenn er eine ganze Legion von Mechs kommandiert.

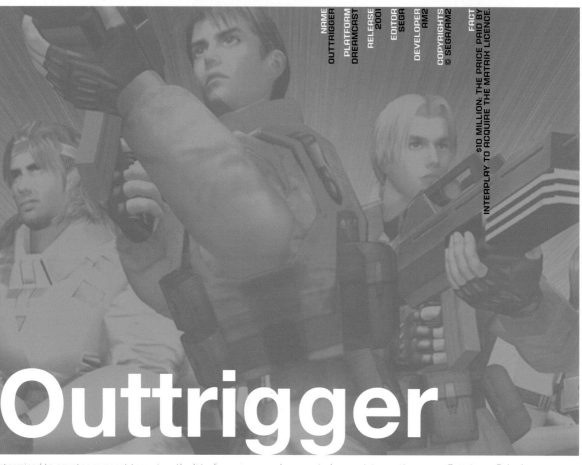

NAME
OUTTRIGGER
PLATFORM
DREAMCAST
RELEASE
2001
EDITOR SEGA
DEVELOPER
AM2
COPYRIGHTS
© SEGA/AM2
FACT
$10 MILLION: THE PRICE PAID BY
INTERPLAY TO ACQUIRE THE MATRIX LICENCE.

Outtrigger

Determined to counter rampant terrorism, the Interforce company has created a new intervention group, Outtrigger. Only the most war-hardened combatants come through the rigorous Outtrigger training. Then begins the struggle against international terrorism. Perilous missions take them to every corner of the globe. They fight in ruined castles, astronomic observatories and abandoned railway stations. The best become squad leaders, commanding four specialists (explosives, heavy weapons, sniper, and energy-weapons). The formidable squad arsenal includes flame-throwers, photon-torpedoes, fragmentation grenades, portable lasers and missile-launchers. Go for it!

« »

Afin de contrer la menace terroriste de plus en plus forte, la société Interforce a créé un nouveau groupe d'intervention internationale, Outtrigger. Seul les combattants les plus aguerris achèvent l'entraînement rigoureux d'Outtrigger et peuvent se lancer dans la lutte contre les organisations terroristes internationales, dans des missions périlleuses qui les feront voyager aux quatre coins du globe, les entraîneront dans des châteaux en ruine, des observatoires astronomiques ou encore des stations ferroviaires abandonnées. Les plus méritants auront le privilège de devenir chefs d'escouade et de prendre en main le destin d'une escouade de quatre soldats (démolisseur, armes lourdes, tireur d'élite, spécialiste en armes à énergie), dotés d'un arsenal meurtrier, dont des lance-flammes, des torpilles à photons, des grenades à fragmentation, des lasers portatifs ou encore des lance-roquettes.

« »

Um sich gegen die immer stärker werdende terroristische Bedrohung zur Wehr zu setzen, hat die Interforce eine neue internationale Einsatzgruppe gegründet: Outtrigger. Nur die zähesten Männer schaffen die harte Ausbildung für die Spezialgruppe und können den Kampf gegen die internationalen terroristischen Vereinigungen aufnehmen. Ihre gefährlichen Missionen verschlagen sie in alle Himmelsrichtungen, in verfallene Schlösser, in Sternwarten und in verlassene Bahnhöfe… Die verdienstvollsten Kämpfer können zum Truppenchef aufsteigen und das Schicksal einer jeweils aus vier Soldaten bestehenden Truppe (Zerstörer, schweres Geschütz, Scharfschütze, Spezialist für Energiewaffen) in die Hand nehmen. Zu ihrer Unterstützung erhalten sie ein mörderisches Waffenarsenal, darunter Flammenwerfer, Photonentorpedos, Splittergranaten, Laserpistolen in Taschenformat und sogar Raketenwerfer.

NAME PHANTASY STAR ONLINE

PLATFORM DREAMCAST-PC-GAMECUBE-XBOX

RELEASE 1999

EDITOR SEGA

DEVELOPER SONIC TEAM

COPYRIGHTS © SONIC TEAM/SEGA

FACT 16,000: THE MULTIPLAYER CAPACITY OF AN ELEMENTAL SAGA SERVER.

Phantasy Star Online

Approaching planet Ragol, the settlers in spaceship Pioneer 2 are expecting to rejoin their friends and families, who travelled on the first interstellar transport, Pioneer 1. But contact with the colony has been lost. A group is sent down to investigate, but only a handful return. Catastrophe: the colony is in ruins, there is no sign of survivors, and the planet is teeming with ferocious monsters. The mission's leaders ban all civilian access to the planet, and dispatch the Hunters, a team of mercenary warriors, magicians and mechanics to explore the situation. A superlative role-playing actioner, *Phantasy Star Online* was also the first online multi-player for console.

« »

À l'approche de la planète Ragol, les colons du vaisseau Pioneer 2 pensaient retrouver leurs proches, arrivés dans le premier transporteur interstellaire, Pioneer 1, déjà installés sur la planète. Mais la colonie ne répond pas aux communications, et seule une poignée des premiers explorateurs de Pioneer 2 dépêchés sur place reviennent, porteurs d'informations fragmentaires et catastrophiques : la colonie est en ruines, aucun colon ne donne signe de vie et pire encore, la planète est envahie de monstres sauvages et sanguinaires. Afin de découvrir ce qui a pu se passer sur Ragol, les dirigeants de Pioneer 2 en interdisent tout accès aux civils, et n'autorisent que les Hunters, des mercenaires guerriers, magiciens et mécaniques, à explorer la planète...

Jeu de rôles et d'action 3D superbe, *Phantasy Star Online* est également le tout premier jeu multijoueurs sur Internet pour une console, la Dreamcast de Sega.

« »

Beim Anflug auf den Planeten Ragol glaubten die Siedler an Bord des Raumschiffes Pioneer 2, bald ihre Angehörigen wiederzusehen, die mit dem ersten interstellaren Transporter Pioneer 1 gelandet waren und sich auf dem Planeten niedergelassen hatten. Aber die Kolonie reagiert nicht auf die Funksignale und lediglich eine Hand voll der zur Erkundung ausgesandten Besatzungsmitglieder der Pioneer 2 kehrt mit bruchstückhaften Katastrophenmeldungen zurück: Die Kolonie gleicht einer Ruine, es gibt keinerlei Lebenszeichen mehr von den Siedlern, und schlimmer noch, der Planet wurde von wilden und blutrünstigen Monstern heimgesucht. Um herauszufinden, was sich wirklich auf Ragol abgespielt hat, untersagen die Führer der Pioneer 2 den Zivilisten jeglichen Zugang zum Planeten Ragol. Die Erforschung des Planeten ist nur den Hunters erlaubt, den kriegerischen Söldnern und Cyborgs mit Zauberkraft...

Phantasy Star Online ist ein super 3-D-Rollen- und Actionspiel und zugleich das erste Online-Multiplayerspiel für eine Konsole, und zwar für die Dreamcast von Sega mit eingebautem Modem für den Zugang zum Internet.

NAME
PROJECT EDEN

PLATFORM
PC - PLAYSTATION 2

RELEASE
2001

EDITOR
EIDOS INTERACTIVE

DEVELOPER
CORE DESIGN

COPYRIGHTS
© EIDOS INTERACTIVE/CORE DESIGN

FACT
4 BILLION: THE NUMBER OF WEB PAGES
ON THE INTERNET IN FEBRUARY 2001
ACCORDING TO CYVEILLANCE.

Project Eden

In a none-too-distant future, the world has become a single, gigantic megapolis: overpopulation has attained critical levels and skyscr apers cover the earth. As a result of this extreme urban density, the swarming mass of humanity is divided into two very distinct categories. The lower storeys of the cities are swarming with the poor, while a handful of the privileged enjoy the light of day. In the lower depths, criminal gangs, psychopaths and ultra-violent sects battle it out for mastery of a metal jungle, while the police force, the Urban Protection Agency, struggles to regain control. Four members of the UPA experience a descent into hell when they discover sinister plots intended to solve overpopulation by the most drastic means. Only their combined talents can avert this threat; meanwhile, Carter, who heads the group, Minoko, the computer specialist, André, master-mechanic, and Amber the cyborg must pool their talents merely to survive their journey through this urban jungle where the sun never rises.

« »

Dans un futur assez proche, la terre n'est plus qu'une gigantesque mégapole : la surpopulation a atteint un stade critique, et les gratte-ciel recouvrent la surface de la planète. Conséquence de cette extrême urbanisation, la grouillante humanité se divise en deux catégories très distinctes : les masses pauvres occupent les bas étages des cités, et une poignée d'influents ont seuls la chance de voir la lumière du soleil. Au sous-sol, gangs criminels, psychopathes en tous genres et sectes ultra violentes font régner le chaos dans cette jungle de métal où les forces de l'ordre, l'UPA, peinent à la tâche. Quatre membres de l'UPA vont vivre une véritable descente aux enfers et découvrir de sombres complots visant à résoudre de la plus atroce façon le problème de la surpopulation. Seuls leurs talents conjugués leur permettront d'écarter la menace, aussi Carter, chef du groupe, Minoko, spécialiste en informatique, André, mécanicien hors pair et Amber, le cyborg devront-ils travailler de concert pour survivre dans cette jungle urbaine que n'éclaire jamais la lumière du jour.

« »

In naher Zukunft wird die Erde nur noch ein gigantischer Megapol sein: Die Überbevölkerung hat ein kritisches Stadium erreicht und der Planet ist mit Wolkenkratzern übersät. Als Folge dieser krassen Verstädterung teilt sich die wimmelnde Menschheit in zwei extrem unterschiedliche Lager: Die armen Massen belegen die unteren Etagen der Städte, eine Hand voll Einflussreicher dagegen genießt das Privileg des Sonnenlichts. Im Untergrund sorgen kriminelle Banden, Psychopathen aller Art und ultragewalttätige Sekten in diesem Metalldschungel für Chaos, dem die Ordnungskräfte der Urban Protection Agency, kaum noch Herr werden. Vier Mitglieder der UPA erleben einen regelrechten Abstieg in die Hölle. Dabei decken sie finstere Komplotte auf, die auf ganz abscheuliche Weise das Problem der Überbevölkerung lösen sollen. Nur durch vereinte Anstrengungen können sie der Gefahr ausweichen. So müssen Carter, der Gruppenchef, Minoko, die EDV-Spezialistin und Hackerin, André, der unübertreffliche Automechaniker, und Amber, der Cyborg, eng zusammenarbeiten, um in diesem ewig finsteren Stadtdschungel eine Überlebenschance zu haben.

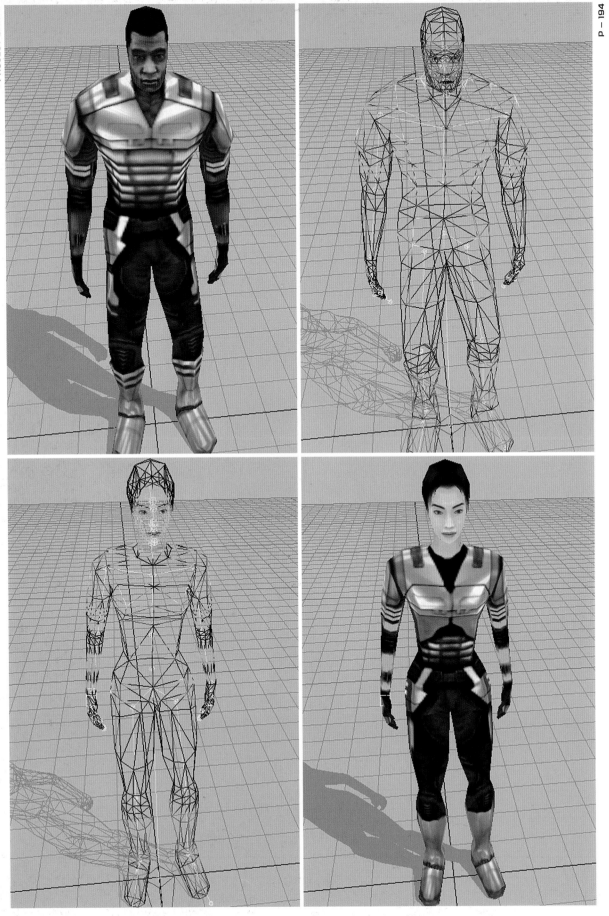

NAME STARCRAFT
PLATFORM PC
RELEASE 1998
EDITOR BLIZZARD ENTERTAINEMENT
DEVELOPER BLIZZARD ENTERTAINEMENT

FACT
IN KOREA, STARCRAFT HAS BECOME A VERITABLE NATIONAL SPORT, CREATING ITS OWN CELEBRITIES. THE BEST GAMERS LIVE ON WHAT THEY EARN IN STARCRAFT COMPETITIONS, AND THE FINEST MATCHES GO OUT LIVE ON TELEVISION.

Starcraft

In a distant future, a small colony of humans is exiled to the very borders of the known universe. Cut off from their world of origin, these colonists are building a new nation by exploiting the meagre resources of the solar system to which they are confined. After many years' effort, the Terran nation is born, but almost immediately its future is threatened by lack of raw materials. Determined to survive at any cost, the Terrans turn their gaze toward the rich resources of their extraterrestrial neighbours, the strange Protoss, who possess psionic powers. War breaks out between these two races for the possession of the scant energy sources of the system. But while Terrans and Protoss are locked in battle, a new threat invades their solar system, destroying everything in its path: the Zergs, terrifying and utterly ruthless creatures organised like a giant colony of ants and directed by the abominable Overmind.

« »

Dans un futur lointain, une petite colonie d'humains se retrouve exilée aux confins de l'univers connu. Coupés de leur monde originel, ces colons bâtissent une nouvelle nation en exploitant les rares ressources du système solaire où ils ont échoué. Après bien des années d'efforts, la nation Terran naît, mais se retrouve rapidement menacée par la pénurie de matières premières. Décidés à survivre à tout prix, les Terrans se tournent vers les riches ressources de leurs voisins extraterrestres, les étranges Protoss dotés de pouvoirs psioniques. La guerre explose entre les deux races qui se disputent farouchement les maigres sources d'énergie disponibles. Terrans et Protoss s'affrontent sans merci, mais un autre danger les menace : une troisième espèce envahit le système solaire, détruisant tout sur son passage : les Zergs, créatures terrifiantes et sans pitié, organisées comme une gigantesque fourmilière et dirigées par une créature abominable, l'Overmind.

« »

In einer weit entfernten Zukunft ist eine kleine Gruppe von im Exil lebenden Menschen dazu verdammt, am Rande des Weltraums ums nackt Überleben zu kämpfen. Von ihrem Ursprungsplaneten sind sie völlig abgeschnitten. Mit den wenigen Ressourcen, die ihnen das Sonnensystem bietet, bauen die Siedler in jahrelanger Anstrengung eine neue Nation auf. Doch schon bald gehen die lebensnotwendigen Rohstoffe zur Neige. Die Terraner, die um jeden Preis überleben wollen, haben es nun auf die reichen Bodenschätze ihrer außerirdischen Nachbarn abgesehen, der geheimnisumwitterten Protoss, die mit psionischen Fähigkeiten ausgestattet sind. Es kommt zum Krieg zwischen den beiden Rassen, die nun unerbittlich um die wenigen noch verfügbaren Energievorräte kämpfen. Während Terraner und Protoss sich erbarmungslose Kämpfe liefern, droht eine weitere Gefahr: Eine dritte Spezies namens Zerg ist in das Hoheitsgebiet der Protoss eingedrungen und zerstört nun alles, was sich ihr in den Weg stellt. Es sind Furcht erregende Kreaturen, die kein Mitleid kennen und wie ein riesiger Ameisenstaat organisiert sind, mit dem abscheulichen Overmind an der Spitze.

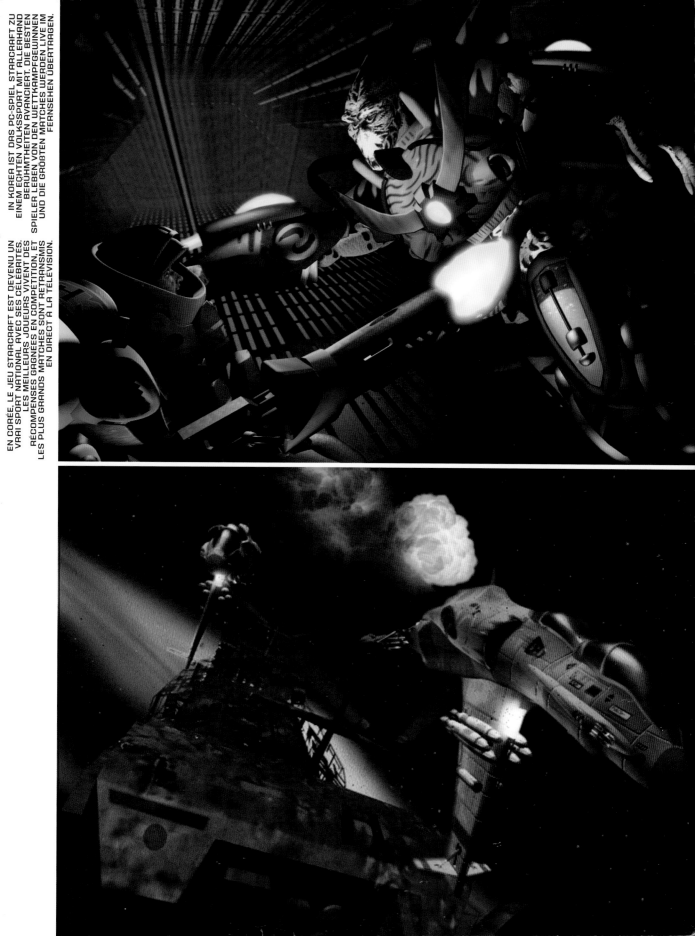

IN KOREA IST DAS PC-SPIEL STARCRAFT ZU
EINEM ECHTEN VOLKSSPORT MIT ALLERHAND
BERÜHMTHEITEN AVANCIERT. DIE BESTEN
SPIELER LEBEN VON DEN WETTKAMPFGEWINNEN
UND DIE GRÖßTEN MATCHES WERDEN LIVE IM
FERNSEHEN ÜBERTRAGEN.

EN CORÉE, LE JEU STARCRAFT EST DEVENU UN
VRAI SPORT NATIONAL AVEC SES CÉLÉBRITÉS.
LES MEILLEURS JOUEURS VIVENT DES
RÉCOMPENSES GAGNÉES EN COMPÉTITION, ET
LES PLUS GRANDS MATCHES SONT RETRANSMIS
EN DIRECT À LA TÉLÉVISION.

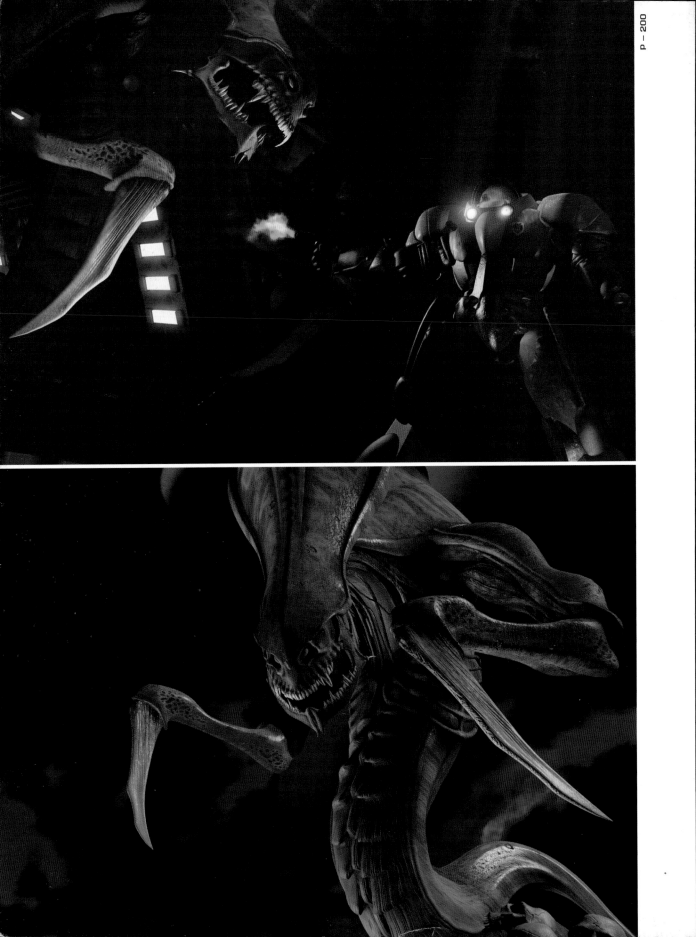

NAME
STARLANCER

PLATFORM
PC – DREAMCAST

RELEASE
2000

EDITOR
MICROSOFT (FOR PC)
CRAVE ENTERTAINMENT (FOR DREAMCAST)

DEVELOPER
DIGITAL ANVIL (FOR PC)
WARTHOG (FOR DREAMCAST)

COPYRIGHTS
© MICROSOFT
© CRAVE ENTERTAINMENT

FACT
3,000-4,000: THE NUMBER OF LINES OF
DIALOGUE SPOKEN BY THE VARIOUS CREATURES
IN STAR WARS EPISODE I: PHANTOM MENACE.

Starlancer

Ask the pilots of space-fighters what they think of ANS Reliant, they immediately reply that its volunteer crew - not invariably well-trained - is renowned for taking on the most dangerous missions with the most obsolete of equipment. They may show a degree of contempt for the Reliant crew-members, but they secretly respect the courage of these men and women, who alone have the courage to take on the most delicate assignments in the remotest areas of the galaxy. Amongst the best known crew-members are Captain Robert Foster, who, after a prestigious career, preferred the Reliant captaincy to retirement; Maria "Red Fox" Enriquez, who chose to devote her piloting and tactical brilliance to these lost causes; Mike "Moose" Horrigan, who refuses promotion in order to stay in the thick of things, and Jean-Marc "French" Baptist, a bit of a sociopath, but very handy in a punch-up.

« »

Si vous leur demandez de vous parler de l'ANS Reliant, tous les pilotes de chasse spatiaux vous répondront que son équipage, composé de volontaires parfois peu entraînés, est réputé prendre en charge les missions les plus dangereuses avec le plus obsolète des équipements. S'ils affichent un certain dédain pour les membres du Reliant, il y a fort à parier que tous respectent tout de même le courage de ces hommes et de ces femmes, qui seuls ont le courage d'affronter les plus délicates assignations dans les régions les plus reculées de la galaxie. Parmi les plus célèbres figures du Reliant, citons le Capitaine Robert Foster qui, après une prestigieuse carrière, a décidé de rempiler à un poste délicat ; Maria « Red Fox » Enriquez qui a décidé de mettre ses grands talents de pilote et de tacticien au service des causes perdues ; Mike « Moose » Horrigan qui a refusé maintes opportunités d'avancement pour rester au cœur de l'action, ou encore Jean-Marc « Frenchy » Baptist, personnage quelque peu asocial, mais combattant émérite.

« »

Auf die Frage, was sie von der „ANS Reliant" halten, gibt es unter Weltraum-Jagdpiloten wohl nur eine einzige Antwort: Deren Besatzung - bestehend aus Freiwilligen, zuweilen ohne entsprechende Ausbildung - sei bekannt dafür, die gefährlichsten Missionen zu übernehmen, und das mit einer völlig veralteten Ausrüstung. Und obwohl eine gewisse Geringschätzigkeit für die Crew der Reliant nicht zu überhören ist, bewundern doch alle den Mut dieser Männer und Frauen, die ohne mit der Wimper zu zucken die schwierigsten Einsätze in die entlegensten Teile der Galaxie fliegen. Zu den bekanntesten Crew-Mitgliedern der Reliant gehören Captain Robert Foster, der sich nach einer glänzenden Karriere der Erledigung heikler Aufgaben verschrieben hat; Maria „Red Fox" Enriquez, die beschlossen hat, ihre großen fliegerischen und taktischen Talente in den Dienst einer verlorenen Sache zu stellen; Mike „Moose" Horrigan, der so manche Gelegenheit zur Beförderung ausgeschlagen hat, um immer mittendrin dabei zu sein; oder Jean-Marc „Frenchy" Baptist, ein etwas asozialer Charakter, aber dafür ein erfahrener Kämpfer.

ZWISCHEN 3.000 UND 4.000: ANZAHL DER DIALOGZEILEN, DIE VON DEN VERSCHIEDENEN CHARAKTEREN IN STAR WARS EPISODE 1: DIE DUNKLE BEDROHUNG GESPROCHEN WURDEN

ENTRE 3000 ET 4000: C'EST LE NOMBRE DE LIGNES DE DIALOGUES PARLÉES PAR LES DIFFÉRENTES CRÉATURES DANS LE JEU STAR WARS ÉPISODE 1 : LA MENACE FANTÔME.

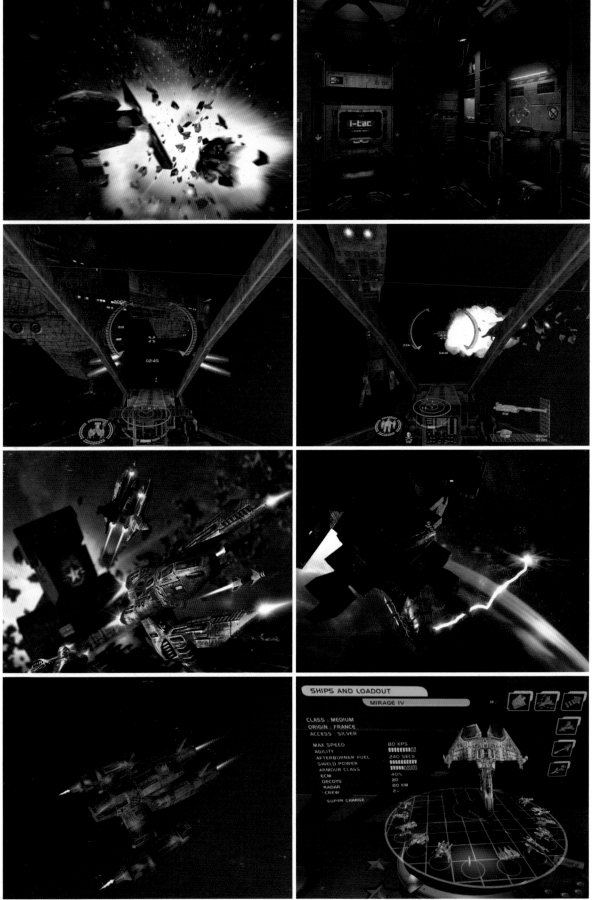

NAME
STARTOPIA
PLATFORM
PC
RELEASE
2001
EDITOR
EIDOS INTERACTIVE
DEVELOPER
MUCKY FOOT
COPYRIGHTS
© EIDOS INTERACTIVE/MUCKY FOOT
FACT
5 MILLION: THE (VIRTUAL) AMOUNT YOU WIN FOR
EACH GOOD ANSWER IN THE QUIZ INCLUDED IN
THE GAME WEALTH OF THE WORLD.

Startopia

Any hotel manager will tell you, it's no easy business meeting your clients' demands; everyone has different needs and desires. So you can imagine how difficult it is to organise an intergalactic holiday resort, with clients who come from every corner of the galaxy. Each race demands its own environment: furniture to suit its form (biped, quadruped, tentacular, or gaseous), its own private weather (torrid heat, cold ammoniac air), and activities exactly like those on its home planet. And then there is diet (which sometimes comprises members of other races on holiday at the same resort), space pirates, and competitors trying to grab your customers and leave you bankrupt. Ah, who'd want to be an orbiting holiday-camp manager?

« »

Tout gérant de station balnéaire vous le dira : accéder aux demandes des clients est loin d'être une mince affaire, chaque personne ayant des besoins et des désirs différents. Imaginez alors à quel point l'organisation d'une station de vacances intergalactique peut être une entreprise de grande envergure, avec des clients venus des quatre coins de la galaxie. Chaque race demande en effet un environnement adapté : des meubles épousant ses formes (que ses membres soient bipèdes, quadrupèdes, tentaculaires, gazeux), une météorologie particulière (atmosphère torride, air froid chargé d'ammoniac), des loisirs identiques à ceux de sa planète d'origine etc. Ajoutez à cela des régimes particuliers (parfois composés de membres d'autres races, elles aussi en vacances dans la même station orbitale), des pirates spatiaux ou des concurrents qui s'installent dans la même station et attirent vos clients, au risque de vous mettre en faillite, et vous aurez une idée de ce qui peut attendre les responsables de ces camps de vacances orbitaux...

« »

Jeder Manager eines Seebades kann ein Lied davon singen: Allen Gästen gerecht zu werden, ist wahrlich nicht einfach - zu unterschiedlich sind die Bedürfnisse und Wünsche der Einzelnen. Wenn man sich dann einmal vorstellt, welches Ausmaß an Organisation die Leitung eines intergalaktischen Ferienortes annehmen kann, an dem Gäste aus allen Teilen der Galaxie Erholung suchen. Da fordert jede Rasse eine auf sie abgestimmte Umgebung: formgerechte Möbel (für Zweibeiner wie für Vierbeiner, für Tentakelige wie für Gasförmige), besondere klimatische Bedingungen (glühende Hitze, mit Ammoniak angereicherte Kaltluft), die gleichen Freizeitmöglichkeiten wie auf dem Heimatplaneten. Aber auch spezifische Regierungsformen müssen berücksichtigt werden (manchmal verbringen Mitglieder unterschiedlicher Rassen ihre Ferien auf der gleichen Orbitalstation), oder es droht Gefahr von Weltraumpiraten und anderen Konkurrenten, die sich in derselben Ferienstation einnisten und euch die Kunden streitig machen wollen oder versuchen, euch in den Bankrott zu treiben. Sicher könnt ihr euch vorstellen, was die Manager eines solchen Feriencamps erwartet...

NAME
UNREAL 2003
UNREAL TOURNAMENT 2
UNREAL CHAMPIONSHIP

PLATFORM
PC - XBOX

RELEASE
2002

EDITOR
INFOGRAMES

DEVELOPER
EPIC MEGAGAMES

COPYRIGHTS
© INFOGRAMES

FACT
1976: THE YEAR IN WHICH
DEVELOPMENT OF THE
ATARI 2600 BEGAN AT ATARI CORP.

Unreal

Just one rule: kill or be killed. Arms and ammo are everywhere, concealed only by the complex architecture of the elegant arenas in which the futuristic gladiators of Unreal Tournament entertain the masses by killing one another. Combats last till there's only one man or one clan standing. So precision reflexes and teamwork are essential. The gladiators' arsenal is startlingly diverse, running from missile-launchers to a hydraulic hammer that crushes bodies at a single blow. Every participant chooses his own speciality - sniping, hand-to-hand combat, whatever. The variety of arms and the way they balance out allows the best fighter to win through, however lightly armed; just shoot first and avoid enemy fire.

« »

Une seule règle : tuer. Au cœur d'arènes à l'architecture complexe cachant dans leurs entrailles les armes les plus puissantes et leurs munitions, les gladiateurs futuristes de Unreal Tournament s'entre-tuent pour le plaisir des masses, dans des combats à la fin desquels il ne peut rester qu'un seul participant, ou des affrontements en clans, où la précision et les réflexes se partagent la vedette avec l'esprit d'équipe. L'arsenal mis à leur disposition est des plus hétérogènes, allant du marteau hydraulique pouvant broyer un corps en un unique coup au lance-roquettes. Chaque participant trouvera sa spécialité, du sniper au spécialiste du combat rapproché. La variété des armes, l'équilibre entre leurs divers effets permettent au meilleur des combattants, même s'il ne possède qu'une arme légère, de vaincre ses adversaires s'il frappe le premier et sait éviter avec maestria les tirs adverses.

« »

Es gibt nur eine einzige Regel, und die heißt: Töte. In verwinkelten Arenen, wo die schlagkräftigsten Waffen und die dazugehörige Munition versteckt liegen, metzeln sich die futuristischen Gladiatoren von Unreal Tournament zur Belustigung der Massen gegenseitig nieder, bis am Ende nur einer übrig bleibt beziehungsweise Teams sich gegenüberstehen, für die Präzision und Reaktionsschnelligkeit genauso wichtig sind wie Teamgeist. Im Kampf stehen den Gladiatoren die verschiedensten futuristischen Waffen zur Verfügung: vom Impact-Hammer, der einen Körper mit einem einzigen Schlag zerquetschen kann, bis zum Raketenwerfer. Jeder Kämpfer findet sein Spezialgebiet, sei es als Heckenschütze oder als Nahkampfexperte. Durch die Vielfalt der Waffen und das Gleichgewicht der Kräfte ist es möglich, dass der beste Kämpfer, selbst wenn er nur leichte Waffen benutzt, seine Gegner ausschalten kann, sofern er als Erster abdrückt und den feindlichen Angriffen geschickt ausweichen kann.

1976: JAHR, IN DEM MIT DER ENTWICKLUNG DER KONSOLE ATARI-2600 VON ATARI CORP. BEGONNEN WURDE

1976: C'EST L'ANNÉE DU DÉBUT DE DÉVELOPPEMENT DE LA CONSOLE ATARI 2600 DE ATARI CORP.

IZADIAN CONCEPT 02A

SKAARI CONCEPT 01
(NO ARMOR)

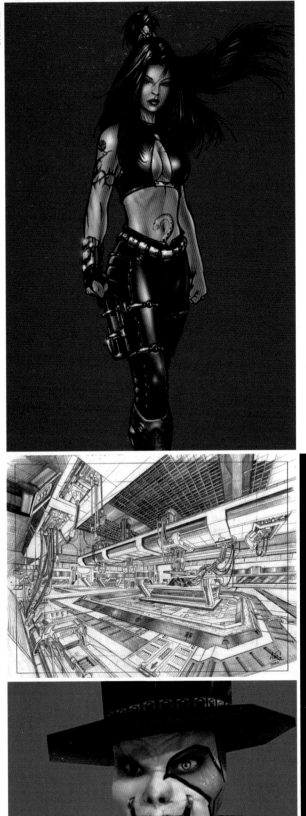

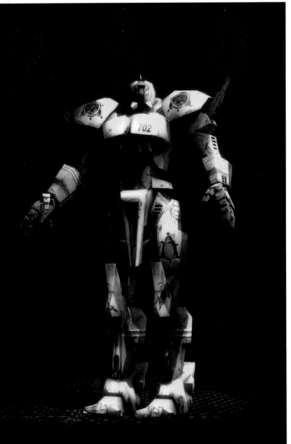

NAME
VIRTUAL ON: ORATORIO TANGRAM

PLATFORM
DREAMCAST

RELEASE
2001

EDITOR
SEGA

DEVELOPER
AM3

COPYRIGHTS
© SEGA/AM3

FACT
3 GAMES A SECOND: THE RATE OF SALES CLAIMED BY NINTENDO WORLDWIDE DURING ITS FIRST 12 YEARS OF GAMES PRODUCTION.

Virtual On

The discovery of the Lunar Portal dramatically modified the course of history. At the heart of the Portal, the mysterious V-Crystal offered mankind an apparently infinite source of psychic energy. To exploit this power, the DN Group, the only corporation authorised to exploit the V-Crystal, constructed nine factories in which it manufactured the most redoubtable combat machines ever designed by humanity, gigantic robots called Virtuaroids. But a corrupt DN Group member sold the factories to rival corporations... Faced with ruin and torn apart by internal dissension, the DN Group has divided into two factions, the DNA and the RNA. Each of them launches their own assault on the nine factories, which are defended by the fearsome robots.

Virtual On belongs to the great tradition of Japanese giant-robot narratives, and, as the humanoid robots belabour each other with missiles and lasers, offers a festival of spectacular combat.

« »

La découverte du Portail lunaire a dramatiquement modifié le cours de l'histoire. Au cœur du Portail, le mystérieux V-Crystal offrait aux hommes une nouvelle source d'énergie psychique, apparemment inépuisable. Afin d'exploiter cette puissance, le DN Group, seule organisation autorisée à exploiter le V-Crystal, construisit neuf usines où furent fabriquées les plus redoutables machines de combat jamais conçues par l'homme, les virtuaroïds, de gigantesques robots. Mais un membre corrompu du DN Group vendit les usines à des corporations rivales... Au bord du gouffre et déchiré par les brouilles internes, le DN Group se divise en deux factions, les DNA et les RNA, qui chacune de leur côté se lancent à l'assaut des neuf usines sévèrement protégées par de redoutables virtuaroïds.

Dans la grande tradition des robots géants du divertissement japonais, *Virtual On* est un festival de combats spectaculaires où s'affrontent des robots humanoïdes à grand renfort de missiles et autres puissants rayons laser.

« »

Die Entdeckung des Mondportals hat den Lauf der Geschichte dramatisch verändert. Im Herzen des Tores verbarg sich der geheimnisvolle V-Kristall, der den Menschen eine neue und scheinbar unerschöpfliche psychische Energiequelle verschaffte. Zur Erschließung dieser Kraft errichtete die DN Group, die einzige zur Ausbeutung des V-Kristalls bemächtigte Organisation, neun Werke, in denen die furchterregendsten Kampfmaschinen gebaut wurden, die je ein Mensch erdacht hat: die Virtuacyborgs, riesige Roboter. Aber ein korrumpiertes Mitglied der DN Group verkaufte die Werke an Konkurrenzunternehmen... Am Rande des Abgrunds und von internen Streitereien zerrissen, spaltet sich die DN Group in zwei Fraktionen, die DNA und die RNA, die nun getrennt die neun, von gefährlichen Virtuacyborgs scharf bewachten Werke angreifen.

In der großen Riesenroboter-Tradition der japanischen Unterhaltung ist *Virtual On* ein Festival spektakulärer Kämpfe, in denen sich menschenähnliche Roboter mit ihren Raketen und starken Laserstrahlen gegenüberstehen.

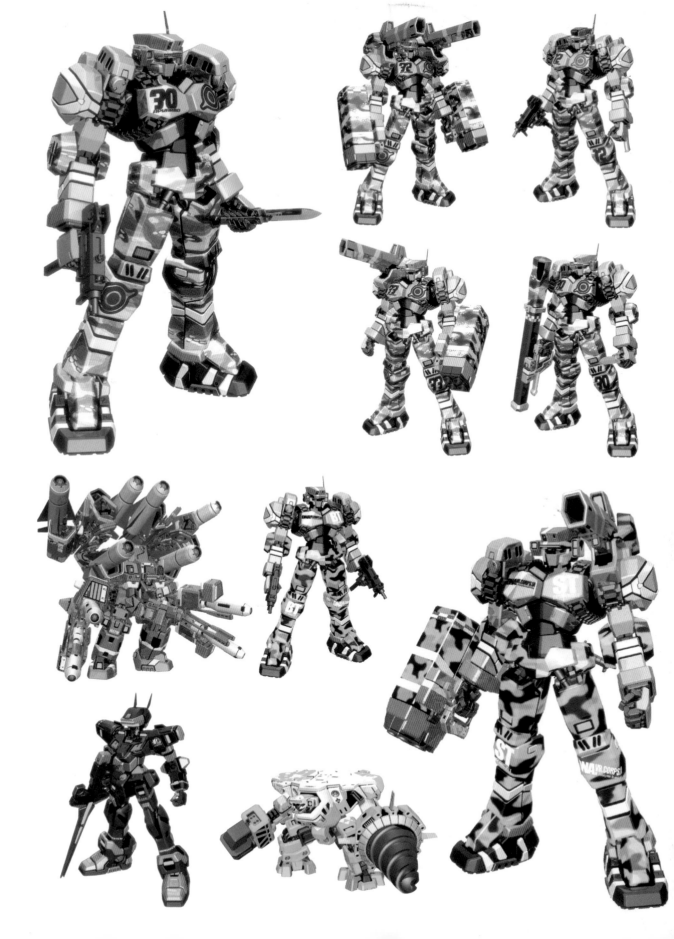

NAME
XENOSAGA EPISODE I : DER WILLE ZUR MACHT

PLATFORM
PLAYSTATION 2

RELEASE
2002

EDITOR
NAMCO

DEVELOPER
MONOLITH

COPYRIGHTS
© NAMCO

FACT
17 X 14.1 MM. THE MEASUREMENTS OF THE EMOTION ENGINE, THE PLAYSTATION 2 PROCESSOR.

Xenosaga

In a distant future, humankind, having bled Earth dry and abandoned it, has spread through the entire galaxy. An alliance of some 500,000 planetary systems has been formed: the Galactic Federation. Exploration of the galaxy continues thanks to the Unus Mundus Network, a space/time-travel technology that crosses light-years in an instant. But humanity is not alone in the galaxy. A hostile race, Gnosis, is discovered, whose object is to destroy humanity. Faced with Gnosis' combat-androids, the Galactic Federation sends its army, equiped with the AGWS (Anti Gnosis Weapon System), whose soldiers repel the extraterrestrial assault aboard their impressive battle-robots, the KOS-MOS. The young Shion Uzuki has sworn to avenge the death of her parents, who were killed during a Gnosis raid; she finds herself at the heart of a terrifying adventure whose astonishing dénouement sees the collapse of the Gnosis Empire.

« »

Dans un futur éloigné, les hommes se sont éparpillés dans la galaxie, après avoir abandonné la terre exsangue. Une alliance de plus de 500 000 systèmes planétaires s'est formée, la Fédération Galactique. L'exploration de la galaxie continue cependant grâce au Unus Mundus Network, une technologie de voyage spatio-temporel permettant de traverser des années-lumière en un instant. Mais les hommes ne sont pas seuls dans la galaxie et se heurtent à une race hostile, les Gnosis, qui veulent détruire l'humanité. Face aux androïdes de combat Gnosis, la Fédération Galactique envoie son armée de l'AGWS (Anti Gnosis Weapon System), dont les soldats repoussent les assauts extraterrestres à bord de leurs impressionnants robots de bataille, les KOS-MOS, à la pointe de la technologie. La jeune Shion Uzuki, qui s'est juré de venger la mort de ses parents, tués lors d'un raid Gnosis, se retrouvera au cœur d'une formidable aventure dont l'incroyable dénouement mènera à l'écroulement de l'empire Gnosis.

« »

In einer weit entfernten Zukunft lebt die Menschheit, nachdem sie die ausgeblutete Erde verlassen hat, in der Galaxie verstreut und hat sich der Galaktischen Föderation mit über 500 000 Planetensystemen angeschlossen. Unterdessen wird die Erforschung des Weltraums weiter vorangetrieben, und zwar durch das Unus Mundus Network, das mit Hilfe neuester Technologie Raum-Zeit-Reisen in Sekundenbruchteilen möglich macht. Doch die Menschen sind nicht alleine in der Galaxie. Sie treffen auf eine feindselige Rasse namens Gnosis, deren erklärtes Ziel es ist, die Menschheit zu vernichten. Um dieser Bedrohung etwas entgegenzusetzen, sendet die Galaktische Föderation ihre Armee mit den AWGS (Anti Gnosis Weapon Systems) aus. Die Soldaten sollen die außerirdischen Angriffe an Bord ihrer hoch entwickelten KOS-MOS-Kampfroboter abwehren. Die junge Ingenieurin Shion Uzuki, die sich geschworen hat, ihre bei einem Angriff der Gnosis getöteten Eltern zu rächen, steht im Mittelpunkt eines fesselnden Abenteuers, dessen spektakuläres Ende zum Untergang des Gnosis-Imperiums führt.

あんたの邪魔はしない
目的は一緒　だろ？

全ての事象は
この秩序の羅針盤が指し示す通りに動く

だからって　他人を殺してもいいってことには
ならないのよ

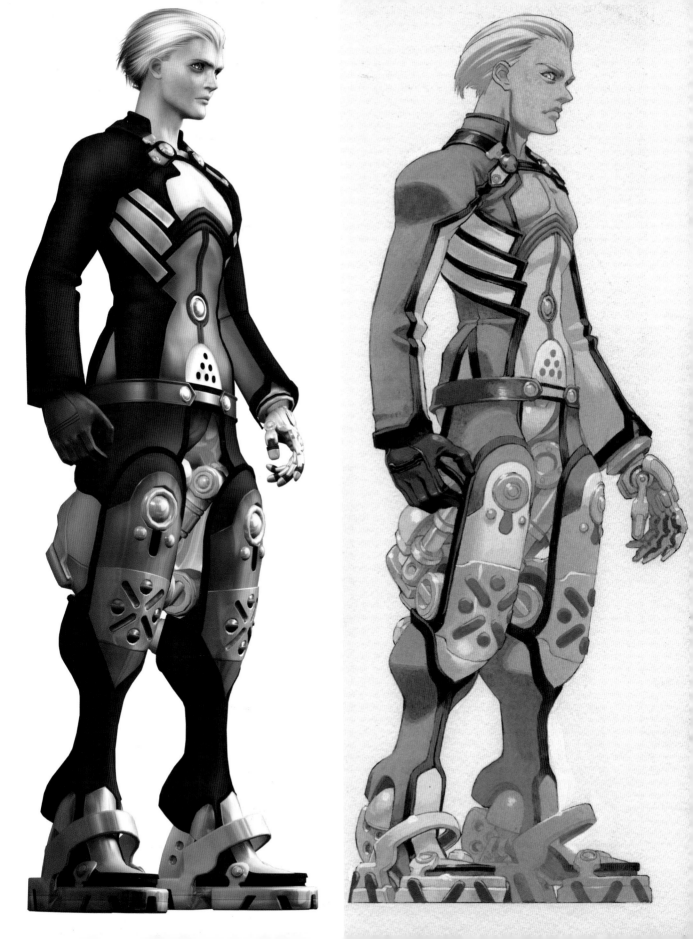

Dブロックを包囲しろ
前後から挟撃するのだ

グノーシスより怖いもんなんか
この世の中に山程あらぁ

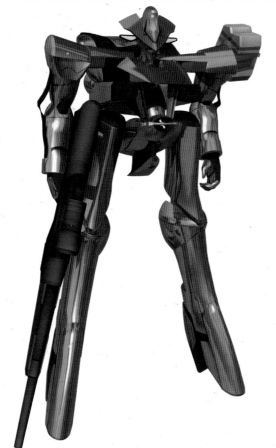

全ては脆い"ヒト"の生み出した
生ぬるい幻想の世界だ

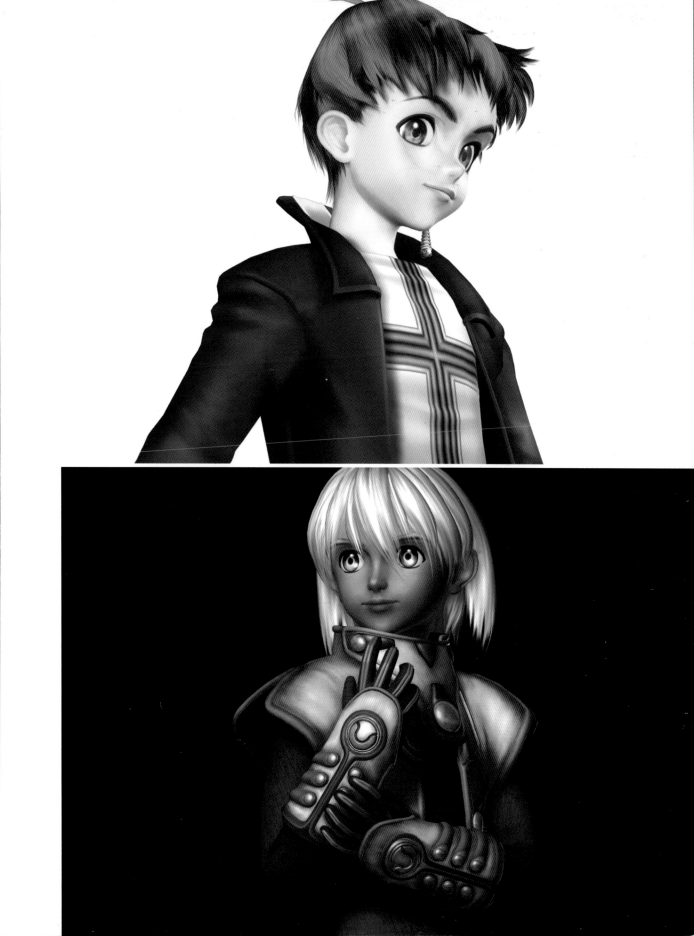

NAME
ZONE OF ENDERS

PLATFORM
PLAYSTATION 2

RELEASE
2001

EDITOR
KONAMI

DEVELOPER
KONAMI

COPYRIGHTS
© KONAMI

FACT
500,000: THE NUMBER OF VIDEO-GAMS
FOR GAME BOY SOLD DURING THE FIRST
THREE WEEKS OF THEIR AVAILABILITY
IN JAPAN, IN FEBRUARY 1999.

Zone of Enders

There was no warning. Space station Antilla, in orbit around Jupiter, suddenly fell victim to massive Martian attack. During the first onslaught, teenager Leo Stanbuck escaped into the station's military stockpile, taking refuge in a prototype fighter, the Jehuty. His friends didn't get off so lightly: seeing them executed by the Martians, Leo, bursting with fury, activates the fighter's controls. Piloting seems to be hardwired into him; the Jehuty responds to his every desire. This is the beginning of his story: Leo and the Jehuty quickly attain heroic status, becoming the Martian's main target. Under relentless assault, Leo must, all by himself, fight off the innumerable Martian space-ships and repel these savage invaders if Antilla is to be saved.

« »

Rien ne laissait présager l'attaque massive par les armées martiennes de la station spatiale Antilla, en orbite autour de la planète géante Jupiter. Lors du premier assaut, Léo Stanbuck, adolescent qui avec quelques amis s'était discrètement infiltré dans un entrepôt militaire secret de la station, se réfugie dans le cockpit d'un prototype de robot de combat, le Jehuty. Ses amis n'ont cependant pu s'échapper : les voyant exécutés par les troupes martiennes, Léo éclate sous l'emprise de la colère et active le Jehuty, se découvrant un étonnant instinct de pilote : le Jehuty répond à ses moindres désir, tel une extension de son propre corps. Son histoire ne fait cependant que commencer : bien malgré lui, Léo gagnera son statut de héros à bord de l'engin de guerre, objectif principal des assauts martiens. Sans répit, Léo devra combattre les innombrables vaisseaux martiens et peut-être sauver à lui seul la station Antilla et repousser les farouches envahisseurs.

« »

Der massive Angriff der Marsarmee auf die um den Riesenplaneten Jupiter kreisende Raumstation Antilla war nicht vorhersehbar. Beim ersten Ansturm gelingt es dem jungen Leo Stanbuck, der sich mit ein paar Freunden in ein verborgenes Militärlager der Station eingeschlichen hat, sich im Cockpit eines Kampfroboter-Prototypen namens Jehuty zu verstecken. Alleine allerdings, denn seinen Freunden ist die Flucht nicht gelungen. Als Leo Zeuge des Gemetzels wird, das die Marstruppen unter seinen Freunden veranstalten, überkommt ihn eine unsägliche Wut. Er setzt Jehuty in Gang und entdeckt dabei sein erstaunliches Talent: Jehuty reagiert auf jeden noch so kleinen Wunsch; er kann bei-spielsweise seinen Maschinenkörper beliebig ausdehnen. Und das soll erst der Anfang der Geschichte sein: Denn Leo wird gegen seinen Willen zum Helden an Bord des Kriegsflugkörpers, den die Marsarmee zu ihrem Hauptangriffsziel erkoren hat. Pausenlos muss er den Angriffen der zahllosen Marsraumschiffe trotzen. Vielleicht gelingt es ihm, die Station Antilla im Alleingang zu retten und die fanatischen Eindringlinge zurückzuschlagen.

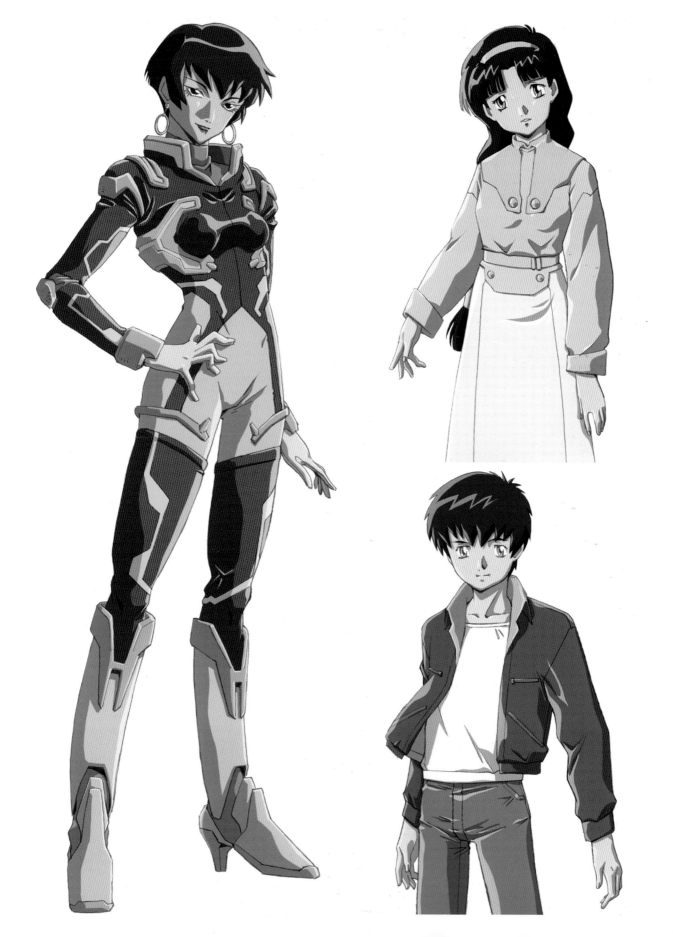

«Kings of Action»

Action games are often arraigned for their violence. But do they inspire real-world violence? Such, at least, is the accusation.

The titles most often indicted are the least likely suspects. The games at the heart of this debate feature a frenzied violence quite unlike anything seen in reality, indeed, the mayhem is often self-evidently farcical. Alongside them are other games, generally overlooked in the rush to condemn, which might more reasonably be presented as evidence. These games are more in tune with cruel reality. No supermen here to dance through the exploding warheads; no monsters to disembowel. The conventions are those of human frailty: one bullet can kill, and the 'bots' behave just as human enemies might.

But if any blame does attach to such games, they share it with TV news and film and books, all of which can be vectors of a violence still more shocking. Horses for courses: there are audiences for which some video-games are unsuited, and this holds for works of film and literature too. The fact that a game features war, crime or blood-thirsty combat should not therefore be considered an incitement to any of these activities. Those unfamiliar with action games will no doubt continue to think otherwise. But gamers know: a game is a game.

« »

Souvent pointés du doigt pour leur violence, les jeux d'action sont-ils aussi responsables de certaines violences de faits divers que certains veulent le laisser entendre ?

Les titres régulièrement accusés sont certainement de mauvaises cibles. En effet, ceux qui se sont retrouvés au cœur du débat sont essentiellement des jeux dont la violence, loin de refléter une condamnable réalité, est des plus paroxystiques. Aux côtés de ces farces si extrêmes qu'elles ne peuvent décemment trouver reflet dans le monde réel, se trouvent d'autres jeux oubliés des accusateurs qui seraient plus à même d'être montrés du doigt. Ces jeux sont en effet plus en phase avec la dure réalité. Ici, point de surhomme pouvant survivre à des explosions de roquette de plein fouet ou de monstres à étriper. Ces jeux prennent le parti de coller à la réalité : une seule balle peut tuer, les adversaires informatiques se comportent comme le feraient de vrais ennemis.

Mais n'imaginons pas les blâmer pour autant, en tout cas pas plus qu'on ne saurait blâmer journaux télévisés, films et livres véhiculant également une certaine violence, parfois plus dure. Comme certaines œuvres littéraires ou cinématographiques, tous les jeux vidéos ne sont pas pour tous publics. Aussi si certains mettent en scène la guerre, certaines criminalités ou des séquences sanglantes, ils ne doivent pas pour autant être considérés comme incitatifs. Ceux qui ne connaissent pas les jeux d'action pensent peut-être différemment, mais tous ceux qui y ont joué savent que ces jeux ne sont que des jeux.

Sind die Actionspiele, die wegen ihrer Gewalt häufig angeprangert werden, wirklich für den einen oder anderen Gewaltakt aus den Nachrichten verantwortlich, wie so oft behauptet wird?

Die Titel, die regelmäßig unter Beschuss geraten, sind ganz bestimmt keine gute Zielscheibe. Denn bei den besonders heiß debattierten Spielen handelt es sich fast ausschließlich um solche, deren Gewaltdarstellungen weit davon entfernt sind, eine verwerfliche Realität zu reflektieren: Vielmehr sind sie sehr oft Ausdruck einer aufs Höchste gesteigerten Erregung. Diese Farcen sind so extrem, dass wohl niemand ernsthaft behaupten wird, sie könnten in der Realität nachgeahmt werden. Daneben gibt es jedoch andere Spiele, die von den Anklägern vergessen werden, auf die mit dem Finger zu zeigen aber durchaus gerechtfertigt wäre. Diese Spiele sind auf der gleichen Wellenlänge wie die harte Realität. Kein Übermensch nirgends, der den Angriff mit einer Panzerfaust oder die Begegnung mit einem blutrünstigen Monster überlebt. Diese Spiele streben eine große Realitätsnähe an: Eine einzige Kugel kann tödlich sein, die virtuellen Gegner verhalten sich so, wie wahre Feinde es tun würden.

Aber wir wollen sie jetzt nicht stärker kritisieren als nötig, zumindest nicht mehr und nicht weniger, als es Nachrichten, Filme oder Bücher verdient hätten, die ebenfalls Gewalt transportieren, und mitunter sogar eine noch härtere. Ebenso wie bestimmte literarische oder kinematografische Werke sind auch einige Videospiele nicht für jedes Publikum geeignet. Wenn Spiele also Krieg, Kriminalität oder blutige Szenen in den Mittelpunkt stellen, müssen sie noch lange nicht zur Nachahmung inspirieren. Diejenigen, die Actionspiele nicht kennen, denken vielleicht anders darüber, aber diejenigen, die damit vertraut sind, wissen, dass diese Spiele eben nur Spiele sind.

NAME
ACE COMBAT 4

PLATFORM
PLAYSTATION 2

RELEASE
2001

EDITOR
NAMCO

DEVELOPER
NAMCO

COPYRIGHTS
© NAMCO

FACT
$250 MILLION: THE APPROXIMATE PROFITS
MADE IN JUST 24 HOURS IN THE USA BY THE
SALE OF 500,000 PLAYSTATION 2 CONSOLES,
INCLUDING ACCESSORIES AND SOFTWARE.

Ace Combat

Early in the 21st century, the fictive world power Erusia is kept under close surveillance by the ISAF (Independent States Allied Force). The Erusian armies have, after all, just invaded a peaceful neighbour-state to lay hands on 'Stonehenge', an electromagnetic gun formidable against aircraft and powerful enough to pulverise a meteor approaching the planet. This redoubtable weapon cannot remain in Erusian hands, and the ISAF decrees a large-scale aerial assault. But the target-country has excellent defences. Only the most talented ISAF pilots will survive their missions.

Flying one of the many fighters available in this game (F-14, F-22 Raptor, Mirage 2000, Rafale, etc), you are armed with nearly thirty different bombs and missiles; your mission is to save world peace while earning the highest military accolades.

« »

En ce début de XXIe siècle, la nation fictive Erusia est une force militaire surveillée de près par l'ISAF (Independent States Allied Force). Les armées d'Erusia ont en effet bombardé et envahi un pays voisin pacifique afin de s'emparer de l'arme spéciale « Stonehenge », un canon électromagnétique redoutable contre les assauts aériens, suffisamment puissant pour pulvériser un météore approchant de la planète. Une telle arme aux mains d'une nation aussi belliqueuse qu'Erusia est une menace que l'ISAF décide d'endiguer, en lançant des assauts aériens de grande envergure sur Erusia. Mais cette nation est redoutablement bien défendue et seuls les meilleurs pilotes de l'ISAF pourront mener à bien les périlleuses missions qui les attendent.

A bord de l'un des nombreux avions de chasse du jeu (F-14, F-22 Raptor, Mirage 2000, Rafale) et armé de près de trente bombes et missiles différents, le joueur devra mériter les plus hautes décorations militaires et sauver la paix dans le monde.

« »

Wir stehen am Beginn des 21. Jahrhunderts. Die fiktive Nation Erusia, eine Militärmacht, wird von der ISAF (Independent States Allied Force) streng bewacht. Denn die Erusia-Streitkräfte haben ein friedliches Nachbarland angegriffen und besetzt, um sich seiner Spezialwaffe „Stonehenge" zu bemächtigen. Diese elektromagnetische Kanone ist stark genug, um einen herannahenden Meteor auszuschalten. In den Händen einer so kriegerischen Nation wie Erusia stellt eine derartige Waffe eine Bedrohung für alle dar. Deshalb beschließt die ISAF, Erusia durch breit angelegte Luftangriffe zu schwächen. Diese Nation aber hat ein verdammt gutes Verteidigungssystem und nur die besten Piloten der ISAF werden ihre gefährlichen Missionen überleben.

An Bord eines der zahlreichen Jagdflugzeuge des Spiels (F-14, F-22 Raptor, Mirage 2000, Rafale), ausgestattet mit über dreißig verschiedenen Bomben und Raketen, muss sich der Spieler um die höchsten militärischen Auszeichnungen bemühen und der Welt den Frieden wiederbringen.

250 MILLIONS: C'EST ENVIRON LE MONTANT EN DOLLARS DE CE QU'A RAPPORTE EN 24 HEURES SEULEMENT LA VENTE DES 500 000 EXEMPLAIRES DE LA PLAYSTATION 2 AUX ETATS-UNIS, EN INCLUANT LA VENTE D'ACCESSOIRES ET DE LOGICIELS.

250 MILLIONEN: GEWINN IN US-DOLLAR, DER IN DEN USA INNERHALB VON 24 STUNDEN DURCH DEN VERKAUF VON 500.000 PLAYSTATION-2 -GERÄTEN, EINSCHLIEßLICH ZUBEHÖR UND SOFTWARE, ZUSAMMENGEKOMMEN IST

NAME
COMMANDOS 2: MEN OF COURAGE

PLATFORM
PC - PLAYSTATION 2

RELEASE
2001

EDITOR
EIDOS INTERACTIVE

DEVELOPER
PYRO STUDIOS

COPYRIGHTS
EIDOS INTERACTIVE/PYRO STUDIOS

Commandos

What if the greatest Allied victories in the Second World War had been won not on the battlefields of Europe but in the heart of the occupied territories, by a handful of terrifyingly efficient soldiers? To them the most dangerous missions were entrusted. One condition: they must never be detected. Nothing is impossible to the complementary talents of these nine heroes. The team comprises Jerry 'Tiny' McHale, close-combat expert, Thomas 'Inferno' Hancock, explosives specialist, James 'Fins' Blackwood, combat diver supreme, René 'Spooky' Duchamp, infiltration specialist, Paul 'Lupin' Toledo, master-thief, and Sir Francis T. 'Duke' Woolridge, redoubtable marksman. Then come the sublime Natasha 'Lips' Niukochevki, renowned spy, and the lovable dog Whiskey, who has been trained to create diversions and lure adversaries to their doom!

« »

Les plus grandes victoires alliées de la Deuxième Guerre mondiale n'ont peut-être pas eu lieu sur les champs de bataille, mais au cœur même des territoires occupés par les Nazis, et elles ont été remportées par une poignée de combattants aussi discrets qu'efficaces. Les missions les plus dangereuses leur sont en effet attribuées, et ils devront les mener à bien sans jamais être repérés. Grâce à la complémentarité de leurs talents, rien n'est impossible aux neuf héros : l'équipe se compose de Jerry «Tiny » McHale, expert en combat rapproché, Thomas « Inferno » Hancock, pour qui les explosifs n'ont aucun secret, James « Fins » Blackwood, nageur de combat émérite, Sid « Tread » Perkins, pilote hors pair, Rene « Spooky » Duchamp, spécialiste de l'infiltration, Paul « Lupin » Toledo, talentueux voleur et Sir Francis T. « Duke » Woolridge, redoutable tireur d'élite. Les deux derniers membres du commando sont la sublime Natasha « Lips » Niukochevki, espionne de grande renommée et l'adorable chien Whiskey, dressé pour faire diversion et attirer les adversaires dans les pièges tendus par ses maîtres.

« »

Im Zweiten Weltkrieg haben die Alliierten ihre größten Siege vermutlich nicht auf den Schlachtfeldern erzielt, sondern inmitten der von den Nazis besetzten Gebiete. Errungen wurden sie von einer Hand voll Soldaten, die sich durch Verschwiegenheit und Tüchtigkeit auszeichneten. Sie bekommen die gefährlichsten Missionen zugewiesen, die sie im Verborgenen durchführen müssen. Doch da sich ihrer aller Fähigkeiten vortrefflich ergänzen, ist für die neun Helden nichts unmöglich. Die Einheit besteht aus dem Nahkampfexperten Jerry „Tiny" McHale, Thomas „Inferno" Hancock, der sich ausgezeichnet auf Sprengstoffe versteht, dem ehemaligen Wettschwimmer James „Fins" Blackwood, dem unübertroffenen Piloten Sid „Tread" Perkins, dem Infiltrationsexperten Rene „Spooky" Duchamp, dem Meisterdieb Paul „Lupin" Toledo und dem brandgefährlichen Elite-Schützen Sir Francis T. „Duke" Woolridge. Das Schlusslicht bilden die sagenhafte Natasha „Lips" Niukochevki, eine hoch angesehene Spionin, und der entzückende Hund Whiskey, der darauf dressiert ist, die Feinde abzulenken und sie in die Fallen seiner Herrchen zu locken.

NAME
DARK PROJECT
DARK PROJECT 2: THE METAL AGE

PLATFORM
PC

RELEASE
1998

EDITOR
EIDOS INTERACTIVE

DEVELOPER
LOOKING GLASS STUDIO

COPYRIGHTS
© EIDOS INTERACTIVE/
LOOKING GLASS/ION STORM

Dark Project

The most talented member of the Guild of Thieves, Garrett, is offered the most arduous assignments, which are, natch, the most remunerative. But the burglaries Garrett is currently planning - they promise mountains of loot - take him into the invisible warzone where devotees of magic and partisans of technology duel for supremacy. Garrett's life is at stake; he has to make expert use of his burglarious talents to survive perils he could never even have imagined. These include mechanical traps and human sentinels, which he has to avoid or neutralise in the early parts of the game; later come fatal occult snares and terrifyingly complex Golems. Garrett can duke it out with the best, but he prefers to rely on cunning, along with his many kleptocrat's gadgets - grappling hooks, water and fire-arrows, invisibility potions - the usual stuff...

« »

Parce qu'il est reconnu comme étant le plus talentueux des membres de la guilde des Voleurs, Garret se voit proposer les missions les plues ardues, qui évidemment sont aussi celles qui rapportent le plus. Mais les cambriolages que Garrett s'apprête à effectuer, appâté par de mirobolantes récompenses, feront de lui un acteur involontaire d'une guerre invisible entre les adeptes de la magie et les partisans de la technologie. Emporté dans une aventure où il jouera sa vie, Garrett devra exploiter au mieux ses talents de voleur et affrontera des périls qui dépassent son imagination. Aux simples pièges mécaniques et aux sentinelles humaines qu'il devra éviter ou neutraliser au début de l'histoire succéderont de mortels traquenards occultes et d'effrayants golems aux rouages complexes. Bien que Garrett sache se battre, il préférera utiliser son ingéniosité et ses nombreux accessoires de cambrioleur (grappins, flèches d'eau ou de feu, potions d'invisibilité) pour survivre aux incroyables obstacles qui se dresseront sur sa route.

« »

Garrett bekommt als Meisterdieb stets die schwierigsten Aufgaben übertragen, aber die bringen natürlich auch am meisten ein. Doch bei diesem Beutezug nun, zu dem sich Garrett mit der Aussicht auf eine fantastische Belohnung aufmacht, gerät er unfreiwillig in einen unsichtbaren Krieg zwischen Anhängern der Zauberei und Technik-Freaks. Es geht um sein Leben. Garrett muss alle seine Talente als Meisterdieb aufbieten und sich dabei Gefahren aussetzen, die jenseits seiner Vorstellungskraft liegen. Am Anfang seiner Mission warten auf ihn einfache mechanische Fallen, aber auch Wachposten, die er umgehen oder ausschalten muss. Im weiteren Verlauf lauern tödliche Geheimfallen und schreckliche Golems. Obwohl Garrett sich zu wehren weiß, benutzt er lieber seinen Scharfsinn und sein umfangreiches Einbruchswerkzeug (darunter Steigeisen, Wasser- oder Brandpfeile), um die Hindernisse, die sich ihm entgegenstellen, aus dem Weg zu räumen.

FRONT BOX POSE
NOT FOR USE ON ADD

NAME
DRIVER 2

PLATFORM
PLAYSTATION

RELEASE
2000

EDITOR
INFOGRAMES

DEVELOPER
REFLECTIONS SOFTWARE

COPYRIGHTS
© INFOGRAMES

FACT
500: THE NUMBER OF CARS
AVAILABLE IN GRAN TURISMO 2.

Driver

Tanner has also already infiltrated and dismantled one criminal organisation. Now a new further exploit awaits him: the accountant Solomon Cain, a new criminal capo, has allied himself to his chief's greatest rival, Brazilian gangster Alvaro Vasquez. Gang warfare is in the offing, and with it the prospect of violence spreading through the country as a whole. Joined by another police officer, Tobias Jones, Tanner contrives to be taken on by Cain. He must win the confidence of his fellow-gangsters by accepting the most dangerous missions: high-speed chases through the streets of Chicago, Las Vegas, Havana and Rio, brutal tit-for-tat killings and many other criminal assignments. And try explaining that to your colleagues without blowing your cover! So they're after him too...

« »

Tanner, courageux policier qui a déjà réussi à démanteler une organisation criminelle organisée en s'y infiltrant, doit reprendre du service : le comptable de Solomon Cain, un nouveau leader criminel aux Etats-Unis s'allie au plus grand rival de son chef, un gangster brésilien du nom d'Alvaro Vasquez. Une guerre des gangs s'annonce, qui risque de mettre les Etats-Unis à feu et à sang. Rejoint par un autre policier, Tobias Jones, Tanner réussit à se faire engager par Cain et devra gagner la confiance des gangsters en acceptant des missions aussi dangereuses qu'explosives : courses-poursuites dans les rues de Chicago, Las Vegas, La Havane et Rio, règlements de comptes musclés entre gangs rivaux, braquages et bien d'autres activités criminelles l'attendent. En outre, Tanner devra subir les assauts de ses collègues policiers sans leur dévoiler sa véritable mission, afin de ne pas risquer de perdre sa couverture.

« »

Der wagemutige Cop Tanner, der bereits ein Verbrecher-Syndikat zerschlagen hat, weil es ihm gelang, sich in die Organisation einzuschleusen, wird erneut gebraucht. Denn als Pink Lenny, der Buchhalter des amerikanischen Gangsterbosses Solomon Cain, sich mit dessen größtem Rivalen, einem brasilianischen Verbrecherkönig namens Alvaro Vasquez verbündet, droht ein verheerender Bandenkrieg in den Vereinigten Staaten auszubrechen. Zusammen mit seinem Partner Tobias Jones kann Tanner sich bei Cain einen Job verschaffen und muss nun versuchen, das Vertrauen der Gangster zu gewinnen, indem er Aufträge ausführt, die ebenso brisant wie gefährlich sind: Verfolgungsjagden durch die Straßen von Chicago, Las Vegas, Havanna und Rio, handfeste Auseinandersetzungen zwischen rivalisierenden Banden, um alte Rechnungen zu begleichen, bewaffnete Raubüberfälle und allerlei andere kriminelle Aktivitäten erwarten die beiden. Darüber hinaus muss Tanner die Angriffe seiner Kollegen über sich ergehen lassen und Stillschweigen über seine Mission bewahren, damit seine Tarnung nicht auffliegt.

MEHR ALS 500: ANZAHL DER VERFÜGBAREN AUTOS IN GRAN TURISMO 2

PLUS DE 500: C'EST LE NOMBRE DE VOITURES DISPONIBLES DANS GRAN TURISMO 2.

NAME
GHOST RECON

PLATFORM
PC

RELEASE
2001

EDITOR
UBI SOFT

DEVELOPER
RED STORM ENTERTAINMENT

COPYRIGHTS
© UBI SOFT

FACT
BATTLEZONE: THE FIRST GAME USED BY
THE US ARMY FOR MILITARY TRAINING.

Ghost Recon

For masters of infiltration like the Ghost Recon unit, high-risk missions are everyday fare: lightning capture of jungle training-camps, mountain ambushes, taking out heavily-guarded convoys, rescuing hostages or kidnapping terrorist leaders, all this is meat and drink to them. Their forte is teamwork; each commando-member has a clearly defined role and very specific talents. The scouts detect and observe the enemy; the sappers lay and defuse explosives, while the camouflaged marksmen can eliminate their adversaries unseen. The gamer plays each of these characters in turn, while his team mates capably respond to his instructions. Intuition, tactics and adaptability no less than your reflexes will keep you alive as the game proceeds through theatres of combat ranging from tropical forest and arid desert to central European towns ravaged by bombing.

« »

Rompus aux missions d'infiltration, les militaires de l'unité Ghost Recon sont habitués aux missions les plus dangereuses : assauts-éclair sur des camps cachés au cœur de la jungle, embuscades dans les montagnes, attaques de convois surprotégés ou encore sauvetage d'otages ou kidnappings de leaders terroristes sont leur lot quotidien. Si le travail d'équipe est leur principale force, chaque membre du commando a un rôle bien défini et des talents particuliers : les éclaireurs savent repérer les ennemis en toute discrétion ; les explosifs à poser ou désamorcer n'ont aucun secret pour les démolisseurs et les tireurs d'élite, savamment camouflés dans la végétation savent éliminer les menaces en restant invisibles. Le joueur peut incarner tour à tour chacun de ces militaires, les coéquipiers se comportant seuls avec talent suivant ses indications. L'intuition et le sens tactique sont ainsi aussi cruciaux que des réflexes acérés et une capacité d'adaptation aiguë, et ce dans tous types de théâtres d'opération, de la forêt tropicale au désert brûlant, en passant par des environnements urbains, comme des villes d'Europe centrale ravagées par des bombardements.

« »

Das Eindringen in fremde Gebiete gehört zu den Aufgaben der Spezialeinheit Ghost Recon. Die Soldaten dieser Einheit sind mit den gefährlichsten Missionen vertraut, und so gehören der Blitzangriff auf versteckte Camps im Dschungel, der Hinterhalt in den Bergen, der Angriff auf stark bewachte Konvois, die Geiselbefreiung oder das Kidnapping von Terroristenführern für sie zum Alltag. Teamarbeit ist zwar ihre größte Stärke, trotzdem hat jeder einzelne Soldat eine genau definierte Rolle und verfügt über besondere Fähigkeiten. Der Spähtrupp kann den Feind ganz unauffällig ausfindig machen. Bomben und Minen legen oder entschärfen ist für das Sprengstoffkommando kein Problem. Und die Schützen der Elitetruppe können als Meister der Tarnung Gefahren in der Umgebung ausschalten und trotzdem unsichtbar bleiben. Der Spieler kann nach und nach in die Rolle eines Soldaten schlüpfen, während die übrigen Mitglieder der Truppe ihren Fähigkeiten entsprechend seinen Anweisungen folgen. Entscheidend bei diesem Spiel sind nicht nur Intuition und Taktik, sondern auch blitzschnelle Reflexe sowie eine sehr gute Anpassungsfähigkeit, und das an allen Fronten: ob im tropischen Regenwald oder im heißen Wüstensand, aber auch in europäischen Metropolen nach einem verheerenden Bombenangriff.

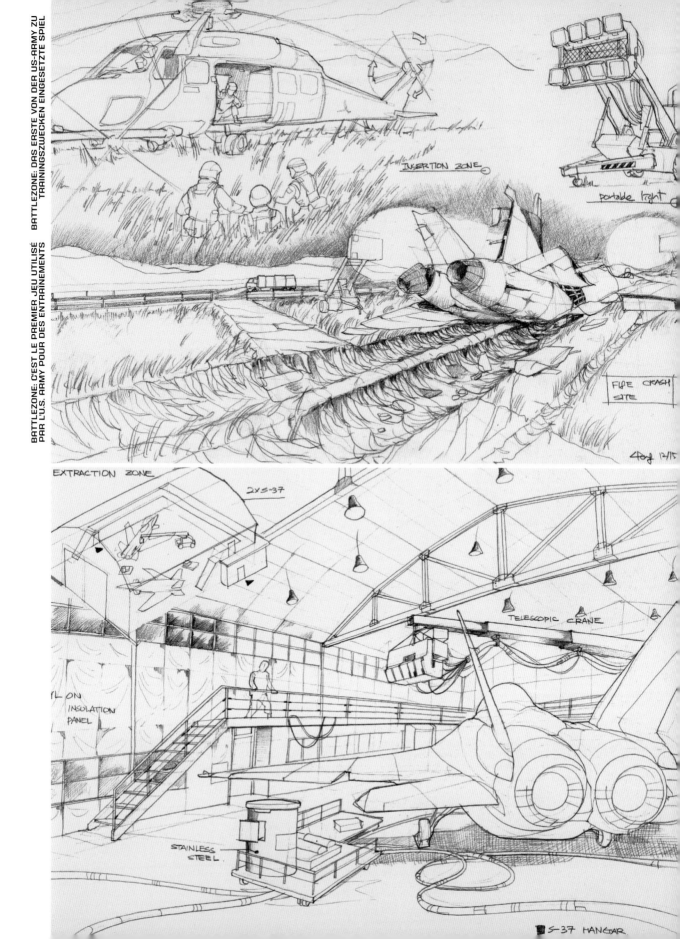

INSERTION ZONE

portable light

FIRE CRASH
SITE

EXTRACTION ZONE

2×S-37

TELESCOPIC CRANE

...L ON
INSOLATION
PANEL

STAINLESS
STEEL

S-37 HANGAR

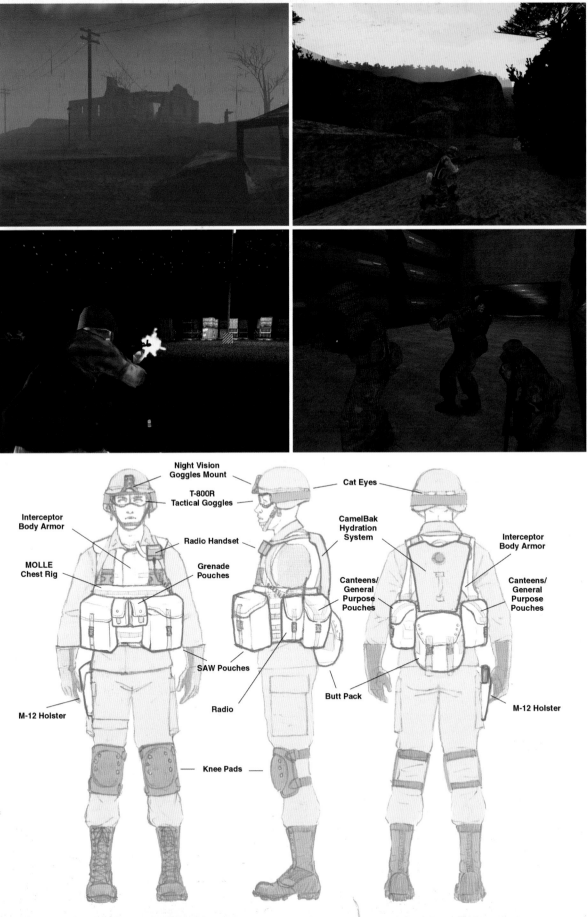

Night Vision
Goggles Mount

Cat Eyes

T-800R
Tactical Goggles

Interceptor
Body Armor

CamelBak
Hydration
System

Radio Handset

Interceptor
Body Armor

MOLLE
Chest Rig

Grenade
Pouches

Canteens/
General
Purpose
Pouches

Canteens/
General
Purpose
Pouches

SAW Pouches

M-12 Holster

Radio

Butt Pack

M-12 Holster

Knee Pads

NAME HEADHUNTER
PLATFORM DREAMCAST - PLAYSTATION 2
RELEASE 2001
EDITOR SEGA
DEVELOPER AMUZE
COPYRIGHTS © SEGA

Headhunter

In a not-so-distant future, the most valuable merchandise is human spare-parts. And they're not just used to cure the sick; you can use them cosmetically, or to prolong life. One large company, Biotech, has a monopoly. Most of the population can afford artificial implants, but only the rich get the real thing. And if you have to harvest organs from some group or other, how about using up the criminal population? Result: bounty-hunting is a high-earning profession.... Jack Wade is one of the most famous hunters, or, to be exact, he was. His new adventure begins when he wakes up in a strange prison, his memory gone. All the same, he hasn't forgotten how to fight, and he quickly escapes. He pieces together the fragments of his memory with the help of Angela, a rich young woman who takes him under her wing, setting him to discover who murdered her father, the former MD of Biotech. To do so, Jack has to climb back up through the ranks of the bounty-hunters, starting from scratch.

« »

Dans un avenir pas très lointain, la marchandise la plus courue est l'organe humain, non seulement pour parer à des défaillances physiques, mais aussi pour l'esthétisme et l'allongement de la durée de vie. Une seule grosse société, la Biotech, en a le monopole. Si les implants artificiels sont accessibles à la majeure partie de la population, les implants naturels sont prisés par les riches. Et quelle meilleure source d'approvisionnement que les criminels ? Implication logique de cet état de fait, le métier de chasseur de primes est fort prisé. Jack Wade en est un des plus célèbres représentants, ou plus exactement, l'était ... Car sa nouvelle aventure commence alors qu'il se réveille dans une étrange prison, amnésique. Cela ne l'empêche cependant pas de retrouver ses réflexes de combattant et de s'évader. Il pourra rassembler les premiers fragments de sa mémoire grâce à une jeune femme riche, Angela, qui le prend sous son aile et lui donne pour mission de découvrir qui a tué son père, ex-PDG de Biotech. Pour ce faire, Jack devra gravir de nouveau les échelons du métier de chasseur de primes, en repartant de zéro...

« »

In nicht allzu ferner Zukunft wird das menschliche Organ das gefragteste Handelsobjekt sein, nicht nur aus medizinischen Gründen, sondern auch aus Gründen der Ästhetik und zur Verlängerung des Lebens. Als einzige große Organisation hat Biotech das Monopol darauf. Während sich die breite Masse der Bevölkerung nur künstliche Implantate leisten kann, legen die Reichen Wert auf echte menschliche Organe. Was liegt näher, als sich bei Kriminellen damit einzudecken? Dementsprechend ist der Beruf des Kopfgeldjägers hoch angesehen. Und Jack Wade ist einer der berühmtesten Vertreter dieser Headhunter, besser gesagt: Er war es... Denn sein neuestes Abenteuer beginnt damit, dass er in einem merkwürdigen Gefängnis erwacht und feststellt, dass er unter Gedächtnisverlust leidet. Was ihn aber nicht daran hindert, seine Kampfreflexe wieder aufflackern zu lassen und zu fliehen. Bruchstückhaft kommen ihm erste Erinnerungen. Das verdankt er Angela, einer reichen und jungen Schönen, die ihn unter ihre Fittiche nimmt und ihm den Auftrag erteilt, den Mörder ihres Vaters, des ehemaligen Generaldirektors von Biotech, zu finden. Dafür muss Jack erneut das Handwerk eines Kopfgeldjägers erlernen, das heißt praktisch wieder bei null anfangen...

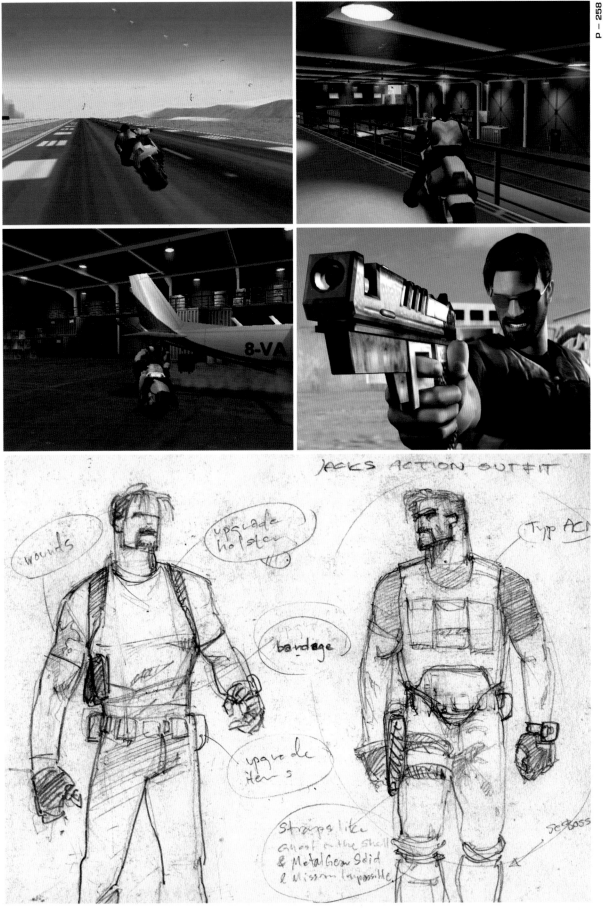

NAME
HITMAN 2

PLATFORM
PC – PLAYSTATION 2

RELEASE
2000

EDITOR
EIDOS INTERACTIVE

DEVELOPER
IO INTERACTIVE

COPYRIGHTS
EIDOS INTERACTIVE/IO INTERACTIVE

FACT
145 MILLION: THE NUMBER OF AMERICANS WHO PLAY VIDEO-GAMES, ACCORDING TO A POLL BY THE DIGITAL SOFTWARE ASSOCIATION CONDUCTED IN NOVEMBER 2000. THAT IS 3 OUT OF EVERY FIVE AMERICANS. THE AVERAGE AGE OF GAMERS IS 28 YEARS AND 43% ARE WOMEN.

Hitman

The first perceptions of the hitman? The blank walls of his tiny padded cell. Then a first view of his emaciated features and shaven head. All memories of the past have vanished; in their place is a strange bar-code on the back of his neck. Intensive training follows: an unknown voice from loud-speakers hidden in the walls reveals his talents as master-assassin. He is inch-perfect in every department of weaponry, from blade to sniper's rifle. Now the downtown missions begin, ordered by the mysterious agency that runs him. Hidden on a roof above the villa, he catches the magnate in the cross hairs. Infiltrating an organisation, he retrieves secret documents. Two gangs, each believing the other to have committed 47's crimes, are set at each other's ears. Through a succession of contracts, his own origins - and the goals of the Agency - begin to come into focus...

« »

Les premiers aperceptions du tueur à gages sont les murs aseptisés d'une minuscule cellule capitonnée. Puis vient la découverte de son visage émacié, au crâne rasé. Sur sa nuque, un étrange code barre le surprend plus encore que l'absence de toute mémoire personnelle. Puis viennent les entraînements intensifs où le tueur, guidé par une voix inconnue que crachent des haut-parleurs cachés dans les parois, se découvre d'incroyables talents d'assassin, une maîtrise des armes inouïe, du simple couteau au fusil à lunette. S'ensuivent des missions au cœur des villes, pour le compte de la mystérieuse agence qui le manipule : assassinat-éclair au fusil à lunette du haut d'un toit donnant sur la villa d'un magnat du crime, infiltration et cambriolage de documents secrets, intervention discrète menant à une guerre entre gangs rivaux, s'imputant respectivement les crimes commis par 47, etc. Les contrats de meurtre se succéderont, donnant au fur et à mesure au numéro 47 des indices sur ses origines et la raison d'être de l'Agence.

« »

Als er das Bewusstsein wiedererlangt, nimmt der Auftragskiller als Erstes die sterilen Wände der gepolsterten Minizelle wahr. Als nächstes bemerkt er sein ausgemergeltes Gesicht mit dem glatt rasierten Schädel. Ein merkwürdiger Strichcode auf seinem Nacken überrascht ihn noch mehr als sein kompletter Gedächtnisverlust. Dann beginnt ein Intensivtraining unter der Anleitung einer unbekannten, krächzenden Stimme aus Lautsprechern in der Wand. Dabei entdeckt der Killer ungeahnte Talente an sich. Er beherrscht unzählige Waffen: vom einfachen Messer bis zum Gewehr mit Zielfernrohr. Es folgen Einsätze in Städten für die geheimnisvolle Organisation, die ihn manipuliert: der Blitzangriff mit einem Scharfschützengewehr vom Dach eines Hauses auf die Villa eines Großkriminellen oder der Diebstahl von Geheimakten, die versteckte Intervention, die einen Bandenkrieg auslöst und ihm angelastet beziehungsweise den von Nummer 47 begangenen Verbrechen zugerechnet wird. Ein Mordauftrag löst den anderen ab. Nach und nach lichtet sich für Nummer 47 das Dunkel seiner Vergangenheit und er kommt dem Grund seiner Arbeit für die Organisation auf die Spur.

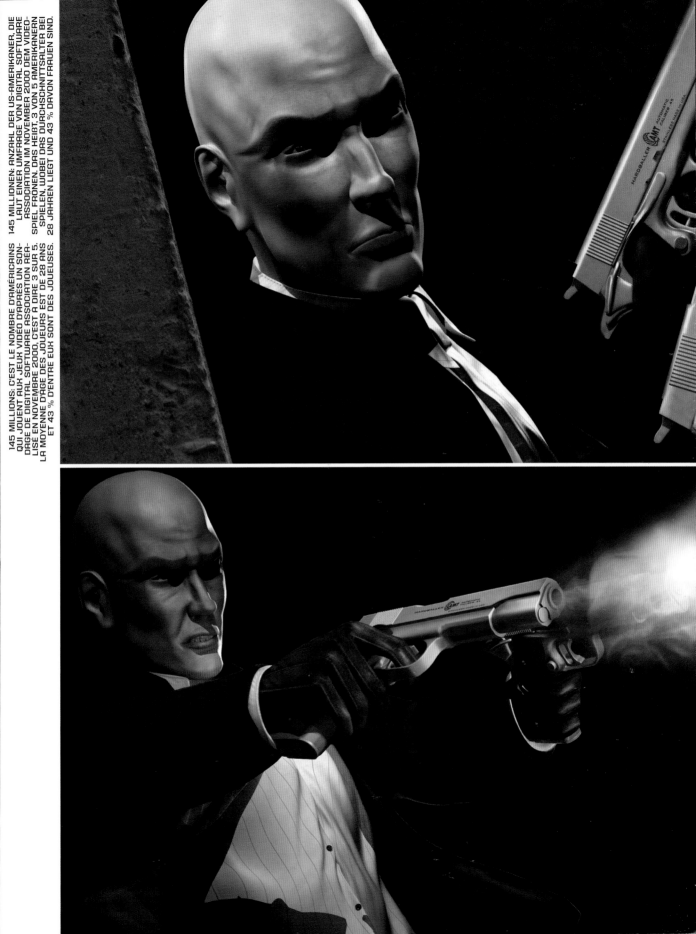

145 MILLIONS: C'EST LE NOMBRE D'AMÉRICAINS QUI JOUENT AUX JEUX VIDÉO D'APRÈS UN SONDAGE DE DIGITAL SOFTWARE ASSOCIATION RÉALISÉ EN NOVEMBRE 2000, C'EST À DIRE 3 SUR 5. LA MOYENNE D'ÂGE DES JOUEURS EST DE 28 ANS ET 43 % D'ENTRE EUX SONT DES JOUEUSES.

145 MILLIONEN: ANZAHL DER US-AMERIKANER, DIE LAUT EINER UMFRAGE VON DIGITAL SOFTWARE ASSOCIATION IM NOVEMBER 2000 DEM VIDEOSPIEL FRÖNEN. DAS HEIßT, 3 VON 5 AMERIKANERN SPIELEN, WOBEI DAS DURCHSCHNITTSALTER BEI 28 JAHREN LIEGT UND 43 % DAVON FRAUEN SIND.

NAME
METAL GEAR SOLID 2: SONS OF LIBERTY
PLATFORM
PLAYSTATION 2
RELEASE
2001
EDITOR
KONAMI
DEVELOPER
KONAMI
COPYRIGHTS
© KONAMI

Metal Gear Solid

Solid Snake is a legendary loner, a master warrior and infiltrator. He has been declared dead after an operation aboard a cargo-ship blown up off New York. On that spot, The Big Shell, a pollution-processing plant, has been built; or so, at least, the government is saying. But Snake seems to have survived. Now he heads up the Sons of Liberty, a faction set on destroying the Metal Gears, giant hi-tech combat robots. In a baptism of fire, the young Raiden, a man already with a shady past, infiltrates the Big Shell, which is in the hands of terrorists with a prize hostage: the President of the United States. But these terrorists are none other than the Sons of Liberty, and over the course of his adventures, Raiden will discover the incredible truth. He must face down not only ferocious adversaries such as Fortune, Vamp and Fatman, but the scarcely more credible story of his own origins.

Born of the imagination of Hideo Kojima, Solid Snake, the hero of the *Metal Gear* series, quickly became a video-game legend. His adventures marked the advent of a new genre, fusing adventure with combat and infiltration. In addition to their gaming qualities, it was the quality of their scenarios that made these sagas so striking; they were worthy of the great Hollywood action films. The developers also worked very hard on the psychology of the characters and their interactions, thus bestowing real conviction on their cocktail of sci-fi and realism. In 2001, *Metal Gear Solid 2: Sons of Liberty* pulverised all sales records, shifting half a million copies in four days in Japan, and two million in the first fortnight on the USA market.

« »

Solid Snake, le légendaire combattant solitaire, le maître de l'infiltration, a été déclaré mort suite à une opération sur un cargo explosé au large de New York – là où se trouve aujourd'hui The Big Shell, une usine de traitement de la pollution. C'est du moins ce que le gouvernement a annoncé. En fait, Snake serait encore en vie et à la tête des Sons of Liberty, un groupuscule voué à la destruction des Metal Gears, robots de combat géants à la technologie très avancée. Pour son baptême du feu, le jeune Raiden, au passé trouble, s'infiltre sur la Big Shell qui est aux mains de terroristes ayant pris en otage le président des Etats-Unis en visite sur la plate-forme. Ces terroristes ne seraient autres que les Sons of Liberty, mais Raiden découvrira la vérité au fil de ses aventures, qui le mettront non seulement face à de redoutables adversaires tels Fortune, Vamp et Fatman, mais surtout lui dévoileront l'incroyable réalité de sa propre histoire…

Né de l'imagination de Hideo Kojima, Solid Snake, héros de la série *Metal Gear*, est rapidement devenu une légende du jeu vidéo. Ses aventures ont en effet marqué la naissance d'un genre nouveau, mêlant aventure, combat et infiltration. Outre leurs qualités ludiques, les jeux de la saga ont marqué les esprits grâce à la qualité de leurs scénarios, dignes de grands films d'action hollywoodiens, et aussi à cause de l'extrême travail des créateurs sur la psychologie des personnages et de leurs interactions, qui rend crédible le cocktail de science-fiction et de réalisme des jeux Metal Gear. En 2001, la sortie du jeu *Metal Gear Solid 2 : Sons of Liberty* a battu tous les records de vente, avec un demi-million d'exemplaires vendus en quatre jours au Japon et plus de deux millions aux Etats-Unis sur les quinze premiers jours.

« »

Der legendäre Einzelkämpfer und Meister der Infiltration, Solid Snake, wird nach einer geheimen Operation auf einem vor der Küste von New York explodierten Frachter für tot erklärt. An der Explosionsstelle befindet sich jetzt die Wasserreinigungsanlage The Big Shell. Das ist zumindest die offizielle Verlautbarung der Regierung. In Wahrheit ist Snake noch am Leben und Kopf der Sons of Liberty, einer kleinen Gruppe, die sich die Zerstörung der Metal Gears, sehr hoch entwickelter, riesiger Kampfroboter, zum Ziel gesetzt hat. Die Feuertaufe des jungen Raiden, eines Typen mit dunkler Vergangenheit, besteht darin, sich auf Big Shell einzuschleusen. Die Anlage ist in der Gewalt von Terroristen, die den Präsidenten der USA während eines Besuchs auf der Plattform als Geisel genommen haben. Bei den Terroristen handelt es sich um die Sons of Liberty. Raiden deckt diese unglaubliche Wahrheit während seiner Mission auf, die ihn nicht nur mit

gefürchteten Gegnern konfrontiert, sondern ihm vor allem die unglaubliche Wahrheit über seine eigene Vergangenheit enthüllt...
Solid Snake, der Held der *Metal Gear*-Reihe, aus der Feder von Hideo Kojima, ist in kürzester Zeit zu einer Legende des Videospiels geworden. Seine Missionen haben tatsächlich ein ganz neues Genre entstehen lassen, eine Mischung aus Abenteuer, Kämpfen und Infiltration. Neben den spielerischen Qualitäten besticht die Spiele-Saga durch ihre tollen Szenarien, die es durchaus mit den Action-Klassikern Hollywoods aufnehmen können. Hinzu kommt, dass die Entwickler sehr viel Mühe darauf verwendet haben, die psychologischen Aspekte der Charaktere und ihrer Handlungen herauszuarbeiten, was diese Mischung aus Science-Fiction und Realität so glaubwürdig macht. Als im Jahre 2001 *Metal Gear Solid 2: Sons of Liberty* auf den Markt kam, brach der Verkauf alle Rekorde: Innerhalb von nur vier Tagen gingen in Japan eine halbe Million Exemplare über den Ladentisch, während in den USA in den ersten zwei Wochen über zwei Millionen Spiele verkauft wurden.

NAME SOLDIER OF FORTUNE 2: DOUBLE HELIX
PLATFORM PC
RELEASE 2002
EDITOR ACTIVISION
DEVELOPER RAVEN SOFTWARE
COPYRIGHTS © RAVEN SOFTWARE/ACTIVISION
FACT TREND REZNOR: THE LEADER OF THE GROUP NINE INCH NAILS CREATED THE MUSIC AND SOUND EFFECTS OF THE GAME QUAKE.

Soldier of Fortune

John Mullins is a mercenary, as hard-boiled as they come, a man able to perform ultra-violent commando operations in jungle or snow-covered mountains as well as the most delicate town-centre hostage-rescue missions. As a member of the international association Soldier of Fortune, John has access to the most powerful weapons and he certainly knows how to use them. Whether it's a razor-sharp blade for discreetly eliminating guards, a pump-action shotgun so powerful it blows its victims apart, or a long-range sniper's rifle, for Mullins, mastery of his arsenal is second nature. His gaming appearances have been somewhat controversial: his adventures are both very violent and very realistic. The environments in which he moves and the adversaries he gleefully massacres are entirely convincing, so these games are not for the sensitive.

« »

John Mullins est un mercenaire, un dur de dur, rompu aux missions impossibles et ultra violentes telles des opérations commando dans des jungles ou des montagnes enneigées ou de plus délicates missions de sauvetage d'otages en plein cœur de la ville. Membre de l'association internationale Soldier of Fortune, John a accès aux armes les plus puissantes et sait parfaitement s'en servir. Du couteau affûté comme un rasoir lui permettant d'éliminer un garde en toute discrétion au fusil à pompe suffisamment puissant pour démembrer une victime à bout portant, en passant par le fusil à lunette lui permettant de faire mouche à des centaines de mètres de distance, utiliser tout l'arsenal du parfait mercenaire est pour Mullins une seconde nature. Ses apparitions dans le jeu vidéo sont matière à polémique car ses aventures sont à la fois très violentes et réalistes : les environnements où il évolue, les adversaires qu'il massacre sont criants de vérité, aussi mieux vaut déconseiller les jeux où il apparaît aux âmes sensibles.

« »

John Mullins ist ein hartgesottener Söldner, einer, der auf scheinbar aussichtslose und extrem gewalttätige Missionen abonniert ist, so auch auf Kommandounternehmen im Dschungel oder im verschneiten Gebirge oder aber auf heikle Geiselbefreiungen in der City. Als Mitglied der internationalen Organisation Soldier of Fortune hat John Zugang zu den schlagkräftigsten Waffen und kann auch bestens damit umgehen. Das Waffenarsenal reicht von der rasiermesserscharfen Klinge, mit der er einen Wachposten lautlos um die Ecke bringen kann, über das Scharfschützengewehr, mit dem er aus einer Entfernung von mehreren hundert Metern ins Schwarze trifft, bis zur Pumpgun, mit der er ein Opfer aus nächster Nähe regelrecht zerfetzen kann. Der Umgang mit all diesen Waffen ist Mullins inzwischen zur zweiten Natur geworden. Über die Häufigkeit, mit der diese Waffen im Videospiel auftauchen, lässt sich streiten. Die Abenteuer von John Mullins sind äußerst brutal und realistisch zugleich: Man denke an die Schauplätze, auf denen er sich bewegt, oder die Gegner, die er niedermetzelt und die täuschend echt schreien. Darum sind die Spiele mit John Mullins nichts für Leute mit schwachen Nerven.

NAME
STUNTMAN
PLATFORM
PLAYSTATION 2
RELEASE
2002
EDITOR
INFOGRAMES
DEVELOPER
REFLECTIONS SOFTWARE
COPYRIGHTS
© INFOGRAMES
FACT
534,000. THE NUMBER OF GBAS SOLD BY
NINTENDO IN JAPAN THE DAY IT
WAS PUT ON THE MARKET.

Stuntman

The greatest spectacle in action films is often in the stunts and car chases. *Stuntman* pays homage to the daredevils who brave all for the camera. You're a novice to begin with: modest productions, relatively simple stunts. Keep at it, and you climb the rungs of the profession, reaching seriously remunerative contracts; then, in big-budget films, you can stage those really explosive sequences. But before you attain such giddy heights, you get to write off innumerable jeeps, and racing, touring and police cars. Off to the scrapyard with them! Here's hoping the same doesn't happen to the stuntman... Since this is Hollywood, the gamer can also action-replay his best stunts, editing them to perfection before saving them for posterity.

« »

Nombre de films d'action ont marqué les esprits grâce à d'époustouflantes séquences de cascades et poursuites en voiture. Le jeu *Stuntman* rend hommage aux « têtes brûlées » anonymes que sont les cascadeurs qui bravent le danger devant la caméra. Dans la peau d'un cascadeur novice, le joueur débute dans de modestes productions pour des séquences relativement simples et gravit les échelons de la profession afin de décrocher les contrats les plus mirifiques, dans des films à grand budget, pour des séquences explosives plus extrêmes les unes que les autres. Mais avant d'atteindre cette consécration, gageons que d'innombrables jeeps, bolides de course, voitures de tourisme ou de police et autres finiront à la casse... en espérant que le cascadeur, lui, s'en sorte indemne. Hollywood oblige, le joueur pourra également revisionner à loisir ses séquences, les monter à son gré et les sauvegarder pour la postérité.

« »

Zahlreiche Filme sind durch atemberaubende Stunts und Verfolgungsszenen im Auto zu unvergesslichen Leinwandabenteuern geworden. Das Spiel *Stuntman* ist eine Hommage an die draufgängerischen Stuntmen, die jeder Gefahr vor der Kamera standhalten. Der Spieler, der zunächst in die Haut eines Stuntman-Neulings schlüpft, beginnt in bescheidenen Produktionen mit eher leichten Stunts, um dann auf der Leiter des Erfolgs in budgetkräftigen Filmen geradezu fantastische Verträge für mitreißende, spektakuläre Szenen zu ergattern. Bis dahin werden jedoch zahllose Jeeps, Rennwagen, Pkws und Polizeiwagen draufgehen in der Hoffnung allerdings, dass der Stuntman unversehrt davonkommt. Und dabei kann der Spieler, Hollywood verpflichtet, seine Filmsequenzen jederzeit Revue passieren lassen, je nach Lust und Laune Montagen anfertigen und sie für die Nachwelt sichern.

NAME
SYPHON FILTER 3

PLATFORM
PLAYSTATION

RELEASE
2001

EDITOR
SONY COMPUTER ENTERTAINMENT

DEVELOPER
SONY COMPUTER ENTERTAINMENT

COPYRIGHTS
SYPHON FILTER IS A TRADEMARK OF SONY
COMPUTER ENTERTAINMENT AMERICA INC.
© 2001 SONY COMPUTER
ENTERTAINMENT AMERICA INC.

FACT
$500: SONY'S CAPITAL WHEN THE
FIRM WAS STATED IN 1946.

Syphon Filter

Gabe Logan, a special forces secret agent, has completed a succession of missions for the US government. But the public will never hear about these anti-terrorist strikes, lightning attacks on Soviet forces during the 80s, and political assassinations intended to ensure US security and world peace. Now his career, and maybe his life, are up for grabs: Logan is accused of exceeding orders and committing gratuitous acts of violence. At his court martial, Logan has to defend himself by bringing to light his top-secret missions to Costa Rica, Ireland, Africa, Japan, Australia and even Washington DC. In the witness box is another secret agent who played a big part in his adventures, the beautiful but formidable Lian King. Will his former ally testify in his favour - or help convict him?

« »

Agent secret des forces spéciales, Gabe Logan a rempli pour le compte du gouvernement américain de nombreuses missions qui resteront à jamais dissimulées au public : lutte anti-terroriste, opérations-éclair contre les forces soviétiques des années 80 et assassinats pour le compte de la nation et la sauvegarde de la paix mondiale. Mais sa carrière, voire même sa vie, est aujourd'hui en péril : Logan est accusé d'avoir outrepassé ses ordres et s'être livré à des actes de violence gratuits que réprouvent ses supérieurs. En cour martiale, Logan va devoir se défendre en faisant resurgir à la surface ses missions les plus secrètes au Costa Rica, en Irlande, en Afrique, au Japon, en Australie et même à Washington, et affronter à la barre un autre agent secret qui partagea ses aventures, la belle mais redoutable Lian King. Celle qui l'épaula bien souvent sera-t-elle son alliée ou condamnera-t-elle son ancien compagnon d'armes ?

« »

Geheimagent Gabe Logan hat für die amerikanische Regierung viele Missionen ausgeführt, die der Öffentlichkeit für immer verborgen bleiben werden. Darunter antiterroristische Kampfeinsätze, Überraschungsangriffe gegen die soujetischen Streitkräfte in den 80er Jahren wie auch Attentate im Auftrag des Staates und zur Rettung des Weltfriedens. Doch jetzt ist seine Karriere, ja sogar sein Leben in Gefahr. Logan wird beschuldigt, seine Befugnisse überschritten und grundlos Gewaltakte verübt zu haben, und das verurteilen seine Vorgesetzten. Logan wird vor das Kriegsgericht gestellt. Zu seiner Verteidigung muss er seine Geheimaufträge in Costa-Rica, Irland, Afrika, Japan, Australien und auch in Washington offen legen und kommt nicht umhin, dem Gericht seine Begleiterin preiszugeben, die ebenfalls für den Geheimdienst arbeitet: die schöne, aber auch gefürchtete Lian King, die ihm aus so mancher Notlage geholfen hat. Wird sie zu ihm halten oder wird sie sich an ihrem alten Kampfgefährten rächen?

500 $: C'EST LE CAPITAL DE DÉPART
DE SONY LORS DE LA CRÉATION DE
L'ENTREPRISE EN 1946.

500 $: STARTKAPITAL VON SONY BEI DER
FIRMENGRÜNDUNG IM JAHRE 1946

NAME
TIME CRISIS 2

PLATFORM
ARCADE – PLAYSTATION 2

RELEASE
2001

EDITOR **NAMCO**

DEVELOPER **NAMCO**

COPYRIGHTS **© NAMCO**

FACT
4 MILLION: THE NUMBER OF QUARTERS SPENT ON PAC-MAN IN ARCADES IN THE USA DURING ITS FIRST YEAR OF EXISTENCE, 1980.

Time Crisis

The Neodyne Corporation is implementing its most ambitious project, the Starline Network. Sixty-four satellites are launched; their goal is jam the communications of the same number of military satellites, thus taking control of the missile-delivery systems of every nation in the world. The world will fall hostage to Neodyne's directors, unless... VSSE sends Christy Ryan to infiltrate Neodyne's HQ, a deep-sea platform guarded by hundreds of heavily-armed hoodlums. Christy fails. VSSE is forced to send in its forces of last resort, special agents Robert Baxter (codename 'Griffon') and Keith Martin ('Cherub'). Can they save their colleague, destroy the Neodyne HQ, and eliminate its leaders, the former general Ernesto Diaz and his henchmen Wild Dog and Jacob Kinisky?

« »

La Corporation Neodyne met en œuvre son plus ambitieux projet, le Starline Network. Soixante-quatre satellites sont lancés en orbite autour de la terre, avec pour objectif de parasiter autant de satellites militaires, et prendre le contrôle des puissances offensives de toutes les nations. Pour éviter que le monde ne devienne otage des dirigeants de Neodyne, l'organisation VSSE envoie Christy Ryan infiltrer le quartier général de la corporation, une plate-forme maritime sévèrement gardée par des centaines de combattants surarmés. L'espion de charme échoue, aussi la VSSE décide-t-elle d'employer ses derniers atouts, les agents spéciaux Robert Baxter (nom de code : Griffon), Keith Martin (nom de code : Cherub), qui auront pour mission de sauver leur camarade, mais aussi de détruire le QG de Neodyne et de mettre hors d'état de nuire ses dirigeants, l'ex-général Ernesto Diaz et ses bras droits Wild Dog et Jacob Kinisky.

« »

Die Neodyne Corporation tritt mit ihrem ehrgeizigsten Projekt in Erscheinung, dem "Starline Network". Vierundsechzig Satelliten werden in die Erdumlaufbahn geschickt, um möglichst viele Militärsatelliten mit Parasiten zu infizieren und die Angriffswaffen sämtlicher Nationen unter Kontrolle zu bringen. Damit die Welt jedoch nicht zur Geisel der Neodyne-Clique wird, schleust die VSSE Christy Ryan in das Hauptquartier der Corporation ein, einen Marinestützpunkt, der von hunderten schwer bewaffneten Kämpfern bewacht wird. Da der charmante Spion scheitert, beschließt die Organisation VSSE, ihre letzten Trümpfe auszuspielen, und entsendet die Spezialagenten Robert Baxter (Codename: Griffon) und Keith Martin (Codename: Cherub). Sie erhalten den Auftrag, ihren Kameraden zu retten, aber auch das Hauptquartier von Neodyne zu zerstören und seine Führung, den Ex-General Ernesto Diaz und seine Helfershelfer Wild Dog und Jacob Kinisky, unschädlich zu machen.

NAME   TUROK EVOLUTION
PLATFORM   PLAYSTATION 2 - GAMECUBE - XBOX
RELEASE   2002
EDITOR   ACCLAIM ENTERTAINMENT
DEVELOPER   ACCLAIM ENTERTAINMENT
COPYRIGHTS   © ACCLAIM ENTERTAINMENT
FACT   1991: THE YEAR IN WHICH THE DINOSAUR
                        YOSHI FIRST APPEARED, IN
                        SUPER MARIO WORLD ON SNES.

Turok

Fatally wounded during a battle in which his tribe, the Saquin, was defeated by the American cavalry under the blood-thirsty Captain Tobias Brucknet, Tal'Set dies in a cavern whose walls are covered with strange symbols. The magic of the site carries his body away to another universe, where he is resuscitated by the mysterious Seer TarKeen. The Seer takes him to the chief of the River people, who live in a strange world still roamed by dinosaurs. For them, Tal'Set's arrival fulfils a prophecy: he is Turok, Son of the Stone, Defender of the River People. His heart and memory still full of the massacre of his tribe, Tal'Set refuses this role and plunges into the jungle, alone with his anger and grief, despite the supplications of the beautiful Mayana. After a period in which he struggles with his own inner demons, Tal'Set emerges from the jungle to aid the river people in their war against their sworn enemy, Lord Tyrannus, leader of the reptilian hordes.

« »

Blessé à mort lors d'une grande bataille opposant sa tribu, les Saquin, à la cavalerie américaine sous les ordres du sanguinaire capitaine Tobias Brucknet, Tal'Set le brave expire dans une caverne dont les parois sont couvertes d'étranges symboles. La magie du lieu emporte son corps vers un autre univers où il sera ressuscité par le mystérieux Seer TarKeen. Celui-ci le mènera au chef du peuple de la rivière, pour qui l'arrivée de Tal'Set est la concrétisation d'une prophétie : Tal'Set est Turok, Fils de la Pierre et Défenseur du peuple de la rivière de cet étrange univers où vivent encore les dinosaures. Le cœur et l'esprit encore emplis des images du massacre de sa tribu, Tal'Set refuse d'endosser ce rôle et s'enfonce dans la jungle, seul avec sa colère et sa peine, malgré les supplications de la belle Mayana. Après avoir quelque temps combattu ses propres démons, Tal'Set reviendra aider le peuple de la rivière à combattre son ennemi juré, le Lord Tyrannus, leader des hordes reptiliennes.

« »

Bei einer großen Schlacht, die der Stamm der Saquin gegen die unter dem Befehl des blutrünstigen Captain Tobias Brucknet stehende amerikanische Kavallerie ausfocht, wird der mutige Tal'Set tödlich verletzt und haucht in einer mit seltsamen Symbolen übersäten Höhle sein Leben aus. Ein Zauber dieses Ortes versetzt seinen Körper in ein anderes Universum, in dem er von dem mysteriösen Seer TarKeen zu neuem Leben erweckt wird. Dieser führt ihn zum Oberhaupt des Flussvolkes, das in der Ankunft von Tal'Set die Erfüllung einer Prophezeiung sieht: Tal'Set ist Turok, der Sohn des Steins und Verteidiger des Flussvolkes, das in einer sonderbaren Welt lebt, in der noch immer Dinosaurier beheimatet sind. Aber in seinem Herzen und seinem Geist spuken nach wie vor die Bilder des Massakers, das seinen Stamm ausgelöscht hat. Deshalb verweigert er diese Rolle und flüchtet, alleine mit seinem Zorn und seinem Leid, in den Dschungel. Auch das Flehen der schönen Mayana stimmt ihn nicht um. Nach einem verzweifelten Kampf mit sich selbst kehrt Tal'Set einige Zeit später wieder zurück, um das Flussvolk in seinem Krieg gegen die fürchterlichen Feinde, Lord Tyrannus und seine Reptilienhorden, zu unterstützen.

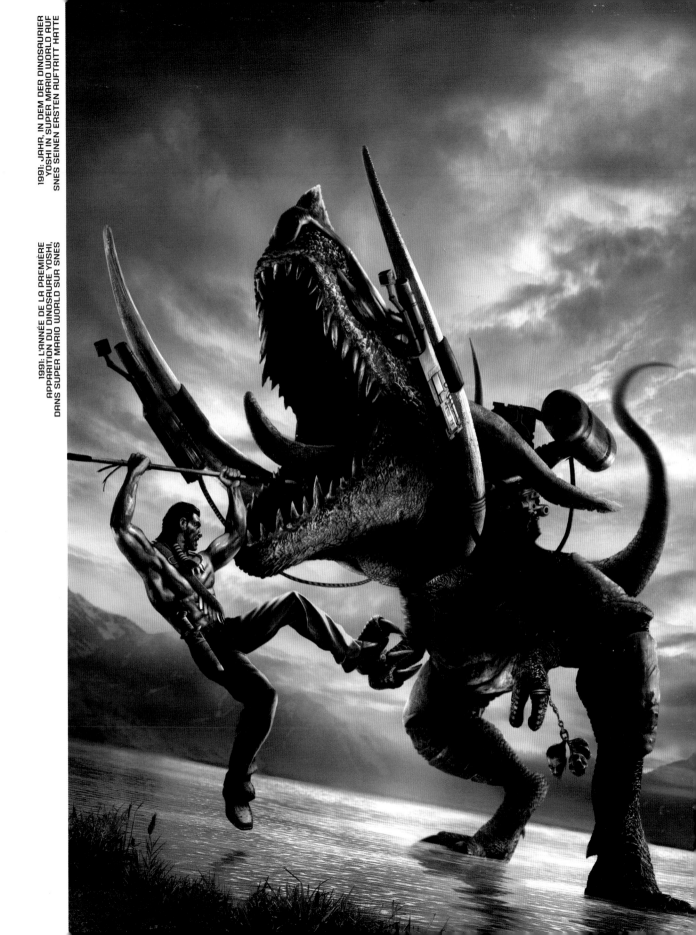

1991: JAHR, IN DEM DER DINOSAURIER YOSHI IN SUPER MARIO WORLD AUF SNES SEINEN ERSTEN AUFTRITT HATTE

1991: L'ANNÉE DE LA PREMIÈRE APPARITION DU DINOSAURE YOSHI, DANS SUPER MARIO WORLD SUR SNES

NAME
VIRTUA COP

PLATFORM
ARCADE - PC
GENESIS - DREAMCAST

RELEASE
1994

EDITOR
SEGA

DEVELOPER
AM2

COPYRIGHTS
© SEGA/AM2

FACT
COMPUTER SPACE: THE VERY FIRST ARCADE
GAME, WHICH APPEARED BEFORE PONG

Virtua Cop

A heavily-armed gang is terrorising Southern California, and two policemen are sent out against it. The first *Virtua Cop* (1994) set the standards for first-person shooters in scenario-based 3D. The gamer (or gamers, since two can play simultaneously), armed with a light-sensitive pistol, shoots down the hordes of adversaries that well up on screen in precisely defined order. You have to be fast and accurate to eliminate your enemies before they fire - and mind those hostages! Ammo-management also features: you fire outside the screen to reload. *Virtua Cop* was a big arcade hit, and its success was repeated on the Saturn console; just add a light pistol to shoot'em up in the comfort of the home.

« »

Deux policiers sont envoyés à l'assaut d'un gang armé jusqu'aux dents qui terrorise le sud de la Californie. Le premier *Virtua Cop* posa en 1994 les bases du jeu de tir au pistolet dans un univers 3D ultra scénarisé. Le joueur (ou les joueurs, l'expérience pouvant être vécue à deux simultanément), armé d'un pistolet doté de capteurs lumineux, se retrouve face à l'écran et doit tirer sur les hordes d'adversaires qui surgissent dans un ordre défini à l'avance. La précision et les réflexes du joueur devront être affûtés, afin d'éliminer les ennemis avant qu'ils ne fassent feu et d'éviter de tirer sur les otages qui apparaissent à l'écran. La gestion des munitions était elle aussi reproduite, le joueur devant tirer hors de l'écran pour recharger son six-coups. Le succès de *Virtua Cop* en salle d'arcade se répéta sur la console Saturn, grâce à un pistolet lumineux qui permettait de reproduire les mêmes sensations, confortablement installé chez soi.

« »

Zwei Polizisten werden zum Einsatz gegen eine bis zu den Zähnen bewaffneten Gang geschickt, die den Süden Kaliforniens terrorisiert. Das erste *Virtua Cop* legte 1994 die Grundlagen des Ballerspiels in einem 3-D-Universium mit einem bestens durchdachten Szenario. Der mit einer Pistole mit Laserpointer bewaffnete Spieler (oder die Spieler, die simultan spielen können) sitzt vor dem Bildschirm und muss auf die feindlichen Horden schießen, die in einer zuvor festgelegten Reihenfolge plötzlich hervortreten. Treffsicherheit und Reflexe des Spielers sollten Topniveau haben, um die Feinde auszuschalten, bevor sie das Feuer eröffnen. Nur so lässt sich verhindern, dass sie auf die Geiseln zielen, die auf dem Bildschirm erscheinen. Dabei ist die Rationierung der Munition gut durchdacht, denn der Spieler gibt einen Schuss neben den Bildschirm ab, um seine Waffe wieder aufzuladen. Dank der Leuchtpistole, die den gleichen Effekt bringt wie die Pistole mit Laserpointer, war *Virtua Cop* für die Saturn-Konsole so erfolgreich wie in den Spielhallen, mit dem Vorzug, dass man es sich zu Hause bequem machen kann.

COMPUTER SPACE: ALLERERSTES ARCADE-SPIEL, DAS NOCH VOR PONG AUF DEN MARKT KAM

COMPUTER SPACE: C'EST LE TOUT PREMIER JEU DE BORNE D'ARCADE, QUI PARUT AVANT PONG

NAME
WHITE FEAR

PLATFORM
PC-PLAYSTATION 2

RELEASE
2002

EDITOR
MICROÏDS

DEVELOPER
MICROÏDS

COPYRIGHTS
© MICROÏDS

FACT
16 JUNE 2000: THE DATE AT WHICH GAME BOY
ATTAINED 100,000,000 SALES WORLDWIDE.

White Fear

In the infinite frozen wastes of the Arctic, Iru, a young shaman, must save his people and the ecology of the ice-floes from the magical attacks of Sukko, a powerful wizard of very unfriendly intentions. Iru's quest forces him to scour the vast tracts of snow and the immense caverns hidden beneath the ice in search of the magic Spirits with the aid of whose powers he can overcome the dark wizard. Sukko in his turn will do everything in his power to stop Iru, setting a thousand fatal traps in his way, and unleashing his hordes of supernatural monsters against the youthful shaman, who has only his harpoon and some magical powers to defend him. Inspired by Inuit mythology, Iru's quest combines exploration, enigma and spectacular battles with terrifying creatures. The wonderful world of the ice-floes is a landscape rarely seen by gamers. This is a disconcerting adventure full of magic and freighted with the ecological wisdom of the Inuit.

« »

Au cœur des infinies étendues glacées de l'Arctique, Iru, un jeune chaman, doit sauver son peuple et l'équilibre de la banquise des attaques magiques de Sukko, un sorcier aussi puissant que maléfique. Sa quête le fera sillonner les régions enneigées et les immenses cavernes cachées sous les glaces, à la recherche des Esprits magiques dont le pouvoir lui permettra de terrasser le mage maudit. Sukko fera tout pour empêcher le chaman d'atteindre son but, dressant d'innombrables pièges mortels sur sa route et envoyant ses hordes de monstres surnaturels à l'assaut du jeune homme armé d'un simple harpon et de quelques pouvoirs magiques. Inspirée de la mythologie Inuit, la quête d'Iru mêle exploration ponctuée d'énigmes et combats spectaculaires contre d'effrayantes créatures, dans un monde neigeux superbe et rarement exploité dans le jeu vidéo. Une aventure dépaysante pleine de magie et porteuse d'un sage message écologique.

« »

Inmitten der unendlichen Weite der arktischen Eises hat der junge Schamane Iru die Aufgabe, sein Volk und das Packeis vor den magischen Angriffen des ebenso mächtigen wie gefährlichen Zauberers Sukko zu retten. Seine abenteuerliche Reise führt ihn durch schneebedeckte Regionen und riesige, unter dem Eis versteckte Höhlen, immer auf der Suche nach Geisthelfern, mit deren magischen Kräften er den bösen Zauberer besiegen kann. Sukko seinerseits setzt alles daran, den Schamanen von seinem Ziel abzubringen. Er stellt ihm entlang des Weges viele tödliche Fallen und schickt ihm reihenweise seine schrecklichen Monster auf den Hals, während der junge Iru lediglich mit einer einfachen Harpune und ein paar magischen Kräften ausgestattet ist. Die Abenteuer des Iru sind der Mythologie der Inuit nachempfunden. Es ist eine gelungene Mischung aus einer mit Rätselaufgaben gespickten Entdeckungsreise und spektakulären Kampfszenen gegen Furcht erregende Monster, und das vor dem Hintergrund einer atemberaubenden Schneelandschaft, wie sie in Videospielen bisher selten zu sehen war. Ein ungewohntes Abenteuer voller Magie und mit einer eindeutigen ökologischen Botschaft.

NAME
SHIGERU MIYAMOTO

BORN
1952

HOME TOWN
SONEBE, JAPAN

OCCUPATION
GENERAL MANAGER, NINTENDO CO LTD.

KEY TITLES
THE LEGEND OF ZELDA (2002)
SUPER MARIO SUNSHINE (2002)
PIKMIN (2001)
LUIGI'S MANSION (2001)
MARIO KART 64 (1997)
SUPER MARIO 64 (1996)
LEGEND OF ZELDA: OCARINA OF TIME (1998)
STARFOX (1994)
F-ZERO (1991)
THE LEGEND OF ZELDA (1986)
SUPER MARIO BROS. (1985)
DONKEY KONG (1980)

«Legends of Video Games»
Shigeru Miyamoto

Since Mario first appeared in his first video game in 1981, his legacy has played a significant part in redefining video gaming history and he continues to be one of the most recognisable faces worldwide.

When Mario first appeared alongside Donkey Kong in their first Donkey Kong arcade adventure he was originally called "Jumpman" because of the way he could jump across the screen. I heard that in the office of Nintendo of America at that time, Nintendo's landlord was called Mario and his face resembled Jumpman so much that we decided to rename the character "Mario" in his next game.

My original idea behind Mario was not to have him being a super-hero with extraordinary powers, but for him to be a likeable and very accessible character to play - I was thinking of him being roughly mid-20s in age. Over the last 20 years, players have already been able to enjoy his different adventures on consoles such as NES, SNES, Game Boy, Nintendo 64, Game Boy Advance and now on the Nintendo GAMECUBE. In each game, the Mario series has offered fans innovative and fun gameplay, but we have not changed what players love most about the character - from the famous phrases he uses, the way he jumps and defeats enemies, to the design of his dungarees and moustache. Mario has continued to be a famous video game icon because, I believe, whenever this loveable and familiar character appears in a new game he provides the players with lots of fun as well as brand new and unique surprises, completely different from his preceding adventures.

At the beginning of each game design, I look at what excites the player and then sketch out the types of situations and emotions within the gameplay I would like them to experience. It's only then that I look at the different characters and plot within the game.

Frequently, the ideas and backdrops to the games derive from my everyday observations and my very own childhood experiences. For example, part of the concept behind Pikmin, my newest creation for the Nintendo GAMECUBE, came to me while I was gardening at home. The backdrop to the game uses a lot of natural imagery and I was intrigued by the mysterious structure and design of the plants, the details of which I had not cared to observe even though they were around me all the time. I was also attracted by the movement of a group of ants and thought it would be fun if we could move them just as we wish. With these thoughts in mind, we created an alien planet, inhabited by helpful, small plant like creatures called Pikmin, who help to rebuild the crash-landed space ship. However, the planet is also home to some other hostile creatures that eat the Pikmin. Is the player using Pikmin to escape from the planet? Or is it the Pikmin who are making use of the player in order to eradicate their natural enemy? The game will surely make you wonder. In nature, there is an obscure line between good and bad. The strong prey upon the weak. Those natural laws are alive in this unprecedented game.

At the time of writing this, we are in the very final development phase of Super Mario Sunshine, and most of our time is now devoted to the new Legend of Zelda game for Nintendo GAMECUBE. I am testing the controls everyday in order to make sure that what we want players to feel and experience through Link's character are actually and exactly reproduced there. Though we have different languages, different cultures and difference environments to live in, emotions such as joy, anger, fear and sadness must be common for all human beings and they can be experienced through Mario, Luigi, Donkey Kong, Zelda, Kirby, Metroid, Star Fox, Pokemon, and so on. Many ask why Nintendo games are so loved by so many people right around the world. It must be because, I believe, through the eyes and ears and bodies of these accessible characters people can virtually experience things that are impossible in the real world.

I am happy that gamers have enjoyed Nintendo's characters and games and we hope to continue creating fresh entertainment that will surprise people around the world for a very long time to come.

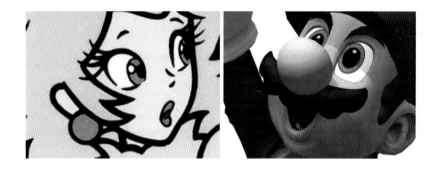

Depuis la première apparition de Mario dans un jeu vidéo en 1981, son héritage a joué un rôle important dans la redéfinition de l'histoire du jeu vidéo, et il reste l'un des visages les plus reconnaissables dans le monde entier.

Lorsque Mario est apparu aux côtés de Donkey Kong dans leur première aventure d'arcade, il se nommait « Jumpman » (« L'homme qui saute »), de par sa façon de sauter à l'écran. J'entendis, dans les bureaux de Nintendo of America, que le propriétaire se prénommait Mario et que son visage ressemblait à celui de Jumpman, aussi nous décidâmes de nommer le personnage « Mario » dans son prochain jeu.

Mon idée originale pour Mario était qu'il ne soit pas un super-héros doté de pouvoirs extraordinaires, mais un personnage attachant et facile à jouer – je l'imaginais âgé d'environ 25 ans. Pendant ces vingt dernières années, les joueurs ont pu apprécier ses diverses aventures sur des consoles comme la NES, la SNES, la Game Boy, la Nintendo 64, la Game Boy Advance et maintenant sur la Nintendo GAME-CUBE. Chaque jeu de la série Mario a offert aux fans une manière de jouer innovante et divertissante, mais nous n'avons pas changé ce que les joueurs préféraient chez le personnage -- des fameuses phrases qu'il lance à l'allure de sa salopette et de ses moustaches, en passant par sa façon de sauter ou de vaincre ses ennemis.

Si Mario n'a cessé d'être une célèbre icône du jeu vidéo, c'est je crois parce que chaque apparition de ce personnage familier et attachant dans un nouveau jeu vidéo apporte au joueur beaucoup de plaisir et de nouvelles surprises, complètement différentes de ses précédentes aventures.

Au début du développement d'un nouveau jeu, je regarde ce qui plaît au joueur et j'esquisse les situations et émotions que je désire lui faire expérimenter. Ce n'est qu'ensuite que je travaille sur les différents personnages et sur l'histoire du jeu.

Régulièrement, les idées et toiles de fond des jeux s'inspirent de mes observations quotidiennes et de mes propres souvenirs d'enfant. Par exemple, une partie du concept de Pikmin, ma dernière création en date pour la Nintendo GAMECUBE, me vint alors que je jardinais chez moi. La toile de fond du jeu se sert énormément d'imagerie naturelle et j'étais intrigué par les mystérieuses structures des plantes, des détails que je n'avais jamais vraiment observés, bien qu'ils fussent toujours autour de moi. J'étais également fasciné par les mouvements d'un groupe de fourmis et je pensais qu'il serait amusant de les faire se déplacer à notre guise. A partir de ces réflexions, nous avons créé une planète extraterrestre peuplée de petites créatures-plantes amicales appelées Pikmin, qui aident à la reconstruction d'un vaisseau spatial échoué. Mais la planète abrite également des créatures hostiles qui se nourrissent de Pikmin. Est-ce le joueur qui utilise les Pikmin pour fuir cette planète étrangère ? Ou sont-ce les Pikmin qui se servent du joueur pour éradiquer leurs ennemis naturels ? Le jeu vous amènera certainement à vous poser la question. Dans la nature, la frontière entre le bien et le mal est obscure. Les forts se nourrissent des faibles. Ces forces naturelles sont à l'œuvre dans ce jeu sans précédent.

Au moment où j'écris ces lignes, nous entrons dans la phase finale de développement de Super Mario Sunshine, et la majeure partie de notre temps est dédiée au nouveau jeu Legend of Zelda pour la Nintendo GAMECUBE. Je teste les contrôles chaque jour afin d'être certain que ce que nous voulions faire ressentir aux joueurs par l'intermédiaire du personnage Link est reproduit tel que nous le désirions. Bien que nous ayons des langues, des cultures et des environnements de vie différents, des émotions comme la joie, la colère, la peur ou la tristesse doivent être communes à tous les êtres humains et peuvent être ressenties par l'intermédiaire de Mario, Luigi, Donkey Kong, Zelda, Kirby, Metroïd, Star Fox, les Pokémon, et ainsi de suite. Nombreux sont ceux qui se demandent pourquoi les jeux Nintendo sont aussi appréciés de par le monde. C'est, je crois, dû au fait que par les yeux, les oreilles et le corps de ces personnages accessibles, les gens peuvent expérimenter virtuellement des choses qui restent inaccessibles dans la vraie vie.

Je suis heureux que des joueurs aient apprécié les jeux et personnages de Nintendo et nous espérons pouvoir continuer à créer des divertissements originaux qui surprendront les gens de par le monde, pour de très nombreuses années encore.

Seit seinem Debüt im Jahre 1981 hat der Klempner Mario die Geschichte der Videospiele maßgeblich beeinflusst und er wird auch weiterhin zu den bekanntesten Gesichtern weltweit zählen.

Als Mario erstmals zusammen mit Donkey Kong im ersten Donkey-Kong-Arcade-Abenteuer auftauchte, wurde er noch „Jumpman" genannt, wegen der Art, wie er über den Bildschirm hüpfte. Im damaligen Büro von Nintendo of America erfuhr ich, dass der Vermieter von Nintendo Mario hieß, und da er Jumpman so ähnlich sah, beschlossen wir kurzerhand, den Charakter im nächsten Spiel in „Mario" umzubenennen.

Meine ursprüngliche Vorstellung von Mario war nicht die eines Superhelden mit übernatürlichen Kräften, er sollte vielmehr ein liebenswerter und sehr unkomplizierter Charakter sein – altersmäßig so etwa Mitte zwanzig. Im Laufe der letzten zwanzig Jahre konnten sich die Spieler an seinen diversen Abenteuern auf Konsolen wie NES, SNES, Gameboy, Nintendo 64, Gameboy Advance und neuerdings auch auf dem Nintendo Gamecube erfreuen. Jeder neue Ableger der Mario-Serie versprach den Fans ein innovatives Gameplay und viel Spaß, während das, was die Spieler an der Figur so liebten, unverändert blieb: seine berühmten Aussprüche, seine Art zu hüpfen und wie er Gegner besiegt, aber auch das Aussehen seiner Latzhose und seines Schnurrbartes. Und so ist Mario zu einer echten Kultfigur des Videospiels geworden, denn wann immer dieser sympathische und vertraute Charakter in einem neuen Spiel auftaucht, sorgt er für jede Menge Spaß und tolle, stets brandneue Überraschungen.

Zu Beginn eines jeden Gamedesigns überlege ich mir, was die Spieler wohl begeistern könnte, und skizziere die verschiedenen Situationen und Emotionen, die von ihnen nachempfunden werden sollen. Erst dann stellen sich mir die verschiedenen Charaktere und die Handlung des Spiels vor Augen.

Gelegentlich liefern mir meine alltäglichen Beobachtungen und meine Kindheitserlebnisse die Ideen und Hintergründe zu den Spielen. Das Konzept zu Pikmin, meiner neuesten Schöpfung für den Nintendo Gamecube, kam mir teilweise bei der Gartenarbeit. Viele Darstellungen aus der Natur bilden den Hintergrund des Spiels. Ich war fasziniert von den geheimnisvollen Pflanzen, deren Struktur und Gestalt ich in den Details nie wahrgenommen hatte, obwohl ich ständig von ihnen umgeben war. Ebenso interessant fand ich das Gewimmel von Ameisen und ich überlegte mir, wie toll es wäre, wenn wir sie nach unseren Wünschen leiten könnten. Mit diesen Ideen im Kopf entwickelten wir einen fremden Planeten und bevölkerten ihn mit hilfsbereiten kleinen Kreaturen namens Pikmin, die dem Spieler dabei helfen, ein notgelandetes Raumschiff wieder zusammenzubauen. Dieser fremde Planet wird allerdings auch von anderen, feindlichen Kreaturen bewohnt, die die Pikmin fressen. Wird der Spieler sich die Pikmin zur Flucht von dem Planeten dienstbar machen? Oder bedienen sich die Pikmin des Spielers, um ihre natürlichen Feinde auszuschalten? Das Spiel sorgt garantiert für Verwunderung. In der Natur ist die Grenze zwischen Gut und Böse nicht eindeutig auszumachen. Die Starken fressen die Schwachen. Diese Naturgesetze kommen in dem einzigartigen Spiel deutlich zum Tragen.

Während ich dies schreibe, befinden wir uns in der letzten Entwicklungsphase von Super Mario Sunshine und verwenden nun die meiste Zeit auf die neue Episode von Legend of Zelda für den Nintendo Gamecube. Jeden Tag mache ich Tests vor, um sicherzugehen, dass auch tatsächlich gerendert wird, was wir an Gefühlen und Erfahrungen erzeugen möchten. Trotz unterschiedlicher Sprachen, Kulturen und Lebensumstände sollte es den Menschen möglich sein, Emotionen wie Freude, Ärger, Angst und Traurigkeit miteinander zu teilen; durch Mario, Luigi, Donkey Kong, Zelda, Kirby, Metroid, Star Fox, die Pokemon und andere können diese Gefühle erlebt werden. Wir werden oft gefragt, warum Nintendo-Spiele auf der ganzen Welt so beliebt sind. Ich glaube, es liegt daran, dass die Spieler durch die Augen, Ohren und Körper dieser einprägsamen Charaktere virtuell Erfahrungen machen können, die in der Realität nicht möglich sind.

Ich freue mich, dass die Nintendo-Figuren und -Spiele so begeistert aufgenommen werden. Und wir alle hoffen, auch weiterhin gute und spannende Unterhaltung liefern zu können, von der sich die Menschen rund um den Globus noch in ferner Zukunft faszinieren lassen.

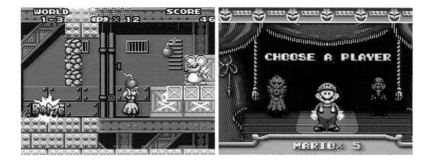

NAME	SUPER MARIO SERIES
PLATFORM	NINTENDO 64, GAME BOY GAME BOY ADVANCE
RELEASE	1996
EDITOR	NINTENDO
DEVELOPER	NINTENDO
COPYRIGHTS	© NINTENDO

Mario

What to make of a little Italian plumber with moustachios and a pot-belly? How about the most famous icon of video-gaming, and the mascot of Japanese giant Nintendo? A product of the fertile imagination of Shigeru Miyamoto, Mario is undoubtedly the key figure in video-games-world wide. As he's grown in stature, his circle of friends have all become major figures too: his brother Luigi, the monkey Donkey Kong (Mario's first adversary), Princess Peach, whom Mario never tires of saving, and the sweet little dinosaur Yoshi. The years have done nothing to diminish Mario's success. On the contrary, he's never worked harder: this hero of platformers is now MC-ing all kinds of tennis, golf, combat, kart and strategy games. Nor has he been spoilt by over-exposure: his presence in a game is an index of success and a guarantee of quality.

« »

Qui aurait cru, voici bien des années, qu'un petit plombier italien rondouillard et moustachu deviendrait non seulement une des plus célèbres icônes du jeu vidéo, mais aussi la mascotte d'un géant japonais, Nintendo. Sorti de l'imagination féconde du créateur Shigeru Miyamoto, Mario est sans conteste la figure de proue du jeu vidéo, et ce dans le monde entier. Sa réputation grandissant, Mario s'est entouré d'amis qui, à leur tour, sont devenus des incontournables de l'industrie : son frère Luigi, le singe Donkey Kong qui fut son tout premier adversaire, la princesse Peach que Mario sauva d'innombrables fois au fil de ses aventures ou encore l'adorable petit dinosaure Yoshi. Les années, loin d'entamer le succès de Mario, l'ont vu s'adonner à d'innombrables activités : le héros de plates-formes est désormais également le maître de cérémonie de jeux de tennis, de courses de karting, de golf, de combats de réflexion etc. Sa polyvalence n'a en rien érodé sa prestigieuse aura, bien au contraire : plus que jamais, la présence de Mario dans un jeu vidéo est non seulement un gage de succès, mais aussi, voire surtout, une preuve de qualité.

« »

Wer hätte es sich jemals träumen lassen, dass ein kleiner stämmiger, oberlippenbärtiger italienischer Klempner nicht nur eine der berühmtesten Ikonen des Videospiels werden würde, sondern auch das Maskottchen eines japanischen Riesen, Nintendo. Aus der unermesslich reichen Fantasie seines Schöpfers Shigeru Miyamoto entstanden, ist Mario unbestritten weltweit zur Symbolfigur des Videospiels geworden. Mit wachsender Bekanntheit gesellten sich Freunde zu Mario, die sich inzwischen einen ebenso festen Platz erobert haben: sein Bruder Luigi, der Affe Donkey Kong, sein allererster Gegner, die Prinzessin Peach, die Mario im Laufe seiner Abenteuer unzählige Male gerettet hat, oder auch der herzallerliebste kleine Dinosaurier Yoshi. Mario hat sich im Laufe der Jahre, die seinem Erfolg bisher nichts anhaben konnten, in zahllosen Aktivitäten bewiesen: Der Held der Konsolenspiele ist nunmehr auch zum Zeremonienmeister des Tennisspiels, des Kartrennens, des Golfspiels, der Kampfspiele, der Denk- und Knobelspiele geworden. Seine Vielseitigkeit hat seiner Aura keineswegs geschadet, ganz im Gegenteil: Mehr denn je ist Marios Präsenz in einem Videospiel nicht nur der Garant für den Erfolg, sondern auch, und vor allem, ein Beweis für Qualität.

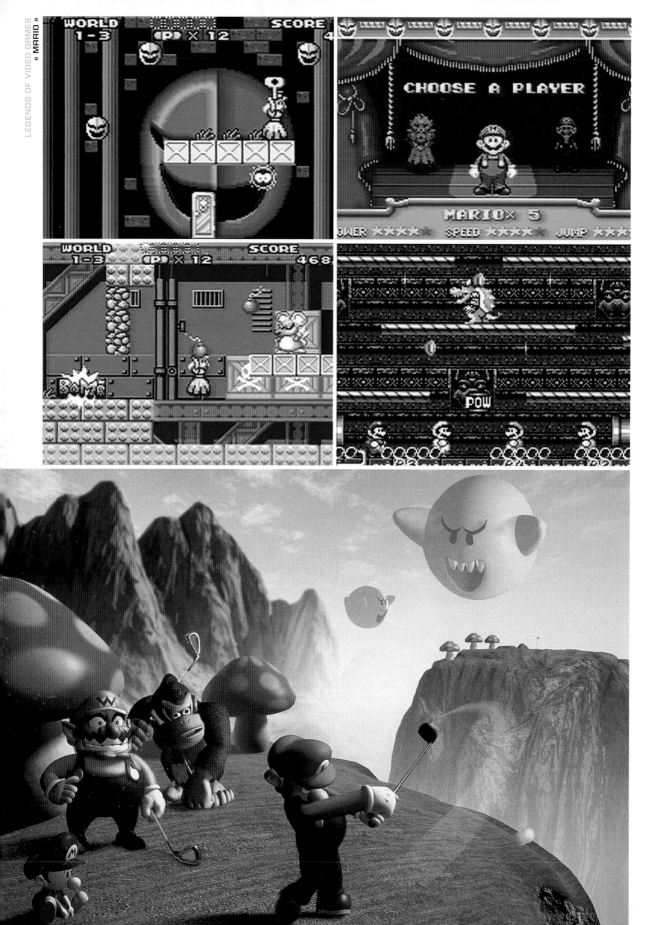

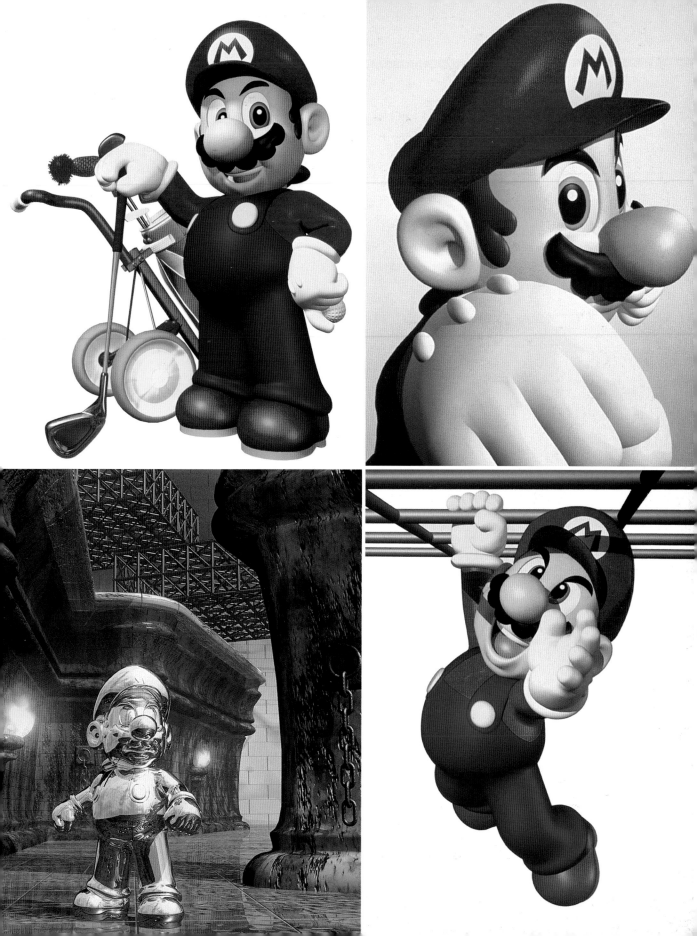

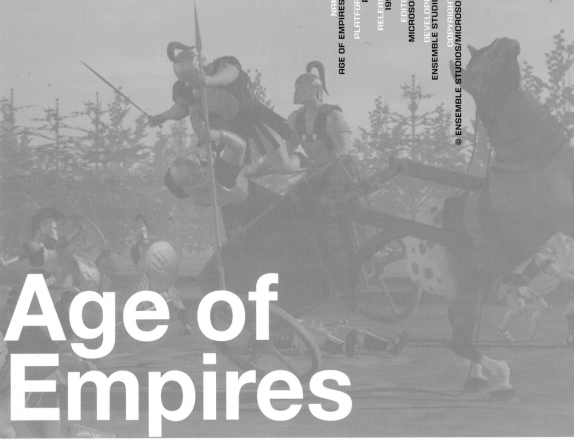

NAME **AGE OF EMPIRES 2**
PLATFORM PC
RELEASE 1997
EDITOR MICROSOFT
DEVELOPER ENSEMBLE STUDIOS
COPYRIGHTS © ENSEMBLE STUDIOS/MICROSOFT

Age of Empires

War is the one constant of human history, and the deeds of the great warriors have brought them legendary status. Alexander the Great, William Wallace, Attila the Hun, and Jeanne d'Arc are just some of the names from classical and medieval history that have left their mark on civilisation, and whose lives and fame the gamer can adopt. But wars are not won on the battlefield alone: diplomacy, economic development and technological research are equally vital. Heading up one of the many civilisations in the *Age of Empires* series, the gamer attempts to lead it to victory. Construct a village, exploit natural resources, manage the peasantry, orchestrate technological advance to increase the efficiency of your armies and facilitate life for the home clan: these are some of the many challenges on the road to a place in history. The greatest challenge is competition from other clan chiefs - the other players, each of them ready to wage merciless war over the Internet.

« »

L'histoire de l'humanité est ponctuée de guerres menées par des guerriers que leurs hauts faits ont fait accéder au rang de légendes. Alexandre le Grand, William Wallace, Attila le Hun, Jeanne D'Arc sont quelques noms antiques ou médiévaux qui ont marqué la civilisation, et dont la destinée peut être prise en main par le joueur. Mais les guerres ne se sont pas uniquement jouées sur les champs de bataille : l'économie, la recherche technologique et la diplomatie ont joué des rôles capitaux. Le joueur, à la tête d'une des nombreuses civilisations disponibles dans la série des *Age of Empires*, devra la mener à la victoire. Construire un village, exploiter les ressources naturelles, gérer ses paysans, orchestrer les avancées technologiques pour augmenter l'efficacité de ses armées, mais aussi faciliter la vie de son clan sont autant de tâches qu'il lui faudra maîtriser pour marquer l'histoire de son empreinte. Son plus grand défi sera de se mesurer aux autres chefs de clans que sont les autres joueurs, prêts à guerroyer dans de grandes batailles par le biais de l'Internet.

« »

Die Geschichte der Menschheit ist gekennzeichnet durch eine Reihe von Kriegen, deren heldenhafte Kämpfer zu Legenden geworden sind. Alexander der Große, William Wallace, Attila der Hunnenkönig und Jeanne d'Arc gehören zu den großen Namen der Antike oder des Mittelalters, die die Zivilisation geprägt haben und deren Schicksal der Spieler nun lenken kann. Kriege finden aber nicht nur auf dem Schlachtfeld statt. Die wirtschaftliche Entwicklung, der Stand der Forschung in Wissenschaft und Technik und die Diplomatie spielen eine nicht minder entscheidende Rolle in der Menschheitsgeschichte. Der Spieler, der an der Spitze einer der Zivilisationen aus der Serie *Age of Empires* steht, verhilft durch sein Geschick einem Clan zum Sieg. Er errichtet ein Dorf, erschließt Bodenschätze, führt seine Bauern und lenkt die technologischen Neuerungen, um die Schlagkraft seiner Armee zu erhöhen und die Lebensbedingungen seines Volkes zu verbessern. Nur wenn er diese Aufgaben richtig erfüllt, kann er in die Geschichte eingehen. Seine größte Herausforderung besteht in der Auseinandersetzung mit den anderen Clanchefs, will heißen, mit den anderen Spielern, die sich über das Internet auf die großen Schlachten vorbereitet haben.

NAME
CIVILIZATION III

PLATFORM
PC

RELEASE
2001

EDITOR
INFOGRAMES

DEVELOPER
FIRAXIS GAMES

COPYRIGHTS
© INFOGRAMES

FACT
EVOLUTIONARY ERROR: IN THE FIRST SERIES OF THE GAME CIVILIZATION, THE ALPHABET HAS TO BE DISCOVERED BEFORE WRITING, REVERSING THE HISTORICAL ORDER.

Civilization

Imagine controlling the destiny of a nation, from first faltering steps to imperial apogee. *Civilization* lets you guide a simple nomadic tribe from prehistory on. Found the first towns, plan expansion, direct intellectual and industrial development; govern diplomatic relations with other civilisations. And if need be, assume plenipotentiary powers at the head of the nation's armies. Sid Meier's *Civilization* series has captivated millions of gamers, who re-write history and test innumerable development strategies. The choice is yours - militaristic or pacific, protectionist or expansionist, democrat, royalist or tyrant, you can fashion every aspect of human existence. More than a game, *Civilization* is a limitless laboratory for political, military, economic and scientific experiment. Make your mark on history: this is the playing field on which battles are really won.

« »

Imaginez pouvoir prendre en main la destinée d'une nation, de ses premiers balbutiements à son aboutissement. Guide d'une simple tribu nomade au sortir de la préhistoire, vous auriez sous votre responsabilité la fondation des premières villes, l'expansion de la nation, l'évolution intellectuelle et industrielle, les relations diplomatiques avec d'autres civilisations... et si besoin, on vous accorderait les pleins pouvoirs à la tête des armées. Née de l'imagination de Sid Meier en 1990, la série des *Civilization* a conquis des milliers de joueurs, qui peuvent à leur gré réécrire l'histoire et expérimenter d'innombrables stratégies d'évolution. Protectionniste ou expansionniste, belliqueuse ou pacifique, démocratique, royaliste ou tyrannique : toutes les facettes de l'histoire de l'humanité peuvent être façonnées à loisir par le joueur-leader. Plus qu'un jeu, *Civilization* est une expérience sans cesse renouvelée, un terrain de jeu politique, militaire, économique et scientifique où chacun peut rêver d'apposer son empreinte sur l'histoire.

« »

Mit nie da gewesener Spannung kann hier das Schicksal einer Nation, von ihren ersten Schritten bis hin zu ihrer Blüte, in die Hand genommen werden. Der Spieler, Anführer eines einfachen Nomadenstammes am Ende des prähistorischen Zeitalters, trägt die Verantwortung für die Gründung der ersten Städte, die Entstehung der Nation, die Entwicklung von Know-how und Industrie, die diplomatischen Beziehungen mit anderen Zivilisationen; mitunter wird ihm sogar die Befehlsgewalt über eine ganze Armee übertragen. Im Jahre 1990 der genialen Schöpferkraft von Sid Meier entsprungen, hat die Reihe der *Civilization* tausende Spieler in ihren Bann gezogen, die mit unzähligen Evolutionsstrategien experimentieren und die Geschichte nach eigenem Gutdünken neu schreiben können. Ob nun protektionistisch oder expansionistisch, kriegerisch oder pazifistisch, demokratisch, royalistisch oder tyrannisch: Der Spieler kann sämtlichen Facetten der Geschichte der Menschheit seinen Stempel aufdrücken. *Civilization* ist mehr als nur ein Spiel. Es bietet stets neue Erfahrungen sowie ein Spielfeld politischen, militärischen, wirtschaftlichen und wissenschaftlichen Schaltens und Waltens, wo dem Spieler der Traum erlaubt ist, den Lauf der Geschichte mitzubestimmen.

THE WARRIOR TRIBES OF THE ZU
FIGHT UNTIL THE LAST BREAT
LEADER: SHAKA ZU
SPECIAL UNIT: IMPI SPEARMA

REWRITE HISTORY
SID MEIER'
CIVILIZATION

JOIN THE MIGHTY LEGIONS OF ROME

CIVILIZATION

CIVILIZATION: UNITED STATES OF AMERICA
LEADER: ABRAHAM LINCOLN
SPECIALIZED UNIT: F15 FIGHTER JET
CAPITAL: WASHINGTON D.C.

REWRITE HISTORY.
SID MEIER'S
CIV 3

The Aztecs
people of gold and silver.

civilization: the aztecs
unit: jaguar warrior
leader: montezuma
capital: tenochtitlan

REWRITE HISTORY.
SID MEIER'S
CIV III

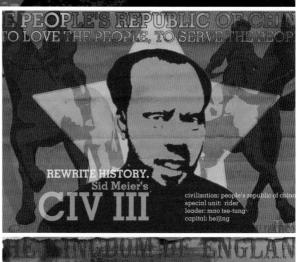

THE PEOPLE'S REPUBLIC OF CHINA
TO LOVE THE PEOPLE, TO SERVE THE PEOPLE

REWRITE HISTORY.
Sid Meier's
CIV III

civilization: people's republic of china
special unit: rider
leader: mao tse-tung
capital: beijing

The Babylonians
the glory of creation

civilization: the babylonians
leader: hammurabi
special unit: bowman
capital: babylon

rewrite history.
sid meier's
III

THE KINGDOM OF ENGLAND
upon which the sun never sets...

WANTED

CIVILIZATION

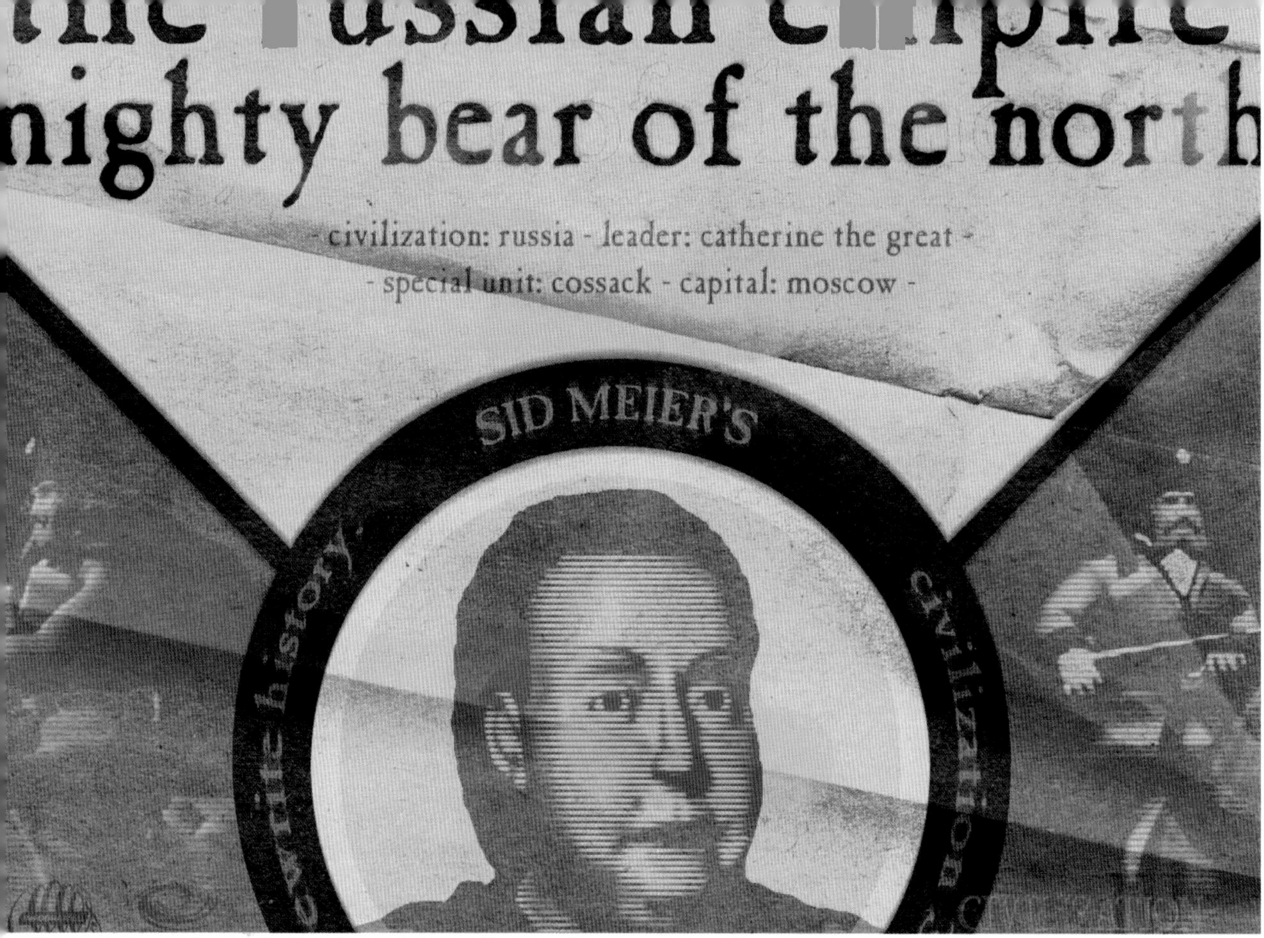

the Russian empire
mighty bear of the north

- civilization: russia - leader: catherine the great -
- special unit: cossack - capital: moscow -

SID MEIER'S
civilize history
civilization

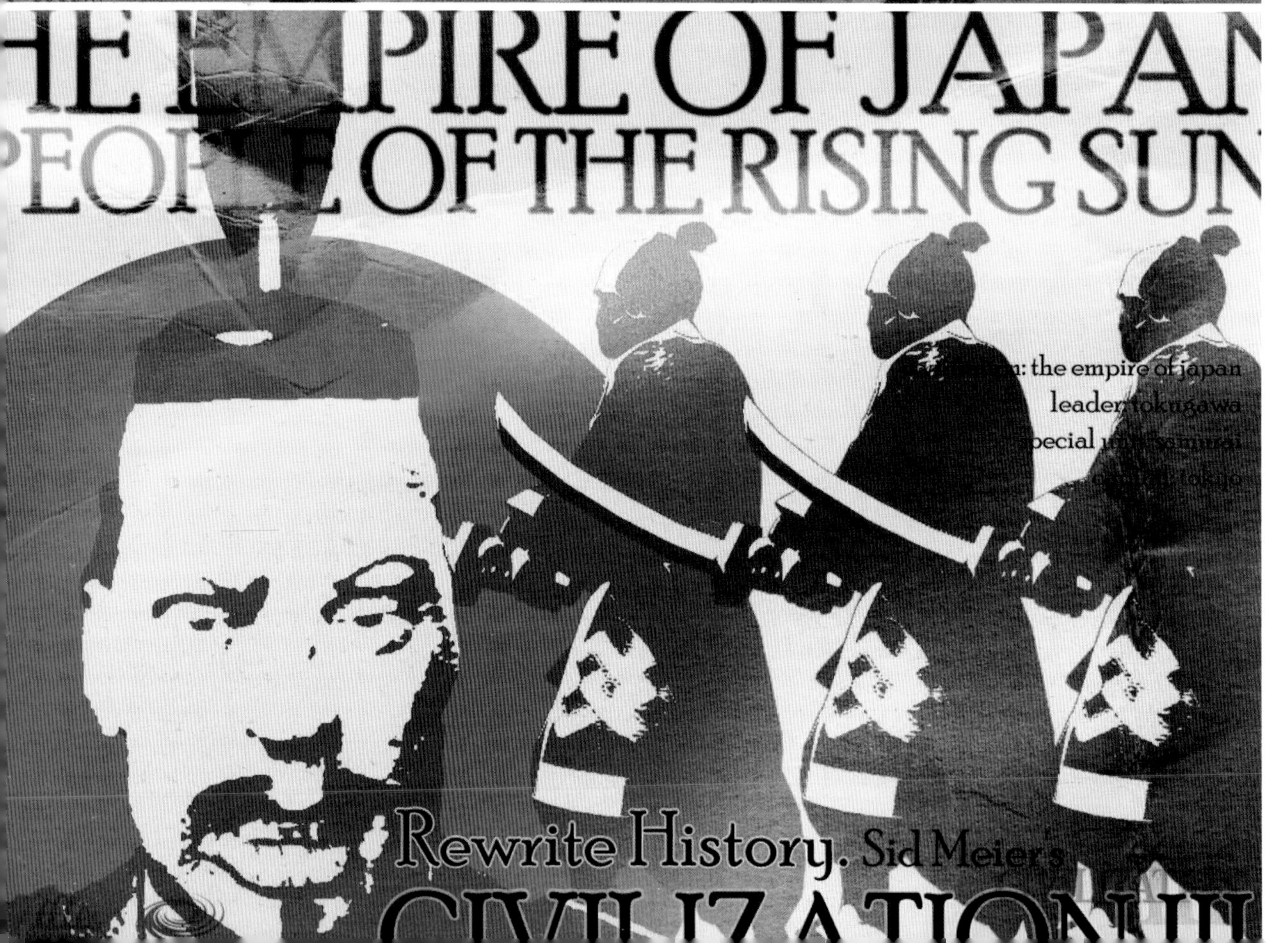

THE EMPIRE OF JAPAN
PEOPLE OF THE RISING SUN

: the empire of japan
leader: tokugawa
special unit: samurai
capital: tokio

Rewrite History. Sid Meier's
CIVILIZATION II

NAME
CRASH BANDICOOT: CORTEX STRIKES BACK

PLATFORM
PS2

RELEASE
2002

EDITOR
UNIVERSAL INTERACTIVE STUDIOS

DEVELOPER
TRAVELLER'S TALES

FACT
2: THE NUMBER OF YEARS REQUIRED BY NAUGHTY DOG TO DEVELOP CRASH BANDICOOT ON PLAYSTATION.

Crash Bandicoot

Any self-respecting comic hero has a sworn enemy - preferably a mad scientist - and Crash Bandicoot is no exception. Crash has always stood between the vile Doctor Neo Cortex and his goal: destroying or dominating the earth, or, for that matter, shrinking it to the size of a grape-pip. Cortex has one even greater priority: killing Crash. And of course, Cortex always fails, thanks to Bandicoot, his sister Coco and their band of friends. To counter Cortex's diabolical machines, Crash and co. need crystals, which are, natch, lying about all over the place. Whatever, Crash is ready to brave every danger; he walks, he flies (by rocket pack), he travels by giant sphere or other surreal form of locomotion, dealing with the many adversaries placed in his path by spinning on his own axis and flinging them into oblivion.

« »

Tout héros humoristique qui se respecte a un ennemi juré, de préférence un savant fou. C'est le cas de Crash Bandicoot, qui s'est toujours dressé sur le chemin de l'infâme docteur Neo Cortex lequel tente sans relâche de détruire la terre ou d'en devenir le maître (voire de la réduire à la taille d'un grain de raisin, allez savoir pourquoi)... avec tout de même une autre priorité : tuer Crash. Evidemment, ses sombres projets se heurtent toujours au courageux Bandicoot, bien décidé à empêcher Cortex d'accomplir ses funestes objectifs. Pour ce faire, Crash et ses amis (dont sa sœur Coco) ont à chaque fois besoin de cristaux, nécessaires pour contrer les machines diaboliques de Cortex, et évidemment disséminés un peu partout. Peu importe : Crash est prêt à affronter tous les dangers à pied, en fusée dorsale, dans de grosses boules ou avec tout autre moyen de transport farfelu et à combattre les maints adversaires qui se dresseront sur sa route, en tourbillonnant sur lui-même avant de les éjecter.

« »

Jeder witzige Held, der etwas auf sich hält, hat einen Erzfeind, am besten einen verrückten Wissenschaftler. So ist es auch bei Crash Bandicoot, der sich immer wieder mit dem fiesen Doktor Neo Cortex anlegt. Cortex versucht unablässig, die Erde zu zerstören oder sie sich untertan zu machen (will sie gar auf die Größe einer Rosine schrumpfen, warum, weiß keiner). Sein eigentliches Ziel, nämlich Crash zu töten, verliert er dabei keine Sekunde aus den Augen. Solche düsteren Pläne stoßen bei dem tapferen Crash jedoch stets auf Widerstand, denn der ist fest entschlossen, Cortex von seinem Vorhaben abzubringen. Dafür brauchen Crash und seine Freunde (darunter seine Schwester Coco) Kristalle. Diese wichtigen Utensilien, die den Teufelsmaschinen von Cortex Einhalt gebieten können, sind aber leider überall verstreut. Egal. Ob zu Fuß, per Rakete, in großen Kugeln oder mit jedem anderen abstrusen Transportmittel: Crash ist bereit, sich allen Gefahren zu stellen und es mit den vielen Gegnern aufzunehmen, die sich ihm in den Weg stellen.

2: ANZAHL DER JAHRE, DIE NAUGHTY DOG FÜR DIE ENTWICKLUNG VON CRASH BANDICOOT AUF PLAYSTATION BENÖTIGTE

2: C'EST LE NOMBRE D'ANNÉES DONT NAUGHTY DOG A EU BESOIN POUR DÉVELOPPER CRASH BANDICOOT SUR PLAYSTATION.

NAME
DIABLO 2

PLATFORM
PC

RELEASE
2000

EDITOR
BLIZZARD ENTERTAINMENT

DEVELOPER
BLIZZARD ENTERTAINMENT

COPYRIGHTS
© 2002 BLIZZARD ENTERTAINMENT.
ALL RIGHTS RESERVED.
BLIZZARD NORTH IS A TRADEMARK AND
BLIZZARD ENTERTAINMENT, BATTLE.NET AND
DIABLO ARE TRADEMARKS OR REGISTERED
TRADEMARKS OF BLIZZARD ENTERTAINMENT
IN THE U.S. AND OTHER COUNTRIES.

FACT
34,000 MILES: THE DISTANCE COVERED
IF ALL THE 181 MILLION VIDEO-GAMES SOLD
IN 1998 WERE PLACED END-TO-END.

Diablo

Surely Diablo was down and out? No, the demon possesses himself of the body of the brave warrior who thwarted him. Then, allying himself with those traditional forces of evil, Mephisto and Baal, he prepares to hurl the mortal world into chaos. The demons unleash their shadowy forces on the Kingdom, and rare indeed are those who can withstand these hordes of skeletons, living-dead, werewolves and other night-mare creatures. A handful of heroes fights for the survival of the world. Their alliance must triumph over profound differences. Thus the Amazon, with her deadly bow, fights shoulder-to-shoulder with the redoubtable Barbarian, who goes into battle a weapon in each hand; the astonishing Necromancer, a sinister magus who can summon the dead and force them to fight at his side, rallies to the side of the Paladin, who is not only a fine swordsman but a White Magician. The shape-changing Druid and the Sorceress - who can command the elements - join forces with the shadowy Assassin. But can even they repel Diablo's infernal hordes?

« »

Après avoir été terrassé par le brave guerrier qui a osé l'affronter, le démon Diablo réussit à prendre possession du corps de son vain-queur et s'apprête à semer le chaos dans le monde des mortels, s'alliant à d'autres forces du Mal originelles, Méphisto et Baal. Les démons lancent leurs troupes ténébreuses à l'assaut du Royaume et rares sont ceux qui peuvent et osent affronter les hordes de morts-vivants, squelettes, gargouilles et autres créatures cauchemardesques qui terrorisent les hommes. Quelques rares héros se battent pour la sur-vie du monde, s'alliant malgré leurs profondes différences : on peut ainsi voir l'Amazone, armée de son puissant arc, se battre aux côtés du redoutable Barbare qui peut se battre une arme dans chaque main. Plus étonnant encore, le Nécromancien, sombre mage pouvant invo-quer les morts et les obliger à se battre à ses côtés peut s'allier au Paladin doté de pouvoirs divins bénéfiques, mais également redouta-ble bretteur. Le Druide métamorphe, la Sorcière maîtresse des éléments et le ténébreux Assassin joignent eux aussi leurs forces afin de repousser les hordes infernales de Diablo.

« »

Kaum hat der heldenhafte Krieger ihn mitsamt dem verfluchten Stein in einer Höhle vergraben, da gelingt es dem Dämon Diablo, vom Körper seines Bezwingers Besitz zu ergreifen. Er verbündet sich mit anderen Urkräften des Bösen, namentlich mit Mephisto, dem Herrn des Hasses, und mit Baal, dem Herrn der Zerstörung, und gemeinsam schicken sie sich an, Chaos im Reich der Sterblichen zu verbreiten. Als die Dämonen den Befehl zum Sturm auf das Reich geben, gibt es nur wenige, die es wagen, sich den finsteren Horden von Zombies, Skeletten Werwölfen und anderen albtraumhaften Kreaturen in den Weg zu stellen. Schließlich finden sich doch ein paar Helden zusammen, die trotz gravierender Unterschiede gemeinsam für das Überleben der Welt kämpfen wollen: Da ist zum einen die streitbare Amazone mit ihrem gewaltigen Bogen, die Seite an Seite mit dem gefürchteten Barbaren kämpft, der beidhändig eine Waffe halten kann. Noch beein-druckender ist der Nekromant, ein finsterer Magier, der die Toten beschwört und sie zwingt, an seiner Seite zu kämpfen. Er kann sich ver-bünden mit dem Paladin, der mit guten göttlichen Gaben ausgestattet ist, aber auch ordentlich zuschlagen kann. Ebenfalls mit von der Partie sind der Druide, der seine Gestalt verändern kann, die Zauberin, die die Elemente beherrscht, und der düstere Mörder. Mit vereinten Kräften versuchen sie, Diablos teuflische Horden zurückzuschlagen.

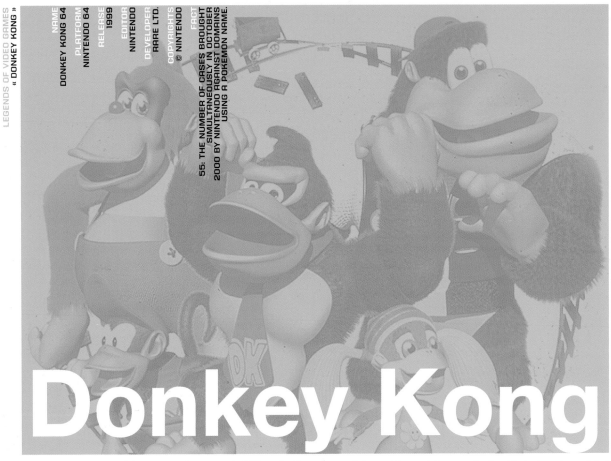

NAME
DONKEY KONG 64

PLATFORM
NINTENDO 64

RELEASE
1999

EDITOR
NINTENDO

DEVELOPER
RARE LTD.

COPYRIGHTS
© NINTENDO

FACT
55: THE NUMBER OF CASES BROUGHT
SIMULTANEOUSLY IN OCTOBER
2000 BY NINTENDO AGAINST DOMAINS
USING A POKEMON NAME.

Donkey Kong

Donkey Kong made his debut on arcade screens in 1981, as the first enemy of the world's most famous plumber, Mario. Largely modelled on King Kong, though noticeably smaller, Donkey Kong kidnapped Mario's fiancée; to liberate his beloved, Mario had to dodge the barrels rolled at him by the gorilla. After this perfunctory go at being the baddy, Donkey Kong joined the side of the angels. From 1994 on, he appeared in a series of platformers, *Donkey Kong Country*. Like most of the major Nintendo figures, Donkey Kong has had a part in a number of board games, and taken on his rivals at golf, tennis, and karting, before settling into the arenas of *Super Smash Brothers*, the combat-game where they all rumble together. The large and amiable Donkey now has a little brother, young Diddy Kong. Having accompanied his elder in a number of adventures, the little fellow got his first starring role in a wacky racer, *Diddy Kong Racing*.

« »

Premier adversaire du célèbre plombier Mario, Donkey Kong est né sur les écrans de bornes d'arcade en 1981. Largement inspiré de King Kong, Donkey Kong, plus petit que son modèle, avait alors kidnappé la fiancée de Mario, ce dernier devant éviter les tonneaux envoyés par le gorille afin de libérer sa belle. Après avoir été le méchant de service, Donkey Kong est devenu à son tour un héros, notamment à partir de 1994 dans une série de jeux de plates-formes, *Donkey Kong Country*. Comme la majeure partie des grands personnages de Nintendo, Donkey Kong a participé à plusieurs jeux de société, affrontant ses semblables au golf, au tennis ou en kart ou dans les arènes de *Super Smash Brothers*, le jeu de combat rassemblant tout ce petit monde. Aux côtés du grand primate sympathique, un autre petit singe est devenu une figure incontournable de Nintendo, le jeune Diddy Kong qui, après avoir accompagné son aîné dans plusieurs aventures, est devenu le héros principal d'un jeu de course débridé, *Diddy Kong Racing*.

« »

Donkey Kong, der erste Gegner des berühmten Klempners Mario, kam 1981 als Ballerspiel in die Spielhalle. In Anlehnung an King Kong, aber kleiner als sein Vorbild, hatte Donkey Kong die Verlobte von Mario gekidnappt. Letzterer musste erst Fässern aus dem Weg gehen, die Donkey Kong auf ihn niederwarf, bevor er seine schöne Braut befreien konnte. Nachdem Donkey Kong zunächst auf den Bösen vom Dienst abonniert war, wurde er später selbst zum Helden, insbesondere ab 1994 in dem Konsolenspiel der Serie *Donkey Kong Country*. Wie die meisten Protagonisten von Nintendo ist Donkey Kong in zahlreichen sportlichen Disziplinen gegen seinesgleichen angetreten, sei es im Golf, im Tennis, im Karting oder in den Arenen von *Super Smash Brothers*, dem Prügelspiel mit den beliebten Nintendo-Figuren. Neben dem sympathischen Gorilla gibt es noch einen kleinen Affen namens Diddy Kong, der ebenfalls zu einer unverzichtbaren Nintendo-Figur geworden ist. Nachdem er seinen älteren Bruder zunächst auf zahlreichen Abenteuern begleitet hat, ist er in *Diddy Kong Racing* nun selbst der Held eines rasanten Rennspiels geworden.

NAME
DRAGON'S LAIR 3D

PLATFORM
PC

RELEASE
2002

EDITOR
UBI SOFT

DEVELOPER
DRAGONSTONE SOFTWARE

COPYRIGHTS
© UBI SOFT

FACT
$8: THE APPROXIMATE PRODUCTION
COST OF A PLAYSTATION CD IN 1999.

Dragon's Lair

Don Bluth is a big name in cartoon strips, and was the first to combine animation and video-gaming in *Dragon's Lair*, the very first interactive cartoon. The adventure draws on medieval chivalry; its hero is Dirk, a clumsy fellow but plucky with it, who faces down the perils lurking in a shadowy castle. His goal, meritorious but oh-so-conventional, is to rescue his beloved, the charming Princess Daphne. She has been kidnapped by a mighty dragon that makes its den in the castle dungeons. The first *Dragon's Lair* was a technological tour de force rather than a successful game - its interactive component was rather slender - but it made its mark all the same, since its graphic quality was quite exceptional for the time. Nearly twenty years later, *Dragon's Lair* has returned in real-time 3D, offering a much-improved gaming experience; the gamer is plunged into peril as he directs Dirk into the murky depths of the dragon's subterranean labyrinth.

« »

Don Bluth, grand nom du dessin animé, a été le premier à accorder le film d'animation et le jeu vidéo avec *Dragon's Lair*, le tout premier cartoon interactif. Dirk, le héros de cette aventure puisant dans les clichés des contes médiévaux, est un chevalier aussi maladroit que courageux qui affrontera les dangers tapis dans un sombre château. Son objectif, aussi louable que conventionnel, est de libérer sa promise, la charmante princesse Daphne, kidnappée par un puissant dragon qui se terre au fond de la bâtisse. Si le premier *Dragon's Lair* était plus une prouesse technologique qu'une véritable réussite ludique, l'aspect interactif y étant fort limité, le jeu a marqué les esprits grâce à sa réalisation graphique, exceptionnelle pour l'époque. Presque vingt ans après le jeu original, Dragon's Lair revient en 2002, tout en 3D temps réel, pour une expérience plus ludique, qui plonge enfin le joueur dans une véritable aventure, où il peut diriger Dirk comme bon lui semble dans les profondeurs de l'antre de la créature.

« »

Der bekannte Cartoonist Don Bluth war der Erste, der den Zeichentrickfilm und das Videospiel mit *Dragon's Lair*, dem allerersten interaktiven Cartoon, verknüpfte. Dirk, der Held der Abenteuers, bedient alle Klischees mittelalterlicher Geschichten. Er ist ein ebenso linkischer wie tapferer Ritter, der den in einer düsteren Burg lauernden Gefahren trotzen muss. Sein Ziel, löblich und klassisch zugleich: die Befreiung seiner Braut, der charmanten Prinzessin Daphne, die von einem mächtigen Drachen entführt wurde, der in dem besagten Gemäuer haust. War die ursprüngliche Version von *Dragon's Lair* wegen der stark eingeschränkten Interaktivität auch nicht der absolute Renner in den Spielhallen, so hat das Spiel dennoch seine Spuren hinterlassen. Aufgrund der grafischen Umsetzung, die für die damalige Zeit sensationell war, galt das Spiel als ein kleines Wunderwerk der Technik. Zwanzig Jahre später – 2002 – erscheint die Neuauflage des Originals, alles in 3-D-Echtzeit und mit garantiertem Spielvergnügen. Den Spieler erwartet ein echtes Abenteuer, bei dem er Dirk ganz nach seinen Vorstellungen in die Höhle des Drachen führen kann.

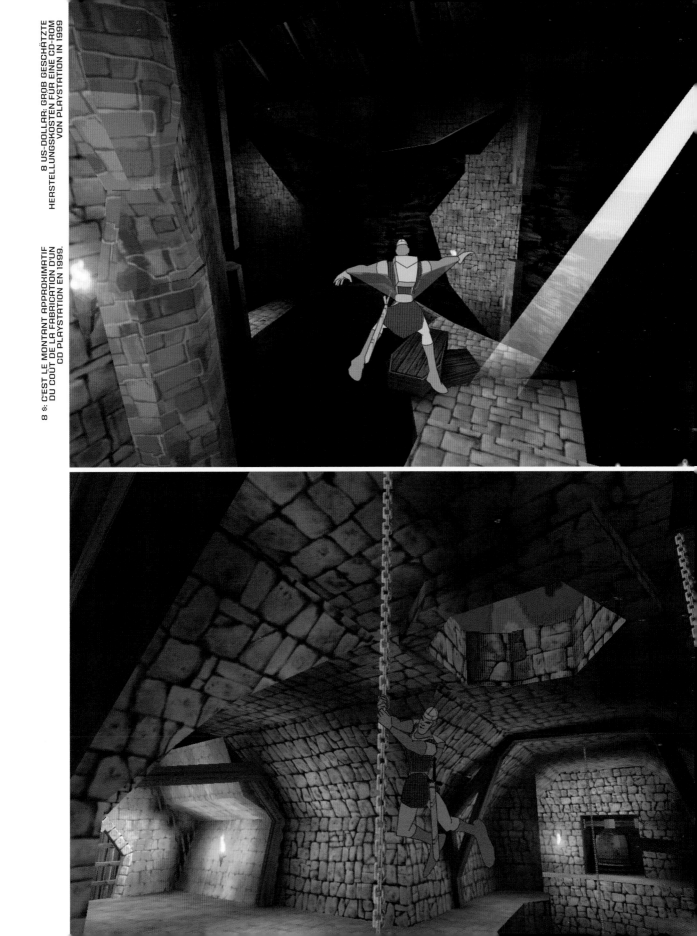

8 US-DOLLAR: GROB GESCHÄTZTE
HERSTELLUNGSKOSTEN FÜR EINE CD-ROM
VON PLAYSTATION IN 1999

8 $: C'EST LE MONTANT APPROXIMATIF
DU COÛT DE LA FABRICATION D'UN
CD PLAYSTATION EN 1999.

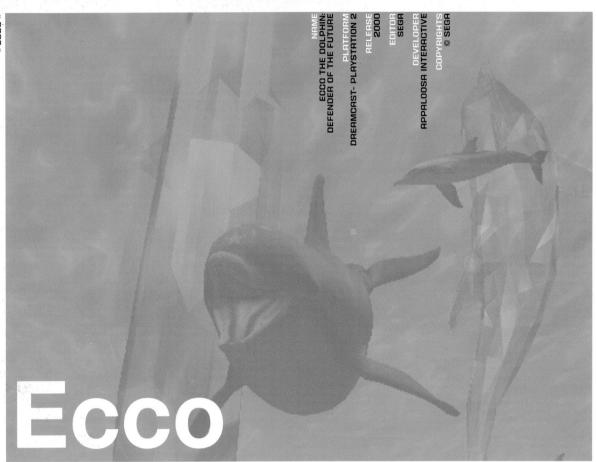

NAME
ECCO THE DOLPHIN:
DEFENDER OF THE FUTURE
PLATFORM
DREAMCAST- PLAYSTATION 2
RELEASE
2000
EDITOR
SEGA
DEVELOPER
APPALOOSA INTERACTIVE
COPYRIGHTS
© SEGA

Ecco

Ecco is not just a playful young dolphin, he is a child of destiny. Only he can save the world from The Foe, a fatal power come from outer space to destroy humanity. Aided by the speaking crystals of the Guardian, Ecco defies The Foe with his natural talents. Thanks to his aquatic mastery, he can reach great speeds and make huge leaps out of the water; he can club sharks and other enemies with his beak, and his song summons other dolphins to his rescue. Ecco's quest leads deep into the ocean, to the sublime underwater cities of Atlantis. There various obstacles await him before he can restart the astounding machines that are his last hope of repelling The Foe.

« »

Jeune dauphin joueur, Ecco est promis à un destin exceptionnel : lui seul pourra sauver le monde de l'invasion de The Foe, une sombre et mortelle puissance venue de l'espace pour détruire l'harmonie terrestre. Aidé par les cristaux parlants du Guardian, Ecco devra repousser The Foe armé de ses talents naturels : grâce à son agilité aquatique extraordinaire, il peut se propulser à grande vitesse et effectuer des sauts prodigieux hors de l'élément liquide ; son solide bec est utilisable comme massue contre d'horribles requins et autres adversaires ; son chant lui permet d'appeler les autres dauphins à l'aide, lorsqu'il se trouve dans une situation périlleuse. La quête d'Ecco l'amènera à redécouvrir les sublimes villes englouties de l'Atlantide, où il devra vaincre les obstacles se dressant sur son chemin avant de remettre en activité les étonnantes machines qui contreront la noire menace issue du fin fond de l'univers.

« »

Dem jungen, verspielten Delphin Ecco ist ein besonderes Schicksal vorbestimmt: Er allein kann die Welt vor der Invasion von The Foe retten, einer finsteren und todbringenden Supermacht aus dem Weltall, die die Harmonie auf Erden zerstören will. Ecco soll, beschützt von den sprechenden Kristallen des Guardian, The Foe zurückschlagen. Dabei vertraut er auf seine natürlichen Talente: Dank seiner außergewöhnlichen Gewandtheit im Wasser kann er sich äußerst rasch fortbewegen und gewaltige Sprünge aus dem Wasser heraus vollbringen; seine robuste Schnauze setzt er wie eine Keule gegen Furcht erregende Haifische und andere Gegner ein; mit seinem Gesang ruft er die anderen Delphine in gefährlichen Situationen zu Hilfe. Auf seiner Suche entdeckt Ecco die prachtvollen versunkenen Städte von Atlantis, in denen er erst einmal Hindernisse überwinden muss, bevor er die wunderlichen Maschinen in Gang setzen kann, die die schwarze Bedrohung aus den Weiten des Universums bezwingen werden.

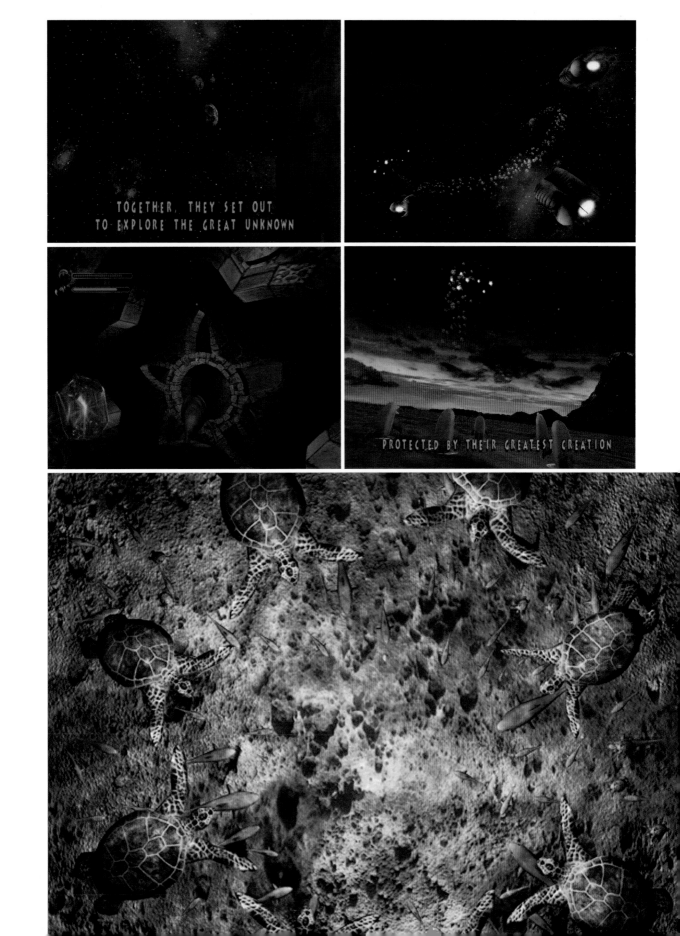

NAME
GOLDEN AXE

PLATFORM
ARCADE - MASTER SYSTEM

RELEASE
1988

EDITOR
SEGA

DEVELOPER
SEGA

COPYRIGHTS
© SEGA

Golden Axe

The evil hordes of Death Adder have invaded the world of Yuria. Seizing village after village and massacring innocents by their thousands, Death Adder takes the king and his daughter hostage and seizes the Golden Axe, a legendary weapon and source of all true power. Only three warriors dare to defy the tyrant: Ax Battler, a barbarian from the plains and master of thunder-magic, Tyris Flare, an Amazon and initiate of fire-magic, and Gilius Thunderhead, a superlative fighter able to use the forces of Earth. *Golden Axe*'s first appearance was an arcade game in 1989; its advanced graphics and immediate playability, along with the facility for two gamers to team up, made it an immediate hit. The players could put astonishing creatures to the sword, ride little dragons and cast spectacular spells. A sequel on the same principle came out in the arcades in 1992, this time allowing four players to set out on a simultaneous adventure. The more anecdotal beat'em-up that came out in 1994 was less of a hit.

« »

Les hordes maléfiques de Death Adder ont envahi le monde de Yuria. Après avoir pris possession de chaque village et tué des milliers d'innocents, Death Adder kidnappe le roi et sa fille et s'empare de la Hache d'Or, l'arme légendaire source de toute puissance. Seuls trois guerriers osent encore défier le tyran : Ax Battler, barbare des plaines qui maîtrise la magie de la foudre, Tyris Flare, l'amazone initiée à la magie du feu et Gilius Thunderhead, combattant émérite capable d'utiliser les forces de la Terre. *Golden Axe*, sorti en arcade en 1989, eut un succès retentissant grâce à des graphismes très avancés pour l'époque, une prise en main immédiate et la possibilité de jouer à deux simultanément, en coopération. Les joueurs pouvaient pourfendre d'incroyables créatures, chevaucher de petits dragons et invoquer des sorts spectaculaires. Une suite reprenant le même principe vit le jour en arcade en 1992, où quatre joueurs pouvaient se lancer dans l'aventure simultanément. Plus anecdotique, un jeu de combat à un contre un sortit en 1994, mais n'eut pas le succès de ses prédécesseurs.

« »

Die unheilvollen Horden von Death Adder sind in die Welt von Yuria eingedrungen. Nachdem sie von jedem Dorf Besitz ergriffen und tausende von Unschuldigen getötet haben, nimmt Death Adder den König und seine Tochter gefangen und bemächtigt sich der Goldenen Axt, einer legendären Wunderwaffe. Nur drei Krieger wagen es noch, dem Tyrannen die Stirn zu bieten: Ax Battler, der Barbar der Ebenen, der die Magie des Blitzes beherrscht; Tyris Flare, die Amazone, die sich auf die Magie des Feuers versteht; und Gilius Thunderhead, erprobter Kämpfer, der die Kräfte der Erde zu nutzen weiß. *Golden Axe*, 1989 als Arcade-Spiel auf den Markt gekommen, war aufgrund der für damalige Verhältnisse sehr ausgefeilten Grafik ein durchschlagender Erfolg. Es bot zudem die Möglichkeit, zwei Spieler gleichzeitig antreten zu lassen, um gemeinsam ungeheuerliche Monster abzuschlachten, auf niedlichen kleinen Drachen zu reiten und spektakuläre Schicksale heraufzubeschwören. 1992 erschien eine Fortsetzung des Ballerspiels, bei dem sich vier Spieler gleichzeitig ins Abenteuer stürzen konnten. Interessanterweise wurde es 1994 als Kampfspiel aufgelegt, doch hatte es nie den Erfolg seiner Vorgänger.

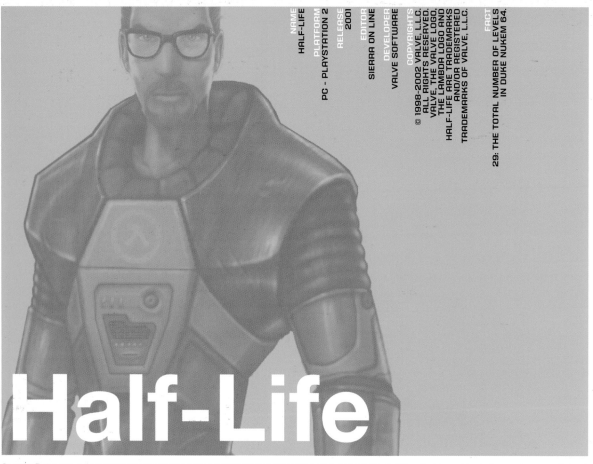

NAME HALF-LIFE

PLATFORM PC - PLAYSTATION 2

RELEASE 2001

EDITOR SIERRA ON LINE

DEVELOPER VALVE SOFTWARE

FACT 29: THE TOTAL NUMBER OF LEVELS IN DUKE NUKEM 64.

Half-Life

Gordon Freeman, a scientist experimenting with extraterrestrial matter in the secret Black Mesa base, accidentally creates a portal out of which stream hordes of horrible creatures. These monsters massacre the Black Mesa staff; Gordon is the only survivor, thanks to his suddenly-revealed combat talents. Can he fight his way out? Escape is the more perilous because a mysterious commando group is attacking Black Mesa, with orders to exterminate all witnesses. Alone against everyone, Freeman fights for his life both in the ruins of Black Mesa, and far from earth, in the unimaginable universe from which the vile invaders originated. Violent struggle, terrifying coups de théâtre and an atmosphere you could cut with a knife: the status of *Half-Life* as an all-time-great among first-person actioners is assured.

« »

Gordon Freeman, scientifique responsable d'expérimentations sur un matériau extraterrestre dans la base secrète de Black Mesa, crée accidentellement un portail d'où jaillissent des hordes d'horribles créatures. Ces monstres incontrôlables massacrent les employés de Black Mesa, et seul Gordon Freeman réussit à survivre, se découvrant de grands talents de combattant. Sa fuite, jalonnée de combats, sera d'autant plus périlleuse qu'outre ces monstres extraterrestres, de mystérieux commandos militaires assaillent Black Mesa, avec pour ordre de ne laisser aucun témoin vivant. Seul contre tous et piégé dans cet enfer, Freeman devra se battre pour rester en vie dans les ruines de Black Mesa, mais aussi loin de la terre, dans l'univers au-delà de toute imagination d'où sont venues les créatures innommables qui ont pris le contrôle de Black Mesa et menacent de s'étendre sur la terre. Affrontements violents, coups de théâtre effrayants et atmosphère à couper le souffle ont fait de *Half-Life* un incontournable du jeu d'action en vue subjective.

« »

Der Physiker Gordon Freeman, der für die Black Mesa Corporation an einem geheimen Regierungsprojekt mit außerirdischem Material arbeitet, errichtet versehentlich ein Portal, dem ganze Horden von bösartigen Aliens entspringen. Die unkontrollierbaren Monster metzeln die Angestellten von Black Mesa nieder. Nur Gordon Freeman kann sich retten. Auf der Flucht entdeckt er seine ungeahnten kämpferischen Fähigkeiten, die er immer wieder unter Beweis stellen muss. Doch nicht nur die Aliens haben es auf sein Leben abgesehen. Es gibt da auch noch eine mysteriöse Armee von Regierungssoldaten, die den Auftrag hat, alle Zeugen zu beseitigen. Und das macht die Mission umso gefährlicher. Allein gegen alle und gefangen in dieser Hölle, muss Freeman in der verwüsteten Black Mesa Corporation um sein Leben kämpfen. Und so auch fernab der Welt, in einem Universum jenseits aller Vorstellungskraft, denn von dort kommen die unzähligen Aliens, die sich der Black Mesa Corporation bemächtigt haben und sich über die ganze Erde auszubreiten drohen. Brutale Kampfszenen, Überraschungseffekte und eine spannungsgeladene Atmosphäre haben *Half-Life* zu einem unvergleichlichen Action-Spiel in First-Person-Perspektive gemacht, das man sich nicht entgehen lassen darf.

Infantry grunt

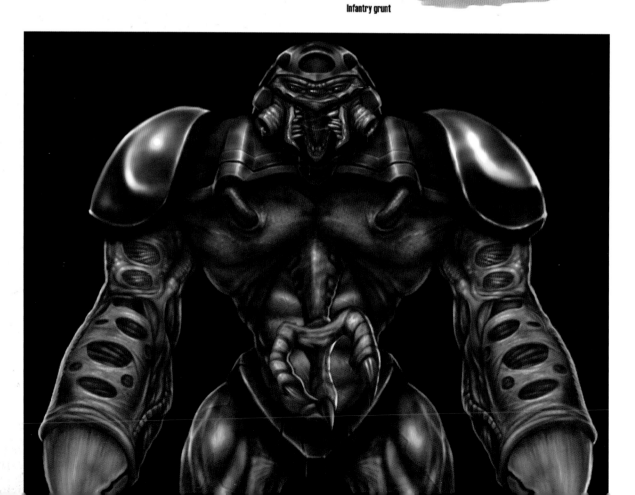

NAME
PAC-MAN SERIES

PLATFORM
ARCADE - GAME BOY
GAME BOY ADVANCE - PLAYSTATION

RELEASE
2002

EDITOR
NAMCO

DEVELOPER
NAMCO

COPYRIGHTS
© NAMCO

FACT
1979: THE YEAR IN WHICH DEVELOPMENT OF PAC-MAN BEGAN.

Pac-Man

What a career Pac-Man has had! This little yellow pill-and ghost-ingurgitating sphere was created by Namco in the prehistory of video-games, and is further proof that a very simply designed character can become a great name and preside over multifarious genres. Ghost-hunting in simple labyrinths won over innumerable gamers, and they were quick to take Pac-Man's fiancée, Miss Pac Man, to their hearts; she too gobbles little white pills and ghosts. With advancing technology, the rough circle of the early years, split by an ear-to-ear smile, has been refined to a perfect sphere. And to meet the needs of new games, Pac-Man has on occasion acquired arms and legs and a little snub nose. Alongside today's games, the original Pac-Man principle can't bring in new gamers, but all those who discovered video-games in his person keep a special place in their hearts for the voracious little bubble.

« »

Quelle consécration pour la petite boule jaune mangeuse de pilules et de fantômes créée par Namco au tout début de l'histoire du jeu vidéo ! Une fois encore, la preuve est faite qu'un personnage au design tout simple peut devenir un grand nom fédérateur. La chasse aux fantômes dans de simples labyrinthes a conquis d'innombrables joueurs qui ont aussi adopté la fiancée de Pac-Man, Miss Pac Man, tout aussi friande de petites pilules blanches et de revenants. Evolution technologique oblige, le cercle approximatif des premiers jeux, fendu d'un énorme sourire, s'est affiné avec le temps, devenant une vraie boule à la courbure parfaite, puis gagnant, pour les besoins de certains jeux, des jambes, des bras et un petit nez retroussé. Si, face aux concepts évolués des jeux d'aujourd'hui, le principe des premières aventures de Pac-Man n'attire plus de nouveaux joueurs, tous ceux qui ont grandi et ont découvert le jeu vidéo avec Pac-Man, réservent une place d'honneur à la boule jaune gourmande.

« »

Was für eine glänzende Bestätigung für die kleine gelbe, Energiepillen und Gespenster verschlingende Kugel, die Namco ins Leben rief, als das Videospiel noch in den Kinderschuhen steckte! Einmal mehr ist der Beweis erbracht, dass eine Figur von schlichtem Design zu einem großen Markennamen avancieren kann. Zahllose Spieler sind der Jagd auf Gespenster in diesen klar gegliederten Labyrinthen verfallen. Und inzwischen haben sie auch Ms. Pac Man ins Herz geschlossen, die genauso hungrig auf die kleinen weißen Pillen und Gespenster ist wie ihr Verlobter. Der eher grob umrissene Kreis mit dem breiten Grinsen wurde mit der Zeit immer raffinierter – technisches Know-how verpflichtet – , und hat sich zu einer wohlgeformten Kugel gemausert, die inzwischen Arme, Beine und eine kleine Stupsnase dazubekommen hat, um so dem einen oder anderen Spiel gerecht werden zu können. Auch wenn das simple Prinzip der ersten Pac-Man-Adventures angesichts der hoch entwickelten Konzeption der heutigen Spiele kaum noch einen neuen Spieler aus der Reserve lockt, so räumen doch all die jenigen, der gefräßigen gelben Kugel einen Ehrenplatz ein, die mit Pac-Man aufgewachsen sind und mit ihm das Videospiel entdeckt haben.

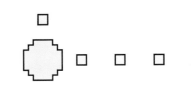

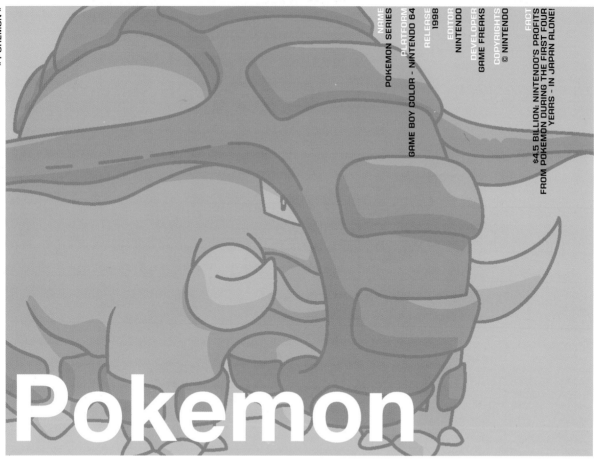

NAME	PLATFORM	RELEASE	EDITOR	DEVELOPER	COPYRIGHTS	FACT
POKEMON SERIES	GAME BOY COLOR - NINTENDO 64	1998	NINTENDO	GAME FREAKS	© NINTENDO	$4.5 BILLION: NINTENDO'S PROFITS FROM POKEMON DURING THE FIRST FOUR YEARS - IN JAPAN ALONE!

Pokemon

Like most boys of his age, Ash dreams of becoming a great Pokemon-trainer. There are dozens of species of Pokemons, all pets, each categorised by its relation to the elements (earth, air, water, fire) and realms (vegetable, mineral). And they can all be trained up for the famous Pokemon tournaments. Ash's aspiration is realised when Professor Shen gives him a young Pokemon - and a mission: to catalogue Pokemons planet-wide. He must scour the globe, catching new Pokemons and pitting himself against the trainers of every town on the road. Somewhere between adventure game and tactical combat, the *Pokemon* series has, over a few short years, become one of the star attractions of video-gaming; players of every age love the innumerable "pocket monsters" and the collection and swapping system that has extended the licence to board games, animations and feature films. At every stage of the saga, new Pokemons have appeared; their world-wide fan-base knows every one of the more than 250 species by heart.

« »

Comme bien des garçons de son âge, Ash rêve de devenir un grand dresseur de Pokemon. Ces animaux, dont on dénombre plusieurs dizaines d'espèces, catégorisées selon leur lien avec les élémentaires (eau, feu, foudre etc.) et les règnes (végétae, minérae etc.), sont autant de compagnons domestiques ou de combattants à manager dans les célèbres tournois Pokemon. Les aspirations d'Ash prennent forme lorsque le professeur Shen lui confie un jeune Pokemon et une mission : répertorier tous les Pokemon de la planète. Sa quête le fera sillonner le monde, attraper de nouveaux *Pokemon* et affronter les plus grands dresseurs de chaque ville. Entre jeu d'aventure et jeu de combat tactique, la série Pokemon est devenue en quelques années un incontournable, les joueurs de tout âge et de tous horizons ayant été séduits par les innombrables Pokemon, le système de collection et d'échange qui a étendu la licence à d'autres supports, comme des jeux de société, des séries animées et des longs métrages. A chaque nouvelle étape de la saga, de nouveaux Pokemon sont apparus, et aujourd'hui les fans du monde entier en connaissent par cœur plus de 250 espèces différentes.

« »

Wie andere Jungs seines Alters träumt auch Ash davon, ein berühmter Pokémon-Trainer zu werden. Diese Tiere, von denen zig Arten bekannt sind, die sich je nach ihrer Verbindung mit den Elementen (Feuer, Wasser, Blitz u.a.) und den Reichen (Pflanzen, Mineralien usw.) einteilen lassen, können sowohl Haustiere als auch Kampftiere sein, die es in den berühmten Pokémon-Turnieren unter einen Hut zu bringen gilt. Der Wunsch von Ash nimmt Form an, als ihm Professor Eich einen jungen Pokémon und einen Auftrag anvertraut: Er soll alle Pokémon des Planeten fotografieren. Seine Suche führt ihn kreuz und quer über den Globus, treibt ihm neue Pokémon ins Netz und lässt ihn gegen die größten Pokémon-Meister jeder Stadt antreten. Die Pokémon-Serie, eine Mischung aus Adventure-Spiel und taktischem Kampfspiel, ist innerhalb weniger Jahre zu einem Muss geworden. Spieler jeglichen Alters und aus allen Himmelsrichtungen haben sich von den unzähligen *Pokémon* verzaubern lassen. Längst gehören neben den Sammel- und Tauschkarten auch Gesellschaftsspiele, Comics und Filme zur Pokémanie. In jeder neuen Episode der Saga treten neue Pokémon auf, und heute kennen die Fans auf der ganzen Welt mehr als 250 verschiedene Arten auswendig.

NAME RAYMAN SERIES

PLATFORM PC-PLAYSTATION-PLAYSTATION 2
DREAMCAST- GAME BOY ADVANCE
XBOX - GAMECUBE

RELEASE 1995

EDITOR UBI SOFT

DEVELOPER UBI SOFT

COPYRIGHTS © UBI SOFT

FACT
650,000: THE NUMBER OF GAME BOY ADVANCE
ON SALE IN JAPAN ON THE DAY OF ITS RELEASE.
IT IS ALSO THE NUMBER OF GBA SOLD DURING
THE FIRST 48 HOURS OF SALES.

Rayman

This round little man, all protuberant nose and hands and feet that float around his body, quickly won the affection of gamers young and old. His naïve, pastel universe is populated by sweet creatures such as the Globox, the Teensies, Carmen the whale and a host of others. Rayman's only weapons are his fists, which he projects at supersonic speeds, and two locks of hair that rotate like heli-blades; with these he takes on the various unsavoury characters attempting to enslave the peace-loving Teensies.

Rayman began as a platform hero, but has since become a major figure in educational software for six to nine-year-olds. He is now a pillar of the industry, with 10 million games sold worldwide in six years (1995-2001).

« »

Tout en rondeurs, doté d'un nez proéminent, de mains et de pieds flottant autour de son corps, Rayman est rapidement devenu une des coqueluches des joueurs, y compris des plus grands. Son univers pastel et naïf est peuplé de créatures plus adorables les unes que les autres, telles les Globox, les Ptizêtres, Carmen la baleine et bien d'autres encore. Armé de son poing qu'il peut projeter à vive allure et aidé de ses deux grandes mèches de cheveux, pouvant faire office de pales d'hélicoptère, Rayman affronte des adversaires peu recommandables qui tous veulent asservir les pacifiques Ptizêtres.

S'il a commencé sa carrière comme héros de jeu de plates-formes, Rayman est aussi devenu le héros de logiciels éducatifs pour les 6-9 ans. Aux côtés des autres grandes figures du jeu vidéo, Rayman est désormais une figure incontournable, avec plus de 10 millions de jeux vendus de par le monde en six ans, de 1995 à 2001.

« »

Rayman, der knuffige Held mit der vorspringenden Nase, hat innerhalb kürzester Zeit die Herzen der Spieler erobert, und nicht nur die der Kinder. In seiner pastellfarbenen, kindlichen Welt leben Kreaturen, von denen eine liebenswerter ist als die andere, zum Beispiel Globox, die Kleinlinge, Carmen, der Wal und viele andere mehr. Mit seiner Faust, die blitzschnell zuschlagen kann, und seinen beiden gewaltigen Haarsträhnen, die ihm als Rotorblätter wie bei einem Helikopter dienen, kämpft Rayman gegen finstere Gestalten, die allesamt die friedlichen Kleinlinge unterwerfen wollen.

Rayman hat seine Karriere zwar als Held von Konsolenspielen gestartet, ist inzwischen aber auch zum Helden von Lernspielen für die Altersgruppe der 6- bis 9-Jährigen avanciert. Neben anderen großen Namen des Videospiels gehört Rayman mit weltweit mehr als zehn Millionen verkauften Spielen innerhalb von sechs Jahren (von 1995 bis 2001) zu den Charakteren, die man unbedingt kennen sollte.

NAME
SHENMUE
SHENMUE 2
PLATFORM
DREAMCAST
RELEASE
1999
EDITOR
SEGA
DEVELOPER
AM2
COPYRIGHTS
© SEGA/AM2

Shenmue

One dark day of November 1986, Ryo Hazuki returns to his home to find his father dying, beaten to death by one Lan Di, a sinister Chinese master whose goal is to recover a sacred medallion (the Dragon Mirror) held by the Hazuki family. Holding back his tears, the young Ryo swears to avenge his father and sets out in search of Lan Di. Ryo's story is still incomplete today. After two episodes, which have seen him travel from Yokosuka through Hong Kong to Kowloon in China, Ryo has acquired considerable experience as a martial arts champion, and met tried and trusty friends such as Ren, a former gang-leader, and Xui Ying Hong, the wonderful woman kung-fu master. Above all, the *Shenmue* adventure has forged Ryo's character; he has matured and discovered the highs and lows of existence. The *Shenmue* series is more than a simple adventure game; it is an incomparable gaming experience. The cohesion and realism of its universe takes the player beyond normal gaming horizons, in an entirely credible virtual world. It is a full-scale initiatory quest, founded on Japanese traditions and values, and superlatively visualized.

« »

En un sombre jour de novembre 1986, Ryo Hazuki rentre chez lui pour trouver son père agonisant, frappé à mort par un certain Lan Di, un sombre maître chinois dont le but absolu est de récupérer un médaillon sacré (le Dragon Mirror) détenu par la famille Hazuki. Ravalant ses larmes, le jeune Ryo jure de venger son père et part à la recherche de Lan Di. L'histoire de Ryo est aujourd'hui encore inachevée. Après deux épisodes qui l'ont fait voyager de Yokosuka à Kowloon en Chine, en passant par Hong Kong, Ryo a su acquérir une grande expérience de champion en arts martiaux et a rencontré de solides amis tels Ren, ancien leader d'un gang ou Xui Ying Hong, femme sublime mais aussi maître en kung-fu. Mais surtout, l'aventure *Shenmue* a forgé le caractère de Ryo, qui a gagné en maturité et découvert les plaisirs et les déconvenues de la vie. Plus qu'un jeu d'aventure, la série *Shenmue* est une expérience ludique encore inégalée : la cohésion et le réalisme de l'univers *Shenmue* mènent le joueur, au-delà du simple jeu, dans un monde virtuel des plus crédibles, autant par sa réalisation extraordinaire que par son histoire, une véritable quête initiatique fondée sur les grandes valeurs et les traditions japonaises.

« »

An einem düsteren Novembertag im Jahre 1986 findet Ryo Hazuki seinen Vater sterbend zu Hause vor, tödlich getroffen von einem gewissen Lan Di, einem zwielichtigen chinesischen Meister, dessen ausschließliches Ziel die Beschaffung des Dragon Mirror ist, eines heiligen Medaillons, das sich im Besitz der Familie Hazuki befindet. Nur mit Mühe kann der junge Ryo die Tränen zurückhalten. Er schwört, seinen Vater zu rächen, und macht sich auf die Suche nach Lan Di. Die Geschichte von Ryo ist bis heute unvollendet. Innerhalb von zwei Episoden, die ihn von Yokosuka über Hongkong bis ins chinesische Kowlon geführt haben, hat Ryo reichlich Erfahrungen als Meister der Kampfkünste sammeln können und zuverlässige Freunde gefunden, darunter Ren, den ehemaligen Bandenführer, oder die großartige Xui Ying Hong, die neben ihren fraulichen Qualitäten auch meisterliche Fähigkeiten im Kung-Fu vorweisen kann. Vor allem aber hat das Abenteuer *Shenmue* Ryos Charakter geformt. Er ist inzwischen reifer geworden und lernt die Freuden, aber auch die Enttäuschungen des Lebens kennen. Die Reihe *Shenmue* hat mehr zu bieten als reines Abenteuer, es ist ein bislang unerreichtes Spielerlebnis, bei dem das kohärente und realistische *Shenmue*-Szenario den Spieler über das einfache Spiel hinaus in eine virtuelle, aber höchst glaubwürdige Welt entführt, und das betrifft sowohl die fantastische grafische Umsetzung als auch die Geschichte selbst. *Shenmue* erzählt von einer wahrhaften Erfahrungssuche, basierend auf den großen Werten und Traditionen des alten Japan.

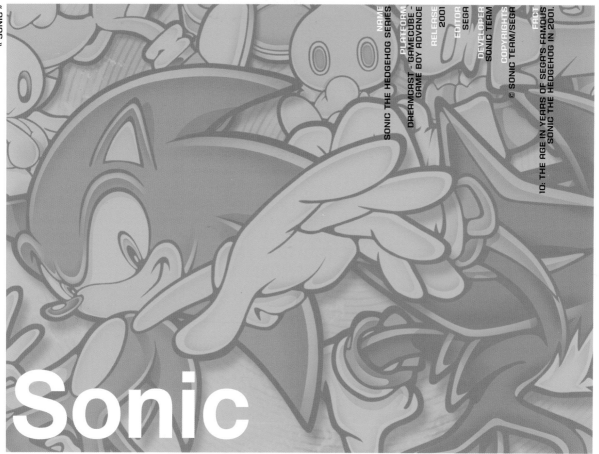

NAME SONIC THE HEDGEHOG SERIES

PLATFORM DREAMCAST - GAMECUBE - GAME BOY ADVANCE

RELEASE 2001

EDITOR SEGA

DEVELOPER SONIC TEAM

COPYRIGHTS © SONIC TEAM/SEGA

FACT 10: THE AGE IN YEARS OF SEGA'S FAMOUS SONIC THE HEDGEHOG IN 2001.

Sonic

Sonic is undoubtedly a major video-game star. Over the course of his adventures, Sega's mascot, a blue hedgehog, has been joined by a whole string of other characters, all intent on defeating the vile Dr Eggman, a mad scientist who transforms peaceful animals into monstrous combat robots. But Sonic, Tails, and Knuckles have other enemies too: Shadow, the black hedgehog secretly created by Eggman to counter his eternal adversaries, and the mysterious Red, a female bat, also set on eliminating Sonic. The hedgehog's incredible agility and ability to run astoundingly fast - especially when rolled up for max velocity - is severely tested by this evil trio. With such fearful opposition, Knuckles, Tail and his other friends naturally have to be supplemented by other adjutants: Tikal, Amy Rose and Chao...

« »

Sonic fait incontestablement partie des figures de proue du jeu vidéo. Au fil de ses aventures, le hérisson bleu, mascotte de Sega, a été rejoint par une ribambelle de personnages qui l'aident à combattre l'infâme docteur Eggman, savant fou transformant de paisibles animaux en monstrueux robots de combat. Mais Sonic, Tails et Knuckles affrontent aussi d'autres ennemis, dont Shadow, le hérisson noir créé en secret par Eggman pour combattre ses éternels adversaires et la mystérieuse Rouge, une chauve-souris femelle, elle aussi vouée à la destruction de Sonic. L'incroyable agilité du hérisson bleu, lui permettant de courir à une allure incroyable, surtout lorsqu'il se recroqueville en boule afin d'atteindre des vitesses encore plus époustouflantes, sera mise à rude épreuve face à ce trio terrifiant. Aussi l'aide de Knuckles, Tails et d'autres protecteurs du bien, comme Tikal, Amy Rose et Chao ne sera-t-elle pas de trop...

« »

Sonic gehört längst zu den Galionsfiguren des Videospiels. Im Laufe seiner Abenteuer gesellte sich eine ganze Schar von Charakteren um den blauen Igel, das Maskottchen von Sega. Sie stehen ihm im Kampf gegen den niederträchtigen und ausgeflippten Wissenschaftler Doktor Eggman bei, der friedliche Tiere in scheußliche Kampfroboter verwandelt. Aber Sonic, Tails und Knuckels bieten auch anderen Feinden die Stirn, wie dem schwarzen Igel Shadow, den Eggman in aller Heimlichkeit geschaffen hat, um seine ewigen Rivalen zu bekämpfen, und der mysteriösen Rouge The Bat, die er auch auf die Vernichtung von Sonic ansetzt. Der unglaublich flinke blaue Igel (zur Kugel gerollt, legt er ein atemberaubendes Tempo an den Tag) wird vor diesem grauenhaften Trio so manche Prüfung zu bestehen haben. Deshalb kommt die Hilfe von Knuckles, Tails und anderen Beschützern des Guten wie Tikal, Amy Rose und Chao keineswegs ungelegen...

10 JAHRE: SO ALT IST SONIC, DER BERÜHMTE BLAUE IGEL VON SEGA IM JAHRE 2001.

10 ANS: C'EST L'ÂGE DE SONIC, LE CÉLÈBRE HÉRISSON BLEU DE SEGA EN 2001.

NAME
SPACE HARRIER
PLANET HARRIERS

PLATFORM
ARCADE – MASTER SYSTEM – GENESIS
GAMECUBE (FOR PLANET HARRIERS)

RELEASE
1985
2002 (FOR PLANET HARRIERS)

EDITOR SEGA

DEVELOPER SEGA

COPYRIGHTS © SEGA

Space Harrier

DragonLand is a peaceful place - or, at least, it was. But Valda the demon decided to invade. The pacifist DragonLanders have only one recourse: Harri the Sentinel. In 1985, *Space Harrier* was a veritable arcade revolution: the immense perspective effects prefigured the 3D backgrounds of today. The gamer steered Harri over-the-shoulder as he zipped over DragonLand, pitting him against enemy hordes whose tiny figures darkened the horizon, growing ever larger as they advanced shooting fireballs and lasers; dodging enemy fire, the gamer responded in kind. Two years later, Sega came up with a similar game-system in *Afterburner*, an airborne shooter with similar sensations of speed and still more striking 3D effects.

« »

DragonLand est un lieu paisible, ou du moins l'était jusqu'au jour où le démon Valda décide de l'envahir. Le peuple pacifiste de DragonLand ne peut envoyer qu'une seule personne combattre l'envahisseur, Harri, la Sentinelle.

Sorti en salle d'arcade en 1985, *Space Harrier* fut une véritable révolution : sa réalisation donnant une impression de perspective immense laissait présager du futur du jeu vidéo dominé par la 3D. Le joueur dirigeait Harri, vu de dos, qui volait à grande vitesse au-dessus de DragonLand, affrontant des hordes d'ennemis qui apparaissaient, minuscules, à l'horizon et grossissaient en s'approchant, crachant boules de feu et rayons laser au héros qui répliquait en évitant les rafales adverses. Selon un système de jeu similaire, Sega sortit deux ans plus tard *Afterburner*, jeu de combat d'avion qui offrait des sensations de vitesse et de profondeur 3D encore plus saisissantes.

« »

DragonLand ist ein friedlicher Ort oder zumindest war er bis zu dem Tag, als der Dämon Valda beschloss, ihn zu überfallen. Die friedfertigen Bewohner von DragonLand haben nur einen, den sie in den Kampf gegen den Eindringling schicken können, und das ist Harri, der Sentinel („Wachposten").

Das 1985 erschienene Ballerspiel *Space Harrier* revolutionierte den Spiele-Markt durch die gelungene perspektivische Darstellung, die bereits erahnen ließ, dass die Zukunft der Videospiele von der 3-D-Optik bestimmt sein würde. In *Space Harrier* sah der Spieler den Helden Harri, den er steuerte und der mit großer Geschwindigkeit über DragonLand hinwegflog, von hinten – der Spieler blickte ihm sozusagen über die Schulter, während dieser gegen feindliche Horden ankämpfen musste. Die Monster erschienen erst winzigklein am Horizont, wurden aber immer größer, je näher sie kamen, und zielten mit Feuerkugeln und Laserstrahlen gegen Harri, der zurückfeuerte und gleichzeitig versuchte, den gegnerischen Angriffen auszuweichen. Nach dem gleichen Muster brachte Sega zwei Jahre später *Afterburner* auf den Markt, ein Action-Spiel um Kampfflugzeuge, das einen noch größeren Geschwindigkeitsrausch und noch mehr dreidimensionale Tiefe bot.

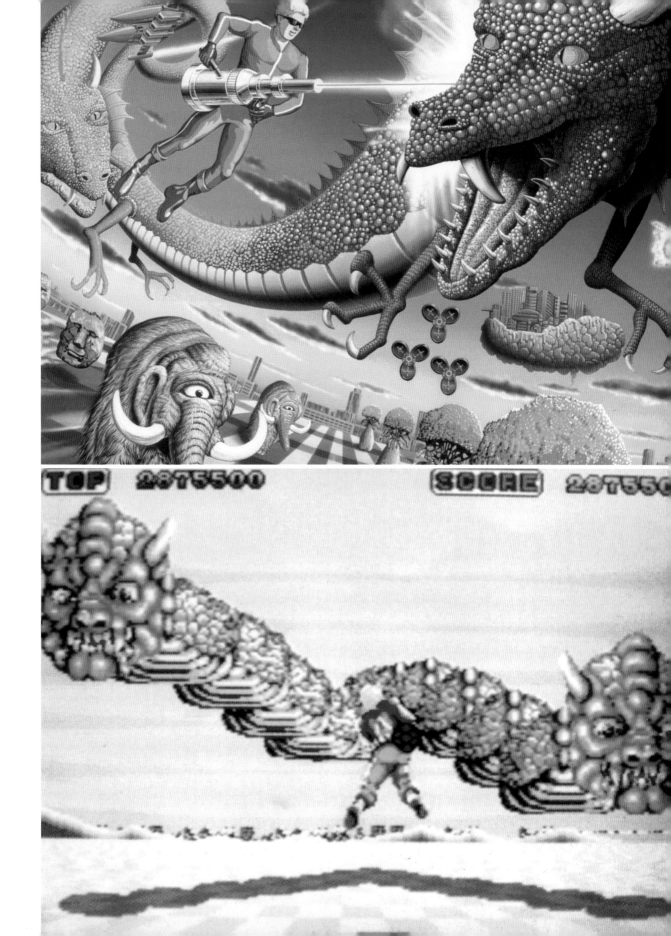

NAME
STARFOX ADVENTURES:
DINOSAUR PLANET

PLATFORM
NINTENDO 64 - GAMECUBE

RELEASE
2002

EDITOR
NINTENDO

DEVELOPER
RARE LTD.

COPYRIGHTS
© NINTENDO

FACT
6.18 MILLION: THE RECORD FOR SALES
OF A SINGLE GAME IN JAPAN, HELD BY
SUPER MARIO BROS. ALL THE POKEMON
VERSIONS PUT TOGETHER 'ONLY' REACHED
6 MILLION COPIES SOLD.

P – 376

Starfox

Having earned his spurs in ferocious space-dogfights, Fox McCloud, no ordinary fox he, lands on a strange planet populated by mutant dinosaurs, intent on discovering the plans of their creator, the infamous General Scales. Armed with a magic wand (with which to strike his adversaries, move objects or transmute his enemies), and assisted by his inseparable comrades, Slippy and Peppy (and any new friends that he makes during his trip), Fox scours the planet on foot, mounted on a triceratops or pterodactyl, and, of course, on board his space fighter Arwing. Having pushed the Super Nintendo and Nintendo 64 technology to its limits with its 3D space-dogfights, the *Starfox* team seems determined to exploit the full technological resources of the new Nintendo console, the Gambecube.

« »

Après avoir acquis ses lettres de noblesse lors de farouches combats spatiaux, Fox McCloud, renard d'élite, atterrit sur une étrange pla-nète peuplée de dinosaures mutants, afin d'enquêter sur les plans sombres de leur créateur, l'infâme Général Scales. Armé d'un bâton magique (pour frapper ses adversaires, déplacer des objets ou transformer ses ennemis) et aidé par ses inséparables compagnons de bataille, Slippy et Peppy (mais aussi de nouveaux amis qu'il rencontrera pendant son périple), Fox sillonnera la planète à pied, sur le dos d'un tricératops ou d'un ptérodactyle et bien sûr, de temps en temps, dans le cockpit de son chasseur spatial Arwing. Après avoir repoussé les limites technologiques de la Super Nintendo et de la Nintendo 64 dans des jeux de combat spatial en trois dimensions, l'équipe de StarFox semble bien décidée à exploiter à l'extrême les capacités de la nouvelle console de Nintendo, la Gamecube.

« »

Nachdem er bei erbitterten Weltraumkampfhandlungen seine Glanzstunde erlebte, landet der Elitefuchs Fox McCloud auf einem sonder-baren, von mutierten Dinosauriern bevölkerten Planeten, um die finsteren Pläne ihres Schöpfers, des anrüchigen General Scales aufzu-decken. Ausgestattet mit einem Zauberstab (um so seine Gegner zu schlagen, Gegenstände zu verrücken oder seine Feinde zu verwan-deln) und unterstützt von seinen unzertrennlichen Kampfgefährten Slippy und Peppy (aber auch von neuen Freunden, die er auf seiner Reise treffen wird), durchstreift er den Planeten zu Fuß, auf dem Rücken eines Triceratops oder eines Pterodactylos und natürlich von Zeit zu Zeit im Cockpit seines Raumflugzeugs Arwing. Nachdem bereits mit Super Nintendo und Nintendo 64 die technologischen Grenzen drei-dimensionaler Spiele nach vorne verschoben wurden, ist das StarFox-Team nun fest entschlossen, die Möglichkeiten der neuen Konsole von Nintendo, des Gamecube, voll auszuschöpfen.

6,18 MILLIONS: C'EST LE RECORD DE VENTES
D'UN JEU À CE JOUR AU JAPON, DÉTENU PAR
SUPER MARIO BROS. TOUTES LES VERSIONS DE
POKÉMON RÉUNIES N'ATTEIGNENT "QUE" LES 6
MILLIONS D'EXEMPLAIRES VENDUS.

6,18 MILLIONEN: VERKAUFSREKORD DES SPIELS
SUPER MARIO BROS. IN JAPAN: ALLE
POKÉMON-VERSIONEN ZUSAMMENGENOMMEN
WURDEN „NUR" 6 MILLIONEN MAL VERKAUFT.

NAME
DAVID CAGE
BORN
1969
HOME TOWN
PARIS, FRANCE
OCCUPATION
C.E.O.
KEY TITLES
FAHRENHEIT (2002) QUANTIC DREAM
OMIKRON: THE NOMAD
SOUL (1999) QUANTIC DREAM

«Licenced Games»
David Cage

Realities and Virtual Worlds

The frontier between fiction and reality is hard to define. Who can say where reality and perception part company? What distinguishes reality from what we think we see? No author conveys this strange dislocation better than Philip K. Dick. His entire oeuvre reflects the schizophrenia of humankind living in a world which is not as it believes. That Dick's theme thus perfectly anticipated developments in our own world of hyper-communication and virtual universes has contributed to the renaissance of his work. Of course, he is not alone in perceiving the ambiguity of our world or worlds. Well before him, the Pre-Socratic philosopher Parmenides had written that the world is not as we see it, and that we perceive only a world of semblance. Plato, too, argued that most of us have access only to a reflection of reality, to imperfect and inexact images in which we can place no trust. The metaphor of the Cave, in which fettered men take shadows for reality, exemplifies this: 'Such men will attribute reality only to the shadows of fabricated objects'.

Interactive fiction is undoubtedly located in the shadowy regions of the cave-wall. But, unlike other forms of fiction, it not only tells a story, but offers access to other worlds, worlds necessarily more exalted than our own.

Philosophy is not the only discipline to have contemplated alternative worlds. Closer to our own lives, quantum physics offers extra-ordinary scope to the imagination within the strictest scientific constraints. In quantum terms, the same experiment conducted under the same conditions does not necessarily produce the same result. A particle will steer now left, now right, for no known reason.

In 1957, the physicist Hugh Everett III propounded a curious theory: there is no such thing as chance - the particle simply did go both ways at once. In 'our' universe, it went left, in another it went right. Every time an alternative arises, each possibility is realised in a parallel universe. There are therefore an infinite number of universes, some similar, some very different to our own.

I have borrowed two things from this. The first is the name of my development studio, Quantic Dream; I wanted it to stand, like quantum physics, half-way between technology and the irrational. The second is the notion of parallel universes.

This concept underpinned my first game: Nomad Soul. I wanted my game-world to be a vision of our own in a parallel universe - as if a tiny evolutionary difference had separated them in a distant past. This disjunction - like the butterfly of chaos theory - has decisively influenced their futures.

There was more to this line of thought. Perhaps each of us has his or her double in parallel universes, beings strictly identical with ourselves but born in a different world and therefore different. Meeting David Bowie allowed me to test this concept. Bowie was happy to consider what he might have become in a different world; indeed, he clearly wanted his parallel self to be diametrically opposed to our own David Bowie. Each of the two roles I suggested reflected a facet of his personality.

He was first and foremost singer of the 'Dreamers', a group banned by the totalitarian government of Omikron for its subversive ideas. To create this character, we used photos of Bowie taken when he was around twenty-five. We made him a rebel against the system, a sort of Futurist troubadour whose mask seemed intended to prove that he could wear more than one face. This version was, of course, inspired by the 'rebel' era of Bowie's career, in which his ideas were considered subversive by 'our' establishment. It also alluded to the many personae that he has since adopted. The poverty of the Dreamers, on the other hand, with their boho life-style, was diametrically opposed to Bowie's own, since he had just founded his own bank and had his back-catalogue listed on the stock-market.

The second character in Bowie's form was Boz, the Virtual Being. Boz was the spiritual master of a sect called the Awoken, whose goal was to open the eyes of the population to the manipulations practised by the Omikron politicians. The government had ordered his execution, but his soul had taken refuge in the Network. He thus became a virtual being, without material existence, immensely old, who could only exist for a few minutes without the Net. For this character, our model was today's Bowie. He had the detachment of a man of

experience, along with a reassuring paternal aspect, and above all, the spiritual master/guru aspect required for the character (he had, after all, just launched his own on-line community, BowieNet). The notion that Boz could not exist without the Network was by no means gratuitous; stars exist by and through the media.

An anecdote: when Loïc Normand, the designer of Nomad Soul, showed me his designs for Boz and the Dreamers' singer, I was a mite nervous. Boz had blue skin, no legs, and holes right through his body, while the singer was wound with rags like bandages. The designs seemed perfect for Omikron, but would Bowie approve? No problem: he immediately gave his consent.

Nomad Soul is a very modest contribution to the myth of Plato's Cave. Literature and cinema have long explored our relation to reality, and the degree in which it exists independent of our senses. Peter Weir's The Truman Show, Philip K. Dick's Ubik, Alex Proyas' Dark City, Mamoru Oshii's Avalon and Adrian Lyne's superlative Jacob's Ladder all ask the same question: is the world that surrounds us really what we think it is?

Video-gaming brings a new dimension to this question. Recent technological advances in 3D and character-AI have made ever more immersive and realistic worlds possible. Video-games do not merely recount these worlds, but integrate gamers into them by offering significant roles. When we describe video-games in these terms, a question inevitably comes to mind: is our own world not, perhaps, some perfectly immersive game, in which we role-play with the fervid conviction of those who leave only through the portal of death?

« »

Réalité(s) et Mondes Virtuels

La frontière entre fiction et réalité est parfois difficile à définir. Qui peut dire où se trouve vraiment la limite entre la réalité et la perception que nous en avons, entre ce qui existe et ce que nous croyons voir ? Aucun auteur n'a mieux retranscrit cet étrange malaise que Philip K.Dick. Toute son œuvre reflète la schizophrénie paranoïde de l'homme vivant dans un monde qui n'est pas celui qu'il croit. Si Dick revient tellement à la mode, c'est aussi parce que sa thématique anticipe parfaitement l'évolution de notre monde moderne, son hyper communication et ses mondes virtuels. Il n'est évidemment pas le seul à avoir saisi l'ambiguïté diffuse de notre monde. Bien avant lui, Parménide, le philosophe présocratique, avait déjà écrit que le monde n'était pas tel que nous le voyons, car il est recouvert par dokos, le voile. Platon avait également acquis la certitude que nous ne percevons qu'un reflet de la réalité, des images inexactes et imparfaites auxquelles on ne peut guère se fier. Sa métaphore de la Caverne où des hommes enchaînés prennent des ombres pour la réalité en demeure le meilleur exemple : « De tels hommes n'attribueront de réalité qu'aux ombres des objets fabriqués. »

La fiction interactive se situe assurément dans la zone d'ombre sur les parois de la caverne. Elle est différente des autres formes de fiction, car elle propose non seulement de raconter une histoire, mais aussi de faire partie d'un autre monde, nécessairement meilleur que le nôtre, et en tous cas plus exaltant.

La philosophie n'est pas la seule discipline à s'être penchée sur l'existence d'autres univers. Plus près de nous, la physique quantique offre à l'imagination un champ extraordinaire reposant sur des fondements scientifiques. Elle a établi que dans des conditions strictement identiques, la même expérience ne produira pas nécessairement le même résultat. Une particule choisira d'aller tantôt à gauche, tantôt à droite, sans raison apparente.

En 1957, le physicien Hugh Everett III propose une curieuse théorie : il n'y a pas de hasard, car la particule a pris les deux directions. Dans « notre » univers, elle est allée vers la gauche et dans un « autre » univers, elle est allée vers la droite. Chaque fois qu'il existe une alternative dans l'évolution d'un système, toutes les possibilités existeraient dans des univers parallèles. Il y aurait donc une infinité d'univers coexistants, très proches ou très différents les uns des autres.

J'ai emprunté deux choses à cette expérience : le nom de mon studio de développement, Quantic Dream, que je voulais — comme la physique quantique — à mi-chemin entre la technologie et l'irrationnel, et le principe des univers parallèles.

Ce concept d'univers alternatifs était à la base de ma réflexion quand j'ai écrit mon premier jeu, Nomad Soul. Je voulais que ce monde soit une alternative très ancienne de notre monde dans un univers parallèle. Une infime différence dans leur évolution les a séparés dans leur passé lointain. Comme dans l'exemple du papillon de la théorie du chaos, cet écart s'est révélé déterminant pour leur avenir.

Poursuivons le raisonnement : peut-être chacun de nous dispose-t-il d'un double dans des univers parallèles, des êtres strictement identiques mais nés dans un monde différent, donc eux-mêmes différents ? La rencontre avec David Bowie m'a permis de tester ce concept. Bowie était très ouvert à l'idée d'imaginer ce qu'il aurait pu être dans un autre monde, avec l'envie évidente de prendre le contre-pied de ce qu'il était dans le nôtre. Les deux rôles que je lui ai proposés reflétaient une facette de sa personnalité tout en jouant avec son image.

Il était d'abord le chanteur des « Dreamers », un groupe interdit par le gouvernement totalitaire d'Omikron en raison de ses idées subversives. Nous nous sommes inspirés de photos de Bowie vers l'âge de 25 ans pour créer ce personnage révolté contre le système, sorte de troubadour futuriste portant un masque sur la tête, comme pour figurer qu'il pouvait avoir plusieurs visages. Ce personnage s'inspirait bien sûr de la période « rebelle » de la carrière de Bowie, celle où ses idées étaient perçues comme dangereuses par l'establishment. Il faisait également allusion aux multiples personnalités qu'il a adoptées depuis. La pauvreté des Dreamers, vivant une vie de bohème dans les rues, était le contre-pied de l'existence réelle du chanteur, lequel venait de fonder sa propre banque et de faire coter son catalogue en bourse.

Le second personnage incarné par Bowie était Boz, l'Etre Virtuel. Il s'agissait du maître spirituel d'une secte appelée « Eveillés » dont le but était d'ouvrir les yeux de la population, de lui montrer les manipulations dont elle était l'objet de la part des politiciens d'Omikron. Alors que le gouvernement avait ordonné son exécution, son âme parvint à se réfugier sur le Réseau. Il devint dès lors un être virtuel, immatériel et suranné, ne pouvant exister que quelques minutes hors du Réseau. Pour ce personnage, nous nous sommes inspirés du Bowie actuel. Il avait le recul de l'homme qui a vécu, l'aspect paternel et rassurant, et surtout, le côté maître spirituel/gourou (il venait de lancer sa propre communauté on-line, « BowieNet ») qui collait parfaitement au personnage. L'idée qu'il ne puisse vivre longtemps en-dehors du Réseau n'était pas innocente. Elle reflétait le principe que les stars n'ont d'existence qu'à travers les médias.

Pour l'anecdote, je dois dire que lorsque Loïc Normand, le designer de Nomad Soul, me présenta ses designs pour Boz et le chanteur des Dreamers, je pris un peu peur. L'un avait la peau bleue, pas de jambes et des trous dans le corps qui permettaient de voir au travers, le second était vêtu très pauvrement, le corps enroulé dans des sortes de bandelettes. Si le design me semblait parfaitement convenir à l'univers d'Omikron, je redoutais quelque peu la réaction de Bowie. Celui-ci sembla d'emblée satisfait et nous donna immédiatement son accord.

Nomad Soul n'est qu'une très modeste contribution au mythe de la Caverne de Platon. Notre rapport à la réalité, son existence objective indépendamment de nos sens, l'existence d'autres réalités sont des sujets amplement explorés par la littérature et le cinéma. The Truman Show de Peter Weir, Ubik de Philip K.Dick, Dark City d'Alex Proyas, Avalon de Mamoru Oshii ou encore l'excellent L'Echelle de Jacob d'Adrian Lyne, tous posent de manière lancinante la même question : le monde qui nous entoure est-il réellement celui que nous croyons ?

Le jeu vidéo apporte une nouvelle dimension à cette interrogation. Les récentes avancées technologiques en terme de rendu tridimensionnel et d'intelligence comportementale lui permettent de recréer des mondes de plus en plus immersifs, de plus en plus réels. Les jeux vidéo ne se contentent plus de raconter ces mondes, ils permettent d'y participer et d'en faire partie intégrante.

« »

Reale und Virtuelle Welten

Die Grenze zwischen Fiktion und Realität ist mitunter schwer zu definieren. Wer kann mit Gewissheit sagen, wo genau die Grenze zwischen der Realität und unserer Wahrnehmung der Realität liegt, zwischen dem, was existiert, und dem, was wir zu sehen glauben. Kein Autor hat dieses seltsame Unbehagen besser beschrieben als Philip K. Dick. Sein gesamtes Werk spiegelt die paranoide Schizophrenie jener Menschen wider, die sich in einer anderen Welt wähnen als in der, die sie umgibt. Wenn Dick erneut in Mode kommt, so auch, weil seine Thematik hervorragend die Entwicklung unserer modernen Welt antizipiert, ihre Hyperkommunikation und ihre virtuellen Welten. Er ist gewiss nicht der Einzige, der die diffuse Ambiguität unserer Welt erfasst hat. Lange vor ihm hatte der vorsokratische Philosoph Parmenides bereits geschrieben, dass die Welt nicht so ist, wie wir sie sehen, da sie von einem *dokos*, einem Schleier, überdeckt ist. Auch Platon war der Meinung, dass wir nur einen Widerschein der Realität sehen, ungenaue und unvollkommene Bilder, denen man kaum vertrauen sollte. Sein Höhlengleichnis, das von Menschen handelt, die seit ihrer Kindheit gefesselt sind und die die Schatten vorübergetragener Geräte für die Realität halten, ist das beste Beispiel dafür: „Diese Leute würden nichts anderes für wahr halten als die Schatten der Geräte."

Die interaktive Fiktion ist zweifellos im Bereich der Schatten auf den Höhlenwänden anzusiedeln. Sie unterscheidet sich von den anderen Formen der Fiktion, da sie nicht nur narrativ, sondern auch Teil einer Welt ist, einer anderen Welt, die zwangsläufig besser ist als unsere oder zumindest aufregender. Neben der Philosophie haben sich weitere Disziplinen mit der Existenz anderer Welten beschäftigt. So bietet beispielsweise die Quantenphysik der Fantasie ein auf wissenschaftlichen Grundlagen beruhendes und außergewöhnlich breites Gedankenfeld. Sie statuiert, dass die Wiederholung einer Erfahrung selbst unter identischen Bedingungen nicht notwendigerweise zu dem gleichen Resultat führen müsse. Ein Teilchen wird für seine Bahn ohne ersichtlichen Grund mal die rechte, mal die linke Richtung einschlagen. 1957 stellt der Physiker Hugh Everett III eine erstaunliche Theorie auf: Es gibt keinen Zufall, da das Teilchen beide Richtungen gewählt hat. In „unserem" Universum hat es links gewählt, und in einem „anderen" Universum rechts. In allen Fällen, in denen es Alternativen in der Evolution eines Systems gibt, existieren ebendiese Möglichkeiten auch in Parallelwelten. Es gäbe also eine unbegrenzte Zahl von nebeneinander existierenden, einander ähnlichen oder sehr verschiedenen Welten.

Ich habe dieser Erfahrung zwei Dinge entnommen: den Namen meines Entwicklungsstudios, Quantic Dream, das ich mir wie die Quantenphysik als eine Schnittstelle von Technologie und Irrationalismus vorstelle, sowie das Prinzip der Parallelwelten. Dieses Konzept alternativer Welten stand am Anfang meiner Überlegung, als ich mein erstes Spiel Nomad Soul entwickelte. Ich wollte, dass diese Welt eine sehr altertümliche Alternative zu unserer Welt in einem Paralleluniversum ist. Ein winziger Unterschied in ihrer Entwicklung bewirkte in der Vergangenheit, dass sie sich trennten. Und wie in dem Schmetterlingsbeispiel der Chaostheorie hat sich diese Abweichung als maßgebend für ihre Zukunft erwiesen.

Spinnt man den Faden dieser Überlegung weiter, so besitzt jeder von uns vielleicht einen Doppelgänger in diesen Parallelwelten, identische, aber in einer anderen Welt geborene Wesen, die folglich anders sind. Die Begegnung mit David Bowie gab mir die Gelegenheit, dieses Konzept zu testen. Bowie stand der Idee, sich vorzustellen, was er in einer anderen Welt sein würde, sehr offen gegenüber. Dabei war er jedoch von dem so verständlichen Verlangen getrieben, sich genau das Gegenteil dessen, was er auf unserer Welt darstellt, zu imaginieren. Die beiden Rollen, die ich ihm vorschlug, reflektierten Facetten seiner Persönlichkeit und waren im spielerischen Umgang mit seinem Image entstanden. Er war zunächst der Sänger der Dreamers, einer Gruppe, die wegen ihrer subversiven Ideen vom totalitären Omikron-Regime verboten worden war. Wir haben uns von seinen Fotos als 25-Jähriger inspirieren lassen, um diese gegen das System revoltierende Figur zu schaffen, eine Art futuristischer Troubadour mit einer Maske auf dem Kopf, die veranschaulicht, dass er mehrere Gesichter haben könnte. Diese Figur nahm selbstverständlich Anleihen bei der „rebellischen" Phase seiner Karriere, als das Establishment Bowies Ideen als gefährlich empfand. Sie spielte auch auf die verschiedenen Persönlichkeiten an, die er sich in seiner Karriere zu Eigen gemacht hat. Die Armut der Dreamers, die ihr Leben als Bohemiens auf der Straße zur Schau stellten, war seiner wirklichen Existenz als Sänger, der gerade seine eigene Bank gegründet hatte und an die Börse ging, diametral entgegengesetzt.

Die zweite, von Bowie verkörperte Figur war Boz, das virtuelle Wesen. Es ging um den spirituellen Meister einer Sekte namens „Die Erweckten", deren Ziel es war, der Bevölkerung die Augen zu öffnen, ihr aufzuzeigen, dass die Politiker von Omikron sie manipulierten. Während die Regierung Boz' Hinrichtung anordnete, gelang es seiner Seele, sich in das Netz zu flüchten. Er wurde von nun an zu einem virtuellen Wesen, immateriell und antiquiert, und war außerhalb des Netzes nur noch für wenige Minuten lebensfähig. Für diese Figur haben wir uns von dem derzeitigen Bowie inspirieren lassen. Sie hatte die Souveränität eines Mannes, der sein Leben gelebt hat, der väterlich ist und zu trösten vermag, sich vor allem aber als spiritueller Meister, als Guru versteht. Bowie hatte erst kurz zuvor seine eigene Online-Gemeinde „BowieNet" ins Leben gerufen, was hervorragend mit dieser Figur in Einklang stand. Die Idee, dass er nicht lange außerhalb des Netzes leben könnte, kam nicht von ungefähr. Sie reflektierte das Prinzip, dass die Stars ihre Existenz allein den Medien verdanken. Dazu fällt mir eine kleine Anekdote ein: Als mir Loïc Normand, der Artdirector von Nomad Soul, seine Entwürfe für Boz und den Sänger der Dreamers zeigte, bekam ich es ein wenig mit der Angst zu tun. Die erste Figur hatte blaue Haut, keine Beine und Löcher im Körper, durch die man hindurchschauen konnte, die zweite war sehr ärmlich gekleidet, von einer Art Bändern umwickelt. Und obwohl dies dem Universum von Omikron ganz und gar angemessen war, fürchtete ich Bowies Reaktion ein wenig. Doch der zeigte sich sogleich sehr zufrieden und gab uns sofort sein Einverständnis.

Nomad Soul ist nur ein sehr bescheidener Beitrag zu Platons Höhlengleichnis. Unser Bezug zur Realität, ihre objektive, von unseren Sinnen unabhängige Existenz, die Existenz anderer Realitäten sind in der Literatur und im Film hinreichend thematisiert worden. Die Truman Show von Peter Weir, Ubik von Philip K. Dick, Dark City von Alex Proyas, Avalon von Mamoru Oshii oder auch der hervorragende Film Jacob's Ladder – In der Gewalt des Jenseits von Adrian Lyne stellen sämtlich immer wieder die gleiche Frage: Ist die uns umgebende Welt wirklich die, für die wir sie halten?

Videospiele bringen eine neue Dimension in diese Fragestellung. Die neuesten Technologien, wie die Dreidimensionalität und das Intelligenzverhalten, ermöglichen es, immer tiefgründigere, immer realere Welten zu erschaffen. Die Videospiele begnügen sich nicht mehr damit, diese Welten zu erzählen, sie lassen uns vielmehr daran teilhaben und machen uns zu einem integralen Bestandteil. Wer kann nach all dem noch mit Sicherheit ausschließen, dass unsere Welt nicht doch ein zur Perfektion getriebenes Videospiel ist, in der wir alle nur Avatars sind?

NAME
NOMAD SOUL

PLATFORM
PC-DREAMCAST

RELEASE
1999

EDITOR
EIDOS INTERACTIVE

DEVELOPER
QUANTIC DREAM

COPYRIGHTS
© EIDOS INTERACTIVE/QUANTIC DREAM

FACT
50,000: THE NUMBER OF PEOPLE EMPLOYED IN
THE VIDEO-GAME INDUSTRY IN THE UNITED
STATES IN 1999.

Nomad Soul

Kay'l and his partner Den are police officers in Omikron, a futuristic parallel world housed in an immense crystal dome. They find themselves at the heart of a complex supernatural plot, confronting formidable beings who trap Kay'l. His soul's desperate calls for help attract a wandering soul, which takes possession of his body in an unknown world in which demons, led by Astaroth, live among humanity and feed on human souls. Able to possess and vacate bodies, and armed with the memories and talents of most of Omikron's inhabitants, the nomadic soul is drawn into confrontation with these malevolent powers. It is assisted by a benevolent virtual being named Boz, who takes the physical form of rock artist David Bowie. Bowie and Reeves Gabrels were responsible for part of the soundtrack of the game, and Bowie himself makes other appearances in *The Nomad Soul*, as a singer or dancer in a series of rather insalubrious bars. Remarkably coherent, the Omikron universe offers a harmonious mix of sci-fi, supernatural and fantasy.

« »

Kay'l et son partenaire Den sont des policiers d'Omikron, monde parallèle et futuriste recouvert d'un gigantesque dôme de cristal. Tous deux se retrouvent au cœur d'une intrigue complexe et surnaturelle, face à de redoutables entités qui piègent Kay'l. Les appels désespérés de son âme désincarnée attirent une âme errante qui prendra possession de son corps, dans un monde inconnu où les démons, menés par Astaroth, se mêlent aux hommes et se nourrissent de leurs âmes. L'âme nomade sera amenée à affronter ces forces maléfiques, armée du pouvoir de se désincarner et de prendre possession du corps, des souvenirs et des talents de la plupart des habitants d'Omikron. L'âme sera aussi épaulée par une entité virtuelle bénéfique, Boz, à laquelle la célèbre rock star David Bowie a prêté ses traits. L'artiste qui, avec son complice Reeves Gabrels, a signé une partie de la bande-son du jeu *The Nomad Soul* apparaît aussi sous d'autres aspects dans le jeu, en chanteur ou danseur de bars plus ou moins respectables. Envoûtant et d'une remarquable cohérence, l'univers étonnant d'Omikron, mêle harmonieusement science-fiction, surnaturel et fantastique.

« »

Kay'l und sein Partner Den sind Polizisten auf Omikron, einer futuristischen, mit einer gigantischen Kristallkuppel überdachten Parallelwelt. Beide sind in eine komplizierte und übernatürliche Intrige verstrickt und stehen zweifelhaften Wesenheiten gegenüber, die Kay'l in eine Falle locken. Die verzweifelten Rufe seiner des Körpers beraubten Seele ziehen die Aufmerksamkeit einer umherirrenden Seele auf sich: In einer unbekannten Welt, in der sich von Astaroth angeführte Dämonen unter die Menschen mischen und sich von ihren Seelen ernähren, schlüpft sie in Kay'ls körperliche Hülle. Die umherziehende Seele, die die Kraft besitzt, sich ihres Körpers zu entledigen und den Körper, die Gedanken und Talente einiger Bewohner von Omikron in ihren Besitz zu nehmen, wird dazu gebracht, den Unheil bringenden Kräften die Stirn zu bieten. Unterstützung erhält die Seele von einem Glück bringenden virtuellen Wesen, Boz, dem der berühmte Rockstar David Bowie seine Züge geliehen hat. Der Künstler, der mit seinem Partner Reeves Gabrels für einen Teil der Tonaufnahmen von *The Nomad Soul* verantwortlich zeichnet, tritt in dem Spiel auch als Sänger oder Tänzer in mehr oder weniger angesehenen Bars auf. Packend und von einer bemerkenswerten Stimmigkeit, vereint das merkwürdige Universum von Omikron aufs Beste Science-Fiction, Mystik und Fantasy.

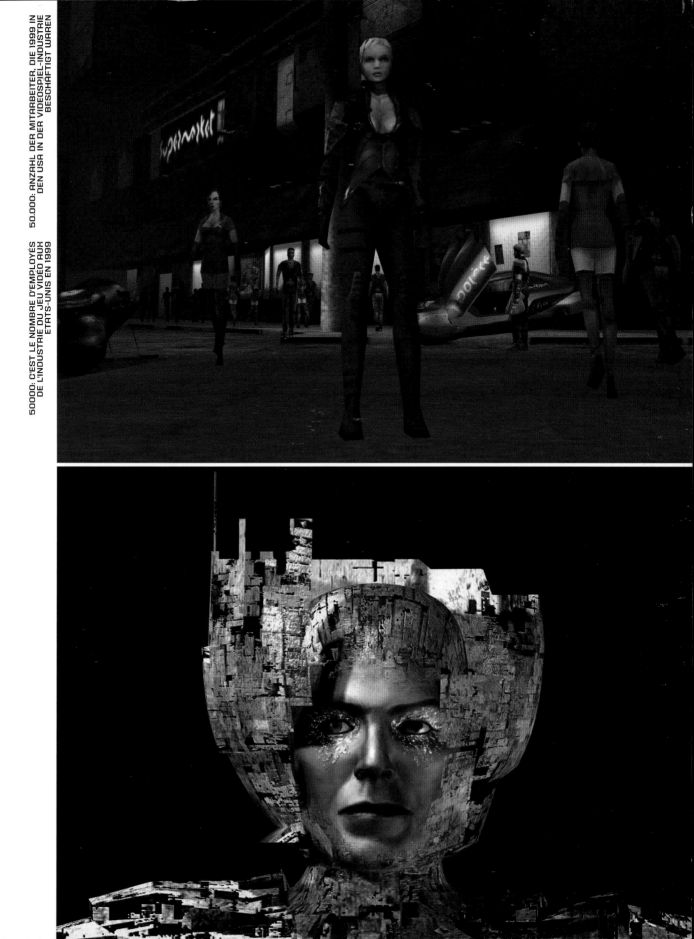

50000: C'EST LE NOMBRE D'EMPLOYÉS
DE L'INDUSTRIE DU JEU VIDÉO AUX
ETATS-UNIS EN 1999

50.000: ANZAHL DER MITARBEITER, DIE 1999 IN
DEN USA IN DER VIDEOSPIEL-INDUSTRIE
BESCHÄFTIGT WAREN

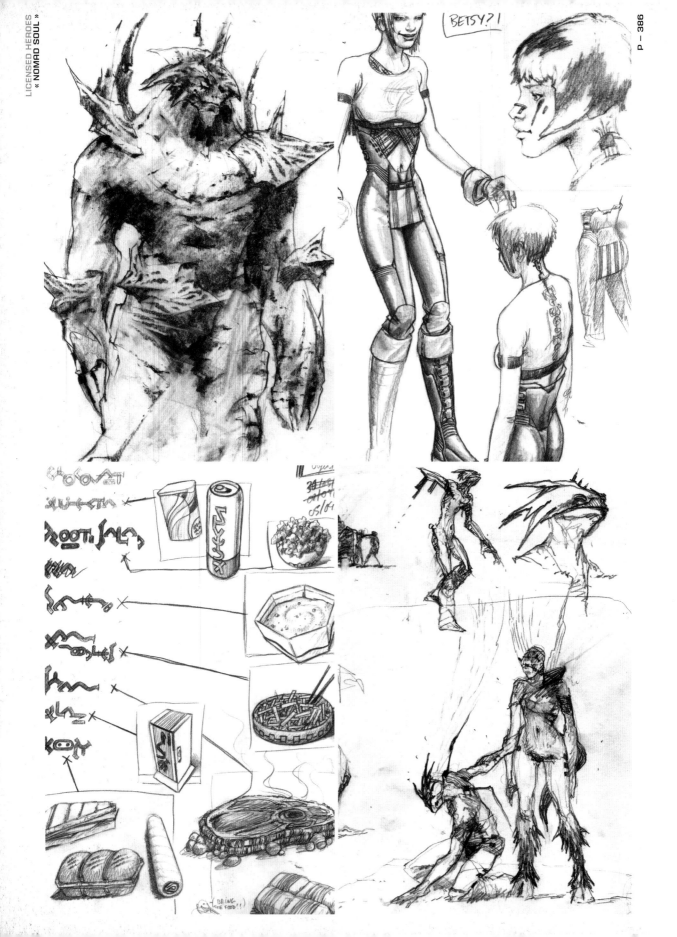

BETSY?!

NAME ALIENS VS PREDATOR 2
PLATFORM PC
RELEASE 2001
EDITOR FOX INTERACTIVE
DEVELOPER MONOLITH SOFTWARE
COPYRIGHTS © 2001TWENTIETH CENTURY FOX FILM CORPORATION. ALL RIGHTS RESERVED. ALIENS VS PREDATOR, FOX INTERACTIVE, AND EACH APPLICABLE LOGOS ARE TRADEMARKS TWENTIETH CENTURY FILM CORPORATION. © 2001 SIERRA ENTERTAINMENT, INC. ALL RIGHTS RESERVED.

Aliens vs Predator

In the film *Predator 2*, cine-goers glimpsed an *Alien* skull in a glass case, and were left to dream of a face-off between these two extra-terrestrial stars... Not for long. The Hollywood sci-fi monsters battle it out in two games, which also feature the Marines. The humans have ultra hi-tech weapons and armour, but they stand little chance against these ferocious hunters from outer space. When the three species meet, each has its own moves. The Aliens have vicious claws and tails like razors, and swarm over walls, ceilings and floors alike. Thanks to its hunt-and-kill gadgetry, the Predator can vanish into any environment, lying in wait with its energy-blasters. The first and last its victim sees is the red triangle of its laser sight. Next to these born killers, the Marines look a little exposed. Their weaponry includes a movement-detector, but panic and death are never far off.

« »

Les cinéphiles auront pu apercevoir dans le film *Predator 2* un crâne d'Alien dans une vitrine du vaisseau Predator, et rêver de voir un jour ces deux races extraterrestres s'affronter... Leur rêve se réalise avec deux jeux qui mettent en scène ces deux pointures du cinéma hollywoodien de science-fiction, aux prises l'une avec l'autre, mais aussi avec des Marines humains qui malgré leurs armes hyper-techno-logiques et leurs armures supra blindées n'ont que peu de chances face à ces chasseurs venus du fin fond de l'espace. Si ces trois espè-ces se rencontrent, chacune se comporte à sa façon : les Aliens n'ont pour armes que leurs crocs acérés et leur queue aiguisée comme un rasoir, mais se déplacent aussi aisément sur les murs et plafonds qu'au sol. De son côté, grâce à ses gadgets de chasseur, le Predator peut se camoufler dans tous les types d'environnement et user avec discrétion de ses armes à énergie. Sa victime n'a que le temps de voir le triangle rouge du viseur laser du Predator avant de rendre l'âme... Entre ces deux races nées pour combattre, le Marine humain fait pâle figure : si ses armes lui permettent de survivre quelques minutes aux assauts de ses ennemis, repérés grâce au détecteur de mou-vements intégré à son attirail militaire, il est constamment en proie à la panique. Si cette dernière survient, ses secondes sont comptées.

« »

Kinofans werden sich bestimmt an den Film Predator 2 erinnern, in dem der Schädel eines Aliens im Predator-Raumschiff hinter Glas aus-gestellt war. Und insgeheim werden sie gehofft haben, dass sich die beiden außerirdischen Rassen eines schönen Tages gegenüberstehen... Ihr Traum ist Wirklichkeit geworden mit zwei Spielen, die die beiden Hollywood-Größen der Science-Fiction in Szene setzen und gegen-einander kämpfen lassen.

Mit von der Partie sind die Marines, Soldaten, die trotz ihrer hoch technisierten Waffen und ihrer High-Tech-Schutzanzüge kaum eine Chance gegen ihre Verfolger aus den Tiefen des Weltraums haben. Wenn die drei Fraktionen aufeinander treffen, verhalten sie sich artgemäß: Die Aliens haben keine anderen Waffen als ihre spitzen Zähne und ihren stacheligen, rasiermesserscharfen Schwanz, können sich aber auch bequem an Wänden und Decken sowie auf dem Boden fortbewegen. Der Predator seinerseits kann sich dank seiner Fangvorrichtungen jeder Umgebung anpassen und unauffällig seine Energiewaffen einsetzen. Seinem Opfer bleibt gerade mal die Zeit, das rote Dreieck von Predators Laservisier zu erblicken, bevor es den Geist aufgibt... Zwischen diesen beiden Kämpfernaturen wirkt der Marine ziemlich blass und unscheinbar. Er kann zwar den Angriffen seiner Kontrahenten ein paar Minuten standhalten, weil ein in seiner Kampfausrüstung eingebauter Bewegungsmelder die Feinde ortet, aber er droht ständig in Panik zu geraten. Und wenn das passiert, sind seine Sekunden gezählt.

NAME
AMERZONE

PLATFORM
PC

RELEASE
1999

EDITOR
MICROÏDS

DEVELOPER
MICROÏDS

COPYRIGHTS
© MICROÏDS

FACT
77: THE NUMBER OF COUNTRIES THAT HAVE
BOUGHT AN AUDIOVISUAL LICENCE FOR
WHO WANTS TO BE A MILLIONAIRE?

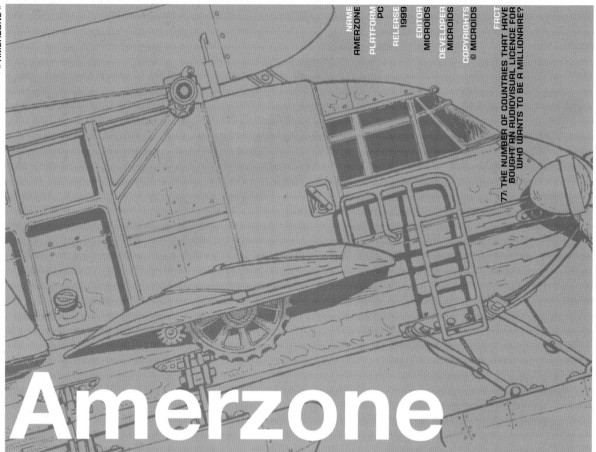

Amerzone

On his deathbed, an aged explorer confides his terrible secret to a young journalist: a little known species, the great white birds of Amerzône (a small country in Central America), is endangered, and its survival lies in the hands of the dying man. He bequeaths this burden to the journo, placing in his hands the last great-white-bird egg and exhorting him to make the trip. The journo sets off. In Amerzone, an enchanted plant kingdom awaits him. But it is threatened by the madness of humanity. Mankind is attacked by an unknown fever, and corrupted by its craving for power.

Amerzone-the-game was put together by the artist Benoît Sokal on the basis of his cartoon books; he has expertly remade his universe in 3-D. The player plunges into the heart of the Amerzone jungle, its dream-like universe the backdrop for a dark and fascinating narrative in which politics, ecology and strategy are interwoven like lianas.

« »

Un vieil explorateur lègue en mourant à un jeune journaliste son terrible secret. Une espèce animale peu connue, les grands oiseaux blancs d'Amerzone, petit pays d'Amérique centrale, est en voie de disparition, et du vieil homme seul dépendait la survie de l'espèce. Il confie cette tâche au jeune journaliste, en lui confiant le dernier œuf d'oiseau blanc, et le pousse à se rendre en Amerzone. L'aventure lui fera découvrir un monde végétal enchanteur, menacé par la folie des hommes, victimes d'une fièvre inconnue ou corrompus par leur soif de pouvoir.

Le jeu *L'Amerzone* a entièrement été orchestré par le dessinateur Benoît Sokal d'après sa propre bande dessinée, qui a su recréer son univers en trois dimensions, et permettre au joueur de plonger au cœur de la jungle de l'Amerzone, univers onirique qui sert de théâtre à une sombre et passionnante histoire mêlant politique, écologie et réflexion.

« »

Kurz vor seinem Tod verrät ein alter Forscher einem jungen Journalisten sein schreckliches Geheimnis. Dabei geht es um eine nahezu unbekannte Tierart, die vom Aussterben bedroht ist: die großen weißen Vögel aus Amerzone, einem kleinen Land in Mittelamerika. Das Überleben dieser Vogelart hängt einzig und allein von dem alten Mann ab. Diese Aufgabe überträgt der Alte nun dem jungen Journalisten. Er vertraut ihm das letzte Ei des weißen Vogels an und drängt ihn zum Aufbruch nach Amerzone. Auf seiner abenteuerlichen Reise entdeckt der junge Mann eine faszinierende Pflanzenwelt. Sie wird bedroht von wahnsinnigen Menschen, die ein unbekanntes Fieber befallen hat oder die von ihrem Machtstreben verdorben sind.

Das PC-Spiel *Amerzone* wurde von dem Zeichner Benoît Sokal nach seinem eigenen Comic inszeniert. Ihm ist es gelungen, eine drei-dimensionale Welt zu erschaffen, die es dem Spieler erlaubt, mitten in den Dschungel von Amerzone einzutauchen, in eine Traumwelt, die einer düsteren und spannenden Geschichte um Politik und Ökologie als Bühne dient.

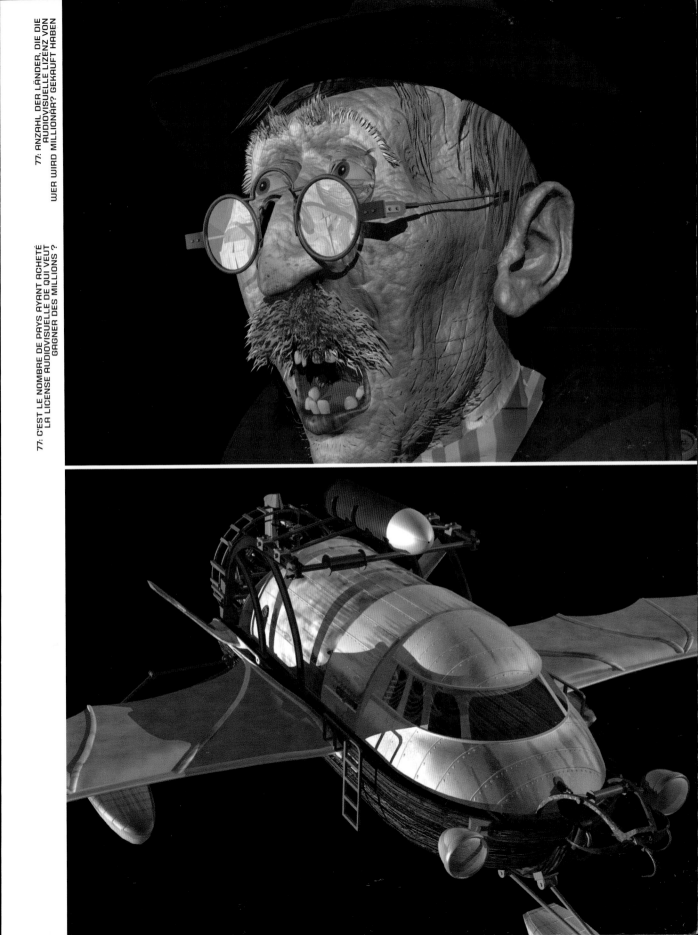

77: ANZAHL DER LÄNDER, DIE DIE
AUDIOVISUELLE LIZENZ VON
WER WIRD MILLIONÄR? GEKAUFT HABEN

77: C'EST LE NOMBRE DE PAYS AYANT ACHETÉ
LA LICENSE AUDIOVISUELLE DE QUI VEUT
GAGNER DES MILLIONS ?

EXPO
ESSAI 1

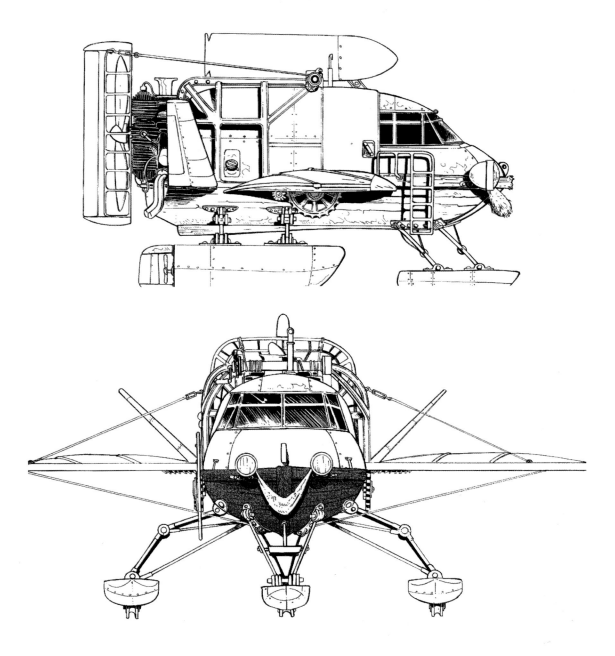
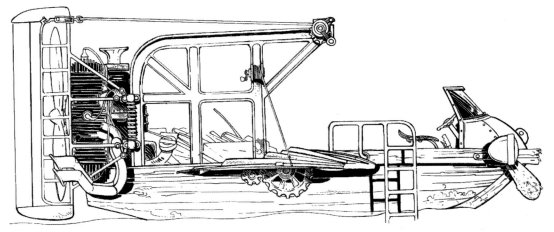

NAME
BATMAN VENGEANCE

PLATFORM
PC-PLAYSTATION 2-XBOX-GAMECUBE
GAME BOY ADVANCE

RELEASE
2001

EDITOR
UBI SOFT ENTERTAINMENT

DEVELOPER
UBI SOFT ENTERTAINMENT

Batman Vengeance

Video-game crime? Call on the super-heroes of American comics! All the major characters from Marvel and DC have been adapted for video-games, with Batman chief among them. The bat-masked dealer of justice tirelessly confronts his sinister adversaries, the Joker, the Penguin and Mr Freeze, in games inspired not just by the original comic strips but by spin-off films and cartoons too. The latest Batman games were spawned by the cartoon *Batman: The Series*. Its dynamic line and vivid colours lend themselves perfectly to video-game. And these games are not just for the younger fans of the super-hero, weaned on his latest adventures; aficionados of his comic-book incarnations will love them too.

« »

Les super-héros des comics américains ne pouvaient laisser passer l'occasion de combattre le crime dans les jeux vidéo. Tous les grands personnages des éditions Marvel et DC ont donc eu droit à des adaptations vidéo-ludiques, Batman étant le plus honoré dans cette caté-gorie. Le justicier au costume de chauve-souris ne se lasse donc pas d'affronter d'aussi célèbres adversaires que le Joker, le Pingouin ou encore Mr Freeze, dans des titres aussi bien inspirés des bandes dessinées qui leur ont donné la vie que des films et dessins animés qui en découlèrent. Les plus récents jeux vidéo dédiés à Batman sont tirés de la série animée *Batman: The Series* dont l'univers graphique sobre aux couleurs contrastées et au trait dynamique s'adapte parfaitement au jeu vidéo et, de plus, s'adresse tant aux jeunes fans du super-héros qui ont découvert ses dernières aventures qu'aux plus anciens amateurs qui ont connu le personnage dans les pages des comics.

« »

Die Superhelden der US-amerikanischen Comics auf Verbrecherjagd in Videospielen – eine Chance, die man sich nicht entgehen lassen darf. Alle bekannten Comic-Figuren der Verlage Marvel und DC wurden für die Spielkonsole entsprechend bearbeitet, auch der allseits beliebte Batman. Und so kämpft der Rächer im Fledermaus-Kostüm unermüdlich gegen seine berühmt-berüchtigten Gegner wie den Joker, den Pinguin oder auch Mr. Freeze. Die Video-Adaptationen sind entstanden nach Ideen und Vorlagen von Comic-Heften, die diesen Figuren Leben eingehaucht haben, und den daraus entwickelten Spiel- und Zeichentrickfilmen. Die neuesten Batman-Videospiele basieren auf der Trickfilmserie *Batman*. Mit ihrer eingängigen grafischen Ausstattung in kontrastierenden Farben und der ihr eigenen Dynamik ist diese Serie wie geschaffen für Videospiele. Darüber hinaus spricht sie ein breites Publikum an: die jungen Fans des Superhelden, die soeben seine neuesten Abenteuer entdeckt haben, wie auch die älteren Batman-Freunde, die ihr Idol noch aus Comic-Zeiten kennen.

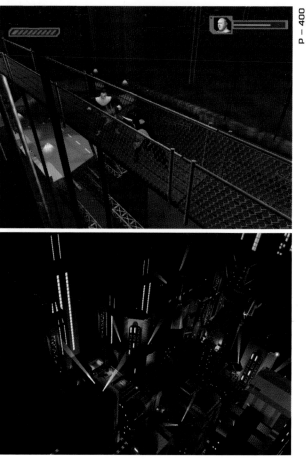

NAME
FLIGHT SIMULATOR 2002

PLATFORM
PC

RELEASE
2002

EDITOR
MICROSOFT

DEVELOPER
MICROSOFT

COPYRIGHTS
© MICROSOFT

FACT
3 YEARS: THE TIME WITHIN WHICH A COMPUTER
LOSES ALL COMMERCIAL VALUE, ACCORDING TO
THE MARKET RESEARCH CONSULTANCY IDC.

Flight Simulator

Detailed and realistic as it may be, even today, a pilot sim can't imitate the vibration of the cabin and the thrill of seeing the ground whizz past a hundred metres beneath one's feet. But in successive versions of *Flight Simulator*, Microsoft has got pretty close, and the latest version is not far short of reality, placing the virtual pilot at the controls of many airliners and tourist craft whose flight behaviour is perfectly reproduced. Equally successful are the environments, very faithful to reality and very like what the passenger sees from an aeroplane window. You can cross the Atlantic at the controls of a 737, with hundreds of passengers in your charge, fly over the summits of the Himalayas for pleasure, and admire Paris or the Grand Canyon. The only limit to this virtual airspace is the imagination of the pilot.

« »

Aussi pointue et réaliste puisse-t-elle être, une simulation de pilotage aérien ne peut aujourd'hui encore imiter intégralement la réalité, les secousses de la carlingue ou l'exaltation de voir défiler la terre à plusieurs centaines de mètres sous ses pieds. Mais Microsoft, au fil de ses versions de *Flight Simulator*, s'en est progressivement approchée et le dernier Flight Simulator en date n'est pas loin de la réalité, offrant au pilote virtuel les commandes de nombreux avions de ligne ou de tourisme aux comportements parfaitement reproduits. Tout aussi réussis sont les environnements fidèles à la réalité et visuellement très semblables à ce que tout passager d'un avion peut voir de son hublot. Faire traverser l'Atlantique à des dizaines de voyageurs aux commandes d'un Boeing 737, survoler pour le plaisir les cimes de l'Himalaya, admirer le Grand Canyon ou Paris : l'espace aérien de la terre n'a aucune limite, si ce n'est la fantaisie du pilote virtuel aux commandes de *Flight Simulator*.

« »

Keiner noch so ausgezeichneten und lebensnahen Flugsimulation gelang es bisher, die Realität in vollem Umfang zu imitieren, die Erschütterungen des Cockpits wiederzugeben oder auch nur dieses Gefühl der Begeisterung zu vermitteln, wenn die Erde hunderte von Metern unter einem vorbeizieht. Das zu verändern, hat sich Microsoft mit seinen regelmäßigen Weiterentwicklungen des *Flight Simulator* zum Ziel gesetzt, und so kommt die neueste Version der Wirklichkeit recht nahe. Dem virtuellen Piloten wird ein Platz im Cockpit zahlreicher Linien- und Charterflugzeuge angeboten, deren Flugverhalten fast perfekt nachgebildet ist. Ebenso gelungen sind die naturgetreuen Landschaften, die den Impressionen sehr nahe kommen, wie sie jeder Passagier während einer Flugreise von seinem Fensterplatz aus hat. Am Steuer einer Boeing 737 Dutzende Reisende über den Atlantik transportieren, einfach aus Spaß die Gipfel des Himalaya überfliegen, den Grand Canyon oder Paris bewundern: Der Luftraum über der Erde ist grenzenlos, wenn der virtuelle Pilot am Steuerknüppel des *Flight Simulator* sitzt.

NAME
GRAN TURISMO 3 A-SPEC
GT CONCEPT

PLATFORM
PLAYSTATION 2

RELEASE
2001

EDITOR
SONY COMPUTER ENTERTAINMENT

DEVELOPER
POLYPHONY DIGITAL

COPYRIGHTS
© 2001 SONY COMPUTER
ENTERTAINMENT INC. ALL MANUFACTURERS,
CARS, BRANDS AND ASSOCIATED
IMAGERY FEATURED IN THIS
GAME ARE TRADEMARKS AND/OR
COPYRIGHTED MATERIALS OF
THEIR RESPECTIVE OWNERS. ALL
RIGHTS RESERVED. PUBLISHED BY
SONY COMPUTER ENTERTAINMENT EUROPE.
DEVELOPED BY POLYPHONY DIGITAL INC.

FACT
500+: THE NUMBER OF CARS AVAILABLE
IN GRAN TURISMO 2.

Gran Turismo

The jewel in the crown of driving sims, *Gran Turismo* allows gamers to take the wheel of hundreds of models of many different makes, all perfectly reproduced in both appearance and performance. But you can't just jump into the Ferraris and take off; you have to earn the right. By passing driving tests, you gain admission to successive races. If you take the chequered flag, you win a new car or cash to up the spec of the old one. Combine perfect mastery at the wheel with mechanical knowledge, and a dream collection of exotic cars awaits you.

« »

Fleuron de la simulation automobile réaliste, la série des *Gran Turismo* permet à chacun de prendre le volant de centaines de voitures de différents constructeurs, parfaitement reproduites tant visuellement que sur le plan de leur comportement routier. Chaque conducteur virtuel doit cependant mériter le plaisir de prendre les commandes de ces véhicules de prestige en réussissant des épreuves de permis, qui l'autoriseront à s'inscrire à maintes compétitions de course. Le pilote victorieux de ces épreuves gagnera une nouvelle voiture ou une certaine somme, cette dernière pouvant être utilisée pour acquérir de nouveaux véhicules chez les concessionnaires ou modifier ceux déjà acquis afin de les rendre plus performants. De petites connaissances en mécanique et une parfaite maîtrise des véhicules sont les clés du succès qui permettront à l'amateur de belles automobiles et de vitesse de devenir propriétaire de la plus grande collection de voitures de rêve...

« »

Die Rennspielreihe *Gran Turismo*, der Höhepunkt der realistischen Automobilsimulation, gibt jedem die Möglichkeit, am Steuer von rund hundert visuell hervorragend wiedergegebenen Autos der verschiedensten Hersteller zu sitzen. Die Fahrzeuge zeichnen sich allesamt durch eine hervorragende Straßenlage aus. Der virtuelle Fahrer muss sich jedoch den Spaß, diese Prestigeobjekte lenken zu dürfen, erst verdienen. Zunächst heißt es nämlich, die Fahrprüfung zu bestehen, eine Voraussetzung, um am Autorennen teilzunehmen. Der Sieger gewinnt ein neues Auto oder erhält eine Geldprämie, die er dazu verwenden kann, bei einem Vertragshändler neue Autos zu erwerben oder seine bereits vorhandenen Fahrzeuge aufzurüsten. Die einen oder anderen Kenntnisse in Automechanik und eine ausgezeichnete Beherrschung der Fahrzeuge sind der Schlüssel zum Erfolg, mit dem der Fan von schönen Karossen und hohen Geschwindigkeiten Eigentümer der größten Kollektion von Traumautos werden kann.

MEHR ALS 500: ANZAHL DER VERFÜGBAREN
AUTOS IN GRAN TURISMO 2

PLUS DE 500: C'EST LE NOMBRE DE VOITURES
DISPONIBLES DANS GRAN TURISMO 2.

NAME
TONY HAWK PRO SKATER 3
MAT HOFFMAN PRO BMX 2
SHAUN PALMER'S PRO SNOWBOARDER
KELLY SLATER'S PRO SURFER

PLATFORM
PC-PLAYSTATION-PLAYSTATION 2
DREAMCAST-XBOX-GAME BOY
GAME BOY ADVANCE-GAMECUBE

RELEASE
2002

EDITOR
ACTIVISION

DEVELOPER
NEVERSOFT

COPYRIGHTS
© ACTIVISION

FACT
$700,000: THE AMOUNT OF THE INITIAL I
NVESTMENT IN ACTIVISION IN 1979.

P – 414

O² Series

By launching its O² series, Activision brought extreme sports to the attention of a wider public, and helped the skateboard, BMX, snowboard and surfer attain their current popularity. The stars who lent names and faces are the first to say so. Tony Hawk, Mat Hoffman, Shaun Palmer and Kelly Slater are delighted with the success of these games, even confessing that these titles turned them into console-artists too. Mat Hoffman says that some of the virtual BMX-stunts became real-life challenges for him... The entire W series brilliantly combines realistic sport, superhuman figures and improbable combination stunts, all for the greater pleasure of gamers, especially those whom the console has introduced to these spectacular disciplines. The landscapes are original, and a touch of the joystick allows you to perform truly acrobatic stunts. Besides, who wouldn't like to be one of these stars for a few hours?

« »

En lançant sa gamme O², Activision a permis aux sports extrêmes de toucher un plus large public, voire a aidé le skateboard, le BMX, le snowboard et le surfer à gagner leurs lettres de noblesse auprès du grand nombre, de l'aveu même des stars de ces disciplines qui prêtent leurs noms et visages aux jeux de cette gamme. Tony Hawk, Mat Hoffman, Shaun Palmer et Kelly Slater sont unanimement ravis du succès de ces jeux, avouant même être devenus pour la plupart joueurs sur consoles avec ces titres. Mat Hoffman signale d'ailleurs s'être tant prêté au jeu que certaines figures qu'il a pu y découvrir sont devenues pour lui des challenges à relever dans la réalité. Tous ces jeux O² mêlent avec brio réalisme du sport, figures surhumaines et enchaînements improbables, pour le plus grand plaisir des joueurs, notamment ceux qui ont découvert par ce biais ces disciplines spectaculaires. Sur des terrains originaux remplis de défis étonnants, des dizaines d'acrobaties sont à portée de manette, tout comme la possibilité d'incarner les nombreux sportifs qui se sont prêté au jeu.

« »

Es ist das Verdienst von Activision und seiner Marke O², dass auch die Extremsportarten der breiten Öffentlichkeit zugänglich gemacht wurden und sich Skateboarder, BMX-Biker, Snowboarder und surfer überall durchgesetzt haben; das zumindest bekennen die Stars dieser Disziplinen, die den Spielen dieser Serie ihre Namen und ihre Gesichter zur Verfügung gestellt haben. Tony Hawk, Mat Hoffman, Shaun Palmer und Kelly Slater sind über den Erfolg dieser Spiele einer Meinung und gestehen in den meisten Fällen sogar, dass sie begeisterte Spieler der Konsole geworden sind. Mat Hoffman erklärt sogar, dass er sich in die Spiele regelrecht hineingesteigert habe. Einige hier entdeckte BMX-Tricks seien für ihn zur Herausforderung geworden und er wolle sie auch in der Wirklichkeit beherrschen. All diese O²-Spiele sind eine gelungene Mischung aus sportlichem Realismus, übermenschlichen Tricks und nahezu unglaublichen Bewegungsabläufen. Ein absoluter Spielgenuss für all diejenigen, die auf diese Weise spektakuläre Sportarten für sich entdecken können. Sensationelle Herausforderungen warten auf originellen Sportplätzen, Dutzende Kunststücke können durch einen Knopfdruck auf dem Joystick im Rampenlicht gesehen werden, und das alles aus der Ego-Perspektive der zahlreichen Sportler.

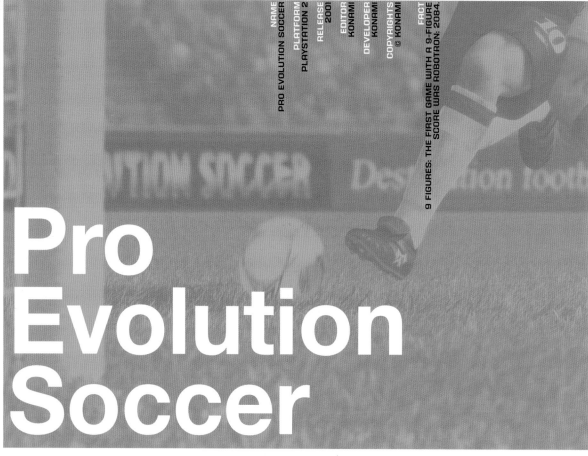

NAME
PRO EVOLUTION SOCCER

PLATFORM
PLAYSTATION 2

RELEASE
2001

EDITOR
KONAMI

DEVELOPER
KONAMI

COPYRIGHTS
© KONAMI

FACT
9 FIGURES: THE FIRST GAME WITH A 9-FIGURE
SCORE WAS ROBOTRON: 2084.

Pro Evolution Soccer

Zidane, Beckham, Ronaldo and other living legends of football have now become stars of video-gaming in the many sims featuring their names, appearances and specialities. Footie fans thus get to borrow their hero's identity, manage the team they support, and arrange the matches they always dreamed of seeing. And it's not just today's great players you get to play; yesterday's stars can also be transferred to the virtual pitch. Create your mythical teams: play Pelé alongside Platini and Maradona. Today, the quality of the graphics, range of movement and realistic soundtrack mean that the best football sims all but rival so-called "real-life" soccer championships and World Cups.

« »

Zidane, Ronaldo et d'autres légendes vivantes du football sont désormais aussi des grands noms du jeu vidéo, grâce à maintes simulations de sport reprenant leurs noms, apparences et spécialités. Certains jeux offrent ainsi aux grands amateurs de football la possibilité d'incarner leurs idoles, de contrôler leur équipe fétiche, voire même de donner vie aux matches dont ils ont toujours rêvé. Car si ces grands joueurs d'aujourd'hui sont au rendez-vous, les légendes du foot peuvent, elles aussi, fouler de nouveau les terrains virtuels : le jeu vidéo permet à chacun de façonner une équipe mythique, où Pelé, Platini et Maradona jouent de concert, dans des rencontres orchestrées par le joueur. Aujourd'hui, de par la qualité des graphismes, la variété des mouvements des sportifs et le réalisme de l'ambiance sonore, les grandes simulations de football n'ont plus grand-chose à envier aux championnats et coupes du monde réels.

« »

Zahlreiche Computersimulationen haben durch Anleihen bei Zidane, Ronaldo und anderen lebenden Fußballlegenden (Namen, Aussehen oder besondere Fähigkeiten) nunmehr auch Sportler zu Größen des Videospiels erhoben. Einige Spiele bieten ihren Fußballfans die Möglichkeit, in die Rolle ihrer Idole zu schlüpfen, ihre bejubelte Mannschaft anzuleiten oder gar lang erträumte Spiele wahr werden zu lassen. Gegen die großen Spieler von heute, die uns nach wie vor auch in den Stadien begeistern, können auf virtuellem Spielfeld sogar die Fußballlegenden von einst antreten: Im Videospiel kann jeder eine Mannschaft nach seinen Vorstellungen zusammenstellen und Pelé, Platini oder Maradona in einer selbst inszenierten Fußballbegegnung gemeinsam spielen lassen. Durch die ausgezeichnete Grafik, die Bewegungsvielfalt der Sportler und die wirklichkeitsgetreue Sounduntermalung stehen die Fußballsimulationen den Weltmeisterschaften und den World Cups in nichts nach.

9 CHIFFRES: LE PREMIER JEU AVEC UN SCORE
MONTRANT A 9 CHIFFRES ETAIT ROBOTRON : 2084

9 ZIFFERN: DAS ERSTE SPIEL MIT EINEM SCORE
VON 9 PUNKTEN WAR ROBOTRON: 2084

NAME
V-RALLY 3

PLATFORM
PLAYSTATION 2 – GAME BOY ADVANCE

RELEASE
2002

EDITOR
INFOGRAMES ENTERTAINMENT

DEVELOPER
INFOGRAMES ENTERTAINMENT

COPYRIGHTS
© INFOGRAMES ENTERTAINMENT

FACT
300,000: THE NUMBER OF PS2 STEERING
WHEELS SOLD IN ONE DAY – THE DAY GRAN
TURISMO 3 A SPEC WAS RELEASED; THE GAME
ITSELF SOLD 720,000 COPIES IN 24 HOURS.

V-Rally

The most prestigious makes are on the starting line for extreme rallying in *V-Rally 3*. Ford, Peugeot, Subaru, Lancia and Mitsubishi put you at the wheel of their rally specials for 24 races in every corner of the globe. From Kenya's dusty tracks to the gravelled forest sections of Great Britain and the snow and ice of Sweden and Finland, the virtual driver must steer and counter-steer with the best and know the car inside out, from gear ratio to choice of tyres. It's up to you! And it isn't just on the course that you have to perform: you also have to organise your budget, choose the right sponsors and maintain morale throughout the team.

« »

Les plus prestigieux constructeurs automobiles se sont donné rendez-vous dans la boue et la poussière pour les plus extrêmes compétitions de rallye dans ce *V-Rally 3*. Peugeot, Subaru, Mitsubishi, Ford, Lancia et autres offrent aux joueurs la possibilité de piloter leurs véhicules spécialement modifiés pour la course de rallye, au fil de 24 épreuves qui les feront voyager de par le monde. Des pistes poussiéreuses du Kenya aux terrains boueux de Grande-Bretagne, en passant par les régions enneigées et verglacées de la Finlande ou la Suède, les pilotes virtuels devront faire montre de grands talents en braquage et contre-braquage, mais aussi de connaissances mécaniques, les réglages de rapports de vitesse, de choix de pneus et autres aspects techniques étant également sous leur responsabilité. La carrière d'un pilote de rallye ne s'arrêtant pas aux épreuves, il faudra également organiser au mieux son budget, choisir les bons sponsors et même gérer le moral de l'écurie au grand complet !

« »

In *V-Rally 3* sind die bekanntesten Automobilhersteller vertreten, um in Schlamm und Staub die extremsten Rennen zu fahren. Autofirmen wie Peugeot, Subaru, Mitsubishi, Ford, Lancia und andere lassen die Spieler ans Steuer ihrer rallyetauglich gemachten Fahrzeuge, wo sie dann in 24 Prüfungsrunden ihre Fahrkünste unter Beweis stellen können. Die Streckenführung reicht von staubigen Pisten in Kenia über verschneite und vereiste Regionen in Finnland bis zu schlammigen Wegen in Großbritannien und verlangt den virtuellen Fahrern geschickte Lenkmanöver, aber auch technisches Verständnis ab. Ob Einstellung des Drehzahlmessers oder die Wahl der richtigen Reifen – für diese und andere fahrzeugtechnischen Aspekte ist der Fahrer selbst verantwortlich. Seine Karriere endet aber nicht mit den Prüfungen, als erfolgreicher Fahrer muss er auch seine Finanzen regeln, zahlungskräftige Sponsoren finden und nicht zuletzt darauf achten, dass die Moral der gesamten Mannschaft des Rennstalls stimmt.

300.000: ANZAHL DER AN EINEN TAG VERKAUFTEN PS2-LENKRÄDER; AM ERSCHEINUNGSTAG VERKAUFTE STÜCKZAHL VON GRAN TURISMO 3 A SPEC, DAS BIS ZU 720.000 MAL IN 24 STUNDEN ÜBER DEN LADENTISCH GING

300000: C'EST LE NOMBRE DE VOLANTS PS2 VENDUS EN UN JOUR; CELUI DE LA SORTIE DE GRAN TURISMO 3 A SPEC, QUI S'EST LUI VENDU À 720 000 EXEMPLAIRES EN 24 H.

NAME XIII
PLATFORM PC–PLAYSTATION 2–XBOX–GAMECUBE
RELEASE 2003
EDITOR UBI SOFT
DEVELOPER UBI SOFT
COPYRIGHTS © UBI SOFT
FACT 7,III,II: THE SCORE ATTAINED BY DONALD HAYES ON 5 NOVEMBER 2000 IN THE GAME CENTIPEDE. IT TOOK HIM 9 HOURS' PLAY. THE PREVIOUS RECORD DATED FROM 28 JUNE 1986: 5,500,000 POINTS.

XIII

The fame of the cartoon story *XIII* by Jean Van Hamme and William Vance, published by Dargaud, has spread through many European countries. The first-person actioner it has inspired remains largely faithful to its spirit. With the authors' permission, some liberties have been taken to show scenes only suggested in the comic, but for the most part it follows the powerful cartoon scenario: a man tattooed with the number XIII wakes up on a beach. He has lost his memory, but acquired the talents of a professional fighter. He is gradually embroiled in a sinister political intrigue, becoming aware of his own central role... Dark plots, disturbing characters and explosive action sequences: all the ingredients that ensured the success of the cartoon strip are present in this adaptation. Homage to the original game is not confined to the scenario. The developers have opted for a 3D cell shading style close to that of the cartoon book: the characters are outlined in black, with hand-painted textures, hefty black shadows and blocks of vivid colour.

« »

Célèbre dans plusieurs pays d'Europe, la bande dessinée *XIII*, signée par Jean Van Hamme et William Vance et éditée par Dargaud, devient un Jeu de Shoot à la première personne qui réussit à rester fidèle à l'esprit de l'oeuvre originale, se permettant quelques libertés validées par les auteurs, mais suivant en grande partie son passionnant scénario : se réveillant amnésique sur une plage, un homme tatoué du chiffre XIII part à la recherche de son passé, se découvrant des talents de commando surentraîné [Why not: talent de combattant professionnel? This would be perfectly comprehensible.] et plongeant peu à peu dans une sombre intrigue politique où lui-même possède un rôle capital... Sombres complots, personnages troubles, séquences d'action explosives : tous les ingrédients qui ont fait le succès de *XIII* sont au rendez-vous dans cette adaptation.L'hommage du jeu à la bande dessinée ne s'arrête pas à son scénario, les développeurs ayant opté avec talent pour des graphismes proche du dessin grâce à la technique du cell shading, avec des personnages aux contours noirs contrastés, des textures peintes à la main, des ombres coupées au couteau et des à-plats de couleurs saisissants.

« »

Der in mehreren europäischen Ländern bekannte Comic *XIII* von Jean van Hamme und William Vance, erschienen bei Dargaud, ist die Vorlage für ein 3-D-Ego-Shooter-Videospiel in 'Unreal'-Technologie, das dem Geist des Originalwerkes weitestgehend treu bleibt, das spannende Szenario der Vorlage also größtenteils übernimmt: Ein Mann wacht am Strand auf. Er hat sein Gedächtnis verloren. Auf seiner Schulter ein Tattoo mit der Ziffer XIII. Er begibt sich auf die Suche nach seiner Vergangenheit. Dabei stellt er fest, dass er ein talentierter Kämpfer ist, aber auch, dass er in eine dunkle politische Intrige verwickelt ist, in der er die Hauptrolle spielt... Finstere Komplotte, zweifelhafte Personen, spannungsgeladene Actionszenen: Das sind Zutaten, die dem Comic *XIII* den Erfolg beschert haben und die sich auch in dieser Adaptation wiederfinden. Die Hommage an die Comic-Vorlage geht weit über das Szenario hinaus; die Entwickler des Spiels haben sich nämlich für eine comicartige Grafik mit "Cell Shading"-Effekten entschieden: Gut gelungen sind das Rendering mit deutlich abgesetzten schwarzen Umrandungen, die handgemalten Texturen, sorgsam ausgeführte Randschatten und eine auffallende Farbsimplizität.

NAME
BILL ROPER

HOME TOWN
IRVINE, USA

OCCUPATION
SENIOR VICE PRESIDENT OF DEVELOPMENT

KEY TITLES
WARCRAFT III : REIGN OF CHAOS (2002) BLIZZARD
DIABLO II (2000) BLIZZARD
STARCRAFT (1998) BLIZZARD
DIABLO (1997) BLIZZARD
WARCRAFT II : TIDES OF DARKNESS (1995) BLIZZARD

«Magical Heroes»
Bill Roper

Blizzard Entertainment's trademark games belong to the tradition of the fantastical tale set in the middle ages; they draw on the works of J.R.R. Tolkien and Michael Moorcock, and by extension on the famous TSR role-player, Dungeons & Dragons. From the eternal wars between fantastical races such as the Orcs, Humans and Elves of the Warcraft saga to the epic quests of the Diablo series, Blizzard has won an almost supernatural reputation. Using scenarios based on worlds with which everyone is familiar, it offers a gaming experience in which ease of immersion and player satisfaction are the overriding values. But Bill Roper, one of the leading lights of the company, is an admirer of another of the fantastical sagas of video-gaming, the classic Final Fantasy series, and in particular Squaresoft's FF VII. The world of Final Fantasy VII is stranger than those of Warcraft or Diablo, but the bones of the story are the same. This is particularly true of Cloud Strife, the hero of the game, as Bill Roper observes:

"Cloud is an amazingly complex character with a deep and engaging path that he walks. At the start of the game, he cares only about himself, taking on missions solely for the money. Representing the very soul of a mercenary, he is willing to change his allegiance to that of the highest bidder at the drop of a hat. However, he begins to slowly realize that something is wrong with both himself and the world around him. Tormented by his horrifying past, he finally emerges as a true hero, accepting his losses and uniting his allies to save the world. Cloud Strife is the model of internal conflict, literally driven by his inner demons. He loses more of himself as the game progresses, and in the process he experiences a psychological break, eventually coming to grips with his true self just long enough to destroy his personal inner demon. In the end he turned out to be everything you could want in a hero - centred, self-aware and powerful. And best of all, he gets the girl in the end!"

« »

Une grande partie des titres signés Blizzard Entertainment sont des hommages au fantastique médiéval traditionnel, puisant dans l'œuvre de J.R.R. Tolkien ou Michael Moorcock, et par extension dans la célèbre saga de jeux de rôles de TSR, Dungeons & Dragons. Des guerres éternelles entre races fantastiques tels les Orcs, Humains ou Elfes de la saga Warcraft aux quêtes épiques d'aventuriers héroïques de la série Diablo, Blizzard a su se forger une réputation quasi surnaturelle, s'appuyant sur des mondes connus de tous pour offrir aux joueurs des expériences ludiques où règnent le plaisir du jeu et la facilité d'immersion. Bill Roper, un des chefs d'orchestre de la société, rend à son tour hommage à une autre grande saga fantastique du jeu vidéo, l'incontournable Final Fantasy et plus particulièrement au septième opus de la série. Si l'univers de Final Fantasy VII est plus particulier que ceux des Warcraft et Diablo, les fondations de l'histoire restent les mêmes, particulièrement si l'on se penche sur le jeune Cloud Strife, héros de cette aventure signée Squaresoft :

« Cloud est un personnage incroyablement complexe, en route vers un destin profond et prometteur. Au début du jeu, il ne se préoccupe que de lui-même, n'acceptant les missions que par appât du gain. Archétype du mercenaire, il peut sans hésitation changer d'allégeance et se mettre au service du plus offrant.

Cependant, il réalisera progressivement que quelque chose ne fonctionne pas, aussi bien dans le monde qui l'entoure qu'en lui-même. Tourmenté par un passé terrifiant, il deviendra un héros véritable, acceptera ses souffrances et unifiera ses alliés pour sauver le monde. Cloud Strife est un modèle de conflit intérieur, littéralement guidé par ses propres démons. Sa personnalité s'effrite au fil du jeu et, dans ce processus, il subira une fracture psychologique, allant jusqu'à affronter son identité profonde et détruire ainsi ses démons intérieurs. Au final, il sera devenu tout ce qu'on peut attendre d'un héros : équilibré, puissant et en accord avec lui-même. Et mieux que tout, il aura ravi le cœur de la belle ! »

Viele Titel von Blizzard Entertainment sind eine Hommage an mittelalterliche Fantasy-Märchen mit Anleihen bei J.R.R. Tolkien oder Michael Moorcock und entfernt auch bei Dungeons & Dragons, dem Rollenspiel von TSR. Mit Spielen, die von Kriegen zwischen Orks, Menschen und Elfen handeln (wie die Warcraft-Saga), bis hin zu den epischen Quests wagemutiger Abenteurer (à la Diablo) hat Blizzard sich einen phänomenalen Ruf erworben. Er gründet sich darauf, dass die Spieler vertrauten Welten Erfahrungen sammeln können, die Spaß machen und leicht nachzuvollziehen sind. Bill Roper, einer der „Drahtzieher" bei Blizzard, huldigt auf seine Weise einer anderen Fantasy-Saga des Videospiels: dem unverzichtbaren Meisterwerk Final Fantasy und ganz besonders der siebten Episode aus dieser Reihe. Die märchenhafte Welt von Final Fantasy VII ist zwar noch komplexer und ausgefeilter als dies bei Warcraft und Diablo der Fall ist, aber die Grundpfeiler der Geschichte sind gleich geblieben, vor allem wenn man den jungen Cloud Strife betrachtet, der als Held aus diesem Squaresoft-Abenteuer hervorgeht:

„Cloud ist ein sehr vielschichtiger Charakter, einer, der einen schweren, aber faszinierenden Weg geht. Zu Beginn des Spiels denkt er nur an sich, übernimmt Missionen nur des Geldes wegen. Er ist der Inbegriff des Söldners und bereit, dem Meistbietenden auf der Stelle zu folgen. Doch ganz allmählich begreift er, dass irgendetwas mit ihm und um ihn herum nicht stimmt. Gequält von seiner schrecklichen Vergangenheit, wird er schließlich zu einem wahren Helden, der seine Verluste akzeptiert und sich mit seinen Verbündeten zusammen-schließt, um die Welt zu retten.

Cloud Strife trägt einen inneren Konflikt aus, er wird geradezu getrieben von seinen inneren Dämonen. Er verliert sich mehr und mehr, je weiter das Spiel fortschreitet, bis etwas Entscheidendes mit ihm passiert: Er setzt sich mit seinem wahren Selbst auseinander und es gelingt ihm schließlich, seinen inneren Dämon zu besiegen. Aus diesem Kampf geht er als der Held hervor, der alle Eigenschaften in sich ver-einigt, die man einem Helden nachsagt: Er hat seine Mitte gefunden, ist selbstbewusst und stark. Und das Allerbeste daran ist, dass er zum Schluss auch noch das Mädchen kriegt."

NAME
PLATFORM
RELEASE
EDITOR
DEVELOPER
COPYRIGHTS

Warcraft

Fifteen years after the Great War between Orcs and Humans, a fragile peace has finally been established. The victorious Human Realms stretch over the surface of the world, and the Humans are convinced that they have finally disposed of their adversaries. In the shadows, the few surviving Orc clans lick their wounds and gather under the banner of a new and visionary leader. But a new threat overshadows the world: Ner'zhul's army of the Dead and the Burning Legion of the Night Elfs are disembarking... A new war is about to break out, featuring four armies all intent on conquering the world, each equipped with specific units, heroes and magic powers.
A major series of real-time strategy games, the *Warcraft* saga first appeared in 1995, and has now, with the very promising *World of Warcraft*, moved into 100% 3D, along with another new dimension, the massive multi-role RPG potential of the Internet.
« »

Quinze années après la fin de la Grande Guerre entre Orcs et Humans, une paix fragile s'est enfin installée. Les victorieux Royaumes Humains s'étendent de par le monde, persuadés d'avoir écarté définitivement leurs éternels adversaires. Dans l'ombre, les quelques clans Orcs survivants pansent leurs blessures et se regroupent sous la bannière d'un nouveau leader visionnaire. Mais une nouvelle menace plane sur le monde : l'armée des Morts de Ner'zhul et la Légion Brûlante des Elfes de la Nuit arrivent... Une nouvelle guerre s'apprête à éclater, mettant en scène quatre armées toutes décidées à conquérir le monde, dotées chacune d'unités, de héros et de pouvoirs magiques spécifiques.
Incontournable série de jeux de stratégie en temps réel, la saga *Warcraft* née en 1995 passe désormais à la 3D intégrale et s'apprête à entrer dans une nouvelle dimension, celle du jeu de rôles massivement multijoueurs sur Internet avec le très prometteur *World of Warcraft*.
« »

Fünfzehn Jahre nach dem Ende des Großen Krieges zwischen Orks und Menschen ist es zu einem unsicheren Frieden gekommen. Die siegreichen Menschenreiche erstrecken sich über die gesamte Welt. Man ist überzeugt, dass die ewigen Feinde endgültig ausgeschaltet sind. Insgeheim versorgen einige überlebende Ork-Clans ihre Wunden und schließen sich unter dem Banner eines neuen visionären Führers zusammen. Aber da droht der Welt schon eine neue Gefahr: Die Armee der Toten von Ner'zhul und die Glühende Legion der Nachtelfen treten in Erscheinung... Ein neuer Krieg zieht herauf, an dem sich vier Armeen beteiligen, die jede für sich die Weltherrschaft anstrebt und die allesamt über Sondereinheiten, Helden und außergewöhnliche Zauberkräfte verfügen.
Die *Warcraft*-Saga aus dem Jahre 1995, eine unverzichtbare Spielserie in 3-D-Echtzeit-Strategie, lässt sich nunmehr in einer neuen Dimension spielen: als Rollenspiel im Mehrspielermodus via Internet und der vielversprechenden *World of Warcraft*-Seite zum Spiel.

NAME

PLATFORM

RELEASE

EDITOR

DEVELOPER

COPYRIGHTS

FACT

Age of Mythology

Dive into the distant past, when myths and legends were the stuff of reality, and the gods fought it out on the surface of the earth with their worshippers at their sides. Take part in the wars between Egyptians, Greeks, and Norsemen and send Cyclops, Dragons and other mythical creatures to fight alongside the soldiers of your chosen civilisation. Invoke the thunderbolts of Zeus or the fire of Ra to blast your opponents in epic battles inspired by legend. Having placed millions of gamers at the head of civilisations classical and medieval in the series *Age of Empires* and *Age of Kings*, Ensemble Studios now offers them a new and magical universe in which several players vie with one another in strategic cunning. Each gamer attempts to lead his civilisation to victory by choosing a protector who will come to its aid. Will the Greek player choose Zeus, Poseidon or Hades? Does the Egyptian gamer idolize Ra, Isis or Set? Who stands behind the Norsemen, Odin, Thor or the cunning Loki?

« »

Plongez dans un lointain passé, où les mythes et légendes étaient réalité et où les Dieux foulaient la terre et s'affrontaient aux côtés de leurs fidèles. Participez aux guerres entres Egyptiens, Grecs, Nordiques et envoyez au combat Cyclopes, Dragons et autres créatures mythiques aux côtés des soldats de chaque civilisation. Invoquez les foudres de Zeus ou le feu de Ra pour terrasser vos adversaires dans d'épiques batailles inspirées des légendes. Après avoir mis d'innombrables joueurs à la tête de civilisations antiques et médiévales dans la série des *Age of Empires* et *Age of Kings*, Ensemble Studios leur offre un nouvel univers magique où exercer leurs talents de stratèges, au fil de passionnantes campagnes ou parties entre plusieurs joueurs. Chaque joueur devra mener sa civilisation à la victoire en se choisissant un protecteur qui viendra l'épauler : qui de Zeus, Poséidon ou Hades sera le Dieu du joueur Grec ? Qui de Ra, Isis ou Set idolâtrera le joueur Egyptien ? Le joueur Nordique sera-t-il adorateur d'Odin, de Thor ou du fourbe Loki ?

« »

Eintauchen in eine weit zurückliegende Vergangenheit, in eine Zeit der Mythen und Legenden, als Götter die Erde bevölkerten und sich mit ihren Getreuen gegenseitig bekämpften. Mitmischen in den Kriegen zwischen Ägyptern, Griechen und Wikingern und dabei Zyklopen, Drachen und andere Fabelwesen zusammen mit Kriegern der jeweiligen Zivilisation in die Schlacht schicken. Zeus um Blitz und Donner oder Ra um Feuer anrufen, um die Gegner in epischen Schlachten zu bezwingen. Nachdem Ensemble Studios mit *Age of Empires* und *Age of Kings* bereits unzählige Spieler in die Antike und ins Mittelalter versetzt haben, präsentieren die Entwickler nun eine neue magische Welt, wo Hobby-Strategen – auch im Mehrspieler-Modus – ihre Fähigkeiten in einer faszinierenden 3-D-Landschaft unter Beweis stellen können. Jeder Spieler hat die Aufgabe, seine Zivilisation zum Sieg zu führen, und dazu muss er sich einen Beschützer suchen, der ihn bei seinen Missionen unterstützt. Welcher Gott wird dem Griechen beistehen: Ist es Zeus, Poseidon oder Hades? Wen wird der Ägypter anbeten: Ra, Isis oder Seth? Und welchen Gott wird der Wikinger erwählen: Odin, Thor oder den arglistigen Loki?

Asheron's Call

The isle of Dereth - an artificial world peopled with wandering monsters - was created by Lord Asheron, the great magus of Empyrea. Hundreds of adventurers, transported to Dereth by strange magic portals, have built towns there in the style of their native planet. But most of Dereth remains unexplored, from the lofty mountains in the North to the baking deserts of the West. Fending off the dreadful creatures of this artificial world, forming themselves into hierarchical castes, and exploring the mysterious underground chambers scattered around the island, the adventurers of Dereth scour this immense territory in quest of adventure, prestige and wealth. This was the first large-scale multi-player RPG from Microsoft.

Asheron's Call is a ceaselessly evolving universe in which thousands of gamers take on the roles of mage and warrior, seeking adventure on their own or creating guilds to help each other fathom the mysteries of Dereth.

« »

Façonnée par Lord Asheron, grand mage d'Empyrea, l'île de Dereth est un monde artificiel peuplé de monstres errants. Des centaines 'aventuriers se sont retrouvés sur Dereth, transportés par d'étranges portails magiques, et ont bâti des villes sur le modèle de leurs nations d'origine. Mais la majeure partie de Dereth est inexplorée, des hautes montagnes du Nord aux déserts brûlants de l'Ouest. Combattant les terribles créatures de ce monde artificiel, explorant les mystérieux souterrains disséminés sur l'île, se regroupant en castes hiérarchisées, les aventuriers de Dereth sillonnent les régions de l'immense territoire en quête d'aventure, de prestige et de richesse.

Premier jeu de rôles massivement multijoueurs de Microsoft, *Asheron's Call* est un univers en perpétuelle évolution où des milliers de joueurs incarnent guerriers et mages, partent à l'aventure en solitaire ou créent des guildes et s'entraident pour percer les mystères de Dereth.

« »

Die von Lord Asheron, dem großen Magier von Empyrea, geschaffene Insel Dereth ist eine künstliche Welt, die von streunenden Monstern bevölkert wird. Dort haben sich hunderte von mutigen Abenteurern versammelt, die über seltsame Zaubertore dorthin gelangt sind und nach dem Vorbild ihres jeweiligen Heimatlandes Städte gebaut haben. Weite Teile der Insel sind jedoch unerforscht: von den hohen Bergen im Norden bis hin zu den Wüstengebieten im Westen. Und so durchstreifen die Neuankömmlinge die Wildnis der riesigen Insel auf der Suche nach Abenteuern, nach Ansehen und Reichtum. Dabei müssen sie gegen schreckliche Monster kämpfen, sich in ein weit verzweigtes Labyrinth unterirdischer Katakomben begeben und strategische Bündnisse eingehen.

Asheron's Call ist das erste Online-Rollenspiel von Microsoft im Multiplayermodus, das in einer Welt spielt, die sich ständig weiterentwickelt und in der tausende von Spielern in die Rolle von Kriegern und Magiern schlüpfen können. Entweder ziehen sie allein ins Abenteuer oder sie verbünden sich mit anderen, um gemeinsam die Geheimnisse von Dereth aufzudecken.

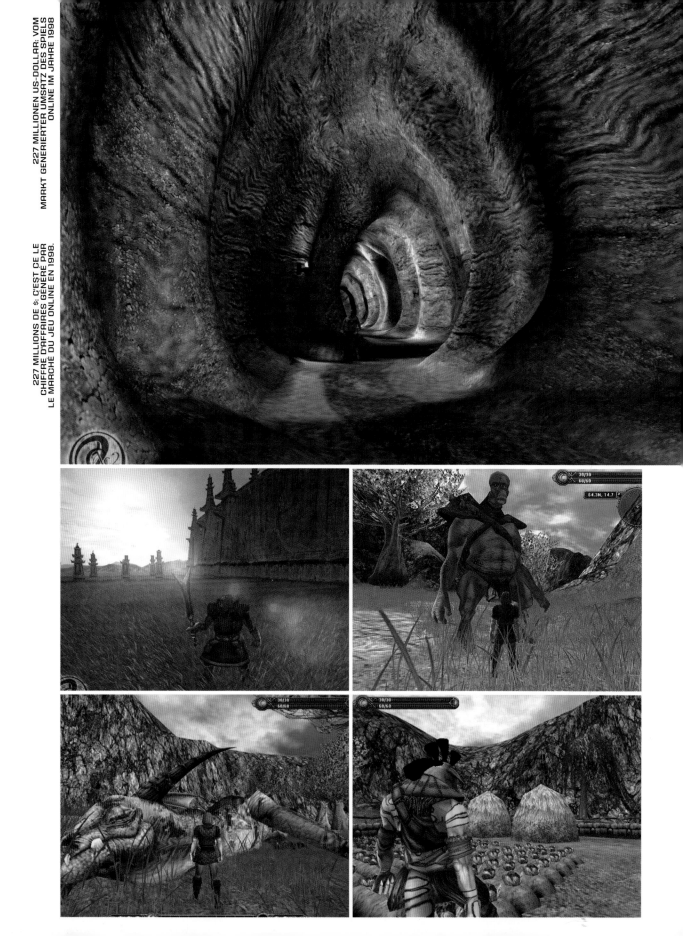

227 MILLIONEN US-DOLLAR: VOM MARKT GENERIERTER UMSATZ DES SPIELS ONLINE IM JAHRE 1998

227 MILLIONS DE $: C'EST CE LE CHIFFRE D'AFFAIRES GÉNÉRÉ PAR LE MARCHÉ DU JEU ONLINE EN 1998.

NAME

PLATFORM

RELEASE

EDITOR

DEVELOPER

COPYRIGHTS

FACT

Azurik

The Lord Guardians of Perathia are responsible for the safety of the four Elemental Disks, the source whence all proceeds. Eldwyn, aged master of the Guild and protector of the disk, shares his wisdom with two young and still inexperienced Guardians before choosing which must succeed him. His preference goes to young Azurik. The other student, the power-hungry Balthazar, is jealous; unable to bear rejection, he sells his soul to the dead, then, invested with shadowy powers, murders his ex-mentor, shatters the four disks of Perathia and scatters the pieces through the kingdom. The young Azurik, determined to avenge his teacher and to prevent Balthazar plunging the world into chaos, sets off in search of the fragments, armed with nothing but a wand, though in his hands this staff has remarkable powers. For Azurik is a magical adept, and can summon the forces of fire, earth, water and air to overcome the myriad dangers he will meet on his way.
« »

Les Lords Guardians de Perathia ont la responsabilité de protéger les quatre disques élémentaires, source de toute chose. Le vieil Eldwyn, maître actuel de la Guilde et protecteur des disques, dispense son savoir à deux jeunes Guardians encore peu expérimentés, avant de choisir celui qui prendra sa succession. Sa préférence va au jeune Azurik, et l'autre étudiant, Balthazar, ne peut le supporter. Jaloux et avide de puissance, Balthazar vend son âme au monde des morts puis, investi de ténébreux pouvoirs, assassine son mentor avant de briser les quatre disques de Perathia et d'en disperser les fragments à travers le royaume. Le jeune Azurik, prêt à venger son professeur et à empêcher Balthazar de plonger le monde dans le chaos, part à la recherche des fragments de disques, armé d'un simple bâton qui, dans ses mains, recèle un grand pouvoir. Adepte de la magie, Azurik peut en effet faire appel aux forces du feu, de l'eau, de l'air et de la terre pour vaincre les mille dangers qui se dresseront sur son chemin.
« »

Die Lord Guardians von Perathia tragen die Verantwortung für die vier Elementarscheiben, aus denen alles hervorgeht. Der alte Eldwyn, derzeitiger Meister der Gilde und Hüter der Scheiben, gibt sein Wissen an zwei junge, noch unerfahrene Guardians weiter, bevor er einen von ihnen zu seinem Nachfolger bestimmt. Seine Wahl fällt auf den jungen Azurik, doch Balthazar, der andere Schüler, kann ihn nicht leiden. Deshalb verkauft der eifersüchtige und machthungrige Balthazar seine Seele ans Totenreich, bringt dann – ausgestattet mit allerlei dunklen Mächten – seinen Mentor um, bevor er die vier Scheiben von Perathia zerschlägt und die Einzelteile über das ganze Reich verteilt. Der junge Azurik, der seinen Lehrer rächen und Balthazar daran hindern will, die Welt ins Chaos zu stürzen, begibt sich nun auf die Suche nach den überall verstreuten Bruchstücken. Als „Waffe" dient ihm ein einfacher Stock, der jedoch in seinen Händen eine große Kraft entfaltet. Als Zauberlehrling kann Azurik natürlich auch die Elementargewalten Feuer, Wasser, Luft und Erde anrufen, um die vielen Gefahren abzuwenden, die unterwegs auf ihn lauern.

MAGICAL HEROES
« BATTLE REALMS »

NAME
PLATFORM
RELEASE
EDITOR
DEVELOPER
COPYRIGHTS

P – 448

Battle Realms

A great epic of initiation awaits the young Kenji. On his return from seven long years of exile, he finds his homeland in ruins; the shadowy armies of the Horde have burst forth from Hell, massacred his Clan, and are transforming medieval Japan into a wasteland. The future of his country depends on Kenji. But what of his own destiny? Will he, with the aid of the noble Dragon Clan, save Japan? Or will he be tempted by Evil and swear allegiance to the sinister Serpent Clan, as his father did? Half-way between strategy game and fantasy fiction, *Battle Realm* is all coherent settings and vivid characters. Traditional tales have fed into both its scenario, which borrows liberally from Japanese myth, and its graphic environment; the result is a handsome mix of Asian folklore, characters inspired by mangas, and Western fantasies of the heroic.

« »

Une grande et épique quête initiatique attend le jeune Kenji qui, après sept longues années d'exil, revient chez les siens pour ne trouver que ruines. Son Clan a été anéanti par les ténébreuses armées de La Horde, débarquées de l'Enfer et menaçant de transformer le Japon médiéval en terre brûlée. De Kenji dépendra l'avenir de sa terre, mais son destin n'est cependant pas tracé : tentera-t-il de sauver le Japon à l'aide du noble Clan du Dragon ou sera-t-il tenté par le Mal en prêtant allégeance au sombre Clan du Serpent comme le fit son père ? Entre stratégie et récit fantastique, le jeu *Battle Realms*, dont Kenji est le héros, réussit à harmoniser l'aventure et la tactique, grâce à un monde cohérent où évoluent des personnages hauts en couleurs. Le jeu rend avec réussite hommage aux contes traditionnels, tant grâce à son scénario qui puise avec liberté au cœur des mythes japonais, qu'avec son environnement graphique, mêlant agréablement folklore asiatique, personnages inspirés de mangas et heroic-fantasy occidentale.

« »

Eine große und epische Quest erwartet den jungen Kenji, der nach sieben langen Jahren im Exil nach Hause zurückkehrt und dort alles zerstört vorfindet. Sein Clan wurde vernichtet von finsteren Armeen. Diese Horde, die geradewegs der Hölle entstiegen ist, droht nun das mittelalterliche Japan in brennende Erde zu verwandeln. Von Kenji hängt die Zukunft seines Landes ab, doch sein Schicksal ist keineswegs vorbestimmt: Wird er versuchen, mit Hilfe des edlen Drachen-Clans Japan zu retten, oder wird er sich vom Bösen in Versuchung führen lassen und dem düsteren Schlangen-Clan Gehorsam leisten wie einst sein Vater?

Battle Realms - ein Mittelding zwischen Strategiespiel und fantastischer Erzählung mit Kenji als dessen Held - gelingt es, Abenteuer und Taktik geschickt miteinander zu verbinden. Das liegt an der harmonisch gestalteten Spielwelt mit ihren farbenprächtigen Charakteren. Das Spiel ist eine Hommage an die traditionellen Erzählungen - hinsichtlich des Szenarios mit seiner starken Anlehnung an japanische Mythen und hinsichtlich der grafischen Ausstattung, die eine gelungene Mischung aus asiatischer Folklore, japanischen Comic-Figuren (Mangas) und westlichen Fantasy-Geschichten ist.

NAME

PLATFORM

RELEASE

EDITOR

DEVELOPER

COPYRIGHTS

FACT

Dark Cloud

Nothing but burnt earth remains of the once peaceful kingdom after its destruction by a terrifying evil genie. If its former splendour is to be restored, only one hope remains: the magic spheres of Atlamillia. For the spirit of the king contrived to save a part of the population by protecting it in magical spheres, the Atla, which were dispersed during the genie's attack. If they could be gathered in one place, the kingdom might regain its former beauty. Youthful and happy-go-lucky, Toan is nevertheless entrusted with this perilous mission. To aid him in his quest, the spirit of the king bestows a magic jewel on him, the Atlamillia, which confers magic powers and will allow him to muster the spheres. Innumerable enemies and dangers threaten the young Toan and the companions who join him in his quest: the beautiful Ruby, the muscular Goro, the agile Ungaga, the astonishing Ozmond and the lovable Xiao.

« »

Autrefois paisible et accueillant, le royaume, détruit par un effrayant génie maléfique, n'est plus que terre brûlée. Un espoir subsiste encore pour rendre sa splendeur à ce monde désolé : les sphères magiques d'Atlamillia. L'esprit du roi a en effet réussi à sauver une partie de la population en la protégeant dans plusieurs sphères magiques, les Atla, qui ont été dispersées lors de l'attaque du génie. Si elles venaient à être rassemblées, le royaume pourrait retrouver sa splendeur d'antan. Malgré sa jeunesse et son apparente insouciance, Toan est investi de cette périlleuse mission. Pour l'aider dans sa quête, l'esprit du roi lui confie une gemme enchantée, l'Atlamillia, qui le dotera de pouvoirs magiques et lui permettra de rassembler les sphères. D'innombrables ennemis et dangers guettent le jeune Toan et les compagnons qui viendront le rejoindre au cours de sa quête : la belle Ruby, le musclé Goro, l'agile Ungaga, l'étonnant Ozmond et l'adorable Xiao.

« »

Das einst friedliche und gastfreundliche Königreich wurde von einem Furcht erregenden bösen Dschinn angegriffen und komplett zerstört. Es besteht aber noch Hoffnung, dass der verwüstete Ort wieder in seiner alten Pracht erstrahlt, und zwar mit Hilfe der Zauberkugeln des Atlamillias. Der Feenkönig hat es im letzten Moment geschafft, einen Teil der Bewohner zu retten, indem er sie in viele kleine Zauberkugeln, so genannte Atla, transferiert hat, die beim Angriff des bösen Dschinns in alle Winde zerstreut wurden. Gelingt es, sie einzusammeln, könnte das Königreich wieder in seiner früheren Pracht und Herrlichkeit erstrahlen. Der noch junge und offensichtlich sehr leichtsinnige Toan wird für die gefährliche Mission ausgewählt. Um ihm bei seiner Suche zu helfen, vertraut ihm der Feenkönig einen verzauberten Edelstein an, das Atlamillia, das mit magischen Fähigkeiten ausstattet ist und ihm helfen soll, die Kugeln zu finden. Unzählige Gegner und Gefahren warten auf den jungen Toan und seine Gefährten, die schöne Ruby, den muskulösen Goro, die flinke Ungaga, den sagenhaften Ozmond und den fabelhaften Xiao, die sich nach und nach zu ihm gesellen.

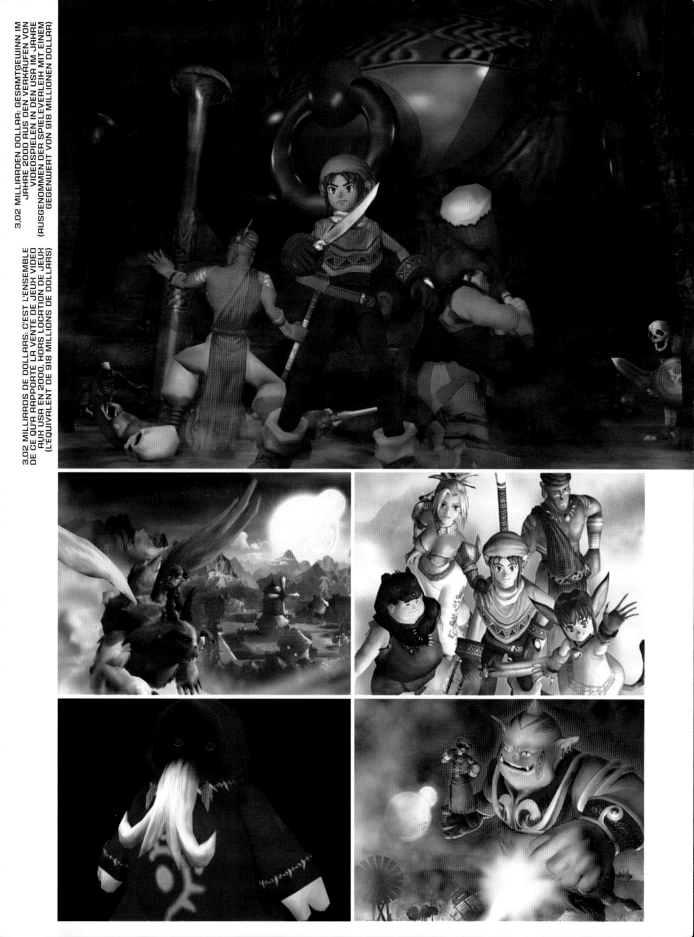

MAGICAL HEROES
« DUELFIELD »

NAME
PLATFORM
RELEASE
EDITOR
DEVELOPER
COPYRIGHTS
FACT

P – 456

DuelField

In the beginning, a single entity reigned over the universe. To escape eternal solitude, it dispersed itself into the millions of souls at loose in the cosmos. It thus engendered the powerful deities, along with various species of inferior creature. All creatures are linked to one of the six original element-deities: Earth, Nature, Air, Water, Fire and Limbo. But the deities are quick to come to blows, each attacking the others with the help of the creatures dependent on the same element. Though deities can overcome their fellow-gods in these duels, war will never be over; the deities themselves are immortal and their conflicts can never end... *DuelField* was inspired by the famous collector-card game *Magic: The Gathering*. It can be played only on the Internet and allows the gamer to assume the role of the various deities. The rules are easy to grasp, but, as the player gains experience, the game opens up to reveal its underlying strategic complexity.

« »

Au commencement, une seule entité régnait sur l'univers. Afin de combattre son éternelle solitude, elle se dispersa en millions d'âmes de par le cosmos, engendrant des êtres puissants, les déités et des espèces inférieures, les créatures, toutes liées à l'un des six éléments originels que sont la Terre, la Nature, l'Air, l'Eau, le Feu et le Néant. Les déités ne tardèrent cependant pas à s'entre-déchirer, chacune affrontant les autres par l'intermédiaire des créatures dépendantes du même Elémentaire. Si les déités peuvent vaincre leurs semblables lors de ces duels, cette guerre ne s'achèvera jamais : les batailles peuvent être gagnées ou perdues, mais les déités sont immortelles et s'affronteront jusqu'à la fin des temps... S'inspirant des échecs et du célèbre jeu de cartes à jouer et collectionner *Magic: The Gathering*, *DuelField* est un titre uniquement jouable sur Internet et permettant aux joueurs d'incarner différentes déités dans des parties aux règles simples à assimiler, mais dotées d'une grande profondeur qui se dévoile avec l'expérience, et offrent de nombreuses stratégies complexes.

« »

Am Anfang herrschte eine einzige Wesenheit über das Universum. Um ihrer ewigen Einsamkeit ein Ende zu setzen, zerstreute sie sich in Millionen Seelen über den Kosmos. Dabei brachte sie mächtige Wesen, die Gottheiten, und niedere Spezies, die Kreaturen, hervor, die allesamt mit einem der sechs Grundstoffe, also der Erde, der Natur, der Luft, dem Wasser, dem Feuer und dem Nichts, in Verbindung standen. Es dauerte nicht lange, da begannen sich die Gottheiten gegenseitig zu bekriegen, und zwar mit Hilfe der Kreaturen, die den jeweiligen Elementen zugeordnet waren. Tragen die Gottheiten bei diesen Duellen den Sieg über ihresgleichen davon, wird der Krieg niemals aufhören: Die Schlachten können gewonnen oder verloren werden, aber die Gottheiten sind unsterblich und werden bis zum Ende aller Zeiten kämpfen... *DuelField*, das mit Anleihen beim Schachspiel und bei *Magic: The Gathering*, dem berühmten Sammelkartenspiel macht, lässt sich nur übers Internet spielen. Die Spieler können in den Kämpfen die Rolle von Gottheiten übernehmen. Die Partien sind nach einfachen Regeln aufgebaut, glänzen aber durch große Spieltiefe, die sich mit zunehmender Erfahrung offenbart, und bieten außerdem jede Menge komplexer Strategien.

900: ANZAHL DER AUFGENOMMENEN FILMSZENEN FÜR DAS SPIEL UCIU MAYHEM AUF PLAYSTATION.

900: C'EST LE NOMBRE DE SCÈNES RÉALISÉES EN MOTION-CAPTURE POUR LE JEU UCIU MAYHEM SUR PLAYSTATION.

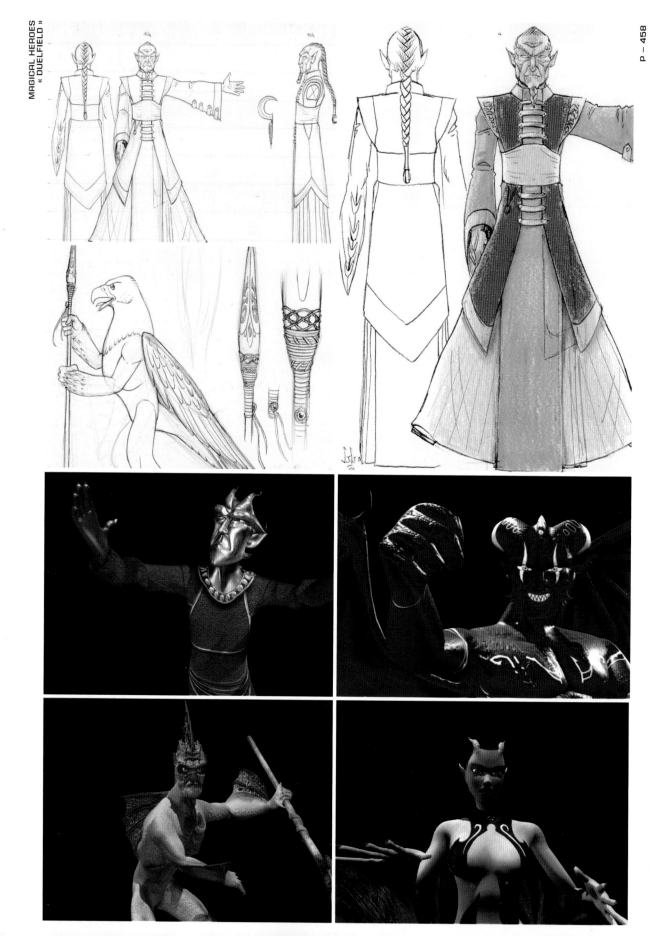

NAME
PLATFORM
RELEASE
EDITOR
DEVELOPER
COPYRIGHTS

FACT

Dungeon Siege

Protected by vast fortifications and the redoubtable Tenth Legion, the Kingdom of Ebh is the youngest of the nations bordering the sinister Plain of Tears. Till now, the fortifications, manned by the specially trained troops of Legion-Commandant Mage Merik, have protected Ebh from the malevolent creatures of the Plain. But now, the hordes of the Plain have somehow defeated Merik's army, and nothing is left to protect the Kingdom from the depredations of the Krugs, Skeletons, Darklings and other plug-ugly creatures. The inhabitants of the Kingdom can only pray to their god Azunai for a miracle. But Ebh finds an unlikely saviour: a young farmer resists the invaders from the Plain, at first alone, then joined by other heroes. Can they repel the shadowy hordes eradicating all vestige of life in the Kingdom?
« »

Protégé par de grandes fortifications et par la Dixième Légion redoutée, le Royaume d'Ehb est la plus jeune nation bordant la sombre Plaine des Larmes. Jusqu'alors, la muraille et les troupes entraînées du Mage Merik, commandant de la Légion, ont su protéger Ehb des raids des créatures maléfiques de la Plaine. Mais sans que personne ne sache comment, les hordes de la Plaine des Larmes réussissent à envahir Ehb et vaincre l'armée de Merik. Plus rien ne protège désormais Ehb des assauts des Krugs, Squelettes, Darklings et autres créatures de la Plaine. Désormais, les pacifiques citoyens du Royaume ne peuvent plus que prier leur dieu Azunai pour qu'un miracle les sauve. Un jeune fermier que rien ne semblait prédestiner à devenir le sauveur d'Ehb affrontera les envahisseurs de la Plaine, seul puis rejoint par d'autres héros qui, à ses côtés, sauront peut-être repousser les hordes ténébreuses menaçant toute vie dans le Royaume.
« »

Hinter einer mächtigen Befestigungsanlage und beschützt von der gefürchteten Zehnten Legion liegt das noch junge Königreich Ehb am Rande der düsteren Ebene der Tränen. Bisher boten das Bollwerk und die Truppen unter der Führung des Magiers Merik genügend Schutz vor den Angriffen der finsteren Kreaturen aus der Ebene. Doch irgendwie gelingt es den Horden aus dem Umland, in Ehb einzudringen und Meriks Legion zu besiegen. Niemand beschützt fortan Ehb vor den Übergriffen der Krugs, Skelette, Darklings und anderer Furcht erregender Kreaturen. So bleibt den friedlichen Bewohnern des Königreichs nichts anderes übrig, als zu ihrem Gott Azunai zu beten, damit er sie durch ein Wunder rette. Ein rechtschaffener Bauer, der sich eigentlich durch nichts für seine Aufgabe als Retter von Ehb prädestiniert, nimmt den Kampf gegen die Eindringlinge auf, zuerst im Alleingang. Doch schon bald schließen sich Gleichgesinnte an. Vielleicht schaffen sie es ja gemeinsam, den marodierenden Horden Einhalt zu gebieten.

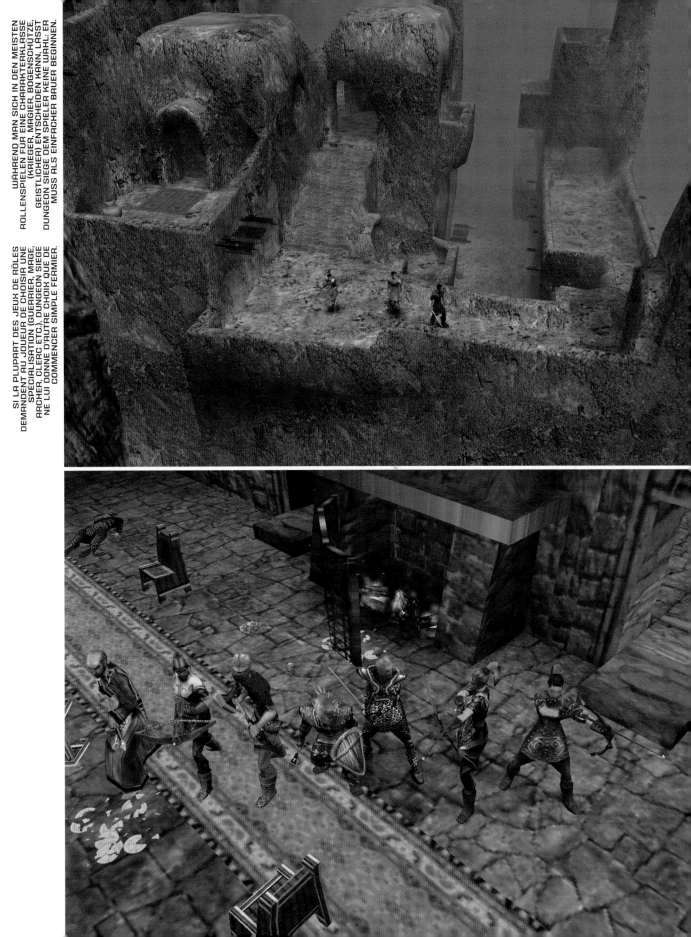

WÄHREND MAN SICH IN DEN MEISTEN ROLLENSPIELEN FÜR EINE CHARAKTERKLASSE (KRIEGER, MAGIER, BOGENSCHÜTZE, GEISTLICHER) ENTSCHEIDEN KANN, LÄSST DUNGEON SIEGE DEM SPIELER KEINE WAHL: ER MUSS ALS EINFACHER BAUER BEGINNEN.

SI LA PLUPART DES JEUX DE RÔLES DEMANDENT AU JOUEUR DE CHOISIR UNE SPÉCIALISATION (GUERRIER, MAGE, ARCHER, CLERC ETC.), DUNGEON SIEGE NE LUI DONNE D'AUTRE CHOIX QUE DE COMMENCER SIMPLE FERMIER.

NAME
PLATFORM
RELEASE
EDITOR
DEVELOPER
COPYRIGHTS

Etherlords

In this medieval universe, White Ether is everything. Those who master its powers dominate the world. But White Ether is ephemeral, degenerating into four lesser forms, each linked to a particular reign: the Red Ether of Chaos, the Blue Ether of Kinetics, the Green Ether of Life, and Black Ether, the magic of Synthesis. When these Ethers merge, the explosion of energy gives rise to worlds like that of the Lords, beings who partly control the Ether. But an influx of White Ether has plunged their world into chaos, and each Lord craves sole mastery; waging all-out war, scouring the world for Ether sources, they dispatch their troops into battle. Their armies are led by magi capable of summoning supernatural creatures to their aid, and no sacrifice is too great if it makes their Lord sole master.

« »

Dans cet univers médiéval étrange, l'Ether blanc est la source de tout. Ceux qui savent maîtriser l'extraordinaire puissance de ce flux d'énergie peuvent dominer le monde, mais l'Ether blanc est éphémère et se transforme rapidement en quatre déclinaisons moins puissantes, chacune liée à un règne : le rouge Ether du Chaos, l'Ether bleu de la Cinétique, l'Ether vert de la vie et l'Ether noir, magie de la Synthèse. Il arrive que ces Ethers fusionnent, l'énergie ainsi dégagée donnant naissance à des Mondes tel celui des Seigneurs, êtres capables d'utiliser partiellement la puissance des Ethers. Suite à un influx d'Ether blanc, le Monde des Seigneurs est plongé dans le Chaos. Tous avides de devenir l'unique maître de leur monde, les Seigneurs se livrent alors des guerres sans merci, sillonnant le monde pour s'accaparer les sources d'Ether et envoyant leurs troupes au combat. Menées par des mages capables d'invoquer des créatures surnaturelles, les armées des Seigneurs se livrent d'incessantes batailles, prêtes à tous les sacrifices pour que leur maître devienne le divin souverain de leur monde.

« »

In dieser unheimlichen Welt des Mittelalters ist der weiße Äther die Quelle allen Lebens und Geschehens. Nur wer die außergewöhnliche Kraft dieses Energieflusses zu lenken versteht, kann die Welt beherrschen. Der weiße Äther aber ist vergänglich und besitzt die Fähigkeit, sich rasch in vier weniger mächtige Ströme zu teilen: in den roten Äther des Chaos, den blauen Äther der Bewegungsenergie, den grünen Äther des Lebens und den schwarzen Äther, der die Zauberkraft der Synthese verkörpert. Mitunter können diese Äther miteinander verschmelzen. Die daraus entstehende Energie gebiert neue Welten. So die Welt der Lords, jener Wesen, die sich zum Teil der Kraft der Äther zu bedienen wissen. Unter dem Einfluss des weißen Äthers wurde die Welt der Lords in das Chaos gestürzt. Die Lords - sämtlich vom Willen besessen, einziger Herrscher über ihre Welt zu werden - führen gnadenlos Krieg gegeneinander, um der Quellen des Äthers habhaft zu werden. Angeführt von Magiern, die in der Lage sind, den Beistand übernatürlicher Kreaturen zu rufen, liefern sich die Armeen der Lords fortwährend Gefechte. Die Truppen sind zu jedem Opfer bereit, damit ihr Gebieter der göttliche Herrscher ihrer Welt wird.

NAME
PLATFORM
RELEASE
EDITOR
DEVELOPER
COPYRIGHTS
FACT

Grandia

Yep! It's an RPG… meaning the young hero is apparently doomed to an ordinary life, till all of a sudden destiny speaks, and he alone is able to overcome the unspeakable dangers threatening the universe. In the *Grandia* universe, the young hero is named Ryudo; his adversary is the demon Valmah, about to resuscitate after a short nap of some thousand years or so. To bring this horrific deity back to life, his henchmen are gathering up his body parts, which a higher power named Granas had dispersed after a gruelling battle. Elena, a young priestess and guardian of Valmah's wings, is possessed by the demon while under Ryudo's protection, and he will face down any danger to save her. This is a story of the fantastical, full of highly original monsters, fairy-tale environments and dazzlingly improbable architecture.
« »

Comme c'est très souvent le cas dans les jeux de rôles sur ordinateur et consoles, le joueur incarne un jeune héros que rien ne semblait lier à une destinée extraordinaire, mais qui seul saura vaincre d'indicibles dangers menaçant de détruire le monde. Dans l'univers de *Grandia II*, ce jeune héros répond au nom de Ryûdo et sera amené à combattre le démon Valmah qui s'apprête à ressusciter après 1000 ans de sommeil. Pour réveiller la terrifiante divinité, les sbires de Valmah doivent rassembler les fragments du corps de leur maître qu'une autre puissance supérieure, nommée Granas, a dispersés de par le monde après une âpre bataille. Elena, une jeune prêtresse qui gardait les ailes de Valmah, est possédée par le démon alors qu'elle se trouvait sous la protection de Ryûdo qui affrontera mille danger pour la sauver… Véritable conte fantastique, le jeu brille par des monstres au look fort original, des environnements féeriques et des bâtiments aux architectures aussi improbables qu'éblouissantes.
« »

Wie so oft bei Rollenspielen auf dem PC oder der Konsole schlüpft der Spieler auch hier in die Rolle eines jugendlichen Helden, bei dem eigentlich so gar nichts auf ein außergewöhnliches Schicksal hindeutet, der aber als Einziger imstande ist, die unsäglichen Gefahren zu bannen, die die Welt zu zerstören drohen. In der Welt von *Grandia II* heißt dieser jugendliche Held Ryudo und ist dazu auserkoren, gegen das Böse zu kämpfen, in diesem Fall gegen die böse Gottheit Valmar. Dessen Wiedergeburt steht nach tausendjährigem Schlaf kurz bevor. Doch zuvor müssen seine Schergen die Einzelteile seines Körpers wieder zusammensetzen, die von einer anderen höheren Macht namens Granas nach einem heftigen Kampf über die Welt verstreut wurden. Die junge Priesterin Elena, die Valmars Flügel hütete, ist von dem Dämon besessen, steht aber unter dem Schutz von Ryudo, der sich tausend Gefahren stellt, um sie zu retten…
Grandia II ist ein echtes Fantasy-Märchen, das sich auszeichnet durch knackige Monster, reizvolle Landschaften und Gebäude von so haarsträubender wie verblüffender Architektur.

160: ANZAHL DER LIEDER, DIE NOBUO UEMATSU UEMATSU A COMPOSÉ POUR FINAL FANTASY IX.

160: C'EST LE NOMBRE DE CHANSONS QUE NOBUO FÜR FINAL FANTASY IX KOMPONIERT HAT

MAGICAL HEROES
« NEVERWINTER NIGHTS »

NAME
PLATFORM
RELEASE
EDITOR
DEVELOPER
COPYRIGHTS
FACT

P – 474

Neverwinter Nights

The *Baldur's Gate* Saga, and its latest manifestation, *Neverwinter Nights*, are in the great tradition of the heroic fantasy (and more particularly of the role-playing universe of TSR's *Dungeons and Dragons*). The gamer takes on the identity of a hero, within a narrative in which the destiny of the world rests, curiously enough, on the bravery of a handful of heroes. Whether they be Paladin, Ranger, Magus or Thief, human, elf, or goblin, these heroes must combat the forces of darkness, whose demon legions infest the plains, mountains, cities and castles of the Forgotten Kingdoms. This is a vast world, and innumerable perilous quests and prestigious feats of arms are open to anyone who chooses to enter this elaborate fantastico-medieval universe. Here the goal is the perfection of self, as each adventurer gains experience over the course of the quest, acquiring new strength, agility and magical powers.
« »

Dans la grande tradition de l'heroic fantasy, et plus particulièrement de l'univers du jeu de rôles Donjons et Dragons de la société TSR, la saga *Baldur's Gate*, dont *Neverwinter Nights* est le dernier représentant en date, offre à chacun de devenir un héros et de vivre des aventures où le destin du monde est entre les mains d'une poignée de héros. Qu'ils soient Paladin, Ranger, Mage ou Voleur, qu'ils soient des elfes, des humains ou des nains, ces héros devront combattre les forces des ténèbres qui ont envoyé leurs légions démoniaques infester les Royaumes Oubliés, ses plaines, ses montagnes, ses villes et ses donjons. Un monde gigantesque à parcourir, d'innombrables quêtes périlleuses et exploits prestigieux sont à portée de main de tous ceux qui rêvent d'entrer dans un univers fantastico-médiéval élaboré, pour vivre des aventures dont le grand aboutissement est l'accomplissement de soi, chaque aventurier acquérant de l'expérience au fil de ses pérégrinations, et donc plus de force, d'agilité ou de pouvoirs magiques.
« »

In der großen Tradition der Fantasy-Heldengeschichten, allen voran die Burgen- und Drachenrollenspiele der Firma TSR, bietet die Saga *Baldur's Gate*, die mit *Neverwinter Nights* ihre jüngste Kreation auf den Markt bringt, jedem Spieler die Möglichkeit, in die Rolle eines Helden zu schlüpfen und sich in Abenteuer zu stürzen, die das Schicksal der Welt in die Hände einiger Helden legen. Ob nun Paladin, Ranger, Magier oder Dieb, Elfen, Menschen oder Zwerge, die Helden müssen die Kräfte der Finsternis besiegen, die ihre dämonischen Legionen ausgeschickt haben, um die Vergessenen Reiche, ihre Ebenen, Gebirge, Städte und Burgen zu verseuchen. Eine gigantische Welt gilt es zu durchqueren, zahllose gefährliche Quests zu überstehen, und schon warten glänzende Heldentaten auf all diejenigen, die immer davon geträumt haben, eine spannende mittelalterliche Fantasiewelt zu betreten. Der Erfolg eines jeden Spielers ist die Verwirklichung seiner selbst, denn jeder Abenteurer wird im Laufe seiner Reisen an Erfahrung reicher und gewinnt auf diese Weise an Stärke, Gewandtheit und magischer Kraft.

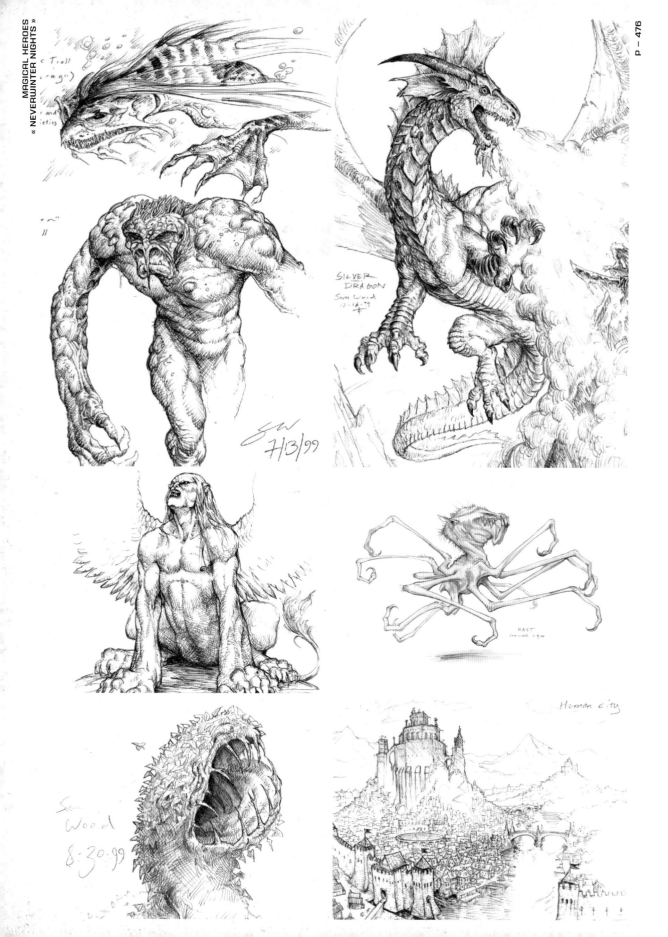

SILVER
DRAGON
Sam Wood
12·16·99

SW
7/13/99

RAST
Sam Wood 3·9·00

Sam
Wood
8·30·99

Human city

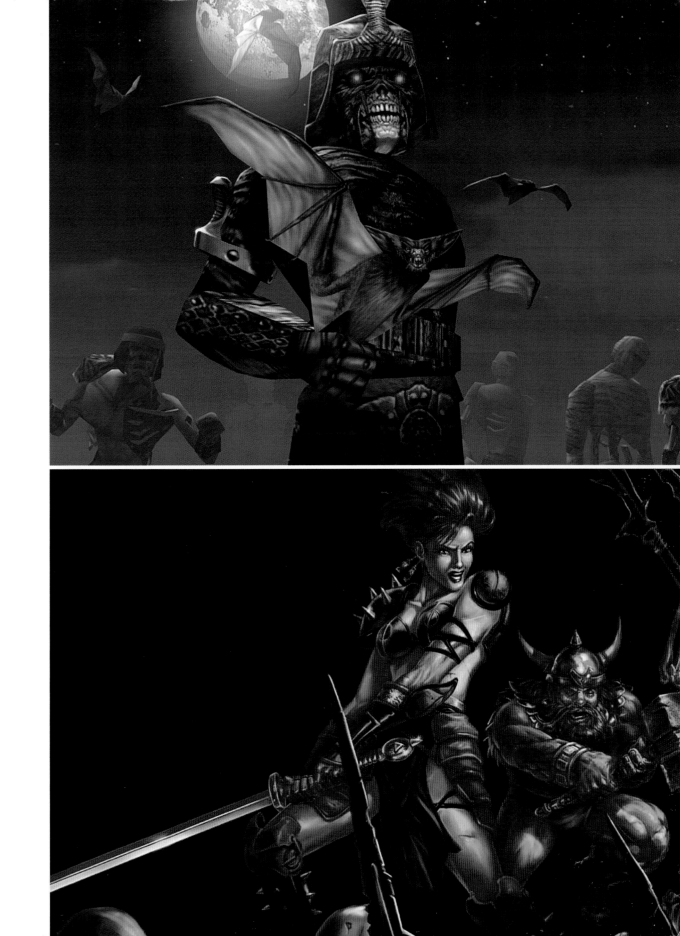

NAME
PLATFORM
RELEASE
EDITOR
DEVELOPER
COPYRIGHTS
FACT

Project Ego

Nothing marked you out for a life of adventure, let alone that of a hero famous throughout Albion. While still a child, you came home one day to find your family brutally murdered. Despite your youth, you swore to discover the culprits and avenge your loved ones. For Peter Molyneux, its creator, *Project Ego* is the next step in RPGs: a world in which the character you adopt matures and develops as experience and life-events ordain. As a gamer, you see your character's talents and physique change over the course of your adventure: wounds leave scars, a spell in a sunny country leaves a tan, and musculature responds to training and choice of weapon. In order to immerse the gamer still further in the virtual world of Albion, *Project Ego* will be a living world, in which each inhabitant has his or her own preoccupations, memories, friends and enemies. The reputation forged by your adopted self can earn you not just friends but enemies...

« »

Rien ne vous prédestinait à une vie d'aventurier, voire de héros célèbre dans tout Albion. Encore enfant, vous rentrez chez vous pour découvrir votre famille sauvagement assassinée. Malgré votre jeune âge, vous jurez de retrouver les coupables et de venger ceux qui vous sont chers. Project Ego est pour son créateur, Peter Molyneux, la prochaine étape du jeu de rôles informatique : un monde où le personnage incarné par le joueur vieillit et évolue en parfaite adéquation avec son expérience et les événements qui ponctuent son histoire personnelle. Le joueur verra se façonner le physique et les talents de son avatar au fil de l'aventure : les blessures en combat laisseront des cicatrices, la peau se burinera si le personnage reste dans des contrées ensoleillées, sa musculature changera suivant son entraînement et ses armes de prédilection... Afin d'ancrer plus encore le joueur dans la réalité virtuelle d'Albion, Project Ego sera un monde vivant, où chaque habitant aura ses préoccupations, ses souvenirs, ses amis et ennemis. Les actes de votre avatar lui forgeront une réputation qui pourra aussi bien lui apporter des partisans que lui créer des ennemis.

« »

Nichts deutete darauf hin, dass Sie ein Leben als Abenteurer führen oder gar in ganz Albion als Held gefeiert werden sollten. Sie waren noch ein Kind, als Sie entdeckten, dass Ihre gesamte Familie einem brutalen Mord zum Opfer gefallen war. Trotz Ihres jungen Alters schwören Sie, die Schuldigen zu finden und Ihre Angehörigen zu rächen. Project - Ego ist für seinen Schöpfer Peter Molyneux die nächste Etappe des elektronischen Rollenspiels: eine Welt, in der die vom Spieler verkörperte Figur altert und einen durch ihre persönlichen Erfahrungen und Erlebnisse geprägten Reifeprozess durchlebt. Der Spieler wird im Laufe der Abenteuer Veränderungen seines Äußeren wie auch der Talente seines Avatars beobachten: Die durch die Kämpfe erlittenen Wunden hinterlassen Narben, der Aufenthalt in sonnigen Gegenden gerbt die Haut, stetes Training und der Umgang mit Waffen straffen die Muskulatur...Um den Spieler noch stärker in die virtuelle Realität von Albion einzubinden, wird Project - Ego zu einer durch und durch lebendigen Welt werden, in der jeder Bewohner seinen Beschäftigungen nachgeht, seine Erinnerungen, seine Freunde und Feinde hat. Die Handlungen Ihres Avatar prägen seinen Ruf, der ihm sowohl Anhänger als auch Feinde einbringen wird.

1980: JAHR, IN DEM SICH DIE EINKÜNFTE VON
ATARI VERDOPPELTEN, WEIL SPACE INVADERS
AUF DER KONSOLE ATARI 2600
HERAUSGEKOMMEN WAR

1980: EN 1980, LES REVENUS DE ATARI ONT
DOUBLE GRACE A LA SORTIE DE SPACE
INVADERS SUR LA CONSOLE ATARI 2600

NAME
PLATFORM
RELEASE
EDITOR
DEVELOPER
COPYRIGHTS
FACT

Skies of Arcadia

In the aerial world of Arcadia, the population lives on islands that float in the sky beneath six great moons. These moons are the source of Arcadian magic, for rocks from the moons are permeated with strange lunar power. Some Arcadians make use of this magic to improve their living conditions; others once recklessly used it to create gigantic monsters called Gigas, fortunately now extinct. But the army of Valua, one of the six regions of Arcadia, has set off in search of big lunar rocks in order to resuscitate the Gigas and bring Arcadia under the dominion of its cruel leader, Galcian. At first, there was nothing to suggest that Vyse, a young pirate of the Blue Clan, he would stand between Galcian and his sinister objectives. But, in an astounding series of coincidences, he saves the mysterious princess Fina from Galcian's grasp, and in doing so discovers a new resolve; he will stand up to the Valuan armies and prevent the return of the dreadful Gigas.
« »

Arcadia est un monde aérien, et ses habitants vivent sur des îles flottant dans les cieux sous le regard de six grandes lunes. Ces lunes sont la source de la magie de ce monde, possible grâce aux fragments de roche venus des satellites gorgés de l'étrange pouvoir de ces astres. Si certains habitants d'Arcadia utilisent cette magie pour améliorer leurs conditions de vie, d'autres plus téméraires s'en sont servi il y a bien longtemps pour créer de gigantesques monstres, les Gigas, heureusement disparus aujourd'hui. Mais l'armée de Valua, une des six régions d'Arcadia, menée par le cruel Galcian, est partie à la recherche des grandes pierres lunaires, afin de ressusciter les Gigas et de faire tomber Arcadia sous son joug. Rien ne laissait prévoir que Vyse, un jeune pirate du Clan Bleu, serait le héros qui réussira à contrer les sombres objectifs de Galcian. Après avoir, par un étonnant concours de circonstances, sauvé la mystérieuse princesse Fina des griffes de Galcian, Vyse se dressera face aux armées de Valua, bien décidé à empêcher le retour des terrifiants Gigas.
« »

Arcadia ist eine Welt in den Lüften, deren Bewohner auf Inseln leben, die unter einem Himmel mit sechs großen Monden dahingleiten. Diese Monde versorgen Arcadia mit einer magischen Kraft aus den Felsstückchen der Himmelskörper, die von dieser Kraft erfüllt sind. Während einige Bewohner von Arcadia die Zauberkraft darauf verwenden, ihre Lebensumstände zu verbessern, gab es vor langer Zeit wesentlich dreistere Arcadier, die sich dieser Macht bedienten, um riesige Monster zu erschaffen, die Gigas, die heute zum Glück verschwunden sind. Doch nun hat sich die Armee von Valua, eine der sechs Regionen von Arcadia unter der Führung des grausamen Galcian, auf die Suche nach den großen Mondsteinen gemacht, um die Gigas wieder zum Leben zu erwecken und Arcadia zu unterjochen. Nichts deutete darauf hin, dass Vyse, der junge Pirat des Blauen Clans, der auserkorene Held würde. Ihm sollte es gelingen, die bösen Absichten von Galcian zu vereiteln. Nachdem er zunächst mit allerlei widrigen Umständen fertig werden muss und die geheimnisvolle Prinzessin Fina aus Galcians Klauen befreit, stellt er sich der Armee von Valua, fest entschlossen, die Rückkehr der grauenhaften Gigas zu verhindern.

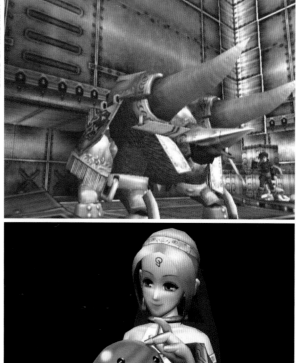

NAME
PLATFORM
RELEASE
EDITOR
DEVELOPER
COPYRIGHTS
FACT

Throne of Darkness

Once a land of miracles, the kingdom of Yamato has become a landscape of desolation. A sinister Black Lord in quest of immortality has liberated Raien, a terrifying demon, and Raien has unleashed his shadow hordes on Yamato. Only seven samurais have survived, but they have sworn to restore Yamato to its former splendour. They are men of complementary talents: the Leader, the Archer, the Sorcerer, the Sabre Master, Bushi, master of many weapons, the powerful Bull and the furious Berserker. Together they combat the armies of evil in the citadel, the sinister dungeons of Raien's fortress and the desolate plains and ravaged villages of Yamato. Zombie-soldiers, dragons, Tengus, Kappas and other extraordinary creatures rise against our seven heroes. But the spirit of their daimyo, who died at Raien's hands, smiles on their cause and, able to resuscitate samurais who perish in battle.

« »

Autrefois terre de prodiges, le royaume de Yamato est devenu un paysage de désolation, un sombre et puissant Seigneur noir en quête d'immortalité ayant libéré Raien, un démon effrayant qui déchaîna ses hordes ténébreuses sur Yamato. Seuls sept samouraïs ont survécu et se sont juré de rendre au royaume sa splendeur d'antan. Ces élus aux talents complémentaires (le Leader, l'Archer, le Sorcier, le Maître du sabre, le polyvalent Bushi, le puissant Taureau et le furieux Berseker) combattront les armées maléfiques du cœur même de leur citadelle aux sombres souterrains dans la forteresse de Raien, en passant par les plaines désolées et les villages ravagés de Yamato. Soldats morts-vivants, dragons, Tengus, Kappas et autres créatures extraordinaires se dresseront sur le chemin des sept héros. Mais l'esprit bienveillant de leur daimyo, tué par Raien, veille sur eux, et il pourra ressusciter plusieurs fois les samouraïs tombés au combat.

« »

Das Königreich von Yamato, einst ein Land der Wunder, ist zu einem Ort der Verzweiflung geworden. Auf der Suche nach dem ewigen Leben hatte ein finsterer und mächtiger schwarzer Herrscher Raien befreit, einen Furcht erregenden Dämon, der seine Heere auf Yamato hetzte. Die sieben überlebenden Samurais schworen sich, das Königreich wieder in seinem einstigen Glanz auferstehen zu lassen. Die Auserwählten, die sich allesamt durch besondere Talente auszeichnen (der Anführer, der Zauberer, der Schwertkämpfer, der vielseitige Bushi, der kräftige Bulle und der zornige Berserker), werden die Mächte des Bösen mitten in ihrer eigenen Zitadelle, in den finsteren Gewölben der Raien-Festung, in den verwüsteten Ebenen und den geplünderten Dörfern Yamatos zur Strecke bringen. Untote Krieger, Drachen, Tengus, Kappas und andere außergewöhnliche Kreaturen stellen sich den sieben Helden in den Weg. Doch der gütige Geist ihres von Raien getöteten Daimyos wacht über sie und wird die mehrmals gefallenen Samurais wieder zum Leben erwecken.

1.000 ZU 1: IM SZENARIO DES SPIELS
BATTLETANK KOMMT AUF 1.000 MÄNNER, DIE
DEN VIRUS ÜBERLEBEN, EINE EINZIGE FRAU.

1000 POUR 1: DANS LE SCÉNARIO DU JEU
BATTLETANK, POUR 1000 HOMMES
QUI ONT SURVÉCU AU VIRUS,
UNE SEULE FEMME Y A ÉCHAPPÉ.

MAGICAL HEROES
« WARRIOR KINGS »

NAME
PLATFORM
RELEASE
EDITOR
DEVELOPER
COPYRIGHTS
FACT

P – 490

Warrior Kings

Torn apart by three contending armies, the world is doomed. Goodbye to the balance of power; the Kingdom can be saved only by the final victory of one of three Warrior Kings. A parody of the struggle of Good and Evil is fought out between the clan of the Celestials and their sworn enemies, the Pagans. Led by the archangel Michael, the fanatical Celestials have launched a Holy War, and tolerance is not on the menu: their goals are inquisition, massacre of the infidel and outright domination of the Kingdom. The Pagans, meanwhile, are practitioners of Earth Magic. Human sacrifice and anarchy are their thing. They want to create a nightmare world of despotism by sorcery. Between these two extremes there is a third choice: technology. The work of the Renaissance clan is commerce and invention. But what price gunpowder and machinery against the terrifying magical powers of their rivals?

« »

Déchiré entre trois armes, le monde court à sa perte. L'équilibre étant définitivement rompu, seule la victoire d'un des clans, mené par un Roi Guerrier, peut éviter l'effondrement du Royaume. La balance du Bien et du Mal est représentée par l'affrontement perpétuel entre les Celestials, fanatiques religieux qui se sont lancés dans une Guerre Sainte ô combien intolérante : inquisition, génocide des incroyants et domination totale du Royaume sont leur objectif. Menés par l'Archange Michael, les Celestials ont pour ennemis jurés les Pagan, menés par le démon Abaddon. Adeptes de la magie de Terre, des sacrifices humains et de l'anarchie, les Pagan veulent transformer le monde en terre de cauchemar, où régnerait la sorcellerie. Entre ces deux extrêmes se dresse un troisième choix, celui de la technologie : loin des buts religieux des Celestials et des Pagan, les adeptes de la Renaissance se vouent au commerce et à l'invention : machines de guerre et poudre à canon pourront-elles se mesurer aux formidables puissances magiques des autres armées ?

« »

Die Welt ist in drei Fraktionen gespalten und völlig aus dem Gleichgewicht geraten. Der Untergang steht bevor. Jetzt kann nur noch der Sieg eines Clans, angeführt von einem Warrior King, den Zusammenbruch des Reiches verhindern. Der immerwährende Kampf zwischen Gut und Böse wird verkörpert durch die Celestials, militante Christen, die voller Fanatismus und mit Unterstützung des Erzengels Michael in einen heiligen Krieg ziehen. Ihre Ziele sind die Inquisition, die Ermordung der Ungläubigen und die totale Herrschaft über das ganze Reich. Erklärte Feinde der Glaubensfanatiker sind die Heiden mit dem Dämonenkönig Abaddon als Anführer. Die Heiden frönen der irdischen Magie, den Menschenopfern und der Anarchie schlechthin. Sie wollen die Welt in einen Ort des Schreckens mit Dämonen und Monstern verwandeln. Zwischen diesen beiden Extremen stehen die Technologiegläubigen. Während Christentum und Heidentum ihre religiösen Ziele durchzusetzen versuchen, haben sich die Anhänger der Renaissance ganz dem Handel und den Erfindungen verschrieben. Aber können mittelalterliche Kriegsmaschinerie und Schießpulver es mit den magischen Superkräften der anderen Mächte aufnehmen?

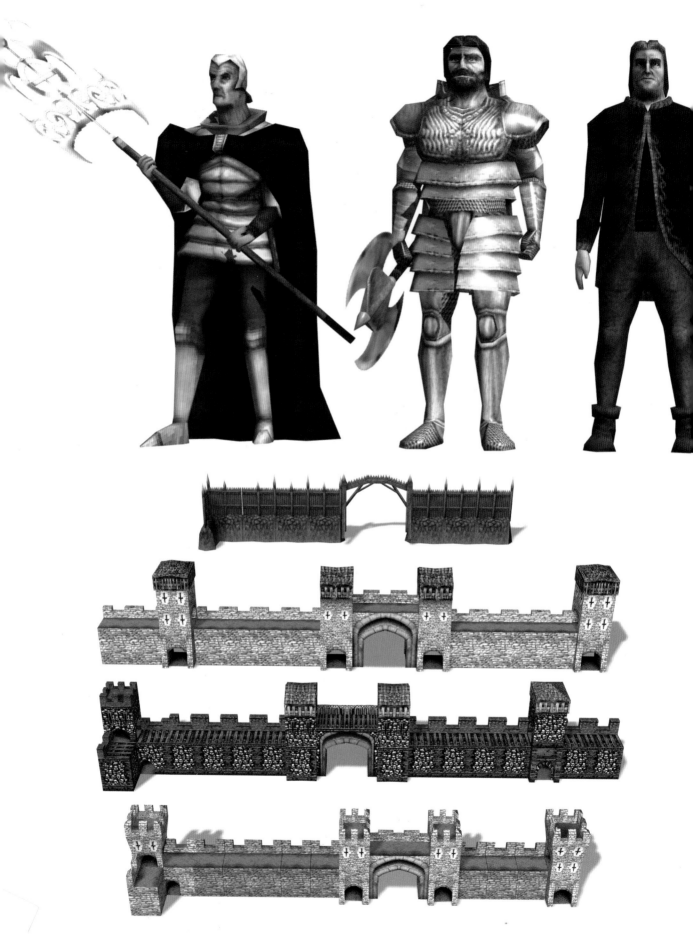

NAME
PLATFORM
RELEASE
EDITOR
DEVELOPER
COPYRIGHTS

Zelda

Link, the young hero of the *Zelda* series, is another major gaming figure born of Shigeru Miyamoto's teeming imagination. From the first title, which appeared in July 1997, to the *Legend of Zelda* (Gamecube 2002), the world of Hyrule - the setting for most of Link's adventures - has grown ever richer and more complex. Link is a valiant young adventurer devoted to Princess Zelda and the Triforce, the source of all energy. He has therefore faced any number of dangers, explored countless subterranean labyrinths, and conquered all the shadowy forces that attempt to invade Hyrule and seize the Triforce. Link's quests have also taken him into the past and future of Hyrule, to the dream island of Koholint and the plains of Termina, where he went disguised as a Mojo child. In *Ocarina of Time* on Nintendo 64 (1998), gamers could also find out about Link's early years, experience the events that forged his character and watch him grow as the adventure unfolded.

« »

Autre icône incontournable du jeu vidéo née de la fertile imagination de Shigeru Miyamoto, Link est le jeune héros des jeux *Zelda*. Du premier titre sorti en juillet 1997 à *Legend of Zelda* (Gamecube, 2002), le monde d'Hyrule où se déroule la majorité des histoires, s'est enrichi, gagnant en complexité au fil des épisodes. Link, vaillant jeune aventurier, protecteur de la princesse Zelda et de la source de toute énergie, la Triforce, a ainsi affronté maints dangers, exploré d'innombrables souterrains et vaincu les forces des ténèbres qui ont tenté d'envahir Hyrule et s'accaparer la Triforce. Ses quêtes ont également emmené Link voyager dans le passé et le futur d'Hyrule, dans l'île du rêve Koholint ou dans les plaines de Termina, transformé en petit être du peuple Mojo. Dans Ocarina of Time sur Nintendo 64 (1998), les joueurs ont également pu découvrir la jeunesse de Link, vivre les évènements qui ont forgé sa personnalité et le voir grandir au fil de l'aventure.

« »

Eine von vielen Kultfiguren des Videospiels aus der fantasievollen Feder von Shigeru Miyamoto heißt Link und ist der Held aus der Zelda-Saga. Seit dem ersten, im Juli 1997 erschienenenspiel bis zu *Legend of Zelda* (Gamecube, 2002) hat die Welt von Hyrule, wo sich die meisten Geschichten abspielen, von Episode zu Episode an Komplexität gewonnen.

Der tapfere kleine Link, Beschützer der Prinzessin Zelda und der Macht des magischen Dreiecks Triforce, hat sich so mancher Gefahr ausgesetzt, unzählige Gewölbe erkundet und die dunklen Mächte bezwungen, die immer wieder versuchten, Hyrule einzunehmen und das Triforce an sich zu reißen. Die aufregenden Missionen führten Link auch mittels Zeitreisen in die Vergangenheit und Zukunft von Hyrule, und als kleines Wesen des Mojo-Volkes reiste er zur Trauminsel Koholint oder in die Ebenen von Termina. In der Episode Ocarina of Time (Nintendo 64, 1998) konnten die Spieler gar in Links Vergangenheit reisen, dort an den Kindheitserlebnissen teilhaben, die seine Persönlichkeit geformt haben, und seine weitere Entwicklung verfolgen.

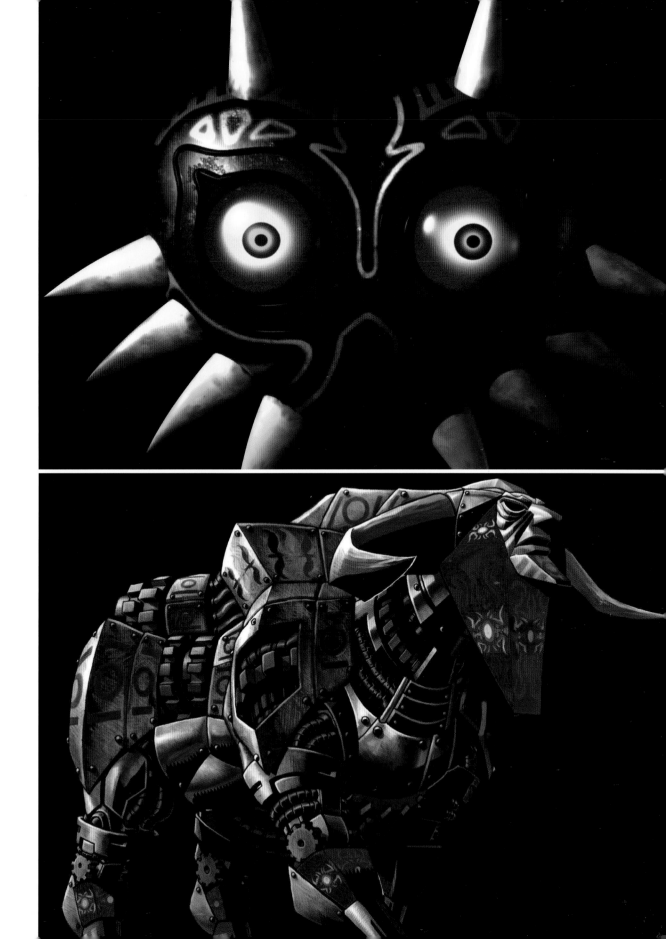

«Sexy Heroes»

If any proof were required to refute the cliché that video-games are strictly for children, the appearance of increasing numbers of heroines in the gaming world will surely suffice. Whether fantasies for men or role-models for women, the advent of virtual heroines confirms the coming of age of video-gaming.

True, few of the heroines represented are an accurate reflection of the woman gamer. Their forms may stress the feminine, but most video-heroines behave in strikingly virile, not to say macho, fashion, with combat their principal raison d'être. It would be facile to define the firearms they wield as phallic symbols, but these heroines still look like sex-objects created for the benefit of men. Joanna 'Perfect' Dark or Cate Archer do indeed seem to be mere James Bonds in body-stockings, while the megastar Lara Croft is just Indiana Jones in drag.

But then there's a simple explanation for this. The creators of these women are men. And what man could ever hope to incarnate even a virtual woman?

« »

La présence de plus en plus affirmée de héros de sexe féminin dans les jeux vidéo balaie aisément le lieu commun selon lequel celui-ci est un loisir réservé aux enfants. Fantasmes pour certains joueurs masculins, possibilité d'identification pour certaines joueuses, les héroïnes virtuelles sont un des signes qui confirment la maturité du jeu vidéo.

Reste que la plupart de ces héroïnes ne sont peut-être pas en premier lieu le reflet des joueuses. Il faut avouer que si leur plastique est ultra féminine, la plupart de ces héroïnes ont un caractère et une activité très masculins, voire machistes, le combat étant leur raison d'être. S'il ne faut pas tomber dans la facilité en transformant les armes à feu que nombre d'entre elles brandissent en symbole phallique, il est certain que ces femmes virtuelles donnent une image de la femme-objet faite pour être contrôlée par l'homme. Joanna « Perfect » Dark ou Cate Archer peuvent en effet être réduites à des James Bond en jarretière et la célébrissime Lara Croft en Indiana Jones au féminin.

Toutefois, il existe une explication toute simple : les créateurs de ces héroïnes sont des hommes. Et quel homme est-il capable de donner corps à une femme, même virtuelle ?

Wenn es noch eines Beweises bedarf, um den Gemeinplatz auszuräumen, das Videospiel sei eine den Kindern vorbehaltene Freizeitbeschäftigung, dann sollte die stetig wachsende Zahl weiblicher Helden in den Videospielen angeführt werden. Ob sie die Fantasien einiger männlicher Spieler wecken oder ob Spielerinnen sich mit ihnen identifizieren können: An den virtuellen Heldinnen entscheidet sich der Reifegrad eines Videospiels.

Aber natürlich sind die meisten dieser Heldinnen nicht unbedingt repräsentativ für die weibliche Klientel, die dem Videospiel frönt. Zugegebenermaßen legen die meisten Heldinnen – abgesehen von ihrem Äußeren – ein eher männliches, wenn nicht sogar machohaftes Auftreten an den Tag und all ihr Sinnen und Trachten gilt dem Kampf. Man sollte es sich zwar nicht so leicht machen, die Feuerwaffen, die so manche von ihnen schwingt, als Phallussymbol zu interpretieren, aber es drängt sich dennoch der Eindruck auf, dass diese virtuellen Frauen dazu geschaffen wurden, dem Mann als williges Lustobjekt zu dienen. Joanna „Perfect" Dark oder Cate Archer lassen sich ohne weiteres auf ihre Rolle als weibliche James Bonds mit Strumpfband reduzieren und die ach so berühmte Lara Croft auf einen Indiana Jones in Frauengestalt.

Dafür gibt es jedoch eine plausible Erklärung: Die Schöpfer dieser Heldinnen sind Männer. Und welcher Mann ist schon in der Lage, einer Frau – wenn auch nur virtuell – Gewicht zu verleihen?

NAME
DEAD OR ALIVE 3

PLATFORM
XBOX

RELEASE
2001

EDITOR
MICROSOFT

DEVELOPER
TECMO

COPYRIGHTS
© TECMO

FACT
15: THE NUMBER OF YEARS ELAPSED BETWEEN
THE ARCADE VERSION OF GAUNTLET (1985) AND
GAUNTLET LEGENDS ON PLAYSTATION

Dead or Alive

Compared to their masculine rivals, the women combattants of *Dead or Alive* have a considerable advantage: their clothes-busting shapes and fatal charms. Within their dream-like forms are concealed superlatively able warriors, whose mastery of the martial arts is no whit inferior to that of their male adversaries. Notable among them are Hitomi, the karateka, Tina, the wrestler, Lei Fang, the T'ai Chi expert, and Ayane the Ninja. None of these woman would look out of place in a beauty competition, but here they are - in the rings of *Dead or Alive*, the martial arts tournament in which nothing is outlawed. Combination blows faster than the eye can see, parries leading straight into attacks and acrobatic immobilisation techniques are standard-issue for these women; hard in the ring, but easy on the eye. The victorious gamer will moreover get a sight of them in new and still more revealing costumes...

« »

Face à leurs rivaux masculins, les combattantes de la trilogie *Dead or Alive* ont un avantage de poids : leurs formes généreuses et leur beauté fatale. Ces silhouettes de rêve dissimulent de grandes spécialistes des arts martiaux, dont les talents guerriers n'ont rien à envier à ceux de leurs mâles adversaires. Citons entre autres Hitomi, la karatéka, Tina la catcheuse, Lei Fang, adepte du T'ai Chi Quan ou encore Ayane la Ninja, qui toutes pourraient aussi bien s'affronter sur des podiums de concours de beauté que sur les rings de Dead or Alive, le tournoi d'arts martiaux où tous les coups sont permis : frappes qui s'enchaînent plus vite que l'œil n'est capable de suivre, parades menant à des contre-attaques plus vives que l'éclair ou immobilisations acrobatiques sont le lot de ces femmes doublement fatales. En incarnant ces combattantes, les joueurs les plus persévérants qui réussiront à les mener à la victoire auront de plus la chance de les admirer vêtues de nouveaux costumes qui dévoilent un peu plus leurs charmes...

« »

Gegenüber ihren männlichen Kontrahenten haben die Kämpferinnen der Trilogie *Dead or Alive* entscheidende Vorteile: ihre üppigen Formen und ihre gefährliche Schönheit. Hinter jeder Frau mit Traumfigur verbirgt sich eine Kampfsport-Expertin, die sich keineswegs vor ihren männlichen Gegnern verstecken muss. Zu den streitbaren Damen gehören unter anderem Hitomi, die Karatekämpferin, Tina, die Catcherin, Lei Fang, eine Tai-Chi-Chuan-Meisterin, und auch Ayane, die Ninja-Kämpferin. Sie alle könnten ebenso gut zu einem Schönheitswettbewerb wie zu einem Match von Dead or Alive antreten. Bei so einem Turnier für atemberaubende Kampftechniken sind übrigens Angriffe aller Art erlaubt: Schläge, die so schnell aufeinander folgen, dass das Auge nicht mehr folgen kann; abwehrende Schläge, die zu blitzschnellen Gegenangriffen führen, oder eine akrobatische Bewegungslosigkeit sind die Stärke der brandgefährlichen Frauen. Wer als Spieler eine dieser mutigen Kämpferinnen verkörpert und wem es gelingt, möglichst viele Gegner zu besiegen, wer also besonders ausdauernd ist, hat außerdem die Chance, die Schönen in immer neuen und zunehmend aufreizenden Kostümen zu bewundern...

成功は成功の元

気楽な抜け忍ね

TEAM BATTLE MODE

CHARACTER SELECT

PLAYER-1

PLAYER-2

VS

LEIFANG

AYANE

T'AI CHI QUAN

NINJUTSU

information

NAME
PLATFORM
RELEASE
EDITOR
DEVELOPER
COPYRIGHTS

Druuna

The sight of the well-endowed *Druuna* lying naked on a chair bristling with wires - the Brainholder - is a compelling one. This chair gives mental access to a parallel world whose population has been corrupted by a virus that leaves them ravening for sex and blood. Druuna's soul is imprisoned in this nightmare, and it's up to you to set her free, by connecting yourself to the Brainholder.

The video-game adventures of this pneumatic brunette are based on the work of the graphic artist Eleuteri Serpieri, in particular the volume *Morbus Gravis* from the saga of Druuna, but for video they have been thoroughly bowdlerized. The violent sexual practices and blood-boltered brutality of the cartoon books are considerably toned down in the video-game, which has no doubt gained a wider audience by this betrayal of its origins.

« »

Vous ne pouvez vous empêcher de frissonner en découvrant la pulpeuse *Druuna*, nue, allongée sur une chaise bardée d'électronique : le BrainHolder. Cette machine permet à l'esprit de voyager dans un monde parallèle peuplé d'individus contaminés par un virus terrible qui les transforme en bêtes assoiffées de sang... et de sexe. L'âme de Druuna est emprisonnée dans ce cauchemar, et c'est à vous qu'incombe de la libérer, en vous connectant à votre tour au BrainHolder.

Si elles sont inspirées de l'œuvre du dessinateur Eleuteri Serpieri, principalement du tome *Morbus Gravis* de la saga de *Druuna*, les aventures vidéoludiques de la pulpeuse brunette sont plus édulcorées que l'original : les pratiques sexuelles violentes et la brutalité sanguinolente de la bande dessinée sont très largement atténuées dans le jeu vidéo ainsi plus à même de s'adresser à un public plus large, mais qui de ce fait s'éloigne grandement de ses origines.

« »

Gänsehaut ist angesagt, wenn man die knackige *Druuna* entdeckt, die sich nackt auf einem total verkabelten Stuhl, dem BrainHolder, rekelt. Mit dieser Apparatur kann der Geist in eine Parallelwelt reisen, deren Bewohner von einem schrecklichen Virus befallen sind, der sie in blutrünstige und sexbesessene Monster verwandelt... Druunas Seele ist in diesem Albtraum gefangen und nur der Spieler kann sie daraus befreien, indem er sich selbst an den BrainHolder anschließt.

Zwar bezieht das Videospiel seine Inspiration aus dem Werk von Eleuteri Serpieri, insbesondere aus dem Band *Morbus Gravis* der *Druuna*-Saga, doch fallen die Abenteuer der üppigen Brünetten viel zahmer aus als im Original: Um ein breiteres Publikum zu erreichen, zeigt das Videospiel die brutalen Sexszenen und die blutrünstige Gewalt des Comics nur in abgeschwächter Form. Dabei entfernt es sich allerdings weit von seiner Vorlage.

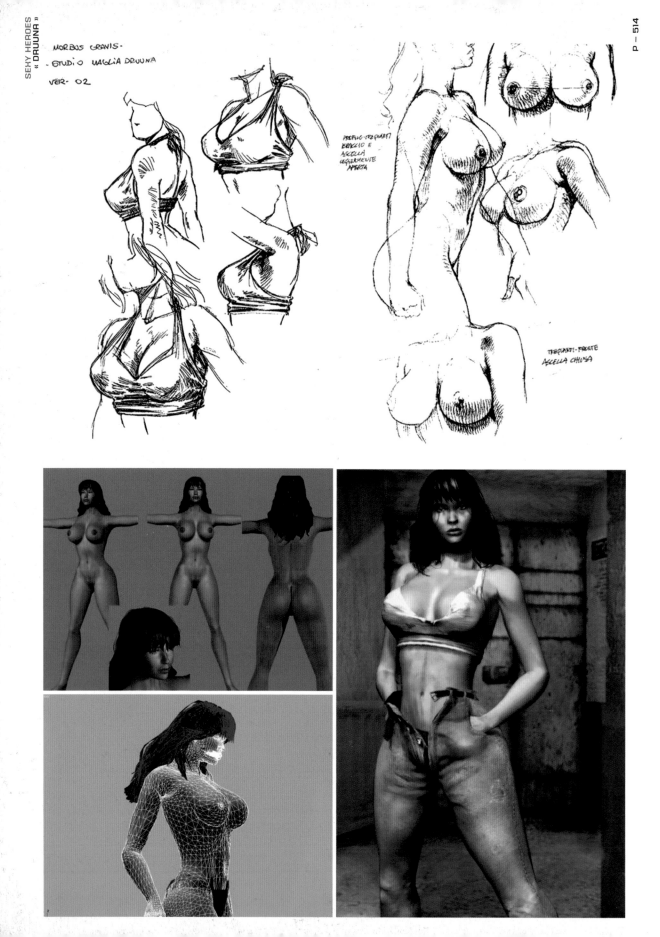

NAME
FEAR EFFECT 2: RETRO HELIX

PLATFORM
PLAYSTATION

RELEASE
2001

EDITOR
EIDOS INTERACTIVE

DEVELOPER
KRONOS

COPYRIGHTS
© EIDOS INTERACTIVE/KRONOS SOFTWARE

FACT
98% THE PERCENTAGE OF VIDEO-GAME BUYERS
WHO ARE OVER 19 YEARS OF AGE

Fear Effect

They don't always go by the rule-book, but then, the mercenaries of *Fear Effect* only ever take on assaults on organised crime. The beautiful Eurasian Hana Tsu-Vachel and her gentle friend, Rain Quin, look somewhat odd alongside Royce Glas, a former US soldier, and Jacob "Deke" Decourt, a cold-hearted killer untroubled by remorse. Appearances are deceptive; slight and frail as they seem compared to their male colleagues, these two women are pretty formidable. Are they just good friends? Hana is a brilliant pilot and marksman, while Rain, whom she discovered in an amnesiac state, is highly erudite and a technological genius; her talents prove indispensable to the group. And faced with the henchmen of international criminal organisations, what could be more useful to Hana and Rain than their sinuous curves and beguiling charm?

« »

Si leurs façons d'agir peuvent parfois sembler condamnables, les mercenaires de l'organisation Fear Effect n'acceptent que des missions de lutte contre le crime organisé. Aux côtés de Royce Glas, ancien membre de l'armée américaine et de Jacob « Deke » Decourt, tueur froid et sans remord, la belle Eurasienne Hana Tsu-Vachel et sa douce amie Rain Quin font étrange figure, leur beauté et leur apparente fragilité contrastant avec les impressionnants gabarits de leurs collègues masculins. Mais toutes deux sont aussi redoutables : pilote émérite et tireuse d'élite, Hana est une combattante hors pair. Rain, découverte amnésique par celle qui deviendra sa meilleure amie, voire plus encore, est un génie de la technologie et une grande érudite, dont les talents s'avèrent indispensables au groupe pour mener à bien les missions qui lui sont confiées. Face aux sbires des organisations criminelles internationales, les meilleures armes de Rain et Hana ne seraient-elles pas leurs formes séduisantes et leur charme exceptionnel ?

« »

Die Söldner der Organisation Fear Effect, deren Vorgehen nicht immer gentlemanlike ist, übernehmen nur Missionen gegen das organisierte Verbrechen. Neben Royce Glas, einem ehemaligen Soldaten der US-Army, und Jacob „Deke" Decourt, einem kaltblütigen Killer ohne Gewissensbisse, wirken die schöne Eurasierin Hana Tsu-Vachel und ihre süße Freundin Rain Quin etwas deplaziert: Ihre Schönheit und ihre scheinbare Zerbrechlichkeit bilden einen augenfälligen Kontrast zur stattlichen Größe ihrer männlichen Kollegen. Doch die beiden Frauen sind ebenfalls nicht ohne: Hana ist eine erfahrene Pilotin und Elite-Schützin und sucht als Kämpferin ihresgleichen. Rain, die einst von ihr mit Gedächtnisschwund aufgefunden wurde und seitdem ihre beste Freundin und mehr ist, ist ein technisches Genie und sehr gebildet. Ihre Fähigkeiten sind für die Gruppe unverzichtbar bei der Durchführung der ihr übertragenen Missionen. Doch Rains und Hanas wirkungsvollste Waffen gegen die internationalen Verbrecherorganisationen sind vermutlich ihre verführerischen Kurven und ihr außergewöhnlicher Charme.

Hana (infiltrator version)

Rain (ALL-American version)

Hana (infiltrator version)

NAME
NOONE LIVES FOREVER

PLATFORM
PLAYSTATION 2

RELEASE
2000

EDITOR
FOX INTERACTIVE

DEVELOPER
MONOLITH

COPYRIGHTS
© FOX. FOX INTERACTIVE, THE OPERATIVE:
NO ONE LIVES FOREVER AND THEIR
RESPECTIVE LOGOS ARE TRADEMARKS OF THE
TWENTIETH CENTURY FOX FILM CORPORATION.

No One Lives Forever

It is hard to imagine, as you admire her perfect curves compressed into pastel latex outfits, that Cate Archer is one of the most redoubtable agents of UNITY, a secret super-organisation dedicated to mercilessly countering the vile crimes and plots of H.A.R.M. Yet UNITY's most dangerous missions are confided to Cate, who can outdrive the baddies at the wheel of any vehicle known to man, outshoot them with sniper's rifle or pistol, overwhelm with grenades and other explosives, and make mincemeat of them hand-to-hand in any combat style. Clearly, faced with the fatal charms of the dazzling Cate, the criminals of H.A.R.M. are onto a loser. *No One Lives Forever* is an actionfest that pays homage to 60s and 70s espionage films, in particular Bond movies. It brilliantly pastiches all the clichés of the genre: sexy heroine, outrageous baddies, and explosive action scenes. And it has a nice line in funky gadgets: robot-poodle, explosive lipstick, flame-throwing cigarette-lighter and a hair-slide that doubles as a Swiss army-knife.

« »

Comment imaginer, en admirant sa silhouette parfaite moulée dans une tenue de latex aux couleurs pastel, que Cate Archer est l'un des plus redoutables agents de l'UNITY, une super-organisation secrète combattant sans relâche les innombrables complots et crimes de l'H.A.R.M. Pourtant, c'est à Cate que l'UNITY confie les missions les plus dangereuses. Seule contre les gangs criminels, Cate est pilote émérite de tous les types de véhicules existants, tireur d'élite aussi à l'aise avec un pistolet, un fusil à lunette qu'avec des grenades et autres explosifs, mais également une lutteuse au corps à corps rompue à tous les types de combat. Face à cette femme fatale armée de tous ces talents et d'un charme éblouissant, les criminels de l'H.A.R.M. n'ont évidemment aucune chance. No One Lives Forever, est un festival d'action rendant hommage aux films d'espionnage des années 60-70, en particulier la saga James Bond, réussissant à pasticher tous les clichés du genre : une héroïne sexy, des méchants caricaturaux, des scènes d'action explosives et bien évidemment des gadgets étonnants, parmi lesquels un caniche-robot, du rouge à lèvres explosif, un briquet lance-flammes ou une barrette à cheveux pouvant servir de couteau ou de passe-partout.

« »

Wer käme beim Anblick dieser perfekt geformten, in pastellfarbenen Latex gekleideten Frau auf die Idee, dass Cate Archer eine der gefürchtetsten Agentinnen der UNITY ist, einer Geheimorganisation, die unermüdlich gegen zahllose Komplotte und Verbrechen der H.A.R.M. ins Feld zieht. Und doch werden Cate die gefährlichsten Missionen anvertraut. Allein gegen kriminelle Gangs, brilliert sie am Steuer sämtlicher Fahrzeugtypen, beweist sich als Eliteschützin, die mit einer Pistole genauso gekonnt umgehen kann wie mit einem Gewehr mit Zielfernrohr oder mit Granaten und anderen Sprengkörpern, und es gibt keine Kampfsportart, die ihr nicht vertraut wäre. Angesichts dieser multitalentierten Femme fatale und ihres atemberaubenden Charmes haben die Verbrecher der H.A.R.M. selbstverständlich keine Chance. No One Lives Forever ist ein Actiongenuss, der die Traditionen der 60/70er Jahre – namentlich die der James-Bond-Saga – weiterführt und sämtliche Klischees des Genres bestens bedient: eine sexy Heldin, karikierte Bösewichter, explosive Actionszenen und selbstverständlich wunderliche Gerätschaften wie etwa ein Roboterpudel, ein explodierender Lippenstift, ein Flammen werfendes Feuerzeug oder eine Haarspange, die sich als Messer oder Passepartout benutzen lässt.

NAME
PERFECT DARK 64

PLATFORM
NINTENDO 64

RELEASE
2000

EDITOR
NINTENDO

DEVELOPER
RARE LTD.

COPYRIGHTS
© RARE LTD./NINTENDO

FACT
40+: THE NUMBER OF ARMS THAT THE GAMER
CAN USE IN PERFECT DARK ON NINTENDO 64.

Perfect Dark

The year is 2023. Humanity is about to perish, destroyed by extraterrestrials who have taken control of powerful corporations. Since this is not common knowledge, the threat must be eradicated discreetly. Clearly a job for the Carrington Institute's special agent Joanna "Perfect" Dark: intelligent, beautiful and lethal, she is a true femme fatale. Her orders are: infiltrate, investigate, destroy. Remove all extra-terrestrial outposts from the face of the earth. Working in the shadows to neutralise her enemies, she must never be seen.

Joanna Dark combines the spying talents of James Bond with the looks and brio of Lara Croft; she turned a lot of heads on Nintendo 64 consoles, and all eyes will be on her again as she debuts on the Gamecube.
« »

En cette année 2023, rares sont ceux qui savent que l'humanité risque d'être bientôt anéantie, détruite de l'intérieurin par des extrater-restres ayant pris le contrôle de puissantes corporations. Pour combattre cette menace le plus efficacement et le plus discrètement pos-sible, l'Institut Carrington envoie son agent spécial Joanna « Perfect » Dark, une femme aussi mortelle que belle et intelligente. Sa péril-leuse mission peut se résumer en trois termes : infiltration, investigation et destruction. Elle devra effacer de la surface de la terre les installations extraterrestres sans jamais se faire repérer et agir dans l'ombre, en longeant les murs, en neutralisant les ennemis avant qu'ils ne la repèrent.

A mi-chemin de James Bond, pour ses talents d'espion et de Lara Croft, pour son charme et son dynamisme, Joanna Dark a conquis nombre de joueurs sur la console Nintendo 64 et devrait bientôt refaire parler d'elle sur la toute nouvelle Gamecube du même constructeur.
« »

Man schreibt das Jahr 2023. Nur die wenigsten wissen, dass die Menschheit von der Ausrottung bedroht ist, durch Zerstörung von innen heraus, weil Außerirdische inzwischen die Kontrolle über mächtige Organisationen haben. Um die drohende Gefahr so effizient und diskret wie möglich abzuwenden, schickt das Institut Carrington seine Spezialagentin Joanna „Perfect" Dark aus, eine ebenso bedrohliche wie schöne und intelligente Frau. Ihre gefährliche Mission lässt sich in drei Worten zusammenfassen: Einschleichen, Ausspionieren und Zerstören. Sie muss die Anlagen der Außerirdischen auf der Erde unbrauchbar machen, ohne sich zu verraten, und dabei im Verborgenen agieren, sich an Mauern entlangschleichen und die Feinde ausschalten, bevor diese sie entdecken.

Mit ihrem detektivischen Spürsinn à la James Bond und ihrem weiblichen Charme à la Lara Croft hat die dynamische Joanna Dark zahlreiche Fans auf der alten Konsole Nintendo 64 begeistern können und wird sicher auch bald auf dem neuen Gamecube desselben Herstellers wieder von sich reden machen.

PLUS DE 40: PERFECT DARK SUR NINTENDO 64 PERMET AU JOUEUR D'UTILISER PLUS DE 40 ARMES DIFFÉRENTES

MEHR ALS 40: IN PERFECT DARK AUF NINTENDO 64 KANN DER SPIELER ZWISCHEN MEHR ALS 40 VERSCHIEDENEN WAFFEN WÄHLEN.

NAME
TOMB RAIDER SERIES

PLATFORM
PC-PLAYSTATION-DREAMCAST-PLAYSTATION 2

RELEASE
2002

EDITOR
EIDOS INTERACTIVE

DEVELOPER
CORE DESIGN

COPYRIGHTS
© EIDOS INTERACTIVE/CORE DESIGN

FACT
181 MILLION: THE NUMBER OF
VIDEO-GAMES SOLD IN THE USA
IN 1998, I.E. TWO PER HOUSEHOLD.

Tomb Raider

Since her first appearance in 1996, Lara Croft, the heroine of the *Tomb Raider* series, has become an international heroine of the virtual. For the first time, a female character has won the heart of the mass gaming audience; her vivid character and pronounced talent for action are major attractions, and, well, she is a nice shape. Lara Croft is a young archaeologist who has explored the ruins of many vanished civilisations, notably those of the Incas and Egyptians, confronting vicious traps and ferocious guardians, along with the kind of animals and supernatural beings invariably found protecting treasures buried in remote and inacessible places. And not all the perils are blasts from the past: Lara also has to thwart unscrupulous archaeologists who covet ancient treasures and magical objects. But her fleetness of foot and thought allows her to see off her adversaries single-handed.

« »

Dès sa première apparition en 1996, Lara Croft, héroïne de la série Tomb Raider, s'est hissée au rang de star virtuelle internationale. Pour la première fois, un personnage du beau sexe a gagné les faveurs d'un très large public, grâce à son charme particulier, qu'expliquent en grande partie son caractère très affirmé et son talent pour l'action. Jeune archéologue, Lara Croft a, au fil de ses aventures, exploré les mystérieuses ruines de maintes civilisations disparues, notamment Inca et égyptienne, et affronté les pièges retors et les gardiens farouches, des animaux et des êtres surnaturels protégeant les trésors enfouis au cœur de ces lieux oubliés. Outre ces périls d'un autre âge, Lara doit aussi se battre contre d'autres archéologues peu scrupuleux, cherchant à s'accaparer les richesses et les objets magiques de ces anciennes civilisations. Grâce à son ingéniosité et son incroyable agilité, Lara Croft réussit cependant à vaincre ses adversaires et leurs sbires, seule contre tous !

« »

Seit ihrem ersten Auftritt 1996 ist Lara Croft, die virtuelle Heldin der Serie Tomb Raider, zum internationalen Star aufgestiegen. Erstmals gelang es einer Vertreterin des schönen Geschlechts, die Gunst eines breiten Publikums zu erlangen. Das ist wohl ihrem besonderen Charme zu danken, ihrer Entschlossenheit und ihrer Vorliebe für Action. Die streitbare junge Archäologin Lara Croft hat im Laufe ihrer Abenteuer die geheimnisvollen Ruinen so manch einer untergegangenen Zivilisation erforscht, insbesondere die der Inkas und der alten Ägypter. Dabei stieß sie auf gemeine Fallen und unerbittliche Wärter, auf wilde Tiere und übernatürliche Wesen, die allesamt die in Tempeln und Gräbern verborgenen Schätze bewachten. Ganz nebenbei musste Lara auch gegen skrupellose Berufskollegen kämpfen, die sich die Reichtümer und magischen Gegenstände dieser alten Zivilisationen unter den Nagel reißen wollen. Mit Köpfchen und einer unglaublichen Beweglichkeit gelingt es Lara Croft jedoch immer wieder, ihre Widersacher und deren Helfer zu bezwingen, und das sozusagen im Alleingang.

NAME
URBAN CHAOS

PLATFORM
PC-PLAYSTATION-DREAMCAST

RELEASE
1999

EDITOR
EIDOS INTERACTIVE

DEVELOPER
MUCKY FOOT

COPYRIGHTS
© EIDOS INTERACTIVE/MUCKY FOOT

FACT
32000: THE NUMBER OF PHOTOS TAKEN BY THE
DEVELOPMENT TEAM IN ORDER TO REPRODUCE
THE CITIES IN METROPOLIS STREET RACER ON
DREAMCAST.

Urban Chaos

Union City, 1999: crime rates are sky-rocketing and police budgets have been pared to the bone. Things are on a war footing as the heavily outnumbered rozzers take on the many criminal gangs and satanic sects who have plunged the city into chaos. The poor city-dwellers, famished and ill, can only look on in horror. Is the Union City Police Department doomed to defeat? Not if our two new recruits have anything to do with it! They still believe in justice... At their head, the beautiful Afro-American D'Arcy Stern, an accomplished athlete and markswoman, and a specialist in unarmed combat. Her right-hand man, Roper McIntyre, is a veritable hulk - and touchy with it; don't cross him, he's an expert in explosives and heavy weaponry. Facing down hordes of gangsters unassisted, they patrol the streets of Union City on foot or by squad-car, hell-bent on dismantling the criminal organisations that terrorise this urban jungle.

« »

Union City, 1999 : la criminalité a explosé alors que les budgets et effectifs de police sont réduits au plus bas. La cité est plongée dans une véritable guérilla urbaine entre les maigres troupes des forces de l'ordre et les nombreux gangs de criminels et sectes sataniques qui plongent la ville dans un innommable chaos, avec pour témoins les pauvres citoyens guettés par la famine et la maladie. Si le combat semble perdu d'avance pour les policiers d'Union City, de fraîches recrues gardent foi en la justice. A leur tête, la belle Afro-américaine D'Arcy Stern, athlète accomplie, tireuse d'élite et spécialiste du combat au corps à corps, et son coéquipier Roper McIntyre, une montagne de muscles susceptible pour qui les explosifs et armes lourdes n'ont aucun secret. Seuls contre des hordes de gangsters, ils parcourent à pied ou en voiture les rues d'Union City, farouchement décidés à démanteler les terribles organisations criminelles qui terrorisent les habitants de cette jungle urbaine.

« »

Union City 1999: Die Kriminalitätsrate ist drastisch gestiegen, nachdem das Budget und die Zahl der Polizeibeamten auf ein Minimum gekürzt wurden. In der Stadt herrscht ein regelrechter Guerillakrieg zwischen den wenigen verbliebenen Ordnungskräften und den zahlreichen kriminellen Banden und Satanssekten, die den Ort in ein furchtbares Chaos gestürzt haben. All dem müssen die von Hunger und Krankheit bedrohten Bewohner der Stadt tatenlos zusehen. Für die städtischen Polizisten scheint der Kampf bereits im Vorfeld verloren, doch da rückt Verstärkung an – im festen Glauben an die Gerechtigkeit: an der Spitze die schöne Afroamerikanerin D'Arcy Stern, ihres Zeichens Vorzeige-Atlethin, Elite-Schützin und Spezialistin im Nahkampf, und ihr Mitstreiter Roper McIntyre, ein sensibler Muskelprotz, für den Sprengstoff und schwere Waffen kein Geheimnis bergen. Zu Fuß oder im Auto durchqueren sie die Straßen von Union City – allein gegen die Verbrecherbanden. Sie sind wild entschlossen, die kriminellen Organisationen zu zerstören, die die Bewohner dieses städtischen Dschungels terrorisieren.

32.000: ANZAHL DER GESCHOSSENEN FOTOS VOM ENTWICKLER-TEAM FÜR DAS RENDERING DER STÄDTE IN METROPOLIS STREET RACER AUF DREAMCAST.

32000: C'EST LE NOMBRE DE PHOTOS PRISES PAR L'ÉQUIPE DE DÉVELOPPEMENT AFIN DE REPRODUIRE LES VILLES PRÉSENTES DANS METROPOLIS STREET RACER SUR DREAMCAST.

NAME
PETER MOLYNEUX

BORN
1960

HOME TOWN
GUILFORD, ENGLAND

OCCUPATION
C.E.O., LEAD DESIGNER

KEY TITLES
PROJECT EGO (2003) BIG BLUE BOX
BLACK & WHITE (2001) LIONHEAD STUDIOS
DUNGEON KEEPER (1997) BULLFROG
THEME HOSPITAL (1997) BULLFROG
MAGIC CARPET (1994) BULLFROG
THEME PARK (1994) BULLFROG
SYNDICATE (1993) BULLFROG
POPULOUS (1989) BULLFROG

«Strange Heroes»
Peter Molyneux

I've always loved the ideas of other worlds. I spent a lot of time as a child imagining lands, continents or planets, and peopling them with beings of my own creation. But instead of making up mysterious places, and marvelling at them, I wanted to own them. I wanted to be the boss, the controller. In fact I wanted to be the god of these beings.

Time and time again, computer game after computer game I've returned to this theme of controlling every aspect of the lives of your minions. The pinnacle of this work has been Black & White. Lionhead managed to do wonders with that game. Every element was exactly how we wanted it to be. It was the ultimate in control, and it had another element which I've been keen to put into a game. A large, dominant being on the landscape. Playing a god is all very well, but I wanted to put something massive and powerful in the world to contrast with the tiny people. Hence the idea of the Creature.

Giving games players a new, separate world is, in theory, easy. All you have to do is fill it. Make it look and feel rich. And of course, no matter how different it is to our own world, you must give it rules which it abides by and which the player can understand. With Black & White we toyed with making the lands hugely different from real life, but we found that in truth it worked better as a mirror of our own world, but compressed. So you get a desert a few hundred metres across, a snow-capped mountain range a hundred metres high, and a vast, deep forest the size of a football pitch. People understand what these things are, and they accept that this is a big mysterious forest, despite the fact that you could cross it in about 20 seconds.

So in order to give people a new world, make it pleasing to look at and fill it with detail. Sim City worked because you could see detail in the places where people lived and worked. It felt like looking down on a real city. Also, it had rules you could apply to make it work. It wasn't alien and odd. This also explains why Black & White incorporated tribes of people similar to those of Earth. Egyptians, Japanese and Celts all lived on the land, and when you saw them you knew certain truths without having to be told. For example, the Egyptians would build huge monuments, the Celts would be fierce warriors and the Japanese would be skilled craftsmen, with their own brand of spirituality.

Once you've created a world, you have to let the player explore it. In Black & White, and also in Project Ego and BC, the games being created at Lionhead's satellite companies of Big Blue Box and Intrepid, the worlds are lush and vibrant, and you have freedom to explore what and where you like. Nothing irritates me more than knowing there's an incredible world in a game, but that I have to progress bit by boring bit to see it.

The advances in graphics and sound and the increase in processor power have meant that game worlds can now come alive like never before. BC boasts individual blades of grass and Ego has beautiful flowers. But what keeps you involved with both games, as with Black & White, are the character progression and the story. A detailed, lush world is no better than a 3D picture if you don't have a strong, engaging reason to exist in it. Whether you're a god, a warrior or a prehistoric man, you have to care about what happens next, and what you're going to do. And that's down to storyline and, the most important thing of all, gameplay.

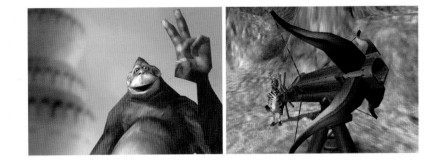

J'ai toujours aimé l'idée que d'autres mondes existent. Enfant, je passais des heures à imaginer des pays, continents ou planètes et à les peupler d'êtres créés par mes soins. Mais au lieu de façonner des lieux mystérieux afin de les admirer, je désirais les posséder. Je voulais être le chef, celui qui a le contrôle. En fait, je désirais être le dieu de ces êtres.

Le temps passant, jeu vidéo après jeu vidéo, je revins sur ce thème — contrôler chaque aspect de la vie de ces êtres. L'apogée de ce travail fut Black & White. Lionhead a fait des miracles avec ce jeu. Chaque élément était exactement tel que nous le voulions. On y avait le pouvoir absolu, mais on y trouvait également un élément que je rêvais d'intégrer à un jeu : un être gigantesque qui dominait le panorama. Jouer à être un dieu était déjà très bien, mais je voulais également ajouter à ce monde quelque chose de puissant et massif, qui contrasterait avec le peuple minuscule. Vint donc l'idée de la Créature.

Donner aux joueurs un monde inédit et indépendant est aisé, théoriquement. Il ne reste qu'à le remplir et le faire s'épanouir. Et bien entendu, aussi différent puisse-t-il être de notre propre monde, il lui faut des règles, dictées et comprises par le joueur.

Avec Black & White, nous nous sommes amusés à créer des mondes très éloignés de la réalité, mais nous avons découvert qu'en vérité, cela fonctionnait mieux si ces mondes était le reflet du nôtre, à des proportions réduites. Ainsi, vous avez un désert de quelques centaines de mètres, une montagne enneigée culminant à quelques centaines de mètres et une vaste forêt profonde de la taille d'un terrain de football. Les gens comprennent ce que sont ces espaces et acceptent que ceci puisse être une grande forêt mystérieuse, bien qu'on puisse la traverser en une vingtaine de secondes.

Il faut donc que ce monde nouveau offert aux joueurs soit plaisant à regarder et foisonne de détails. Le jeu Sim City fonctionnait parce qu'on pouvait examiner en détail les lieux où vivaient et travaillaient les personnages. On avait l'impression de contempler une vraie ville d'en haut. Il fallait aussi appliquer des règles pour que tout marche bien. Cela n'était ni complètement étranger, ni bizarre. C'est pourquoi on retrouve dans Black & White des tribus similaires à des civilisations de la Terre. En voyant des Egyptiens, des Japonais ou des Celtes, vous connaissez d'instinct certaines choses, sans qu'on ait à vous les dire. Par exemple, les Egyptiens construiront de grands monuments, les Celtes seront de fiers guerriers et les Japonais seront de talentueux artisans et tous seront dotés de leur spiritualité spécifique.

Une fois le monde créé, vous devez laisser le joueur l'explorer. Dans Black & White ainsi que dans Project Ego et BC, les jeux actuellement en développement chez Big Blue Box et Intrepid, sociétés satellites de Lionhead, les mondes sont riches et vivants : vous pouvez les explorer comme bon vous semble. Rien ne m'irrite plus que de savoir qu'un jeu possède un monde incroyable, mais que je ne puis le découvrir que petit à petit.

Des processeurs de plus en plus puissants et les évolutions graphiques et sonores permettent aux univers de jeu d'être plus vivants que jamais. BC montre des brins d'herbe individuels et Ego, des fleurs superbes. Mais c'est la progression du personnage et de l'histoire qui vous implique dans ces deux jeux, comme dans Black & White. Un monde riche et détaillé n'a pas plus de valeur qu'une image en 3D si vous n'avez pas une bonne raison d'exister en son sein. Que vous soyez un dieu, un guerrier ou un homme préhistorique, vous devez rester vigilant et penser à ce que vous allez faire. Ce qui nous amène au scénario et, plus important encore, à la jouabilité.

Schon als Kind fand ich die Idee von fremden Welten faszinierend und verbrachte viel Zeit damit, mir Länder, Kontinente und Planeten aus-
zumalen und sie mit meinen eigenen Fantasiewesen zu bevölkern. Doch ich wollte mir die geheimnisvollen Orte nicht nur ausdenken und
darüber staunen, ich wollte sie besitzen. Ich wollte der Chef sein, derjenige, der alles unter Kontrolle hat. Ich wollte sogar ihr Gott sein.
Immer und immer wieder, mit jedem neuen Computerspiel, bin ich auf dieses Thema zurückgekommen: das Leben der Figuren in allen
Einzelheiten kontrollieren zu wollen. Der Höhepunkt meiner Arbeit war Black & White. Lionhead hat mit diesem Spiel wahre Wunder
vollbracht. Jedes Element war genau so, wie wir es wollten. Das Spiel verlieh uneingeschränkte Macht und es hatte ein weiteres Element,
das ich immer schon in ein Spiel einbauen wollte: ein riesiges Wesen, das alles und alle überragt. Gott spielen ist ja ganz schön, doch ich
wollte etwas Gewaltiges und Mächtiges als Kontrast zu den winzigen Menschlein. Daher auch die Idee der Kreatur.

Es ist theoretisch ganz einfach, Spielern eine neue, eigene Welt zu geben. Alles, was man tun muss, ist, sie zu füllen. Und egal, wie sehr sie
sich von unserer realen Welt unterscheidet, man muss Regeln vorschreiben, die zu befolgen sind und die der Spieler verstehen kann. Für
Black & White haben wir zunächst zu unser aller Vergnügen Weltgegenden erschaffen, die von der Realität weit entfernt waren. Aber dann
mussten wir erkennen, dass sie eine stärkere Überzeugungskraft besitzen, wenn sie in verkleinertem Maßstab unsere eigene Welt wider-
spiegeln. Und so gibt es nun die ein paar hundert Meter breite Wüste, eine etwa hundert Meter hohe schneebedeckte Gebirgskette oder
einen finsterer Wald in der Größe eines Fußballfeldes. Die Spieler begreifen, wofür diese Gebiete stehen, und sie imaginieren, dass sie sich
in einem riesigen Zauberwald befinden, obwohl sie ihn in nur 20 Sekunden durchqueren können.

Will man den Leuten also eine neue Welt offenbaren, dann muss man ihr ein gefälliges Aussehen geben und sie ausschmücken. Sim City
überzeugte, weil man genau sehen konnte, wo die Menschen lebten und arbeiteten. Man hatte das Gefühl, auf eine richtige Stadt zu blik-
ken. Außerdem gab es Regeln, die man befolgen konnte und die funktionierten. Nichts war fremd oder merkwürdig. Das erklärt auch, warum
in Black & White Zivilisationen vorkamen, die ähnlich auch auf der Erde existieren. Ägypter, Japaner und Kelten – sie alle lebten dort zusammen, und wenn man sie sah, wusste man bereits bestimmte Dinge über sie, ohne dass dies eigens einer Erklärung bedurft hätte. Die Ägypter bauten zum Beispiel riesige Monumente, die Kelten waren zähe Kämpfer und die Japaner geschickte Handwerker, und alle waren sie
jeweils durch eine eigene Mentalität charakterisiert.

Sobald man eine neue Welt erschaffen hat, muss man dem Spieler Gelegenheit geben, sie zu erkunden. In Black & White, aber auch in
Project Ego und BC – Spielen, die von Lionheads Satellitenfirmen Big Blue Box und Intrepid entwickelt wurden – erwarten den Spieler reich
ausgestattete und lebendige Welten, die er nach Lust und Laune erforschen kann. Nichts ist ärgerlicher, als zu wissen, dass ein Spiel zwar
mit einer irre tollen Welt aufwartet, man sich diese aber nur schrittchenweise erschließen kann.

Die grafischen und soundtechnischen Verbesserungen sowie die erhöhte Prozessorleistung haben dazu beigetragen, dass die Spielewelten
heute so lebendig sind wie nie zuvor. In BC sind einzelne Grashalme zu bestaunen, und in Ego wunderschöne Blumen. Doch das Faszinierende
an den beiden Spielen wie auch an Black & White ist die Weiterentwicklung der Charaktere und der Story. Eine detailgetreue, reich ausgestattete Welt ist nicht besser als ein 3-D-Bild, wenn man keinen triftigen Grund hat, darin zu leben. Ob als Gott, als Krieger oder als prä-
historischer Mensch: Der Spieler muss sich darüber im Klaren sein, dass jede seiner Handlungen und Entscheidungen den weiteren Verlauf
der Story und vor allem das Gameplay beeinflusst.

STRANGE HEROES
« BLACK & WHITE »

NAME
BLACK & WHITE

PLATFORM
PC

RELEASE
2001

EDITOR
ELECTRONIC ARTS

DEVELOPER
LIONHEAD STUDIOS

COPYRIGHTS
© LIONHEAD STUDIOS

P – 546

Black & White

Each world has one or more gods; in the *Black & White* world, the gamer is one of these gods - and wants to be esteemed as such by the tiny humans who inhabit the islands of the Black and White universe. To this end, he must perform miracles of every kind, beneficent or not, to demonstrate his celestial omnipotence and convince frail mankind to adore or fear their god. To further consolidate his power, the gamer has a messenger, a giant animal that he trains to represent him. This creature is a true reflection of the god's personality; living among the natives, he can aid them in their daily tasks or simply terrorise them. But other gods, also accompanied by their representative creatures, haunt this world, and will attempt to face down the gamer with their prodigies and miracles, attempting to lead his worshippers astray. The gamer must defend himself with the same weapons. This unique entertainment unfolds in a universe that the gamer can shape in his own image.

« »

Chaque monde a un ou plusieurs dieux ; dans celui de Black & White, le joueur est l'un de ces dieux et se doit d'être considéré comme tel par les petits humains habitant les îles de cet univers. Pour ce faire, des miracles en tout genre, bénéfiques ou maléfiques, doivent être autant de preuves de la toute-puissance divine, et amener les frêles hommes à adorer ou craindre leur dieu. Pour asseoir plus encore sa puissance, le joueur a un messager, un animal géant qu'il devra éduquer comme il le désire. Véritable reflet de la personnalité du dieu, cette créature vivra parmi les autochtones, les aidera dans leurs tâches quotidiennes ou au contraire les terrorisera. Mais d'autres dieux, eux aussi accompagnés de leurs propres créatures, hantent le monde et affronteront le joueur à coups de miracles prodigieux et mortels pour s'accaparer les fidèles du joueur, qui devra combattre ces autres prétendants avec les mêmes armes. Un divertissement unique, un univers que le joueur peut façonner comme bon lui semble

« »

Jede Welt hat einen Gott oder gleich mehrere. In der Welt von Black & White ist der Spieler ein Gott und muss von den Bewohnern dieser Inselwelt auch als solcher respektiert werden. Deshalb müssen Wunder aller Art, ob positiv oder negativ, ein Beweis für die göttliche Allmacht sein und die schwachen Menschlein dazu bringen, ihren Gott anzubeten oder zu fürchten. Zur Festigung seiner Macht hat der Spieler einen Boten, eine riesige Kreatur, die er nach seinen Vorstellungen erziehen kann. Als exaktes Ebenbild der göttlichen Persönlichkeit lebt die Kreatur unter den Inselbewohnern und hilft ihnen bei der Bewältigung ihrer täglichen Pflichten oder aber terrorisiert sie. Daneben gibt es noch andere Götter, die – ebenfalls mit einem tierischen Begleiter ausgestattet – die Inselwelt heimsuchen und den Spieler mit ihren segensreichen oder tödlichen Wundertaten konfrontieren, wobei sie zugleich dessen Untertanen beeindrucken wollen. Der Spieler muss nun seinerseits versuchen, die Konkurrenten mit den gleichen Waffen zu schlagen. Ein faszinierendes und unterhaltsames Spiel in einem Universum, das der Spieler ganz nach seinen Wünschen gestalten kann.

HUGHBERT ALGERNOD SHAKESWORTHY – CYCLOPEAN GIANT.

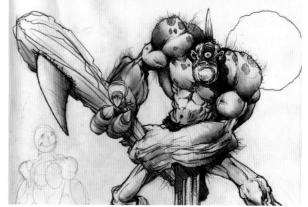

NAME
CHU CHU ROCKET
PLATFORM
DREAMCAST
RELEASE
1999
EDITOR
SEGA
DEVELOPER
SONIC TEAM
COPYRIGHTS
© SONIC TEAM/SEGA

Chu Chu Rocket

The Mice are fed up. Generations have lived in fear of their eternal enemy the Cat. But the Mice are determined to escape those feline clutches; a space-rocket will take them to a new paradise-planet, entirely devoid of Cats. The rocket stands ready, but how are they to reach it? The Mice are none too bright; they can only move in single file, and can change direction only when they face an obstacle or find an arrow drawn to guide them. It requires a superior intelligence to draw the arrows and lead the way to the rocket through the labyrinths in which the Mice are confined. Mouse-life on earth is therefore in the hands of the gamer, who must not only position the arrows right but steer the Mouse-horde clear of fatal felines.

« »

C'en est trop pour les Souris, qui depuis d'innombrables générations redoutent leur éternel ennemi le Chat. Aussi, pour que les générations futures n'aient plus à craindre ce formidable adversaire, les rongeurs ont-ils décidé de fuir leur planète à bord d'une fusée spatiale qui les mènerait vers un monde paradisiaque... sans chat. Mais si la fusée est prête à partir, encore faut-il y accéder. Or, les souris sont un peu stupides, et ne savent que courir en ligne droite, ne changeant de direction que face à un obstacle ou lorsqu'une flèche dessinée au sol leur enjoint de suivre la direction indiquée. Mais seule une puissance supérieure, une intelligence plus évoluée peut dessiner les flèches et trouver le chemin menant à la fusée dans les complexes labyrinthes où sont enfermées les souris... La survie des rongeurs est donc entre les mains du joueur, qui devra poser ses flèches au bon endroit, tout en évitant de voir sa horde de souris croiser le chemin du ou des prédateurs félins.

« »

Jetzt reicht es den Mäusen, die sich seit unzähligen Generationen vor ihrem Erzfeind, der Katze, fürchten. Und damit ihre Kinder und Kindeskinder nie mehr Angst vor dem furchtbaren Gegner haben müssen, beschließen die kleinen Nager, ihren Planeten zu verlassen. Eine Weltraumrakete soll sie in eine paradiesische Welt, in eine Welt ohne Katzen bringen. Die Rakete ist startklar, die Mäuse müssen nur noch hin und einsteigen. Leider sind die Mäuse ein bisschen dumm: Sie können nur geradeaus gehen und die Richtung erst dann ändern, wenn ein Hindernis den Weg versperrt oder ein Pfeil auf dem Boden einen Richtungswechsel vorgibt. Nur eine höhere Macht, eine weiterentwickelte Intelligenz, kann Pfeile auf den Boden zeichnen und die Mäuse somit auf verschlungenen Wegen aus ihrem Labyrinth zur Rakete geleiten. Das Überleben der Nager liegt also in der Hand des Spielers. Er muss seine Pfeile so geschickt positionieren, dass seine Mäuse keiner Katze über den Weg laufen.

NAME
CRIMSON SKIES
PLATFORM
PC
RELEASE
2000
EDITOR
MICROSOFT
DEVELOPER
ZIPPER INTERACTIVE
COPYRIGHTS
© MICROSOFT
FACT
1,000: THE NUMBER OF GAMES PRODUCED FOR
GAME-BOY BETWEEN 1989 AND 1999.

Crimson Skies

In a parallel universe, the year is 1937, but the course of history has changed. The Great Depression and excessive isolationism have torn the United States apart. Anarchy reigns, and, throughout the continent, piracy is crippling the flagging economy. Landborne transport is too dangerous; goods go by air, on gigantic zeppelins. But these too are under attack from air-pirates in their incredible flying machines. Foremost among the air-bandits is that living legend, Nathan Zachary. Chief of the Fortune Hunters, Zachary is the terror of trade and the toast of the pirates. But his true fame is as a Don Juan... If you just happen to be a brigand, a flying ace, an accomplished scrapper and a handsome sort of lad, well, the ladies are bound to react, aren't they?
« »

Année 1937 dans un univers parallèle où le cours de l'histoire a suivi un autre cheminement. Les Etats-Unis d'Amérique ont volé en éclats, à cause de la Grande Dépression et d'un trop grand isolationnisme. L'anarchie règne, et le pays est tombé sous le joug de pirates qui paralysent une économie vacillante. Les voies d'échange terrestre étant devenues trop périlleuses, les marchandises transitent essentiellement par les airs, à bord de gigantesques zeppelins. Les dirigeables sont cependant la proie de criminels des airs, qui attaquent les transporteurs à bord d'incroyables machines volantes, et particulièrement d'une légende vivante, Nathan Zachary. Chef des Fortune Hunters, Zachary est tout aussi craint des commerçants que respecté des autres pirates, mais plus grande encore est sa réputation de Don Juan. Evidemment, être à la fois brigand, as du combat aérien, expert en pilotage, baroudeur accompli et beau gosse ne peut laisser les femmes insensibles...
« »

Wir schreiben das Jahr 1937. In einer Parallelwelt hat die Geschichte einen anderen Verlauf genommen. Die Vereinigten Staaten von Amerika sind infolge der Großen Depression und eines verheerenden Isolationismus zusammengebrochen. Das Land ist der Anarchie anheim gefallen und gerät unter das Joch von Piraten, die die ohnehin schon schwache Wirtschaft völlig lähmen. Da die Handelswege über Land zu gefährlich geworden sind, werden die Waren hauptsächlich mit gigantischen Luftschiffen befördert. Auf eben diese Zeppeline haben es Luftpiraten abgesehen, die die Transporter unter der Führung des legendären Nathan Zachary mit spektakulären Flugmaschinen angreifen. Zachary, Chef der Fortune Hunters, vor dem die Händler zittern und die Piraten sich achtungsvoll verneigen, ist aber vor allem als Don Juan bekannt. Er ist Freibeuter, As im Luftkampf, Ausnahme-Pilot, perfekter Haudegen und dazu noch so gut aussehend, dass wohl keine Frau widerstehen kann...

NAME
EVIL TWIN: CYPRIEN'S CHRONICLES

PLATFORM
PC - PLAYSTATION 2 - DREAMCAST

RELEASE
2001

EDITOR
UBI SOFT

DEVELOPER
IN UTERO

COPYRIGHTS
© UBI SOFT

FACT
37,000 YEN: THE APPROXIMATE PRICE OF
PLAYSTATION WHEN IT WAS FIRST LAUNCHED IN
JAPON ON 3 DECEMBER 1994.

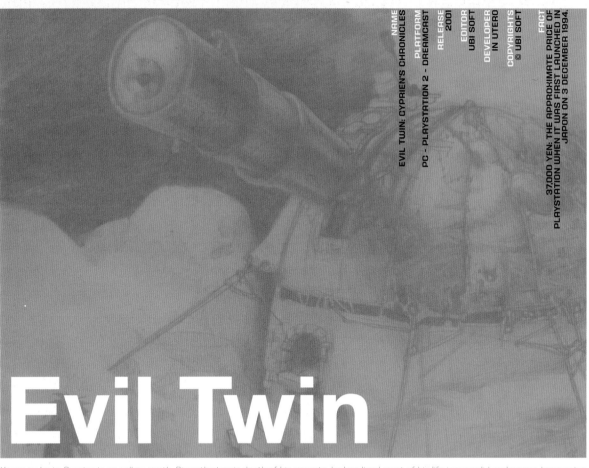

Evil Twin

Young as he is, Cyprien is no callow youth. Since the tragic death of his parents, he has lived most of his life in a sordid orphanage, bemoaning his fate and haunted day and night by terrible nightmares. The frontier between dream and reality is abolished on the date of his tenth birthday (the anniversary of his parents' death): a monster come directly from his nightmares drags him off into the world of dream. There Cyprien has to face down his deepest fears in order to save his friends - they too have been caught up in the nightmare - and above all, learn to love life again. Though Cyprien's imagination thus plunges him into a perilous adventure, it is also his staunchest ally; in his dreams, Cyprien has an alter ego endowed with special powers, and Super Cyp allows him to escape the gravest perils unscathed. Though this is a fairly classic platform-actioner, its hauntingly morbid graphic environment shows considerable originality.

« »

Bien que très jeune, Cyprien est un enfant très mature. Après la mort tragique de ses parents, il a vécu la majeure partie de son existence dans un orphelinat sordide, pleurant ses peines et hanté jour et nuit par d'horribles cauchemars. La frontière entre le rêve et la réalité se déchirera le jour du dixième anniversaire de Cyprien, qui coïncide avec la date du trépas de ses parents : un monstre tout droit sorti des cauchemars de l'enfant l'entraînera dans le monde des songes, où Cyprien devra affronter ses peurs les plus profondes afin de sauver ses rares amis, eux aussi happés dans cet univers de cauchemar, et surtout retrouver goût à la vie. Si l'imagination de Cyprien le plonge dans une aventure périlleuse, elle est aussi sa meilleure arme : dans ses rêves, Cyprien a un alter ego doté de pouvoirs, nommé Super Cyp', qui lui permettra de vaincre les plus grands dangers. Si le jeu est un titre d'action et de plates-formes somme toute classique, son environ- nement graphique torturé et malsain fait, lui, preuve d'une grande originalité.

« »

Cyprien ist für sein Alter ein sehr reifes Kind. Nach dem tragischen Tod seiner Eltern hat er die meiste Zeit seines jungen Lebens in einem schäbigen Waisenhaus verbracht, wo er vor lauter Kummer viel weint und Tag und Nacht von schrecklichen Albträumen geplagt wird. Die Grenze zwischen Traum und Wirklichkeit zerreißt an Cypriens zehntem Geburtstag, der mit dem Todestag seiner Eltern zusammenfällt. Ein geradewegs dem Albtraum des Jungen entsprungenes Monster entführt Cyprien in die Traumwelt. Dort muss er sich seinen schlimmsten Ängsten stellen, um seine wenigen Freunde zu retten, die ihrerseits von diesem Albtraum verschlungen wurden. Vor allem aber gilt es, selbst wieder Lebensmut zu fassen. Seine eigene Vorstellungskraft stürzt Cyprien zwar in ein gefährliches Abenteuer, sie ist aber auch seine stärkste Waffe. In seinen Träumen hat Cyprien ein Alter Ego, das mit allerlei Fähigkeiten ausgestattet ist, und dieser Super Cyp' mei- stert die größten Gefahren.
Obwohl das Spiel ein echter Klassiker im Sinne von Action- und Plattform-Games ist, besticht es durch eine optisch brillante Grafik, die die bedrohliche und quälende Atmosphäre gut wiedergibt.

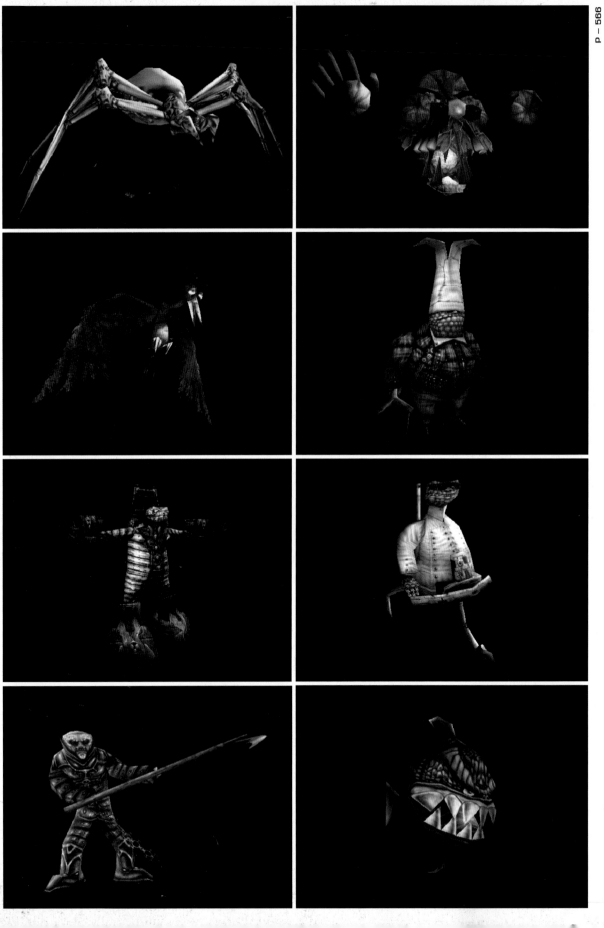

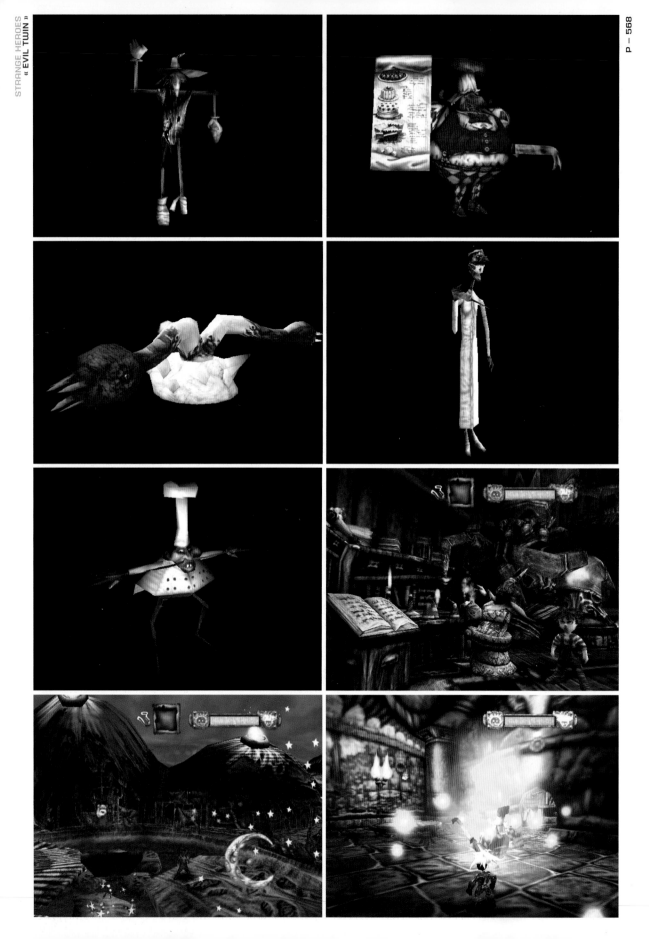

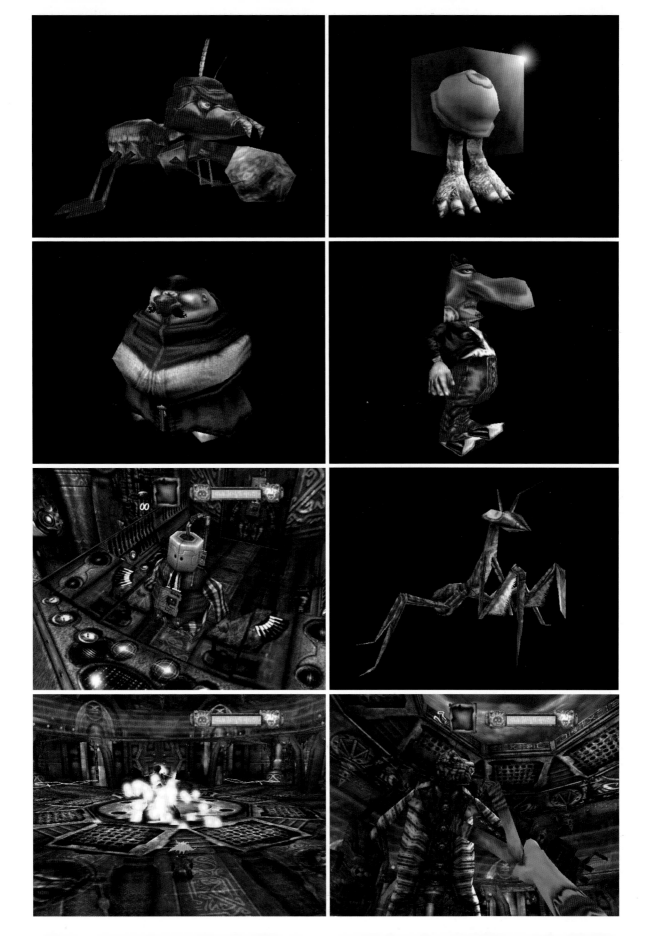

NAME
ICO
PLATFORM
PLAYSTATION 2
RELEASE
2001
EDITOR
SONY COMPUTER ENTERTAINMENT
DEVELOPER
SONY COMPUTER ENTERTAINMENT
COPYRIGHTS
© 2001 SONY COMPUTER ENTERTAINMENT
EUROPE. ALL RIGHTS RESERVED.
DEVELOPED BY SONY COMPUTER
ENTERTAINMENT INC. PUBLISHED BY SONY
FACT
3.3 MILLION: THE NUMBER OF UNITS
OF FINAL FANTASY VIII SOLD ON
PLAYSTATION IN 1 MONTH IN JAPAN ALONE.

ICO

The spell-binding world of Ico is dream-like: pure magic, in fact. The gamer plays the young boy who finds himself inexplicably imprisoned in a mysterious fortress. Escaping from his cell may be child's play, but after that the real fun starts: the building is chock-a-block with fatal traps. Over the course of his quest for freedom, the youth meets a ghostly, speechless young girl whom he must protect from the many dangers of this labyrinthine prison. Pursued by terrifying dark spectres, the two of them live out an adventure in which one wrong step means death. ICO is a unique experience, combining poetry and action in a dazzling graphic presentation. The monochrome aesthetic and richly detailed environment are the perfect vehicles for this superb story, which takes the gamer into its own special world. Here art and playability make a seamless match.

« »

Envoûtant, magique et onirique : tel est le monde de Ico. Le joueur y incarne le jeune garçon se retrouvant inexplicablement prisonnier dans une mystérieuse forteresse. Si s'échapper de sa cellule fut aisé, sortir de la bâtisse est un défi ô combien périlleux, les geôliers ayant truffé la prison de pièges mortels. Au cours de son périple, le jeune homme rencontrera une mystérieuse jeune fille fantomatique et muette qu'il devra protéger des mille dangers de la labyrinthique prison. Poursuivis par d'effroyables spectres noirs, les deux jeunes gens vont vivre une aventure où chaque pas peut mener à la mort. ICO est une expérience unique, mêlant poésie et action, servie par une réalisation graphique éblouissante. L'esthétisme monochromatique du jeu et la richesse de l'environnement visuel servent avec perfection une histoire superbement orchestrée, qui emportera le joueur dans un monde unique, parfait équilibre entre le ludique et l'artistique.

« »

Verzaubert, magisch und traumhaft: Das ist die Welt von Ico. Darin schlüpft der Spieler in die Rolle des Jungen, der sich auf unerklärliche Weise als Gefangener in einer geheimnisvollen Festung wiederfindet. Der Ausbruch aus seiner Zelle ist noch kinderleicht, die Flucht aus dem Gemäuer erweist sich dagegen als ungleich gefährlicher, zumal die Wärter das Gefängnis mit tödlichen Fallen präpariert haben. Während seines Rundgangs begegnet der junge Mann einem geheimnisvollen Mädchen, schemenhaft und stumm, das er vor unzähligen Gefahren, die in dem labyrinthischen Gefängnis lauern, beschützen muss. Außerdem werden die beiden während ihrer abenteuerlichen Flucht von Furcht erregenden schwarzen Phantomen gejagt. Jeder Schritt kann in den Tod führen.

Ico ist ein einzigartiges Adventure-Spiel, in dem sich Poesie und Action vermischen und das von einer fantastischen Grafik unterstützt wird. Die monochromatische Ästhetik des Spiels und das brillante visuelle Beiwerk unterstützen eine meisterhaft inszenierte Story, die den Spieler in eine einzigartige Welt entführt. Ein perfektes Gleichgewicht von Spiel und Kunst.

NAME MYST: EXILE
PLATFORM PC
RELEASE 2001
EDITOR UBI SOFT
DEVELOPER PRESTO STUDIO
COPYRIGHTS © UBI SOFT

Myst: Exile

Atlus and his colleagues have a gift that many dreamers would love to possess; they can make their dream-worlds come true thanks to a lore at once technological and mystic. These universes are created by means of books in which every facet of the universe is noted. It's a Herculean task: no room for error here; the slightest slip will cause the world to degenerate into chaos and may leave its visitors unable to escape. Enchanting or horrifying, these worlds may be natural or mechanical in kind, but they all have one thing in common: their landscapes are breathtakingly beautiful, and comprise strange enigmas, one of whose functions is to lock out the non-initiate bent on reducing the universe to chaos. But when the gamer finds himself imprisoned in a book-world, he needs both logic and intuition to return to reality.
The creators of the universe of Myst, Cyan, revolutionised adventure games by making a major advance in graphic representation: their games were among the first titles to offer detailed synthetic image backgrounds, and have captivated millions of players with their elaborate puzzles since 1994, when the first Myst appeared.

« »

Atlus et ses pairs ont un talent que bien des rêveurs aimeraient posséder : ils peuvent en effet donner vie aux mondes de leurs rêves grâce à une connaissance particulière, à la fois technologique et mystique. Ces univers sont créés à partir de livres détaillant toutes leurs facettes : un travail de titan qui ne laisse aucune place à l'à-peu-près et où la moindre faille peut faire tomber le monde dans le chaos ou emprisonner les visiteurs. Qu'ils soient enchanteurs ou angoissants, voués à la nature ou à la mécanique, ces livres-mondes ont tous un point commun : leurs paysages sont d'une beauté à couper le souffle et renferment d'étranges énigmes qui servent notamment de verrous empêchant les non-initiés de semer le chaos dans ces univers. Mais lorsque le joueur profane se retrouve emprisonné dans un livre-monde, il lui faudra faire preuve de logique et d'intuition pour réintégrer la réalité.
Les créateurs de l'univers de Myst, la société Cyan, ont révolutionné le jeu d'aventure en franchissant une étape graphique importante : leurs jeux faisaient partie des premiers titres à offrir des décors en images de synthèse détaillés, et ont captivé des milliers de joueurs avides de puzzles complexes depuis le premier Myst, en 1994.

« »

Atlus und seinesgleichen haben ein Talent, das manch ein Träumer gerne besäße: Dank besonderer technologischer und mystischer Kenntnisse können sie den Welten ihrer Träume Gestalt verleihen. Diese Welten werden anhand von Büchern geschaffen, die sie detailgetreu beschreiben: Eine titanische Aufgabe, die keinerlei Halbheiten duldet, denn der geringste Fehler kann die Welten in ein Chaos stürzen oder die Besucher hinter Schloss und Riegel bringen. Egal, ob sie den Betrachter verzaubern oder verängstigen, der Natur oder der Mechanik gewidmet sind, all diese Welten-Bücher haben eines gemeinsam: Ihre Landschaften sind von einer atemberaubenden Schönheit und bergen seltsame Rätsel, die vor allem die Nichteingeweihten hindern sollen, Chaos in diesen Welten zu stiften. Wird aber ein uneingeweihter Spieler zum Gefangenen in einem Welten-Buch, muss er Sinn für Logik und Intuition an den Tag legen, um in die Realität zurückzufinden.
Die Schöpfer des Universums Myst von der Firma Cyan leisteten mit der Grafik dieses Adventure-Spiels ganze Arbeit: Ihre Spiele gehörten zu den ersten Titeln, deren Bilder eine hohe Detailgenauigkeit aufwiesen. Tausende faszinierte Spieler warten seit dem ersten Myst aus dem Jahre 1994 auf neue Folgen dieses komplexen Rätselspiels.

NAME	**NIGHTS INTO DREAMS**
PLATFORM	**GENESIS**
RELEASE	**1996**
EDITOR	**SEGA**
DEVELOPER	**SONIC TEAM**
COPYRIGHTS	**© SONIC TEAM/SEGA**

Nights

In everyone's subconscious, there is a zone named Nightopia, in which dreams are created and experienced. There an evil demon, Wizeman the Wicked, piles on magical muscle by stealing the dream-energy of sleeping humans. When fully charged up, he will enter reality, where nothing can stop him. Two children of Nightopia, Claris and Elliot, set out to cut Wizeman down to size; courage like theirs is something he just can't absorb. In this marvellous dream-world, the gamer confronts Wizeman's nightmare henchmen: Reala, a parody of teens everywhere, Gulp, a demon with razor-like teeth, Jackle, a malevolent clown, Gillwing the dragon, along with the terrible Wizeman himself. The game's developers, Sonic Team, have created an astonishing and marvellous world through which the gamer flies at will - why, it's just like a dream...

« »

Dans le subconscient de chacun existe un lieu nommé Nightopia où les rêves sont créés et vivent. Dans ce monde onirique, un être maléfique grandit, volant l'énergie des rêves des humains endormis. Si ce démon, Wizeman the Wicked, réussit à absorber suffisamment d'énergie, il pourra pénétrer dans la réalité où rien alors ne pourra l'arrêter. Deux enfants de Nightopia, Claris et Elliot, vont combattre Wizeman, grâce à leur courage dont le maléfique individu ne peut s'emparer. Dans un univers onirique merveilleux, le joueur affrontera les créatures de cauchemar de Wizeman, dont Reala, parodie des jeunes gens, Gulpo, démon aux dents tranchantes comme des rasoirs, Jackle, un bouffon malfaisant, Gillwing le dragon et Wizeman le terrible lui-même. Les développeurs du jeu, la Sonic Team, ont créé un monde étonnant, merveilleux où le joueur évoluera librement en volant ... comme dans un rêve, bien évidemment.

« »

Im Unterbewussten eines jeden Menschen gibt es einen Ort namens Nightopia, wo Träume entstehen und lebendig werden. In dieser Traumwelt macht sich ein böses Wesen breit, das den Schlafenden die Traumenergie entzieht. Wenn es diesem Dämon namens Wizeman gelingen sollte, genügend Energie abzuzapfen, könnte er in die Realität eindringen, wo ihn nichts und niemand mehr aufhalten kann. Claris und Elliot sind zwei Kinder aus Twin Seeds, die mutig den Kampf gegen Wizeman aufnehmen und dadurch verhindern, dass der Dämon sich ihrer bemächtigt. In einer fantastischen Traumwelt lauern auf den Spieler Wizemans grausige Kreaturen, darunter Reala, eine Parodie auf die beiden Kinder, Gulpo, ein Dämon mit rasiermesserscharfen Zähnen, Jackle, ein boshafter Clown, Gillwing, der Drache, und nicht zuletzt der schreckliche Wizeman. Die Entwickler des Spiels, das Sonic-Team, haben eine staunenswerte Wunderwelt erschaffen, in der sich der Spieler – fliegend – weiterentwickeln kann ... ganz wie im Traum.

NAME
PIKMIN

PLATFORM
GAMECUBE

RELEASE
2001

EDITOR
NINTENDO

DEVELOPER
NINTENDO

COPYRIGHTS
© NINTENDO

FACT
15 MILLION: THE NUMBER OF POKEMON
CARTRIDGES SOLD WORLDWIDE IN 1998.

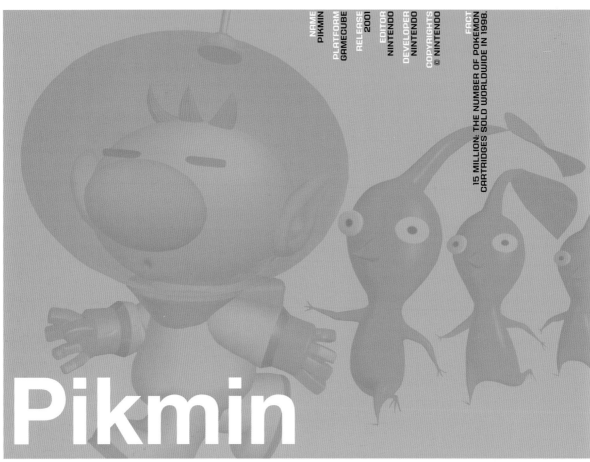

Pikmin

Captain Olimar has made an emergency crash-landing on an unknown planet. He has no choice but to explore it; his spaceship has shattered into some thirty pieces now scattered all over the planet. Coming to after the crash, he finds himself eyeballing a bizarre, giant plant, beside which is a sort of little nest. Moving closer, Olimar sees strange little creatures coming out of it; they have huge eyes and a leaf growing out of their heads. Astonishment gives place to curiosity when these little Pikmins turn out to be friendly - so friendly that they help him to explore their planet and overcome the obstacles in his way. Olimar discovers three species of Pikmin, each with its own talents; some can carry explosives, others are immensely strong or fire-resistant, and so on. Before his astonished eyes, they grow and become flower-beings, ever stronger, faster and more efficient. Pikmin is a peaceful, enchanting game, combining reflection and poetry in a spell-binding environment.

« »

Réussissant in extremis un atterrissage en catastrophe sur une planète inconnue, le Captain Olimar n'a d'autre choix que d'explorer ce nouveau monde, son vaisseau ayant éclaté en une trentaine de morceaux maintenant éparpillés sur la planète. Reprenant peu à peu ses esprits après le crash, Olimar se trouve nez à nez avec une étrange plante gigantesque, près de laquelle se tient ce qui semble être un petit nid. Alors qu'il s'approche, Olimar en voit sortir de bizarres petites créatures dotées de grands yeux et au crâne surmonté d'une feuille d'arbre. L'étonnement d'Olimar cède rapidement la place à la curiosité, d'autant que ces petits êtres, loin d'être agressifs, semblent bien au contraire fort amicaux. Au point où ces créatures, les Pikmin, l'aideront à explorer leur planète et à surmonter les obstacles qui se dresseront sur son chemin. Olimar découvrira trois espèces de Pikmin, chacune dotée de talents qui lui seront bien utiles : porteurs d'explosifs, résistants au feu, costauds etc. Devant les yeux ébahis d'Olimar, les Pikmin grandiront jusqu'à devenir des êtres-fleurs, plus robustes, plus rapides et plus efficaces. Alliant réflexion et poésie, Pikmin est un jeu enchanteur, paisible et incroyablement envoûtant.

« »

In letzter Minute gelingt Captain Olimar eine Bruchlandung auf einem unbekannten Planeten. Da sein Raumschiff jedoch in dreißig Teile geborsten ist, die nun überall verstreut liegen, bleibt ihm nichts anderes übrig, als die Einzelteile wieder einzusammeln. Als er nach dem Aufprall wieder zu sich kommt, sieht er sich einer merkwürdigen Riesenpflanze gegenüber, neben der sich so etwas wie ein kleines Nest befindet. Beim Näherkommen bemerkt Olimar, dass sonderbare kleine Wesen mit großen Augen und einem Blatt auf dem Kopf aus dem Nest hervorkriechen. Seine Verwunderung weicht schnell der Neugier, zumal diese kleinen pflanzenartigen Wesen alles andere als aggressiv sind, ja ihm anscheinend sogar sehr freundlich gesonnen sind. Diese Pikmin, wie Captain Olimar sie nennt, helfen ihm, den Planeten zu erkunden und Hindernisse aus dem Weg zu räumen. Olimar entdeckt drei verschiedene Pikmin-Arten mit jeweils unterschiedlichen Fähigkeiten, die ihm bei der Suche nach den Einzelteilen seines Raumschiffes sehr nützlich sind: So gibt es beispielsweise Pikmin, die Sprengstoff tragen können, andere Pikmin sind resistent gegen Feuer oder sehr robust. Vor den Augen des verblüfften Olimar wachsen die Pikmin zu Blumenwesen heran, die noch widerstandsfähiger, schneller und stärker sind. Diese gelungene Mischung aus Reflexion und Poesie macht Pikmin zu einem wirklich reizvollen Spiel, das friedlich und ungemein sympathisch ist.

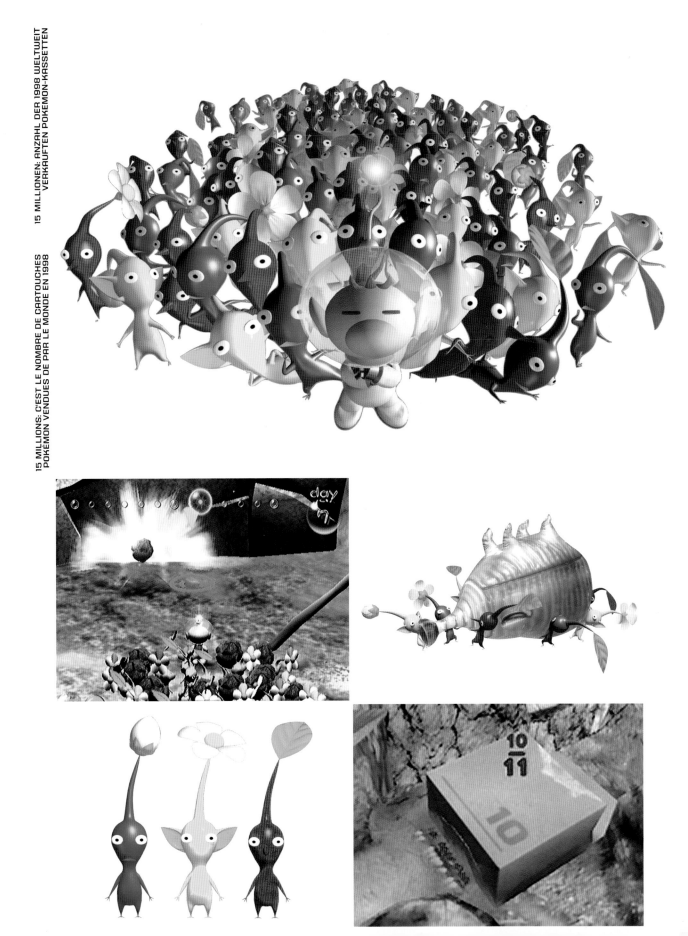

NAME
REZ

PLATFORM
DREAMCAST - PLAYSTATION 2

RELEASE
2001

EDITOR
SEGA

DEVELOPER
UNITED GAME ARTISTS

COPYRIGHTS
© SEGA

FACT
120: THE NUMBER OF ARTISTS WHO TOOK PART
IN SQUARESOFT'S DESIGN FOR FINAL FANTASY
VII ON PLAYSTATION.

Rez

At the heart of network Project K lies Eden, the most advanced form of artificial intelligence. Eden's capacity to form its own thoughts has driven it mad, and its profound depression is imperilling the whole network. The hackers have therefore decided to "cure" Eden, which has barricaded itself at the centre of five circles of cyberspace, each infested with aggressive viruses and protected by powerful fire-shields. The only means of overcoming Eden's shields is to send a computer avatar, Form Zero, capable of paralysing the AI defences by rhythmic sound-impulses. The more of Eden's shields Form Zero deactivates, the more complex and effective it becomes. Rez combines action and musical gaming in a work of interactive art. Its highly original concept will appeal to anyone with an interest in electronic music and digital culture.

« »

Au cœur du réseau Project K trône Eden, la plus avancée des intelligences artificielles. La capacité de celle-ci à former ses propres pensées l'a rendue folle : la dépression existentielle d'Eden met l'ensemble du réseau en péril, aussi des hackers sont-ils engagés pour « guérir » Eden. L'intelligence artificielle s'est barricadée au centre de cinq cercles de cyberspace, chacun étant infesté de virus agressifs et protégé par un pare-feu puissant. Le seul moyen de vaincre les protections d'Eden est d'envoyer un avatar informatique, la Forme Zero, capable de paralyser les défenses de l'I.A. en leur envoyant des impulsions sonores en rythme. Plus la forme Zero désactive de protections, plus elle se complexifie, devenant par là-même plus efficace.

Mêlant jeu d'action et jeu musical, véritable œuvre d'art moderne interactive, Rez est un concept original dans lequel se reconnaîtront nombre d'adeptes de la musique électronique et de la culture digitale.

« »

Mitten im Netzwerk „Project K" thront Eden, die höchstentwickelte künstliche Intelligenz. Ihre Fähigkeit, selbständig zu denken, hat sie in den Wahnsinn getrieben: Edens existenzielle Depression bringt das gesamte Netzwerk in Gefahr. Deshalb wurden Hacker engagiert, um Eden „zu heilen". Die künstliche Intelligenz hat sich hinter fünf Cyberspace-Ringen verschanzt, die allesamt von einem aggressiven Virus verpestet und von einer mächtigen Feuerschneise geschützt sind. Nur eine verhängnisvolle Computermetabolie kann die Schutzwälle von Eden durchbrechen: die Form Zero. Sie allein ist in der Lage, die Verteidigung der künstlichen Intelligenz durch Aussenden von rhythmischen Tonimpulsen zu lähmen. Je mehr Schutzmechanismen Zero außer Kraft setzt, desto komplexer und treffsicherer wird sie.

Die gelungene Kombination aus Action und Musik macht Rez zu einem wahrhaft interaktiven Kunstwerk. Ein originelles Konzept für die Fans von elektronischer Musik und digitaler Kultur.

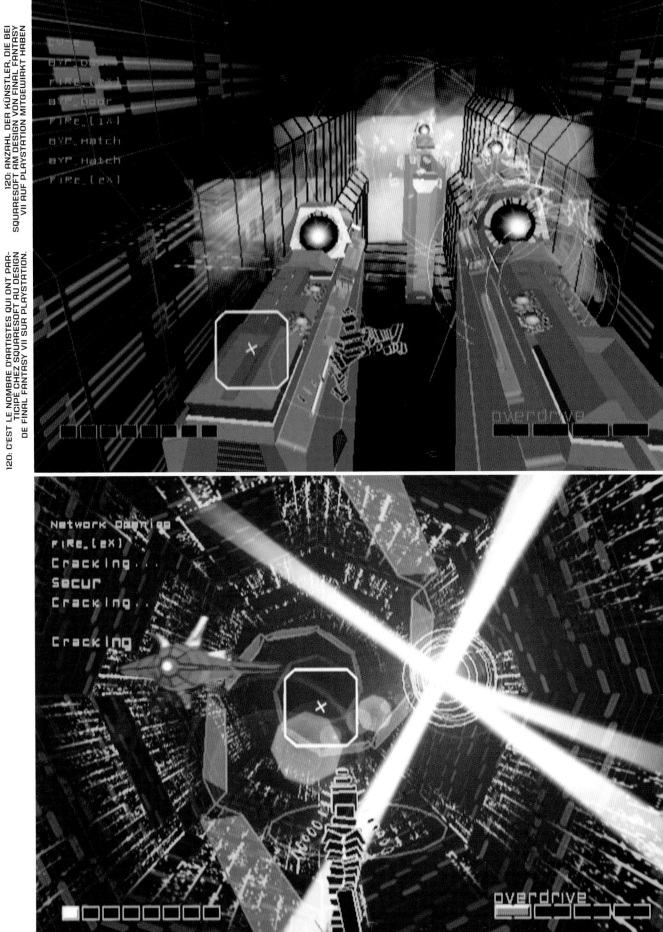

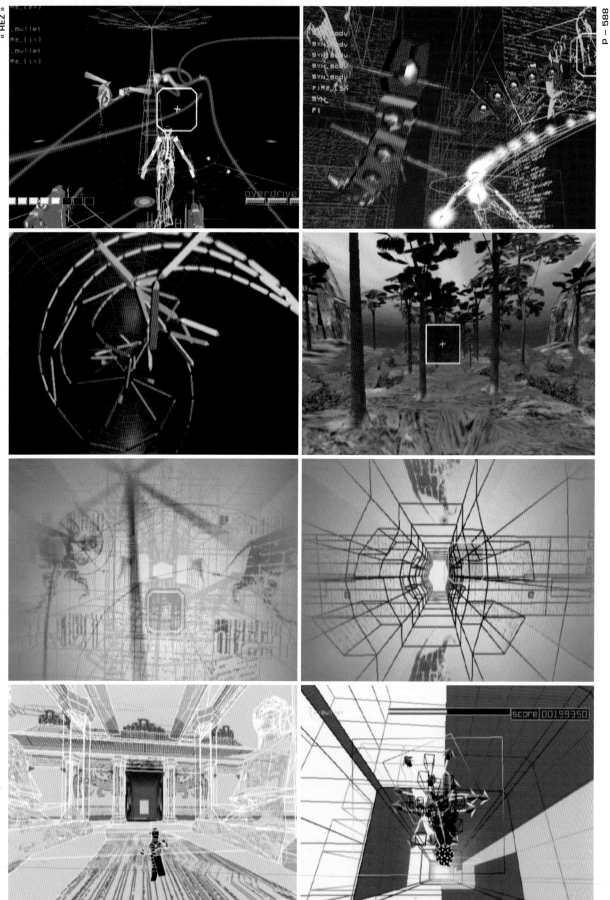

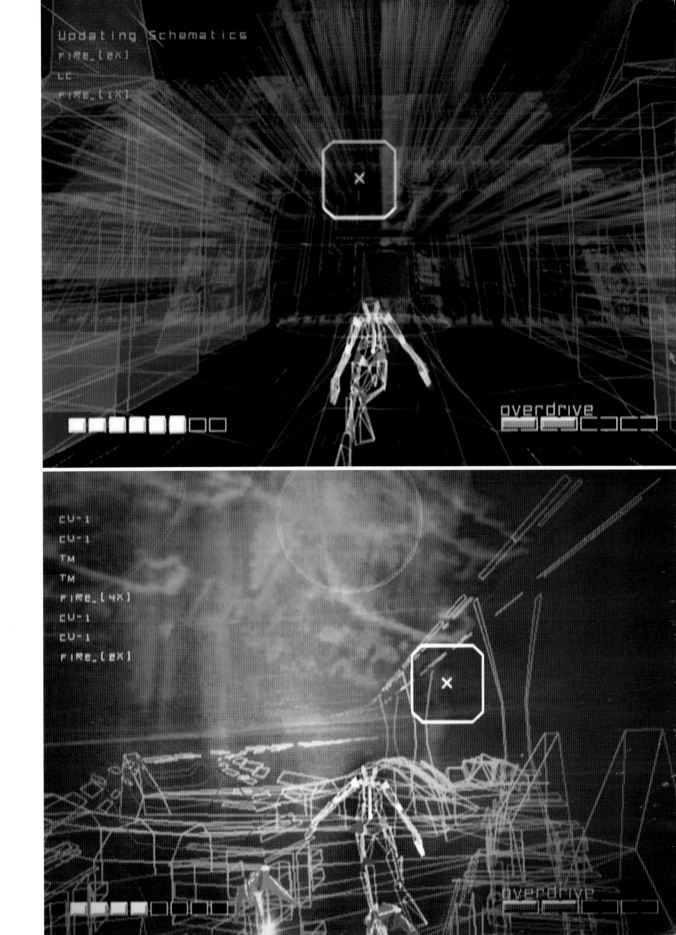

NAME
SCHIZM

PLATFORM
PC

RELEASE
2001

EDITOR
MICROIDS

DEVELOPER
DETALION

COPYRIGHTS
© MICROIDS

FACT
98% THE PERCENTAGE OF WORDS IN WEBSTER'S, THE STANDARD AMERICAN DICTIONARY, ALREADY REGISTERED AS DOMAIN NAMES (BOSTON HERALD).

Schizm

In 2083, a space probe discovers the planet Argilus. The first explorers discover an astonishing spectacle: the planet is covered with human-scale constructions and mysterious machines, but not a single inhabitant is to be seen. All life seems to have abandoned Argilus. To study the planet, and get a line on what happened there, a little colony of scientists is set up. Ten months later, Sam Mayney and Hannah Grant crash-land on Argilus in a supply ship whose controls go haywire as it approaches the planet; they discover that the scientists have vanished. Alone in an unknown world, Mayney and Grant have no choice; if they are ever to return to earth, they must solve the mystery of Argilus.

« »

En l'an 2083, une sonde spatiale découvre la planète Argilus. Les premiers explorateurs à fouler le sol de ce nouveau monde se retrouvent devant un spectacle aussi grandiose que troublant : la planète est couverte de constructions à dimension humaine, de machines étranges à l'utilité mystérieuse, mais… aucun habitant en vue. Toute vie semble avoir disparu d'Argilus. Afin d'étudier la planète et peut-être de comprendre ce qui a pu s'y produire, une petite colonie de scientifiques s'y installe. Dix mois plus tard, Sam Mayney et Hannah Grant arrivent sur Argilus à bord d'un vaisseau de ravitaillement qui se dérègle aux abords de la planète et les oblige à atterrir en catastrophe. Ils découvrent alors que les colons semblent s'être également évaporés. Seuls sur un monde inconnu, Mayney et Grant n'auront donc d'autre choix que de tenter à leur tour de percer le mystère d'Argilus pour espérer s'en sortir.

« »

Im Jahre 2083 entdeckt eine Raumsonde den Planeten Argilus. Den ersten Forschern, die den Boden dieser neuen Welt betreten, bietet sich ein überwältigender und zugleich unerklärlicher Anblick: Der Planet ist mit Bauten menschlicher Dimension und fremdartigen Maschinen unergründlicher Bestimmung übersät. Von seinen Bewohnern jedoch fehlt jede Spur. Jegliches Leben scheint von Argilus verschwunden zu sein. Ein kleines Team von Wissenschaftlern lässt sich hier nieder, um den Planeten zu erkunden und dem geheimnisvollen Verschwinden seiner Zivilisation auf die Spur zu kommen. Zehn Monate später treffen Sam Mayney und Hannah Grant an Bord eines Versorgungsschiffes auf Argilus ein. Beim Anflug auf den Planeten ergeben sich technische Schwierigkeiten und sie müssen notlanden. Bald entdecken sie, dass auch die Forscher spurlos verschwunden sind. Allein in einer unbekannten Welt und in der Hoffnung ihr zu entkommen, werden Mayney und Grant wohl keine andere Wahl haben, als das Mysterium von Argilus selbst aufzudecken.

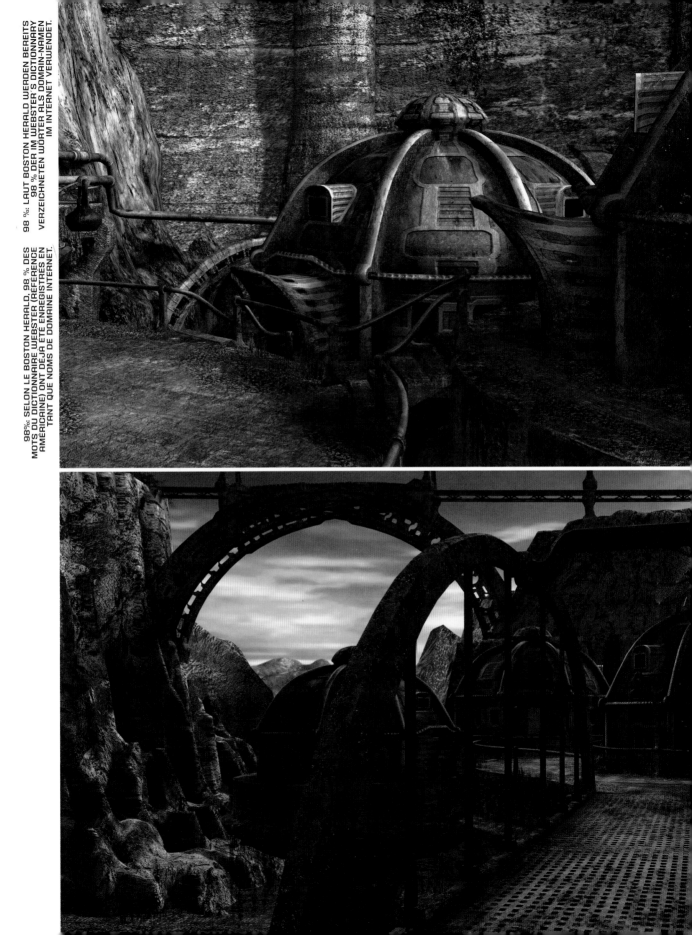

98%: SELON LE BOSTON HERALD, 98 % DES MOTS DU DICTIONNAIRE WEBSTER (RÉFÉRENCE AMÉRICAINE) ONT DÉJÀ ÉTÉ ENREGISTRÉS EN TANT QUE NOMS DE DOMAINE INTERNET.

98 %: LAUT BOSTON HERALD WERDEN BEREITS 98 % DER IM WEBSTER'S DICTIONNARY VERZEICHNETEN WÖRTER ALS DOMAIN-NAMEN IM INTERNET VERWENDET.

NAME
SYBERIA
PLATFORM
PC
RELEASE
2002
EDITOR
MICROIDS
DEVELOPER
MICROIDS
COPYRIGHTS
© MICROIDS
FACT
4000: THE NUMBER OF QUESTIONS AVAILABLE
IN JEOPARDY ON NINTENDO.

Syberia

Kate Walker, a brilliant young New York lawyer, is sent to Europe by the multinational Universal Toys Company to purchase the Voralberg automaton factory, which specialises in complex clockwork and perpetual motion machines. Anna Voralberg, the owner of the factory, is dying, and Kate must therefore find the sole heir, Hans Voralberg, an inventor of genius who disappeared several years before. But before her death, Anna confides to Kate that her son is still alive, and living in Siberia. Kate crosses Siberia, visiting a series of cities in which the inventor has left his mark. She finally discovers him in an extraordinary universe, full of astonishing automata whose job is to guard Hans' terrifying secret. *Syberia* is the second video-game created by the cartoonist Benoît Sokal, who has already adapted one of his works for PC: *Amerzone*. In *Syberia*, he has produced an unprecedented and spell-binding scenario set in a universe of exquisite beauty.

« »

Kate Walker, une jeune et brillante avocate new-yorkaise, est envoyée en Europe par la multinationale Universal Toys Company afin de racheter l'usine d'automates Voralberg, spécialisée dans les machineries à ressorts complexes et le mouvement mécanique perpétuel. Anna Voralberg, propriétaire de l'usine, venant de décéder, Kate doit retrouver son unique héritier, Hans Voralberg, inventeur de génie qui a disparu mystérieusement quelques années plus tôt. Avant de mourir, Anna dévoile à la jeune femme que son fils est toujours vivant, quelque part en Sibérie. Kate traversera la Sibérie, visitant des villes où l'inventeur a laissé son empreinte, avant de se retrouver dans un univers extraordinaire, peuplé d'automates étonnants qui gardent l'incroyable secret du génial Hans. Le jeu Syberia est la seconde créa-tion vidéoludique du dessinateur Benoît Sokal qui avait déjà adapté une de ses œuvres sur PC, L'Amerzone. Il signe avec Syberia une histoire inédite envoûtante et étonnante dans un univers de toute beauté.

« »

Kate Walker, eine junge und erfolgreiche New Yorker Rechtsanwältin, wird von der multinationalen Universal Toys Company nach Europa geschickt. Sie soll den Kaufvertrag für die Automatenfabrik Voralberg unterzeichnen, die spezialisiert ist auf die Herstellung von komplizierten Federungsmaschinen und Perpetuum mobiles. Da Anna Voralberg, die Besitzerin der Fabrik, soeben gestorben ist, macht sich Kate auf die Suche nach ihrem einzigen Erben: Hans Voralberg, ein genialer Erfinder, der vor wenigen Jahren auf mysteriöse Weise verschwunden ist. Denn kurz vor ihrem Tod enthüllte Anna der jungen Frau, dass ihr Sohn noch am Leben ist und irgendwo in Sibirien lebt. Kate reist quer durch Sibirien und besucht die Städte, in denen Hans seine Spuren hinterlassen hat. Dabei gerät sie in ein außergewöhnliches Universum, in dem spektakuläre Automaten das unglaubliche Geheimnis des genialen Erfinders wahren.

Syberia ist die zweite Videospiel-Kreation des Zeichners Benoît Sokal, der schon einmal eines seiner Werke, Amerzone, für den PC adaptiert hat. Mit Syberia liefert er eine bisher unveröffentlichte zauberhafte und höchst verwunderliche Geschichte, angesiedelt in einem Universum von atemberaubender Schönheit.

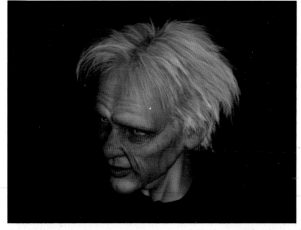

Valadilène:
le caveau familial
des Voralberg.

NAME VEXX

PLATFORM PLAYSTATION PLAYSTATION 2 GAMECUBE – XBOX

RELEASE 2002

EDITOR ACCLAIM ENTERTAINMENT

DEVELOPER ACCLAIM ENTERTAINMENT

COPYRIGHTS © ACCLAIM ENTERTAINMENT

FACT 16.77 MILLION: THE NUMBER OF COLOURS THAT DREAMCAST'S POWER VR GRAPHIC CHIP CAN DISPLAY SIMULTANEOUSLY.

Vexx

The sinister Shadowraith Dark Yabu and his evil hordes invade the planet Astara. Descending on peaceful Rockhaven, they massacre most of the villagers and reduce the survivors to slavery. The village chief is assassinated by Dark Yabu, but his grandson Vexx escapes the Shadowraith by hiding in the depths of Yabu's ship. There he discovers the Astani battle-gauntlets, magic weapons that invest Vexx with their powers. He finds himself selected for a terrifying mission: he alone can defeat Dark Yabu. To do this, he must restore the full power of the gauntlets by finding Reia, the last survivor of the glorious race of Astani. She is a prisoner in the depths of Yabu's fortress. With the gauntlets' powers at last restored, Vexx can hope to overcome the Shadowraith.

« »

Le sombre Shadowraith Dark Yabu et ses hordes maléfiques envahissent la planète Astara, débarquant dans le paisible village de Rockhaven, tuant nombre des habitants et réduisant les autres en esclavage. Seul le jeune Vexx, petit-fils du chef du village assassiné par le cruel Dark Yabu, réussit à s'échapper des griffes du Shadowraith en se cachant dans les profondeurs du vaisseau de celui-ci. Là, il découvrira les gants de bataille Astani, armes magiques qui choisiront de mettre leur pouvoir au service de Vexx. Le jeune garçon se retrouve investi d'une écrasante mission : seul, il devra vaincre Dark Yabu. Pour ce faire, il devra restaurer l'intégralité de la puissance des gants, seuls capables de terrasser le Shadowraith, en retrouvant Reia, la dernière survivante de la glorieuse race des Astani, qui est emprisonnée dans les profondeurs de la forteresse de Dark Yabu...

« »

Als der Bösewicht Dark Yabu und seine dunkle Gefolgschaft über den friedlichen Ort Rockhaven auf dem Planeten Astara herfallen, töten sie zahlreiche Dorfbewohner und zwingen die anderen zur Sklavenarbeit in den Höhlen des nahen Gebirges. Entkommen kann nur der Enkel des von den Eindringlingen brutal ermordeten Dorfvorstehers: der junge Vexx, der sich im Raumschiff des Bösewichtes versteckt. Dort entdeckt er das letzte Paar der Astani-Kampfhandschuhe, die fortan ihre magischen Kräfte in seinen Dienst stellen wollen. Der kleine Kerl sieht sich einer ungeheuer schweren Aufgabe gegenüber: Er ganz allein muss Dark Yabu bezwingen. Das kann er aber nur mit der komplett wiederhergestellten Zauberkraft der Handschuhe, und dafür muss er Reia finden, die letzte Überlebende der glorreichen Astani-Rasse, die in der Festung von Dark Yabu gefangen gehalten wird...

«Heroes Index»
Search by game title

Skeleton
Darklings

Ecco «P—336»
Ecco the Dolphin
Whales
Sharks
Turtles
Moray Eels
Stinging Jellyfish
Manta Rays

Empire Earth «P—164»
Prehistoric Units
Stone Age Units
Bronze Age Units
Dark Age Units
Middle Age Units
Renaissance Units
Imperial Age Units
Industrial Age Units
Atomic Age Units
Digital Age Units
Nano Age Units

Etherlords «P—464»
The Synthets
The Chaots
the Vitals
The Kinets

Evil Twin «P—562»
Cyprien
Super Cyp'

Fear Effect «P—516»
Hana Tsu-Vachel
Rain Quin
Royce Glas
Jacob "Deke" Decourt

Final
Fantasy «P—168»
Tidus
Rikku
Yuna
Wakka
Lulu
Kihmari
The Sin
Auron

Flight
Simulator «P—402»
Cessna 208 Caravan on
Amphibious Floats
Cessna 208 Grand
Caravan
Boeing 747-400
Cessna 172S Skyhawk SP
Raytheon BE58 Baron

Boeing 777-300
Boeing 737-400
Raytheon/Beech King Air
350
Mooney Bravo
Cessna 182S Skylane
Bell 206B JetRanger III
helicopter
Learjet 45 business jet
Cessna Skylane RG
Extra 300S-Patty
Wagstaff's aerobatic
airplane
Sopwith Camel
Schweizer 2-32 sailplane

Fur Fighters «P—104»
Bungalow
Tweek
Roofus
Chang
Juliette
Rico
Viggo

Ghost Recon «P—250»
The Leader
The Sniper
The scout
The demolition man

Golden Axe «P—340»
Ax Battler
Tyris Flare
Gilius Thunderhead
Death Adder

Gran Turismo «P—408»
Acura
Alfa Romeo
Aston Martin
Audi
Chevrolet
Chrysler
Citroën
Daihatsu
Dodge
Fiat
Ford
Gillet
Honda
Jaguar
Lotus
Mazda
Mercedes-Benz
Mitsubishi
Nissan
Opel
Pagani
Peugeot
Renault

RUF
Shelby
Subaru
Suzuki
Tommykaira
Toyota
TVR
Volkswagen

Grandia «P—470»
Ryûdo
Elena
Granas
Valmah

Gunvalkyrie «P—174»
Kelly O Lenmey
Dr. Hebble
Saburouta Mishima
Meridian Poe

Half-Life «P—344»
Gordon Freeman
Scientist
Big Mama
Alien Grunt

Halo «P—176»
The Master Chief
Marines
Covenant Elite
Invisible Elites
Grunt
Hunter
Jackal

Headhunter «P—256»
Jack Wade
Angela Stern
Greywolf
Esteban Ramirez

Herdy Gerdy «P—108»
Gerdy
Sadorf
The Doops
The Gromps

Hitman «P—260»
Code 47

House of
the Dead «P—32»
Harry Harris
Amy Crystal
Zombies

ICO «P—570»
Ico
Yorda

Jak &
Daxter «P—92»
Jak
Daxter
The Eco Sages
Keira

Jet Set Radio «P—180»
DJ. K.
Beat
Gum
Corn
Yyo
Roboy
Combo
Jazz
Clutch
Garam
Soda
The Immortals
The Poison Jam
The Noisetanks
Hayashi
Gouji

Kirby «P—114»
Kirby
Ribbon
King Dedede
Waddle Dee
Adeleine

Klonoa «P—116»
Klonoa
Lolo
Popka
Baguji

Luigi's Mansion «P—120»
Luigi
Professor E. Gadd
Neville "The Bookish
Father"
Lydia "The Mirror-Gazing
Mother"
Chauncey "The Spoiled
Baby"
The Floating Whirlindas
"The Dancing Couple"
Shivers "The Wandering
Butler"
Melody Pianissima "The
Beautiful Pianist"
Mr. Luggs "The Glutton"
Spooky "The Hungry
Guard Dog"
Bogmire "The Cemetery
Shadow"
Biff Atlas "The
Bodybuilder"
Nana "The Scarf-Knitting

Granny"
Miss Pentunia "The
Bathing Beauty"
Slim Bankshot "The
Lonely Poolshark"
Henry & Orville "The Twin
Brothers"
Madame Clairvoya "The
Freaky Fortune-Teller"
Boolossus "Jumbo Ghost"
Uncle Grimmly "Hermit of
the Darkness"
Clockwork Soldiers "The
Toy Platoon"
Sue Pea "The Dozing Girl"
Jarvis "The Jar Collector"
Sir Weston "The Chilly
Climber"
Vincent Van Gore "The
Starving Artist"
King Boo

MechWarrior «P—184»
Atlas
Awesome
Bushwacker
Catapult
Cougar
Daishi
Loki
Mad Cat
Mauler
Nova Cat
Raven
Shadow Cat
Vulture
Thor

Metal Gear
Solid «P—264»
Solid Snake
Raiden
Otacon
Raiden
Vamp
Fortune
Fatman
Solidus Snake
Liquid Snake
Metal Gear Ray
Revolver Ocelot
Emma Emmerich

Myst: Exile «P—574»
Atrus
Catherine
The D'ni
Sirrus
Achenar

«Game Index»
Search by platform

«1000 Game Heroes»
Acknowledgements

Thanks to Luciano Alibrandi (Nvidia), Cécile Caminades (Konami), Jérôme Barbet (Big Ben Interactive), Alexandre Bastien-Riboni (Vivendi Universal Games), Nathalie Baule (Microïds), Cathy Campos (Electronic Arts), Didier Chanfray (Adeline Software), Sophie D'Almeras (Ubi Soft Entertainment), Mathilde Daures (VP Com), Diane de Domecy (Activision), Gregory Delfosse (Sony computer Entertainment France), Takashi Ebiike (Namco), Priscille Demoly (Eidos Interactive), Mark Fisher (Sega), Cécile Fouques-Duparc (Infogrames Entertainment), Frédéric Henry (Frederic Henry Communication), Hans Jurgen Kohrs (Konami), Maryanne Lataif (Activision), Pascal Lecointe (Ubi Soft Entertainment), Anna Mills (Namco Ltd.), Dominique Molinaro (THQ, Inc.), Géraldine Muzzin (Acclaim Entertainment), Tristan Perdriau (Eidos Interactive), Victor Perez (VP Com), Delphine Platten (Ubi Soft Entertainment), Jim Pride (Sega Europe), Agnès Rosique (Microsoft), Sébastien Saligné (Microsoft), Toshi Tokumaru (Capcom), Emmanuel Tremblay (Take 2 Interactive), Alex Waldron (Cake Group Ltd/Nintendo Europe), Natasha Williams (Cake Group Ltd /Nintendo Europe) and all the professionals and friends that contributed to this publication.

Many thanks to David Cage, Shigeru Miyamoto, Peter Molyneux, Frédérick Raynal, Bill Roper and Jason Rubin, who honoured me with their participation.

Special thanks to Julius Wiedemann (Taschen GmbH) for the present this book is for me, all the staff at GameKult.com for their support, Stéphane Belin, who started it all, my wife Natacha for her patience and love, my son Lucas, 6-years old mutant who already beats his father on several games and video games for existing... and of course, to all the game addicts !

P – 608

«1000 Game Heroes»
Imprint

© 2002 TASCHEN GmbH Hohenzollernring 53, D-50672 Köln
www.taschen.com

DESIGN: Sense/Net, Andy Disl and Birgit Reber, Cologne
PRODUCTION: Stefan Klatte
EDITOR: Julius Wiedemann
ENGLISH TRANSLATION: Chris Miller
GERMAN TRANSLATION: Karin Hirschmann
FRENCH TRANSLATION: David Choquet

ISBN: 3-8228-1633-7

PRINTED IN ITALY